FOLK-MEMORY

OR THE

CONTINUITY OF BRITISH ARCHAEOLOGY

ANTIQUITATES SELECTÆ CELTICÆ
ET
SEPTENTRIONALES.

FOLK-MEMORY

OR THE

CONTINUITY OF BRITISH ARCHAEOLOGY

BY

WALTER JOHNSON, F.G.S.

CO-AUTHOR OF 'NEOLITHIC MAN IN NORTH-EAST SURREY,' ETC.

WITH ILLUSTRATIONS BY SYDNEY HARROWING
AND OTHERS

70387

BENJAMIN BLOM, INC.
Publishers, New York 1971

First published London, 1908
Reissued 1971 by
Benjamin Blom, Inc.
New York, N.Y. 10025

Library of Congress
Catalog Card Number 71-173112

Printed in the
United States of America

PREFACE

WHETHER, after the labours of Tylor and Avebury, of Greenwell, Pitt-Rivers, and Mortimer, of Gomme, Haddon, and Clodd, there remains a place on the archaeologist's bookshelf for still another volume, depends necessarily upon the character of the new-comer.

The apology of the claimant is this : since no one individual student can read, much less assimilate, the extensive literature of archaeology, there must be those who would welcome a co-ordination and re-combination of scattered facts selected from the great storehouse. And, as in commerce the middleman may justify his economic existence by specialized knowledge and experience in his department, so the scientific middleman may fairly crave attention if he is able to integrate and to reset some of those isolated truths, which, in themselves, are as old as the hills.

To marshal such truths accurately, and to collate a few new facts, are the objects of this book. Here are set down the results of the spare time of years spent in tramping the country to investigate ancient churches, earthworks, roads, and monuments; in searching for stone implements; in jotting down notes concerning customs and folk-lore; in visiting, whenever possible, British and Continental museums, in studying diligently the best archaeological authorities.

Only one small corner of archaeology is here explored. The size of the volume might easily have been trebled had it been expedient simply to repeat what had been well said already. Notes on the 'Pilgrims' Way', made during personal exploration and study, have been excised unsparingly, because they are now superseded by the writings of Mrs. Ady and Mr. Hilaire Belloc. And, in general, it is hoped that nothing is forced under review without need or connexion. Thus the pages which deal with 'Marling', 'Dene-holes,' and 'Linchets,' were not written until scores

of leisure days, extending over a period of years, had been
spent on field work, usually in the company of competent
geologists or archaeologists.   A like condition was imposed
before giving impressions of the Brandon flint industry.
Mr. Skertchly's 'Memoir' has been freely drawn upon, but
the records have been carefully re-tested, and outstanding
questions settled, by a personal visit to Brandon, followed by
a long correspondence with Mr. F. Snare, the 'King of the
Knappers'.   Of crosses, megaliths, barrows, Roman roads,
dew-ponds, and cultivation terraces, the number inspected
during the past fifteen years is past counting.

Considerable care has been taken in verifying references;
rarely is one given at second-hand.   In accordance with
the plan adopted in a previous work, these particulars are
relegated to a separate chapter, so as not to distract the
reader's attention.   Since references are of two kinds, one
class being inserted merely to substantiate statements, and
the other to form a useful bibliography, an attempt has been
made to indicate the latter group, so as to permit extended
study of any given topic.   The multitude of authorities
cannot be individually acknowledged in this place, but each
case of indebtedness is noted in due order.   No record is
made of references which only duplicate those cited, or of
those quotations which, once discovered to be faulty, are
worse than unprofitable.

For the rest, brief explanations of terms are given by the
way, but some knowledge of archaeology has perforce to
be assumed.   Forgiveness is asked for any monotony in
style and treatment, and for occasional repetitions, inevitable
because archaeology, like natural history, refuses to be
apportioned into arbitrary sections, clean-cut and free from
overlap.

My best thanks are due to Mr. Sydney Harrowing for his
willing help in illustrating the book ; other obligations are
mentioned as they occur

CONTENTS

LIST OF ILLUSTRATIONS

NOTE ON FIG. 1.

An Eighteenth-century Interpretation of Folk-memory. Reproduced from J. G. Keysler's *Antiquitates Selectae* (Hanover, 1720). Despite its crudity, this quaint picture seems to show that Keysler had some idea of mound burial, sun and tree worship, and gods of cultivation. The ' Druid ', apparently waiting for some augury from the sacred horse, prepares the fire on the altar beneath the tree. Supported by a knowledge of the sacrifice, husbandmen prepare for spring sowing, while on the left figures are seen prostrating themselves before fir trees (or larches), and to the sun overhead. A rude tumulus stands in the background, and in the middle distance is an object which may represent an urn or a small shaped menhir.

CHAPTER I

FOLK-MEMORY : ITS NATURE AND SCOPE

WE have long been accustomed to the use of such words as *folk-lore*, *folk-song*, and *folk-speech*, and William Barnes, the Dorsetshire poet and philologist, even advocated the discarding of the familiar ' omnibus ' and the adoption of the simple term *folk-wain*. Naturally, then, a new compound like *folk-memory* finds its pathway already cleared.

By folk-memory we mean the conscious or unconscious remembrance, by a people collectively, of ideas connected with the retention of rites and superstitions, habits, and occupations. Such memory may be clear and sound, the outcome of an unbroken succession of impressions ; it may be dim and fugitive, almost to the point of extinction ; it may be distorted and misleading ; it may, by occasion, represent but the recovery of a clue which has, at an earlier period, apparently been quite lost. Examples of all these transitions will be discussed as we proceed.

Meanwhile, it will be observed that folk-memory is, to a very great extent, correlated with what, in some branches of archaeology, are known as ' survivals ', and again, with that ' superstition ' which, as Dr. Edward Tylor has acutely observed, is etymologically a ' standing-over ' of custom or ceremony,[1] and which may, or may not, involve a derogatory idea.

The memory of an individual person frequently bridges over no inconsiderable period of time. By linking the recollections of two or three such persons we can get a lineal oral tradition which is of great value as an adjunct to written history. Thus, there was living in December, 1905, a North Riding farmer, who, as a boy, in 1827, had talked with a centenarian who had served under the Duke of Cumberland at Culloden in 1746.[2] A long list of such cases might be compiled.

Oral tradition of this kind has, of course, more historical value when the actors concerned belong to the educated class, though unlettered folk may supply the more interesting material. We are often reminded how Dr. Routh, who was for sixty-three years President of Magdalen College, Oxford, and who died in his hundredth year in 1854, had watched Dr. Johnson struggling up the steps of University College, had known a contemporary of Addison, and had talked with a lady whose aunt had seen Charles II walking in the Park at Oxford during the time of the Great Plague. Here the spoken tradition of three generations covers two centuries. Again, Dean Ramsay, who died in 1872, used to relate how he was brought up by an uncle, who gave him an account of the execution of Charles I, as received from an eye-witness.[3]

Numerous other interesting cases might be given, but it is sufficient to note, in passing, that testimony of this kind has been employed with much effect in dealing with historical questions. Professor Saintsbury once made a telling use of overlapping recollections to prove the genuineness of the Shakespearean authorship. The testimony carried onward from father to son will not be lightly esteemed by the archaeologist, who has unfortunately only too often to avail himself of less trustworthy evidence. For it is not to the recollections of individual men and women that he can usually appeal, but only to that common memory which is part of the mental equipment of mankind in the aggregate.

Moreover, the persons who furnish the inquirer with the choicest material are the peasantry, whose recollections must be submitted to every possible test. Lamennais remarks that it is with humanity as with the succession of individuals of which it is composed—memory begins only at a somewhat advanced stage of race development.[4] Hence the earlier traditions must be closely scrutinized; hence, also, as peasants belong to the less progressive section of the race, we must expect discrepancies and contradictions in folk-story.

Of the varying values of evidence take two extreme examples. At the time these words are written, the vicarage of Watford (Herts.) has known only two occupants for 105 years. Making all allowances for human error, the accumulated spoken testimony of the two incumbents would be of priceless worth were all the written annals of the parish by chance suddenly destroyed.

Far otherwise is it with the rural labourer. He, as Stapfer and Joly have incidentally noticed, is like the child—to each there is nothing in antiquity but ' very old '. Do we desire to follow the stream of time backward ? Difficulties soon present themselves. The serf of the Middle Ages, nay, the sage who was his contemporary, made no distinctions in antiquity, pagan, Jewish, or Christian : ' *Il ne connaît que des anciens.*' [5] To the mass. of Englishmen events are simply either of yesterday or of that vague period associated with Cromwell or Julius Caesar indifferently.

Have we, then, nothing on which to rely but the obstinate repetitions of the unlettered hind and the garrulous greybeard ? Happily we have, yet it is difficult to define exactly in what it consists.

We have referred to unconscious memory. The modern psychologist teaches that each human being possesses, besides a conscious personality, a ' sub-liminal self ', an unconscious counterpart, as it were, of the active intelligence, which unobtrusively makes a record of sights and sounds, impressions and conversations. Under abnormal or pathological conditions, when the conscious self is in abeyance, these stored-up records are again brought forth. The fervid revivalist speaks a tongue which he never consciously learnt ; the grown man again recognizes the home of his childhood from which he has long been exiled. A forgotten controversy to which one has unwittingly listened is recalled, unbidden ; a fall from horseback causes concussion of the brain, and a lost memory is restored.[6]

Something like this latent memory exists in a race. At certain times of the year the schoolboy begins to play at marbles or leap-frog ; why, he cannot tell. The city merchant takes to a caravan or goes picnicking, little thinking that the free life and vagabondage of primitive man are reasserting themselves. The slightest spark kindles religious fury, or makes whole nations run amuck and thirst for combat. A long-forgotten sport or homely custom is revived by some trivial incident, after all the efforts of wealth and fashion have failed in the attempt. From the Crusades to the South Sea Bubble, and from these to treasure hunts and whist drives, history is burdened with instances.

The concerted, but not preconcerted, action of masses of people suggests another curious fact. M. Gustave Le Bon, in his ' Psychology of the Crowd ', shows in a convincing manner how certain qualities characteristic of a crowd as a whole, such as generosity, prudence, and animality, are markedly different from the sum total of the same qualities possessed by the constituent units. Thus a mob has greater instinctive chivalry, but more potential brutality, than could be obtained by summing up the endowments of all its separate members.

Mr. Cecil Sharp has compared the growth of a folk-song with the flight of a host of starlings. Erratic invitations to change the direction of the flight come from birds on the margin of the flock. These invitations are ignored, one after another, until a chance suggestion happens to coincide with the will of the majority. The suggestion is accepted ; the flock changes its direction ; a new evolution is initiated. No member of the flock can give a reason ; the community moves as one until the unknown moment for change.

This is exactly what seems to be the plight of folk-memory. Not one amongst the rude forefathers of the hamlet can tell why the local fair is held on a particular day in a field containing a certain ' blue stone ' or barrow, but, to a man, these villagers know that the custom is right and must be followed. Scarcely any one remembers having been distinctly told that the earthwork above the village is ' Roman ', much less has any one made up the legend ; yet there it is, deep-rooted and not to be dislodged.

From these considerations it follows that, although the materials for the study of folk-memory lie ready at hand in the form of superstitions, sayings, ceremonies, and observances, and in customs connected with occupations, food, dress, and dwellings, yet these data must be scrupulously examined if they are to be of any value.

The peasant, as Mr. Grant Allen once remarked, is like the savage in one respect : whilst very incurious about what he deems non-essentials, he is a peculiarly long-headed person in all that concerns his immediate advantage.[7] Both these traits may be turned to profit by the inquirer. The wealth of lore in husbandry, the practical beliefs about weather and soil, the secrets of traditional occupations, aid in establishing connexions with the past. The non-essentials which concern the countrymen so little are, it is true, often the very matters about which the antiquary wishes to hear ; but let him be patient awhile. The narrator loves vain repetitions, and amid these there occasionally stands out a word or phrase which casts light on the quest.

' How can he get wisdom that holdeth the plough, and that glorieth in the goad, that driveth oxen, and is occupied in their labours, and whose talk is of (the breed of) bullocks ? He giveth his mind to make furrows, and is diligent to give the kine fodder.' [8] So the son of Sirach discovered of old, and he who would understand the common folk must lay the truth to heart. He must not only mix with the people, but reflect on that which he sees and hears, thus gaining that insight which the son of Sirach says ' cometh by opportunity of leisure '.[9]

The uneducated countryman, being practical, will carefully hand down to his sons the information which he and his fathers have gained empirically. He discovers that certain building stones, like the ' firestone ' of the Upper Greensand, endure better when surbedded, or placed as they lay when in their natural planes of stratification. In digging chalk for manure, he notices where excavations may be made with least trouble and the minimum of cartage. He has observed that the destruction of the barberry-plant (Berberis vulgaris) tends to prevent rust in the wheat-crop, without knowing the reason—that the shrub is necessary as an intermediate host of the fungoid pest. He finds that the application of lime to the soil will ward off ' finger and toe ' in turnips, and that the continuous cultivation of one crop in the same field will end disastrously. Such knowledge, painfully acquired, is faithfully passed on to the next generation.

Arthur Young, in 1798, found the shepherds in North Lincolnshire trepanning ' giddy ' or ' sturdy ' sheep, and one shepherd was known to be successful in half his cases. The late Mr. John Cordeaux stated that the operation used to be performed within the last fifty or sixty years,[10] and there is a possibility that the practice has come down from remote times. Such wisdom is money to the husbandman, and as his order, like a corporation, is undying, the facts pass onward as long as they are of value.

The case of herbal medicine may be noted. That a knowledge of plants, emanating in part doubtless from monastic sources, was once more widely spread is evinced by the existence of popular plant-names, now to be learned only from textbooks, either directly or indirectly. When the ' doctrine of signatures ' held sway, numbers of plants had virtues ascribed to them. With the birth of medical science, the knowledge dwindled and tradition became blurred. The new men indeed retained some of the simples in the pharmacopoeia, but for information about the excellences of henbane and pellitory and borage and self-heal, one must consult the herbalist, or the wise woman, or the artisan who has a taste for quasi-scientific study. Chickweed tea, infusion of pellitory, coltsfoot wine, and the juice of the greater celandine, are still deemed sovereign remedies in some districts, though, for the reason stated, the reputation of simples has largely died out of folk-memory.

Besides the influence of practical economy on folk-memory, there is that of hereditary occupations, strongest amongst farmers and herdsmen, but felt in many other callings. In 1905, there died at Aston Upthorpe (Berks.) the representative of a family which had held a particular farm in unbroken succession since 1553, in which year the lease was renewed by the monks of Cirencester.[11] Other long leases might be given, and it may be remembered that Richard Jefferies, a son of the soil, often lingers over this theme. If farmers remain farmers for centuries, so is there a like persistence among the labouring class, due allowance being made for exceptional cases. In a Warwickshire parish, Mr. Robert Hudson has traced back family names of peasants to the beginning of the parish register, some centuries ago, and he believes that the lineage of peasant families may be carried to the age of serfdom. Yet in this parish there is not a single landowner whose family record goes back a century.[12] The firm retention of local customs and the corruptions of belief are thus readily explained. That office is performed by the poorer folk.

The peasant is, in some respects, a child as truly as he is physically a healthy human animal. Readers of ' Tess ' will recall with what childish glee old Durbeyfield seizes upon the parson's imprudent remark about Norman ancestry, and how quickly he extends the family tree to the days of Julius Caesar. In making Durbeyfield eke out his scanty knowledge by an appeal to history, warped beyond recognition, Mr. Hardy shows the skill of a master.

But there are other hereditary callings besides those appertaining to the soil. The persistence of the flint-workers at Brandon will be noticed in the sequel. Then there are the lime-burners. Over a century ago, Marshall, visiting the Petworth district of Sussex, found that this occupation was a matter of ' birth and descent ', one worker, then past middle life, being a descendant of four generations of lime-burners.[13] Other trades carried on from father to son were once common ; examples are seen in the Cornish fishers, the Portland quarrymen, the cutlers of Sheffield, the stone-wallers of Derbyshire, and the thatchers of the Wiltshire Downs. Such men have played no mean part in keeping up an inviolable tradition. To a less degree the same remark applies to the hereditary skill, not always, however, involving hereditary descent, of weavers, glass-blowers, and engravers.

It may be urged that knowledge is often irrecoverably lost, that men dispute in vain about the correct method of making Roman cement, or Greek fire, or the colours of the old masters, the gold ink of mediaeval monks, the metal of

ancient bells. The objection is pertinent. These cases are
not uncommon, but for each instance of vanished lore a
reason could probably be given. In most of the examples
secrecy is the explanation, for learned and ignorant alike
can keep a secret at need. Let suspicion, however, become
too powerful, and the knowledge dies with its youngest
possessor.

But the point is precisely this : arts and crafts and customs
may utterly perish when they have ceased to be of immediate
practical use, even when, as in some cases, there was no
purpose in making a mystery.

Ask the native of Kent or Essex the origin and object of
those curious subterranean chambers known as dene-holes,
and no answer is returned. Go to Cheshire and inquire
about the obscured marl-pits, or to Dorsetshire and put
questions about the cultivation terraces on the hill-sides,
or to Cleveland to find out the story of the old disused
excavations for iron-ore ; again there is no reply. The
craft has been lost or diverted, and all the information
gathered will be indefinite talk about battles and treasure-
chambers and giants, valuable only to the discriminating
student of folklore.

The midland or northern farmer who talks of ' boon-
work ' has, of course, not the faintest idea of the old ' bene-
works ' or *precariae*, which were special services demanded
by the manorial lord from his villeins.[14] All that the farmer
knows is that so much boon-work—that is, carting gravel, it
may be, for the parish—means so much money subtracted
from his rates.

The currier who speaks of his smoothing-iron as a ' stone '
or ' sleeker ' knows not that his tool is the direct descendant
of a prehistoric smoothing-stone. The names are mere
literary petrifactions. Leave the age of stone for that of
metal and recollections of the past begin to fly away like
sparks from a crackling fire of sticks. Quite recently
Dr. Roth has found it extremely difficult to collect trustworthy information from the Queensland aborigines concerning stone implements, now that the art of working
timber is almost always performed by scrap-iron or modern

tools.[15] In our own country Dr. T. M. Allison has, after some trouble, succeeded in rescuing facts about British flails, before the last labourer of the old school has passed away. Soon we shall be unable to find a peasant who can do ornamental thatching, or set up decorative oak palings, or even make a ' stake-and-bond ' hedge.

Ascend the scale of intelligence and ask the educated man why yew-trees are planted in churchyards, why hagioscopes were made in church walls, or why the little strips of land composing a farm are often widely scattered : he, too, is at a loss. Yet, in the last-named case, so obstinate was public opinion, that only a century ago Arthur Young and Sir John Sinclair found the open-field system, of which these strips are relics, so firmly established, as it had been from time immemorial, that there was stubborn opposition to any suggested enclosures.[16]

By an extension of the theory of ' immediate advantage ', however, folk-memory retains perverted impressions and beliefs which should be carefully examined. Mythical gold is hidden in burial-mounds ; thunderbolts fall from a stormy sky ; it is dangerous to accept presents of iron ; earthworks were made ' by the Romans, at the time of the war '. By way of supplement, imminent loss or danger has given us the fairies of the barrow, the graveyard ghost, and the incredible monsters of the deep.

In myths, folk-songs, and nursery rhymes we get dim survivals of a long-spent past, with perchance a faint halo of semi-consciousness spread around during the narration. When an actual incident is described, faultiness of memory may be aided by some central idea, such as the familiar notion of buried treasure. This point is illustrated in a story told by Sir Archibald Geikie, who heard it from an aged lady in the Lammermuirs. Before the battle of Dunbar, Cromwell, finding his retreat cut off by Leslie, and his fleet delayed by storms, tried to communicate with his English base by land. With this purpose, so ran the Lammermuir tradition, two men, disguised as natives, were sent on the errand. The messengers got as far as the valley of the Whiteadder, where they were detected and shot.

Sir Archibald continues : 'Miss Darling told me that tradition had always pointed to some old whin-bushes at the opening of the cleugh as the spot where they were buried.' At the lady's instigation the ground was dug up, and among some mouldering bones were found a few decayed buttons and a coin of the time of Charles I.[17]

The story of the buried treasures of the Incas, again, may prove to be well founded, since partial discoveries of treasure were reported from Bolivia in March, 1904. A few months later, a Danish captain, Christian Jensen, returned from an Arctic voyage with news of another kind of discovery, for he announced the existence of giants seven feet and upwards in height, thus partially confirming an old Eskimo tradition.[18]

Superstition carries her treasures carefully. Mrs. Burton-Brown claims as the result of recent discoveries in Rome that the ancient stories, set aside these sixty years as childish inventions, may represent in part actual truths. The old worship of springs and natural forces was indeed already well proven, but we are now told that perhaps even Romulus and Remus existed.[19]

Frequently remembrance is preserved by some childish triviality. Three great events in English history chanced to occur on November 5. On that day in 1605 the Gunpowder Plot was discovered ; on the same day in 1688 William of Orange landed at Torbay; and in 1854, barely two generations ago, be it noted, a great victory was achieved over the Russians at Inkerman. Three momentous crises : one only is remembered, since its events are commemorated by guys and bonfires. Men and boys alike have a born instinct for the joys of bonfires and beacon-fires, and resemble their ancestors, who loved to dance around the roaring flames. The wise folk-lorist repines not, as may the historian ; to the former the least remnant of old custom brings gladness. Even in the most misty legend there may be a basis of reason.

The sheer inertness of custom must also be contemplated. Folk-memory may perish, yet some silly practice may remain. We are told by Professor Seebohm how Bismarck once found a Russian sentinel pacing up and down a lawn in front of a palace. Research made in the military archives showed that in the days of Catherine the Great a snowdrop had appeared on the lawn, a sentinel was placed there to guard it, and the order, never having been revoked, continued to run.

The most curious cases of folk-custom are those industrial practices where distinct breaks appear to have taken place, and methods once lost have been unwittingly resuscitated. For example, the Romans adopted in this country an elaborate system of milestones, yet it is stated that the earliest specimens of post-Roman date are those which were set up between London and Cambridge in A. D. 1729.[20] Again, the Veneti, the old seafaring people of Brittany, who trafficked with Britain in the days of Caesar, used iron chains with their anchors. The invention is believed to have perished, and iron cables did not come in again until 1812, when they were adopted by the British navy.[21] Or consider those thermal springs which are known to have been used as baths by the Romans, but which, having once become ruinous, were not again employed for their first purpose until modern times. Our own springs at Bath, and those of Royat and Mont Dore in France, are a few examples out of many.[22]

From the domain of popular knowledge one instance may be cited. The visitor to the Auvergne district may be astonished to learn, as was the present writer, that the peasants are aware of the volcanic origin of the local mountains. 'Volcano,' 'crater,' 'lava' are common words in the vocabulary of the Auvergnats. Now it happens that relics of primitive rock-shelters have been found beneath the later or Quaternary outflow from the Puy de Tartaret, and it is thought, therefore, that Palæolithic man may have witnessed eruptions from that once-active centre. Further, Professor T. G. Bonney has produced evidence showing that there may have been an isolated outburst occurring so late as the fifth century of the present era ;[23] although Caesar makes no mention of such phenomena in his time. But it would be the rashest simplicity to conclude that there has been a direct tradition of these events. We are told, moreover, that the Auvergnats of the eighteenth century scoffed at Guettard's ideas of the volcanic origin of the puys. We must, then, attribute the present-day knowledge to the influence of the printed book, and to the infiltration of ideas from instructed visitors—two factors which ever tend to mislead the inquirer and to obscure his judgement. Several examples will later receive detailed treatment.

The realm of superstition, with its fairies, witches, and wizards, its sacred animals, trees, and springs, had probably a very early beginning. Briefly, to epitomize this subject we may give the explanation put forth by Mr. G. L. Gomme. He suggests that the British aborigines, whom we may for the moment consider the people of the Newer Stone Age, had belief in their own demoniacal powers. These non-Aryan aborigines had a caste of Druids, who were a kind of hereditary priests or medicine-men. When the ' Aryan ' peoples, let us provisionally say the various Celtic races, conquered the Neolithic folk, they partially adopted the beliefs of the vanquished. A time came, Mr. Gomme supposes, when the blood descent of the Neolithic Druids ceased, and when initiatory descent took its place among the new-comers.[24] The resultant mixture of fairy-craft and witchcraft is very confusing. Druidism also became modified by the introduction of Christianity, and finally died out. From these clashing elements we have to select the origins of later superstitions. Yet there appears to have been no real break. One writer goes so far as to say that it would be a problem of considerable difficulty to fix the point where Irish Druidism, at any rate, ceased, and from which point onwards Christianity could be said to commence. Although this has been termed an extreme view, Sir John Rhŷs would, ' after toning it down a little,' be disposed ' to extend it so as to take in the Celts, not only of Ireland, but of Britain too '.[25]

Those who underrate the value of folk-memory because its conflicting testimonies afford but ' broken lights ', may fairly be reminded of the fallibility of written history. One recalls the old story of Geoffrey of Monmouth, that London was founded by Brutus, son of the Trojan prince Aeneas.

Not that I would decry or belittle the importance of chronicles and documents, much less attack them in the spirit of that unknown cynic—whether it was Charles V, or Lord Melbourne, or some one else—who cried, ' History, I know that to be a fable ! '

Still, it may be pointed out that written history is liable to the unconscious errors of the scribe, to subtle psychological bias, to wilful partisanship, and, most frequently of all, to the sheer mental inability to record accurately scenes, images, and perceptions.

Professor C. Lombroso has given the most startling illustrations of the fallibility of human testimony. Educated eye-witnesses, specially warned beforehand, were asked to give accounts of simple transactions which they had seen. Over and over again, the majority swore to statements which were inaccurate, inexact, and even imaginary.[26]

Another dictum quoted against oral tradition is summarized in the epigram, ' An inch of potsherd is worth all Herodotus.' It is true that objective evidence is of more avail than subjective literature, and is far preferable to verbal testimony. On the other hand, even material documents, such as tiles and columns, have, by their inscriptions, been known to falsify historical facts. The errors were often betrayed only by the anachronisms involved.[27] We may compare the sorts of evidence and perhaps place them in the order just given, and if we are wise we shall let one kind supplement the others.

That folk-memory in its own sphere works well is shown by the accuracy with which the boundaries of parish and township have been handed down by such simple, age-borne methods as beating the bounds and riding the marches.[28] An example of another order is illustrated by the oral transmission, for centuries, of those narrative, impersonal poems known as ballads and folk-songs. Professor F. B. Gummere and Mr. Cecil Sharp have demonstrated how these compositions have come down to us, perchance from early communal dancing-songs, with many variations, essential and unessential, but ever with some unanimity of purpose, betokening the genius of the multitude.[29]

The effort to separate the trustworthy from the erroneous is worth making.   A last word of preparation is necessary. Real continuity is not infrequently overlooked because it is masked by the use of the imperfect term ' survivals '.   The succeeding chapters will deal largely with this question of continuity, and this subject extends beyond the bounds of folk-memory.   Where folk-memory exists we look for its proof in vestigial customs and beliefs.   But the converse is not inevitably true, nor shall we always find it to be so.

CHAPTER II

THE CONTINUITY OF THE AGES OF STONE AND BRONZE

This preparatory chapter will stray beyond the strict limits of folk-memory. In order to avoid undue expansion of the section, some knowledge of prehistoric archaeology is assumed, but the briefest summary must be given so as to acquaint the reader with the ground to be traversed.

The early stages of archaeology, recognizable chiefly by means of the development of man's stone implements, were long ago conveniently marked off by Lord Avebury, who distinguished between the Palæolithic, or Older Stone Age, and the Neolithic, or Newer Stone Age.

To these has now been prefixed the Eolithic period, representing the ' Dawn ' of the Stone Age. Some authorities question the proofs adduced for this period, and a few others, whilst accepting the genuineness of the implements which have evoked the title, contend that these are really of Palæolithic age. The discussion of Eoliths and an Eolithic Age must be considered as not terminated, though the writer may say frankly that he accepts many of the implements put forward by Mr. Benjamin Harrison, of Ightham (Kent), and considers them the work of an early race of low type. Having first approached the matter as a decided sceptic, the writer has the more pleasure in rendering homage to the labours and discoveries of Mr. Harrison.

Much of the misapprehension concerning Eoliths has probably arisen from ignorance of the rude character of some of the older Palæoliths. Confusion is also bound to occur if the expert relies alone on the intrinsic nature of the implement—its shape, patina, and fineness of working—instead of trusting primarily to the stratigraphical position in which the implement is found.

Eoliths of some kind are logically demanded. One

expects them to be rude; to be of few types, answering to primitive needs; and to foreshadow the outlines of the Palæoliths which were to follow.

Of late the attack on Eoliths has been vigorously renewed. Abroad, M. Marcellin Boule is reluctant to admit Eoliths in the absence of osteological corroboration. He claims that they may be formed naturally. At a cement mill near Mantes the chalk is put into a vat filled with water to separate the useless flint from the matrix. A rotary motion is communicated to the water by a horizontal wheel working above the water-level. The wheel has suspended harrows (*herses*) of cast-iron. For twenty-nine hours there is a tumultuous movement, and the nodules of flint, when separated from the chalk, are exposed to every conceivable kind of pressure and shock. The result, says M. Boule, is that the broken flints present all the features of river-gravels, and among the mass are Eoliths, some of which exhibit even the ' bulb of percussion '.[1]

Clearly M. Boule proves too much. Accidental cones and bulbs of percussion may occasionally be made by the pavior's hammer, and may occur fortuitously in river-gravels. But if M. Boule's implication is quite serious, it will rule out many hitherto recognized Palæolithic flakes. It would, however, be passing strange if the revolving spikes of the harrows with their chain attachments, a very artificial arrangement, acting at a definite speed for a definite time, did not sometimes produce bulbs, and it would be equally wonderful if the colliding flints did not get battered edges. The spikes or teeth, catching at the necessary angle a flint imprisoned by the chalky matrix below, would by chance blows form good chipping or knapping agents. Such treatment is but one stage removed from rude, slipshod ' tooling ' by human agency.

Can M. Boule show that the Eoliths of the Kentish plateau have been subjected to the action of such a whirlpool? Among his mill-made specimens can he discriminate four or five well-marked and distinct types, like those of the ' dumb-bell ' and ' double-bow ' patterns? Can he produce deeply-stained flints, occasionally scratched, notched in the hollows and not at the projections, and this frequently from alternate sides, the body of the flints having no chippings or workings ? [2]

From the context, one is driven to believe that M. Boule must be comparing his artificial ' Eoliths ' with the naturally-battered pebbles of the uninformed collector, or with the Miocene ' Eoliths ' of Continental enthusiasts.   As to his demand for osteological evidence, little, from the nature of the case, is likely to be forthcoming.   Dr. H. P. Blackmore claims to have found Eoliths in gravels which, a century ago, yielded the remains of the primitive elephant (*Elephas meridionalis*), at Dewlish, in Dorset; [3] but of this claim there is not complete acceptance.   A similar discovery is recorded from a like horizon at Val D'Arno, in Italy, and St. Prest, in France; but objectors have urged that the implements were in reality Palæolithic.[4]   With the admitted Palæoliths the case is different, bones are available as testimony, though many experts would consider that authenticity could be established independently.

Experiment can be met by experiment, and this has been done by my friend Mr. F. J. Bennett, in respect to Kentish wash-mills and chalk-mills.   Mr. Bennett found that fresh charges of chalk are introduced while the mill is at work, and that some of the flints which had been in the basin only a part of the time sustained fractures and even acquired bulbs, so that, if photographed, they might readily pass for Eoliths.   Photography plays the part of a wizard even with natural flints.   The flints which had been in the mill all the time, and had sunk out of reach of the harrows, were almost perfectly smooth spheres.[5]   Nowhere in nature, save perhaps in a pot-hole or ' giant-cauldron ', can such conditions be postulated.   River-gravels do not usually remain in one spot long enough to receive this special whirlpool treatment.

The most destructive criticism, though not by any means conclusive, yet delivered in England against the Eoliths, is that put forward by Mr. S. Hazzeldine Warren.   He has attempted to prove that Eoliths may be exactly imitated by forces artificially applied, such as stamping with the foot, or crushing in a screw-press. The corresponding natural agencies Mr. Warren looks for in ' soil-creeps ' and earth-movements.[6] Though not convincing, Mr. Warren's arguments may be considered a much-needed corrective to the absurd claims of the extreme school. What has been said in opposition to the views of M. Boule may be repeated to meet those of Mr. Warren. And, above all, if these authorities are right, Eoliths should be found in most river-gravels ; this, however, from long experience and careful examination, I can assert is not the fact.

Finally, we must remember that the Eoliths, as proved by their survival, are presumably among the hardest of the plateau gravels, yet these obdurate nodules display battered or ' worked ' edges. To bruise a flint fresh from the chalk is a different and easy matter, to modify such ' working ' beyond recognition is also readily accomplished.

Having now devoted as much space to this subject as can be spared, we may note that the old classification into Palæolithic and Neolithic is breaking down, and that the archaeologist of the future may perchance see complete continuity established from the earliest stone age to the present day. The old and somewhat arbitrary divisions may, perhaps, be retained popularly, in gratitude for their provisional help in early investigations.

Geologists will call to mind that the history of our knowledge of the Chalk formation reveals a like development. Originally divided into Chalk-with-Flints and Chalk-without-Flints, it was afterwards classified, still on lithological data, into Upper, Middle, and Lower sections. To-day the Chalk has eleven or twelve zones, each based on faunal evidence, and each gradually and imperceptibly merging into its successor.

In the zones of the Chalk, and in the periods of archaeology, the nomenclature tends to look backward rather than forward. A type-fossil of one zone found sporadically in a succeeding zone would not necessarily invalidate the claim of the latter band to separate recognition ; the whole assemblage of fossils must be considered. So with stone implements and weapons, an old type lingering in a new period need not

destroy the label of the later group. All the facts must be
considered—materials, pattern, working, stratigraphy. The
guiding principle is that transitions must be expected, and
neither a geometrical line nor a chronological pendulum can
be employed.

Already two ages of Eolithic implements, representing
differences of type, workmanship, and level, have been
recognized in Kent by Mr. Harrison, Mr. J. Russell Larkby,
and others.[7] The second, or Transitional type, leads on to
the Hill Group, which comprises the oldest Palæolithic tools.
Next come three periods, represented by as many terraces of
river-gravels. The rock-shelters of Ightham seem to furnish
the implements which follow those of the drifts. Messrs.
M. A. C. Hinton and A. S. Kennard, who, after painstaking
labour, claim to have established this succession, state that the
Hill Group of implements, admitted as Palæoliths even by the
orthodox collector, yields ' side-scrapers ', hollow-scrapers,
and flakes showing the characteristic rectangular work of
the Eoliths. Some of the examples so greatly resemble
Eoliths as to indicate attempts to produce artificially the
tabular flints which were prized by the makers of those
primitive implements.[8] The Swanscombe (Kent) river-
gravels have yielded a re-chipped implement of the Hill
Group, remote from the level where it was originally fabricated. Both implements would normally be called Palæoliths, yet a vast period of time elapsed between the deposition
of the two terraces.[9] Incidentally we notice that an implement found in a particular bed may be much older than
the bed itself. A layer of gravel may yield a Palæolith
alongside an Elizabethan coin, and the Thames bed contains
implements of all ages.

On the Continent, M. A. Rutot has divided the pre-
Neolithic implements into ten classes, of which four are
assigned to the Eoliths, four to the older Palæoliths, and
two to the newer.[10] Such a classification, however, must
be deemed tentative only.

English archaeologists have grown accustomed to the
breaking-up of Palæoliths into the drift and the cave types ;
we now see how inadequate is this classification. Such a

grouping does not even take account of the Palæolithic implements discovered under the boulder clay of East Anglia, which indicate man's presence in Britain before the melting of the glaciers.

The term ' Neolithic ' is liable to artificial restriction not warranted by the data. Implements hitherto classed in this period are, as the writer firmly believes, frequently products of a later age. Concerning the flint flakes and scrapers found in Roman, Romano-British, and Saxon settlements the last word has not been uttered. Again, the implements of our Chalk Downs are obviously older than those of our sandy heaths. The ' pigmy ' implements were, perhaps, latest in the period. The evidence demands that we should recognize, at the least, tools of the Æneolithic (Bronze-and-Stone) period; but, as we shall see later, even this intercalation is insufficient in face of a probable steady development.

If the Palæolithic and Neolithic periods, considered separately, must each be subdivided into stages, what is the case for a line of demarcation between these two great periods themselves ?

It was commonly accepted, until within the last decade, that between the Older and the Newer Stone Ages there was a hiatus which could not be filled up. Professor W. Boyd Dawkins thinks that as the Glacial Period passed away, and milder conditions began to prevail, Palæolithic man followed the retreating reindeer Northwards. This authority has even suggested that the modern Eskimos may represent the descendants of these primitive emigrants.[11]

This theory would, of course, involve the existence of a land-bridge from Europe to North-East America in post-glacial times. That such a bridge once existed is agreed, and we need not pause to stir up the vexed question of the date of its disappearance. In any case, if we accept the Eskimo hypothesis, Palæolithic man—man of the drift period—would most probably cross the Border; but as yet his relics have not been discovered in Scotland. It is remotely possible that ice and water have swept away all the drift implements which were left behind in that country; at present we have apparently nothing earlier from Scotland than Mesolithic (Middle Stone Age) objects.   Deniker contends that the supposition of a general European migration to the North is invalidated by the fact that among the shell-heaps or kitchen-middens of Denmark no remains of the reindeer are found.[12]

But why should Palæolithic man follow the reindeer ? The creature was not, seemingly, domesticated to any great extent, some would say not at all.   If pursued Northwards, then, the reindeer would be chased for the sake of food. But a milder climate would bring in an abundant fauna suitable and sufficient for that purpose.   As a fact, the reindeer long survived the new conditions in Britain, for, in the work already referred to, Professor Boyd Dawkins shows that it was living in Caithness as late as A.D. 1159.

When we study the present British types of the Arctic fauna, we shall see that they are isolated in widely-separated localities, and this discontinuity suggests great antiquity. Hence the pre-glacial fauna was probably not exterminated. Authorities like Sir Charles Lyell, Professor G. J. Cole, and Dr. R. F. Scharff hold that extensive glaciation is not incompatible with the existence of sheltered nooks and corners in the unglaciated areas.   Wherever a land-fringe remained unburied by the ice, and especially in Southern England, Palæolithic man, like certain other members of the fauna, and like the modern Lapp, could live and thrive.   The driftless portions of the moorlands of Cleveland, never submerged by the ice-sheet, may have represented areas of refuge.   The Southern Pennines, and the South-East of England, would probably be other areas.

Much has been made of the fact that, accepting the two Palæolithic and Neolithic periods in their old restricted sense, the two corresponding faunas are widely different.   The cave-bear, mammoth, musk-ox, and reindeer are set in contrast to the horse, sheep, dog, and goat.[13]   The change may, however, have been gradual.   Eventually, the larger mammals did disappear, but the result may not have been due to severe cold, even if we admit that the Glacial Period demands a great reduction of temperature.   Algeria has lost its large animals, yet that country was outside the glaciated area.

Dr. Scharff has argued in favour of the existence of a Lusitanian or ' temperate ' fauna throughout the Glacial Period. In Glacial deposits the remains of Arctic and tropical faunas are found at the same levels, and this fact cannot be satisfactorily explained on the assumption of intensely severe conditions, or of great extremes of temperature. Lessen the assumed severity, and the case is explicable. We may approach the problem in another way. Creatures like the reindeer and rhinoceros may not have been so highly specialized with regard to habitat in the Palæolithic period.

Arctic and temperate faunas exist side by side to-day. The tiger, clad in a thicker coat, hunts the reindeer in Manchuria. Animals like the lion have been successfully kept in the open air in the city of Dublin. So with vegetable life : in New Zealand and Switzerland grapes ripen near the foot of great glaciers. Such instances could be extended. On the whole, the Glacial Period is perhaps a more negligible element in the history of man than has hitherto been allowed.

Whether a completely satisfactory transition can now be framed is very doubtful, particularly in the North of England. Remains of Pleistocene mammals, including *Felis spelaea* and *Elephas primigenius*, believed by Mr. Clement Reid to have come from a post-glacial peat-bed in Holderness, are now proved not to have been derived from that deposit.[14] Our bone-caves are few in number. Any Mesolithic surface relics of bones have probably been dissolved or washed away for ever. Or, as may sometimes also be the case with material from the Palæolithic drift, any transitional remains may have become inextricably mixed with the flotsam of later ages. In that event, we are largely thrown back upon the stone implements, which will presently be discussed.

Some writers have argued, with more reason, it would seem, than those of the other school, that during the colder intervals of the Ice Age the stress of the weather drove man Southwards. Remembering that there was at that time land-connexion with the Continental area, emigration and return may have occurred more than once, but it is at least an open question whether there was a general departure. Extinction simple and absolute cannot be seriously propounded, because man, as well as beast, had the power to move from place to place. One important admission must now be made. Between the Cave-man of the Palæolithic period and his successor of the Newer Stone Age there is, in Britain, a ' cultural break '. The fact need not be minimized. The Cave-man could make lifelike carvings on bone and ivory, and could scratch excellent designs on the walls of his rock-home. Neolithic man produced only lines, marks, dots, and zigzags, with herring-bone and rope-work ; these, too, were mainly impressed on pottery.

Is this apparent retrogression consistent with the continuity of races ? On the English evidence alone it would be difficult to prove definitely the affirmative. A few considerations may, however, be set forth. Geometrical forms are not altogether absent in the work of Palæolithic man, for he incised such patterns on his harpoons. Again, different climatic conditions, involving different materials upon which to work, might cause man's artistic skill to change its course. The reindeer had become scarcer, and its antlers objects of value. Tusks of the larger beasts were also correspondingly rare. Somewhere or other the faculty for carving in ivory may have lain in abeyance, for we meet it well developed in early historic times. Mr. Alfred Maskell, in his monograph on ' Ivories ', asserts that though there are many breaks in the chain of examples up to the fourth century of the Christian era, yet onwards, either in Britain or Central Europe, all is complete. This continuity is the more remarkable, seeing that for several centuries after the third no authentic records are left of any other art.[15] It may be fairly argued that the art of carving was lost and re-discovered, but there is a chance that it had never been altogether obsolete.

A secondary explanation of the absence of graving has some force. The Palæolithic cave-man, after a successful hunting expedition, had his hours of idleness, which he probably utilized in carving images of the animals which he had slain. Neolithic man, who was shepherd, husbandman,

hunter, fisherman, weaver, and potter, had scant leisure ;
a life of continuous industry left little time for the practice
of art.[16]

There is, too, always the probability that the Neolithic
folk, finding Britain still partially inhabited by the older
Palæolithic people, first conquered these aborigines, and
afterwards, by sheer force of numbers and the sovereign
power of ignorance, obliterated the artistic instincts of
the vanquished. It is a strange but recognized fact in
ethnology, that the members of a victorious race, even when
moderately civilized, are prone to destroy existing art and
culture whilst unconsciously imbibing the superstitions of
their forerunners on the soil.

Whatever may be the conclusions drawn from the incom-
pleteness of the British evidence, the testimony from the
Continent must secure a clearer verdict. In Austria at
least Dr. Moriz Hoernes claims that there were no yawning
gaps, no catastrophes, but on the contrary a series of imperceptible transitions.[17] Coming nearer home, there is important evidence from France, the more interesting because
Professor Boyd Dawkins asserts that no continuity can be
made out between the Palæolithic man of the Pleistocene
age and any of the races now living in our quarter of the
world, and that between the two periods is an interval
' which cannot be measured in terms of years '.[18]

At Mas d'Azil, on the left bank of the Arise, or Ariége, in
Southern France, there exists a cave or grotto which has
been explored by M. E. Piette, and has yielded evidence of
several stages of transition. There we get relics of the
Equine or Horse epoch, the Cervine or Deer epoch, and the
age of coloured pebbles and shells.[19] The pebbles, which
have coloured spots, and bands, and borders, belong to the
period when the reindeer had practically died out, and art
had entered new channels.

It had previously been argued, on general grounds, that
the so-called ' sterile layers ' of caves and rock-shelters were
probably due to the fact that these abodes often existed at
very slight elevations, and hence a chance inundation
might temporarily drive away the inhabitants. Mas d'Azil

now yields evidence on the positive side. Judged both by stratigraphy and fauna, the gap seems to be closed. To this intermediate period has been given the name Tourassian, from the 'passage-cave' of La Tourasse, in the Haute-Garonne.[20] (Cf. table at end of chapter.)

The disappearance of the reindeer and the subsequent dominance of the red deer testify to a milder climate at Mas d'Azil. But even if man of the Reindeer or Magdalenian (from Madelaine or Madeleine) epoch had pursued his retreating quarry, need we assume that the whole population fled ? The emigration did not take place in a day, or the next day ; it would be gradual. Some members of the human family would probably linger in isolated groups, afterwards to fuse partially with the Neolithic folk.

But mark the changed environment of the primitive race. The reindeer had furnished abundance of food and clothing. Now, if a change of diet were desired, they had to chase the rarer and less-easily captured animal, the fleet-footed deer. The horns of the deer were less easy to engrave. Hence the finely-rounded harpoons of elegant design were replaced by those of deer-horn, and the newer weapons were flatter and rougher in execution. Other instruments of bone, though clearly derived from the Magdalenian epoch, were also less carefully made.[21] Ivory carving was a decaying industry, but the contemporary trade of flint-working was gaining ground.

Besides the retreat of the reindeer, another reason has been assigned for the later desertion of the caves. M. A. Doigneau has ingeniously argued that a milder climate would set up decomposition in the accumulations of animal refuse in and near the caves. Under more glacial conditions, heaps of waste flesh, bones, and skin, would cause little discomfort, but the oncoming of a higher temperature would compel man to flee.[22]

Testimony supplementary to that of Mas d'Azil comes from the sepulchral grottoes of Beaumes-Chaudes in the Lozère. There and elsewhere, in caves of unquestioned Neolithic age, have been discovered human remains which a high authority, Professor G. Hervé, considers to represent a simple variation of the race of Laugerie [23] (Magdalenian or late Palæolithic).   It will be noticed, in passing, that a uniform system of spelling these Continental terms has been adopted.   Out of a wide choice, I have decided to follow De Mortillet's *Magdalénienne*, anglicizing the terminal syllable, and similarly with the other terms.

The conclusion seems to be that the hiatus between the two great periods does not exist in France.   As M. G. de Mortillet has said, ' *il n'existe que dans nos connaissances* '; and again, it is ' *un vide par défaut d'observations* ', not ' *une lacune effective* '.[24]

But there are dissentient voices.   Professor Boyd Dawkins thinks that the Mas d'Azil remains do not show transition, or sequence, but merely mixture.[25]   And we may here note that the Professor considers that no discovery has yet bridged over the two main periods in any part of the world.[26]

The evidence of the implements has now to be taken. It is important to observe that Professor Boyd Dawkins has inferentially admitted the validity of this test ; he employs it to show that the implements of the Thames river gravels are probably older than those of the relic cave at Kent's Hole, Torquay.[27]   This is, moreover, the popular teaching. and it has something to recommend it.   Against this opinion is set the fact that nothing in the character of the faunas warrants the separation.[28]   There are certain rude quartzite implements found in the lower levels of Robin Hood's Cave, Cresswell Crags, Derbyshire, which may have been worked before the furthest advance of the ice-sheet.[29]   Implements of the Mousterian or Middle Palæolithic cave-type are found in England below the boulder clay of the Great Ice Age.[30] Hence, the priority of the drift implements is not strictly proven.

Rudeness of pattern and working does not necessarily attest great antiquity.   Some of the French Palæolithic cave implements and some of our own ' drift ' specimens are of exceeding beauty in shape, bevel, design, and workmanship.   On the other hand, some of the early Neoliths are crude and unshapely, and the roughest of all were found by Professor W. Gowland under the monoliths of Stonehenge, yet these were probably of the late Neolithic period.[31]

Nevertheless, the various types of implements, judged with discretion, have great evidential value, for their development is usually from the simple and crude to the highly-finished article. Professor B. A. Windle's epigrammatic summary of stone tools and weapons will remove much contentious misunderstanding : ' Eoliths are hacked, Palæoliths are chipped, and Neoliths are flaked.'[32] These maxims are generally true, and allowing for exceptions, a little acumen will enable one to trace the pedigree of many implements.

For example, Messrs. Hinton and Kennard, in the paper already alluded to, suggested that the implements of the Ightham rock-shelters might be correlated with those of one of the later French periods, the Solutrean (= Menchecourtian) when men lived not only in caves, but also in open-air settlements. From the upper layers of earth and breccia in Robin Hood's Cave were also dug implements of the Solutrean type.[33] Here, too, were found implements fashioned from bone and antler, as well as a bone engraved with the head of a horse. These last discoveries seem to indicate relationship with the Magdalenian cave-period. Unfortunately, the engraved horse at present stands alone as a representative of Palæolithic art in England.

Mr. Worthington G. Smith has unearthed ' side-scrapers ' from the Palæolithic ' floor ' at Caddington, near Luton, which resemble those of the Mousterian Age.[34] (See table, p. 51.)

From another station, Stoke Newington in the North-East of London, the same worker has adduced evidence of a significant kind. At that spot there formerly existed Mr. Smith's famous ' 12-foot gravel ' bed, which contained Palæolithic implements. On the top of all the older beds there lay ' a surface soil, containing implements of possible Mesolithic age, Neolithic implements, British and Saxon pottery, Roman and mediaeval coins, and objects of recent date '.[35] These Mesolithic, ' Middle Stone Age ', tools demand a little attention, but it should be added that Mr. Smith, discussing the various ages of the Palæoliths at this place, does not himself seem to claim complete continuity. He thinks that Palæolithic man retired before the advancing contorted drift, and that there is no evidence of the genuine Palæolithic savage ever returning to the new surface formed by this material. He may have returned at a later date, but there was a temporary human depopulation.[36] The context does not show whether this retreat is assumed to be of a local or a general character.

Sir A. Geikie has also supposed that the recurring cold periods would drive Palæolithic man out of the country, but that he kept coming back as often as the climate ameliorated.[37] But, accepting the rabbinical doctrine that the great glaciation did not extend south of the Thames, is there proof that the cold was intense enough to banish man—that man who could live alongside the reindeer and mammoth ? Once more, can ' continuation implements ' be produced, or are the Palæoliths and Neoliths sharply severed from each other ? Moreover, whilst such questions as the existence of interglacial periods and the origin of the boulder clay remain unsettled, the archaeologist may claim a little respite before finally accepting the gap theory.

It is commonly said, and the statement is in general true, that the cutting edges of the Palæoliths are at the narrow end, whereas in Neoliths it is the broad end which is chipped for use. Exceptions, however, are met with. Those elongated implements, with approximately parallel sides, conveniently classed as celts, are rightly regarded as typically Neolithic, but this form also has been found in Palæolithic gravels.

The ovoid tools of the Palæolithic drifts near Reading have their successors in the far-separated Neoliths of Suffolk, but here there is no question of Mesolithic tools. We infer, however, that whilst a particular type of implement is justly considered as characteristic of a given epoch, that type may persist long afterwards, and where this happens there can scarcely have been complete severance of continuity.

Flake knives and ' combination tools ' of the two epochs may be selected to match one another very fairly. I have

seen ' multiple ' Palæolithic scrapers from the Thames drift
which are the counterparts, in form, of the Neoliths of the
North Downs, and I have also examined in the museum at
Bourges a Neolith from the department of Indre-et-Loire,
which closely mimics one of our pear-shaped Palæoliths.
Flake knives from the brick-earth of Crayford, which, by
virtue of their stratigraphical position, are commonly
accepted as Palæoliths, would, if not labelled, readily deceive
collectors of tools of the later period. Like Neoliths, the
Crayford specimens are made of flint taken fresh from
the chalk.[38]

Remembering that the implements found in the brick-
earth of Crayford, and those which come from a greater
elevation in the Thames ' High Terrace ' gravels at Swanscombe, a few miles to the east, are alike called Palæoliths,
we see how inadequate is the orthodox classification.
Measured by the enormous amount of lateral erosion, the time
that elapsed between the deposition of the Swanscombe
gravels and the Crayford brick-earth respectively is estimated
to be much greater than the interval between the latter
event and the age in which we live.[39] We should expect
the later Palæoliths 'of the brick-earth to have a closer
Neolithic facies, and such is the case.

Mr. W. J. Lewis Abbott has described implements from
the ' Fourth Thames Terrace ' at Whitehall, which, though
essentially of Palæolithic type as regards quality of work,
seemed by their lanceolate form to foreshadow the Neolithic
pattern.[40]

On or near the Chalk Downs, in districts where no traces
of river drift have been or are likely to be discovered, one
occasionally meets with unabraded tools which belong to an
older type than their neighbours. The author has elsewhere
recorded a good example from Woodcote in Surrey.[41] Here
is no question of stray drift implements, sparse relics of the
now denuded gravels. Survivors of this latter kind I have
discovered on high ground in Wiltshire and Kent, far above
the bed of the present streams, and mixed with true Neoliths.
Mr. J. W. Brooke records a like association of implements
from Pantawick in Wiltshire.[42]

The late Mr. J. Allen Brown considered that he had established continuity at East Dean (Sussex) and elsewhere. He based his conclusion partly upon the character of the deposit, but more especially upon the type of the implements. These were pear-shaped, and of more decided axe form than the true Palæoliths. There were no tools with unworked butts, a common kind among the drift specimens. Many, too, were made of flint taken direct from the chalk.[43]

Other workers think that the rough surface celts of the Downs and the rudely-chipped primitive tools of Cissbury are corroborative of a Mesolithic period. To this supposition there are two objections : roughness is not a complete criterion of age, and the examples from Cissbury may be only half-finished implements. On most sides it is, however, allowed that the tools in question are at least early Neolithic.

A series of Irish finds from White Park Bay, co. Antrim, are of more than transient interest. Amidst an abundance of recognized Neolithic implements, corn-crushers, and animal bones, there were some tools said to be of the Palæolithic type. In the neighbourhood, kitchen middens, containing limpets and periwinkles, were numerous. The explanation offered rests upon the theory of the retreating reindeer ; it is urged that implements corresponding to those of two of the French cave periods continued to be made, whilst an immigration of the Newer Stone men, seemingly from the East, introduced a new phase of progress.[44] The much-debated shell-mounds of Denmark, it may be added, are usually assigned to the earliest Neolithic period,[45] but some writers have deemed them to be older still.

The Scotch evidence is a little stronger. The MacArthur Cave, near Oban, contained what was believed to be a transitional layer. This consisted of a shell-bed enclosing flint scrapers and harpoons of bone. Examination of the harpoons showed that they were of the flattened type, with a double row of barbs and a perforation at the base like those found at the Mesolithic station of Mas d'Azil. Above the shell-bed was a layer of gravel, and overlying this was a kitchen midden. A rock-shelter at Druimvargie, also near Oban, yielded similar remains.[46]

Near Keiss, on the coast of Caithness, an exploration of one of those rude circular structures of stone known as ' brochs ' revealed painted pebbles like those of Mas d'Azil. Whether the pebbles represent mere feats of decorative skill, whether they were counters for games or symbols of a magical character, does not matter ; the fact is, however, noteworthy.[47]

Implements alone, then, plead for the recognition of a Mesolithic group. Professor A. C. Haddon asserts that when a careful comparison is made of the tools and implements in very large collections, it is found that most of the generally accepted theories break down.[48]

From his own experience the writer can support Professor Haddon's assertion. Indeed, as a complement to field-work, there can be no pleasanter method of spending a half-day, either in Britain or on the Continent, than by visiting a well-equipped museum, and inspecting the implements. There one occasionally sees specimens, clearly labelled and well-authenticated, which seem to be out of the natural order of things if we are held bound by arbitrary grouping. The truth seems to be that implements of early Neolithic character appeared ere the Palæoliths had died out, and, contrariwise, rudely chipped tools of the earlier age were employed in times decidedly Neolithic. The sinuous line, seen in the side-view of characteristic Palæoliths, and caused by alternate chipping at the edge, is observable in many ' Mesoliths ' and unquestioned Neoliths.

One remarkable instance I will cite, for its nature cannot be forgotten. In Mr. Harrison's collection at Ightham may be seen a marked type of Eolith of dumb-bell shape. On either side is a hollow, crudely notched. The implement is flattened, and in most cases has one end wider than the other. Among a large assemblage of Palæoliths, implements of this pattern, but of better workmanship, are generally discernible. If we examine collections of Neolithic work, the ' double hollow scraper ' of varying degrees of craftsmanship cannot escape notice. In Fig. 2, four ' dumb-bell ' specimens are shown ; had it been desirable, more telling examples might have been selected. The implements

chosen are in the author's collection.   In looking for these,
the eye lighted upon a Thames drift implement from Hanwell,
which is the exact prototype of the Neolithic horseshoe
scraper.   Ovoid and pear-shaped implements from the three
main groups might also be selected.   A remarkable series of
tools of this nature was exhibited by Mr. E. R. Harrison, son
of the discoverer of the Eoliths, at the Congress of the South-
Eastern Union of Scientific Societies held at Canterbury in
1902.[49]

With respect to the carrying on of the Palæolithic types, it

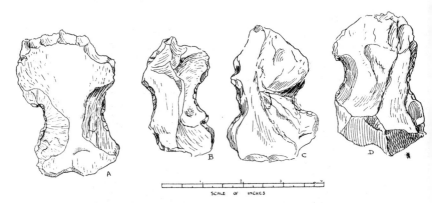

Fig. 2.   Flint implements of the 'dumb-bell' pattern (author's collec-
tion).   A. Eolith from the Kentish plateau.   B. Palæolith, Thames gravels,
Ealing.   c. Mesolith (?), raised beach at Kilroot, co. Antrim.   D. Neolith,
South Downs, near Eastbourne.

may be perhaps argued that these are the result of contact
between the Neolithic folk and the older races of the Continent before the Neolithic invasion of Britain.   But where,
in North-Western Europe, will the catastrophist allow that
such contact may have taken place, if a Mesolithic period be
denied ?   To this plea of oversea influence the transitionist
may oppose two considerations—first, the frequency with
which implements of standard patterns are repeated in
successive ages, and secondly, the merging into one another
of designs of less definite type.

Advocates of the gap theory have been constrained to
argue with Pitt-Rivers that ' form alone is not conclusive

in determining date '. No one should grant the truth of this maxim more freely than the transitionist, from whom indeed the contention would come more naturally. The advocate of transitional implements is aware that designs are carried forward, and that while certain forms persist strongly the criterion of shape is only valid for the more extreme terms of the conventional periods, or for the salient types of an assemblage of implements found on a floor or at some definite horizon.

Before leaving the Mesolithic question, we notice that another supposed line of demarcation may have to be erased. Formerly we were taught that domesticated animals came in with the Neolithic invasion. Bones were, however, found at Mas d'Azil on which were represented a reindeer and horses' heads, with indications of halters.[50] One horse seemed to be adorned with trappings. M. Julien Fraipont, while admitting that the carvings show that man had tamed a few horses and reindeer, urges that these creatures were probably captured young, but that they no more imply domestication than pictures of Roman chariots drawn by tigers and leopards prove the domestication of those fierce animals.[51] Is it quite a fair comparison between the luxurious eccentricities of a civilized people and the newly-awakened desires of a race struggling towards a settled state of existence? Tigers and leopards would be of little use if domesticated by primitive folk, but with horses and reindeer it is otherwise. And, after all, taming is the first step towards domestication.

If the facts be so, why these diversities of interpretation ? some reader may impatiently mutter. One can only reply in the words of Pope :—

> The difference is as great between
> The optics seeing as the objects seen.

For, when the facts have been actually accepted, the trend of opinion lies, now to the newer, now to the older school of archaeologists. All this is inherent in the subject, for archaeology is not an exact science.

The solution of the question is not rendered easier by the uncertainty when the chalk cliffs of Albion became separated from those of the Continent. In the undoubted Neolithic period Britain was ' beclipped all about by the sea '. But there is no decided proof at what period the English Channel was eroded.

Sir A. Geikie considers that when the earliest Neolithic men arrived Britain may have still been a part of the mainland.[52] Mr. Jukes-Browne also deems it quite possible that the new race may have come dryshod across the valley of the Channel.[53]

Professor Boyd Dawkins, on the other hand, contends that Neolithic man came to Britain in his ' dug-out ' canoes.[54] The evidence is at present unsatisfactory. Sir A. C. Ramsay puts the controversy in a nutshell : ' During Tertiary and post-Tertiary times, Britain was again and again united to the Continent.' [55]

Now the ' dug-out ' did not reach its highest development in the Neolithic period, hence, though the Strait was at first narrow, it is a moot point whether such a primitive boat would be fitted for the transport of domesticated animals. The matter is not unimportant, for if there was freedom to cross and recross on foot, it is scarcely credible that an un-mixed race occupied our country in the early Neolithic days.

Dr. John S. Flett has suggested that the separation occurred during the Great Ice Age. If this be so, the ' dug-out theory ' must be accepted. It may fairly be questioned whether the earliest men were pre-glacial and witnessed the oncoming of the ice, but it is almost certain that the Palæolithic inhabitants saw the glaciers begin to disappear. It has now also been shown that Neolithic man was in possession of the country before the last lingering ice-sheets melted away. At Causeway Head, near Stirling, a deer-horn pick and horn-cores of deer (*Cervus elaphus*), associated with smoothed and scratched fragments of the ribs of a whale, have been found on the fifty-foot beach, which represents an old coast-line. The corresponding beach in Sutherland is partly masked by a lateral moraine indicating, as Dr. Flett thinks, that the melting of the glacier was subsequent to the deposition of the beach.[56]

Sir W. Turner believed that the whale's rib, just mentioned, displayed human workmanship, but the evidence did not

convince Dr. Robert Munro.[57] About the deer-horn pick
there was no dispute, and it seemed as if the whale's carcase
had been stripped for the sake of its flesh and blubber.   The
creature had probably been stranded at ebb-tide. At another
place in the Carse of Stirling, on the twenty-five-foot beach,
a post-glacial accumulation of marine origin, a whale's skull
was found, associated with deer-horn picks, two of which
were perforated.[58] The old question recurs, Where was
Palæolithic man during these semi-glacial conditions ? and
the answer usually tendered does not appear satisfactory.

It has seemed advisable thus far to consider these vexed
questions, always attempting to hold an even balance
between the disputants. The progress of archaeological
discovery may eventually compel us to adopt a more complex, but still somewhat arbitrary, system of classification.

One recalls the struggle which was necessary to establish
the genuineness of the Palæoliths. The Eoliths have passed
through a fiercer storm, and are not yet safe. Should the
present temporary classification with its clean-cut boundaries, be abolished, we may witness an unseemly rush to
the victorious side, irrespective of evidence, a result only less
lamentable than unreasoning opposition.

We have said that the Neolithic period can be split into two
divisions, the first being represented by the implements of
the downs and hill-tops, and the second by those of moorlands and sandy regions. Perhaps a third section should be
made to include the delicate, beautifully worked pigmy
flints. Of these latter I have collected many hundreds, and
it is difficult to believe that they do not belong to a late
period. They might possibly be referred to the Age of Metals.

Between the Neolithic and the Bronze Ages is the transitional ' Æneolithic ' age of Sergi and Orsi. This is represented by an overlap of stone and metallic implements.

Setting aside the probable retention of stone tools as
heirlooms, the juxtaposition of objects of flint and bronze in
barrows indicates a gradual disuse of one material and the
adoption of another. Thus, flint arrow-heads continued to be
used in the Bronze Age, and perhaps beyond it. So it is with
perforated stone hammers, but to these I shall refer again.

One case is on record where Neolithic folk appear to have lived continuously on the same site until the Bronze Age. General Pitt-Rivers, in excavating a square camp or village settlement near Rushmore, Wilts., discovered in the lower deposits relics of the Neolithic period, whilst above these were tools and pottery typical of the last days of Bronze, yet there were no traces of iron. The skeletons associated with these remains were of the long-headed Neolithic type.[59]

In several countries it is believed that there was intercalated a Copper Stage before the advent of bronze proper. In Cyprus, for example, where the Stone Age was short, we find plain, unflanged copper celts of a few simple shapes. A brief Copper Age has also been demanded for Ireland, some rude, heavy celts, containing not more than 0·1 per cent. of tin, and reminiscent of stone axes, having been unearthed from time to time.[60] Whether this claim be justified or not, the passage from one period to the other is gentle and easy.

A curious interaction sometimes blends the ages. Professor Ridgeway tells us of stone axes in the Museum of the Royal Irish Academy, which show, in the shape of their faces, the influence of similar tools made of bronze. Some poor men had perchance seen, but could not afford to buy, the more recent implements.[61]

Other stone hatchets are copied from metallic celts whose broad cutting edges were formed by hammering. Danish axes of stone have been found which were actually ornamented with raised lines, imitated from bronze patterns. The holes for inserting the handles, ludicrously small, were in each case removed nearly to the end of the tool.

These ' throw-backs ' are, however, rare. The normal process is the imitation of flint celts by workers in metal. In the Museum at Bourges, previously mentioned, there is to be seen a plain bronze celt, which, in shape, bevel, and thickness, is an almost exact replica of its polished flint predecessor.

The bronze celt was indeed gradually evolved by a series of wonderful adaptations (Fig. 3). From the elementary wide-ended celt with plain sides, copied from an exemplar in

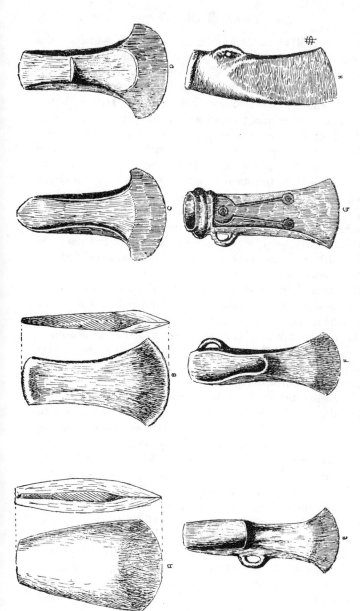

Fig. 3. The Transition from the Stone to the Metal Celt. (Specimens from British Museum and author's collection.) A. A Neolithic flint celt. B. Early copper or bronze celt (the first specimens were hammered, the later were cast). C. Flanged bronze celt. D. Flanged celt with stop-ridge. E. Looped palstave (the flanges have been shortened from below upwards, and now coalesce with the stop-ridge). F. A later palstave (the flanges arched, the socket beginning to be developed). G. Socketed celt, looped and ornamented. H. Iron socketed celt from Walthamstow.

stone, the craftsman developed a tool which had its sides turned up into flanges, so that the cleft handle might be attached more securely. Then came the stop-ridge to prevent the head from splitting the handle. Afterwards the flanges became shortened and were amalgamated with the stop-ridge. Then the tongue which fitted into the prongs of the shaft was made thinner to economize the metal, and a loop was added, giving the so-called palstave. The flanges were now beaten over so as to form a socket. Finally, the middle stop-ridge disappears, and the perfect socket receives a loop high up the side to aid in lashing the handle more firmly, and thus the highest form is reached.[62] This last type has occasionally been found reproduced in iron. With this series may be fitly compared various types of hatchets still used in country districts ; but it is noticeable that the modern mode of mounting is different.

No verbal description can render this quite clear to the novice, and even the advanced student would get a better idea of this fascinating chapter in development by visiting the Department of British Antiquities at the British Museum, and inspecting Wall-Case No. 11. Failing this, he should closely study the letterpress, plates, and illustrations in the ' Guide to the Bronze Age '.

The earlier bronze celts were inserted or forced through their hafts, but in the later stage the handles were made to fit the socket of the implement. An amusing instance, illustrative of the former practice, occurred in connexion with a modern axe-head of iron which was traded off to New Guinea. The native who bought it painstakingly closed the aperture by means of a stone hammer, and then fitted the weapon into a wooden haft. The transformed implement is now to be seen in the Pitt-Rivers Museum at Oxford.[63]

In their highest development, socketed celts not unfrequently exhibited considerable ornamentation, such as curves, ridges ending in knobs, and side rings. These designs represented obscurely the actual materials—hide or twisted grass—with which the celt was lashed to its shaft. The circle was a relic of the loop which aided in the fastening.

To such forms of ornament, demonstrably due to what was once a mode of attachment or structure, Dr. H. Colley March has applied the term ' skeuomorph ' (Gr. τὰ σκεύη = implements, utensils, baggage, tackle, &c.).

Another familiar example of a ' skeuomorph ' is seen in earthenware vessels coming from districts so widely separated as Oceania and Switzerland.   These vessels, decorated with beaded work and twisted designs, are reactions upon, or rather indicate memories of, the crude pipkins embellished by the aid of finger-dents and the impressions of twisted ropes of grass.[64]

The Ages of Bronze and Iron merged into each other quickly, and yet so insensibly that no suspicion of a gap is entertained. No antiquary of experience, Sir John Evans affirms, will deny that many bronze ornaments, and even weapons, remained in use long after steel and iron were known.[65]

A bronze celt was found in a barrow at Market Weighton (Yorkshire) in a Celtic barrow dating from about the time of the Roman invasion.[66]   Bronze pins were especially long-lived ; [67] and bronze mace-heads, cast with heavy rings and spikes, are found to have been made when the true Bronze Age had passed away.[68]   Socketed celts of the Bronze Age pattern, but made entirely of iron, have turned up at Walthamstow (Essex), in North Wales, and near Belfast. Cinerary urns of the common Bronze Age type, but associated with iron relics only, have been discovered in Essex and Berkshire.[69]

Of the Bronze Age proper, no fewer than three divisions have been distinguished, based upon the predominant types of implements in use.   As no question of continuity is involved, these phases may be passed by.

On the Continent the change from Bronze to Iron may be illustrated by a fine series of implements.   Chronologically these transitional implements belong to an earlier date than our own, since the period of Bronze and Iron, though homotaxial, were not everywhere contemporaneous.   At Hallstatt (or Hallstadt), in the Austrian Alps, Professor Oscar Montelius has found abundant relics which are believed to date from B.C. 850–450, and to illustrate many

stages of transition. There are swords made entirely of
bronze, others with iron blades and bronze hilts, and others,
again, made of iron only. There are axe-heads of bronze
alone and of iron alone, while one specimen has the cutting
edge of iron, but the shaft and flanges of the earlier metal.[70]

Other sites have been explored where tools of the Hallstatt
type have been recognized. Lastly, the station at La Tène,
in Switzerland, brings us to the close of the prehistoric age,
and indicates the absorption of the earlier culture into that
of the Iron Age.[71]

As we proceed, numerous philological details will throw
light on our subject. One word may here be noticed. The
Greek for ' blacksmith ', χαλκεύς, originally meant a worker
in copper :[72] thus does the word remain as a silent witness
to man's development. We now give a table, put forward
tentatively, showing the passage from period to period.

[Based on the classifications of MM. De Mortillet, d'Ault, Doigneau, and Rutot, the Rev. Ashington Bullen, Messrs. Hinton, Kennard, Read, Allen Brown, and others. The faunal and climatic conditions are summarized from Boyd Dawkins, Judd, Prestwich, Woodward, and others.]

Geological Period.	Stage.	Subdivisions of periods.[2] Continental.	Subdivisions of periods.[2] British.	Climate.[2]	Fauna.	Industrial remains.
Newer Pliocene or Older Pleistocene. Pre-glacial.	Eolithic.	Puycourian. St. Prest. Reutelian. Mesvinian.	Kent plateau (earlier). [? Cromer Forest Bed.] Transition (Kentish plateau).	Mild at first, then colder.	*Mastodon syn. Elephas meridionalis. Rhinoceros leptorhinus.*	Rudely battered stones. 'Double-bow' shape common. Specialization rare.
Glacial.	Palaeolithic.	Chellean.	Hill group. } Older river-gravels.	Alternations of heat and cold.	*Rhinoceros leptorhinus. Elephas antiquus.*	Coups de poing ('knuckle-dusters'), discoidal or almond-shaped. Hunting.
		Acheulean (Passage period).	100-ft. Thames terrace.	Glaciers, submergence; boulder clay.	*Elephas antiquus.* Mammoth (*Elephas primigenius*).	Implements worked on two faces. Flakes utilized. Hunting.
		Mousterian.	? Mildenhall palaeoliths. Robin Hood's Cave—bottom level. ? Crayford and Caddington brick-earths. ? Kent's Cavern.[1]	Alternations of heat and cold; damp.	Predominance of mammoth and *Rhinoceros tichorhinus* (=*R. antiquitatis*).	Pointed implements. Scrapers, choppers, oval tools, large flakes.
Post-glacial.		Menchecourtian (formerly Solutrean).	Lowest Thames terrace. ? Igthham Rock-shelters.	'Steppe period.' Cold and dry, alternating with warm and moist.	Mammoth. Predominance of horse. Disappearance of rhinoceros.	'Spear-head' type. Flakes well-worked on both sides, longer and narrower.
		Magdalenian.	Robin Hood's Cave—upper levels. ? Uxbridge group. Later floors of some caves.	Cold and dry.	Reindeer predominant. Mammoth continued to live in first part of period.	'Lance-heads', harpoons, needles, graving work on bones and antlers. Hunting, fishing.
'Prehistoric', Proto-historic, and recent.	Mesolithic.	Tourassian (or Asylian).	Scotch bone-caves.	Alternations of temperature.		Coloured pebbles. Harpoons, &c., of red-deer antlers. Rough' Neoliths .
	Neolithic.	Campignian.	White Park Bay. Cissbury.	Moist; forests abundant.	Present fauna (domesticated animals).	Cutting tools. Rough celts. Arrow-heads. Pottery, weaving, agriculture. Long barrows.
	Æneolithic.	Robenhausian.	Implements of sandy settlements. 'Pigmies.'	Present.	"	Polished celts. Arrow-heads. Finer workmanship. Agriculture. Navigation. Long and round Barrows. Megalithic monuments.
Historic and Modern.	Metallic.	Hallstatt (approx.).	Bronze.	Present.	"	Bronze and stone contemporaneous. Then bronze and iron, finally iron alone. Round barrows at first.
		La Tène.	Iron.		"	

Pleistocene. Holocene.

[1] The bottom layer of Kent's Cavern contained implements of the Chellean type. Deniker, *Races of Man*, p. 306.
[2] Deductions as to climate must be accepted with reserve. [See, e.g., G. W. Lamplugh, 'British Drifts and the Interglacial Problem,' *Naturalist*, 1906, pp. 309–10.]

CHAPTER III

FOLK-MEMORY AND RACIAL CONTINUITY

ONE of our modern poets asks his Muse to tell ' What antique wights dwelled ere in this sweet soil '. The difficulty of this task depends upon the precise meaning attached to the adjective ' antique '.

Of the primeval race of beings postulated by an acceptance of the Eolithic theory, we have no direct knowledge. A little inference from the implements left behind, a little comparison with the ways of the rudest savages, that is all.

The discovery (1894), in Java, by Dr. Dubois, of portions of a skeleton of an anthropoid man (*Pithecanthropus erectus*) may eventually help in dispelling the mystery. Both this discovery, however, and the intermittent reports of relics of Tertiary man on the Continent, raise a nebulous controversy, which must be left alone pending further evidence.

Even here, the principle of continuity runs—invisible. For, were there everywhere a gap existing between this period and the next, we should have to demand a special creation to account for the appearance of that Palæolithic being who was unquestionably man.

Descending to that common ground where all archaeologists agree—the Palæolithic period—we ask whether any human influences of this age can be detected among us to-day. Dr. John Beddoe, applying ethnological tests, county by county, thinks that traces of Palæolithic man may be discovered in the modern populations of Wales and the West of England. Here and there one sees men of low stature, having broad cheekbones, a receding forehead, flat nose, narrow chin, and protruding jaws. These features, as well as the oblique or Chinese eye, with its almond-shaped opening and thick upper eyelid, seem to mark off the old ' Eskimo ' or Palæolithic type.[1] Sir John Rhŷs, reasoning on data supplied by philology and folk-lore, leaves room for

Palæolithic vestiges,[2] and Mr. J. Munro suggests that in the fauns and satyrs of classical artists we may have a reminiscence of the Older Stone Age.[3]

Naturally any racial survivals from this far-off time would be very faint and elusive. Those dating from the Neolithic period are not so uncertain. The conclusions of the anthropologist and the ethnologist show that the Neolithic folk, as commonly understood, were a short, dark-haired, dark-eyed race. Their skulls were of the dolichocephalic or narrow kind. Their modern representatives are probably found among the Basques or Iberians of France and Spain.

The ' Celts ', who followed the Neolithic people, came over in several migrations. The Goidels, or Gaels, considered to be the earliest of these immigrants, are believed to have introduced bronze, but they doubtless continued to use stone also until long after their arrival. The later comers, Brythons and Belgae, were acquainted with the use of iron.[4] Some authorities, however, object to the attempt made to connect these races with stages of culture. The Belgae, who, as Caesar observes, had conquered the South-East of Britain before the Roman invasion, were partly of Teutonic extraction.

Let it be said here that, undesirable as may be the terms ' Celts ' and ' Celtic ', when used in the ordinary sense, the plea of convenience must be heard. Throughout these pages the terms refer to peoples having affinities of language. Deniker and other authorities contend that there is neither a single Celtic race nor a Celtic speech. The Celt of tradition is ' found almost everywhere and can be fixed nowhere '.[5] Granting that the words, as employed by the philologist and the archaeologist, involve error, it is more pardonable to retain terms that are understood than to introduce others which create additional complexities.

Deniker classes the Gaels of Scotland and the Irish of Munster as a ' Nordic ', Northern, or Teutonic race ; the Irish of Connaught offer two or three types, variants of a Nord-Occidental, or North-Western group, besides, perhaps, remnants of a Neolithic folk. Cornwall and North Devon furnish attenuated types of an Occidental race.[6] Further,

we learn that it is a misnomer to apply the term ' Celt ' to
the tall red-haired Irishman or Scot. But there is a bond
of union between the Celts of philology and those of history,
since the ' Celts ' (really non-Aryans) of Central Gaul, a
dark-haired, short-skulled people of low stature, spoke in
Caesar's time a Celtic language. This was probably forced
on them by the Southern expansion of the Belgic Gauls,
ethnological relatives of our own Cymry and Gaels.[7] The
Celtic languages of Britain are represented by two dialects,
the Gaelic section, spoken in the North-West of Scotland,
the West of Ireland, and the Isle of Man, and the Cymric or
Welsh of Wales.

Just as the terms ' Celt ' and ' Celtic ' are retained because
they are convenient, so the word ' Aryan ' is often used to
indicate alike Celts and Teutons, as well as the Latins and
Greeks, to say nothing of Slavonic, Lithuanic, and Albanian
peoples. Strictly, ' Aryan ' could only apply to the primitive undivided folk who evolved such root-words as are
common to these languages. Hereafter, the word is used
without prejudice as to the origin of these linguistic groups
of peoples.

The anthropologist, who compares skulls and bones,
heights and angles of features, makes sad work of common
notions as to Aryans and Celts. Roughly, however, we
may take these people to be those who are buried in our
round barrows of the Bronze Age. These folk were tall and
brachycephalic, that is, round-headed. For the present
(and with the reservation that the subject will be discussed
in a subsequent chapter) we may accept the old rule formu-
lated by Dr. J. Thurnam : ' Long heads, long barrows ;
round heads, round barrows.'[8] In other words, the long
barrows have been hitherto referred to the Neolithic folk,
and the round to the Bronze Age people. We repeat that
the maxim has, at most, only a general application, but as
such it is not yet demonstrably erroneous.

After these preliminary cautions, we next ask whether
the pre-Aryan or pre-Celtic people can still be discerned
among us. Dr. W. Z. Ripley, in his learned digest of the
works of the best European ethnologists, states that ' accord-

ing to the testimony of those best fitted to judge ', the primitive Neolithic type of man is still represented in our population.[9] The photographs given in illustration are those of Devonshire people, but the assertion of Dr. Beddoe is quoted to the effect that the type is common enough in other parts of England.

Among the hills of South Wales, the region of the old Silures, non-Aryan descent is traceable in the dark hair, black eyes, and small oval features of the natives. Except in dress and language, the short, swarthy Welshman of Denbighshire is identical with the Basque inhabitant of the Western Pyrenees.[10]

The narrow-headed type is also found in the West country, in the Fens, and around the very towns of the Danelagh, such as Derby, Stamford, and Leicester.[11]

In the Scottish Highlands and the Western Isles, the same dolichocephalic, dark-skinned folk, with a ' strange foreign look ', are met with. Ireland, too, especially to the West of the Shannon, supplies its quota, and, singularly enough, Irish legend tells of a former connexion with Spain.[12] Geologically, there once was doubtless land-connexion, as proved by a comparison of the fauna and flora, but that was at a much earlier period.

Mr. John Munro supplies information about the county of Merioneth, which is difficult to harmonize with our general knowledge. There, he tells us, lives a red-haired, ruddy-skinned people, with receding brows and projecting teeth. These folk, the ' Cochion ', or red ones, can be traced back to the early sixteenth century, when they were known as red goblins or fairies. They dwelt in dens and lived mainly on plunder. Though cannier and fewer than of old, they are still noted for strength, pugnacity, and hot temper. The type is believed to be Finnish, or Ugrian, and of Asiatic origin.[13] Even if we discard the Iberian theory, these hypothetical ' Ugrians ' do not fit in with the usual ideas about the Neolithic race, unless, indeed, we accept two entirely different immigrations. And it is noteworthy that the latest authorities are disposed to believe in two distinct types of Neolithic folk.

Recent expert linguistic testimony discovers slight traces of the non-inflexional Iberian or Mediterranean (=Neolithic) elements in the British Isles, especially in the now extinct dialects of the Picts.[14]   Professor J. Morris Jones considers that the non-Aryan traits of syntax which are found in our insular Celtic point unmistakably to old Egyptian and Berber, and to other idioms of the South Mediterranean Sea.[15]   Evidently influenced by a similar belief, Professor Sayce has compared the natives of Kerry with the Berbers of the hilly regions of North Africa.[16]   In Ireland, it is said, the old Iberian, Iarn (or iron) tongue had not long been extinct in the ninth century.[17]   Canon Isaac Taylor was inclined to limit the survivals to some half-dozen geographical terms, such as Caithness, Hibernia, and Siluria, but Sir John Rhŷs thinks that such names are far more common.[18]

Racial survivals from the Bronze Age are so widespread as to require but a brief notice.   While the ' old black breed ' men of the Neolithic period must be looked for in Scotland chiefly in Shetland, East Sutherland, and Caithness, the Goidelic (Celtic) type abounds there.   Representatives of the round-barrow period are in England most prevalent among the remnants of the yeoman class.[19]   Broadly speaking, the Celts, whether Goidels (Gaels) or Brythons, must be first looked for on the Western fringes of our islands.   Nevertheless, this type is common everywhere, in Gloucestershire, in Warwickshire, and in the Isle of Ely, to mention but three well-known districts.

This brief summary of the race question prepares the way for the sequel.   It proves that there is good reason for assigning an ancient origin to oral tradition as represented in folk-memory.   The old teaching about the extermination of one race by another, whether of Neolithic people by Goidels, of Goidels by Brythons, or of all these by Romans, Saxons, Danes, or Normans, is not now set forth by many writers of repute.   ' Continuity ' is the key which will open many secret chambers.   Partial breaks there must have been, even where a remnant of the vanquished continued to live side by side with the victors.   The tables prepared by Dr. Beddoe show great disparities in the racial

elements of a given county, but a leaven of the older peoples
appears everywhere.

Some curious instances of racial prejudices might be
given.   Consider the belief, not confined to Britain, that,
as Professor Karl Pearson puts it, ' there is something wrong
about red-headed men.' [20]   The notion runs through our
literature.   It is not only recent authors like Sir A. Conan
Doyle, Mr. Anthony Hope, and Mr. G. K. Chesterton, who
have exploited this prejudice.   Shakespearean readers will
remember that Rosalind says to Celia,

> His very hair is of the dissembling colour,

and Celia replies,

> Something browner than Judas'.[21]

And the old saw puts it thus, ' From a black man keep your
wife, With the red man, beware your knife.'   Folk-lore has
comprehensively set down the red man as passionate, fierce-
tempered, deceitful, and cruel.   Not all nations have these
superstitions ;   the Danes, for example, esteem red hair
a mark of beauty.[22]   On the other hand, Aristotle declared
that ' He that has red hair is proud, envious, and deceitful '.
Not to complicate matters, outside nations may be left to
neutralize one another.

History has fortuitously given a little support to the
prejudice, and has also encouraged a misleading theory to
account for it.   Judas Iscariot and Absalom are said to have
possessed red hair.   William Rufus, Red Murdoch, Red
Comyn, among men, and Helen of Troy, Catherine I of
Russia, Lucrezia Borgia, and Mary Stuart, among women,
are a few individuals out of a long list.   All these were
notorious, or in some respects unpopular, and thus the
matter is often supposed to be settled.   But such an explanation falls under De Morgan's humorous ban :

> What hits is history,
> What misses is mystery,

and it takes no heed of red-haired persons like Joan of Arc
and Queen Elizabeth, who were popular.

The principle of accretion might indeed solve the problem
for countries in general, but it would not account for our

strong British prejudice, which exists apart from averages and exaggerations. Moreover, as a fact, Professor Pearson found that, while red-haired children were, on the whole, more liable to quick-temper than black-haired ones,[*] the latter were more sullen, in the proportion of two to one.

We have said that the Danes appreciate red-haired people. The Danes themselves, as well as the Frisians, Jutes, and Saxons, tended to fairness of feature. Recollections of the Danish ' sea-wolves ' might long linger among the residue of Britons of Celtic or Iberian descent. At Wool, in Dorset, there existed until late years a tradition of terrible burnings and slaughter by savage red-haired men ages ago, and Mr. H. J. Moule thinks that the legend refers to the Danes.[23]

The root of the matter lies deeper still. The Celts, or at least large sections of them, were, according to contemporary writers, red-haired people. Professor Windle reminds us that Lucan called the Britons, presumably the Celtic inhabitants—he could not be referring to the dark-haired Neolithic people—*flavi*, or the flaxen folk. Silius Italicus asserts that the hair of the Britons was golden. Vitruvius, in a passage supposed to refer to them, speaks of their red hair ; and Dion Cassius describes Boadicea as having very light hair, which hung in profusion down to the hips.[24]

May we not reasonably argue that the antipathy comes down from the time when the Neolithic folk were subdued by the Celts, that it was strengthened by the struggles of one Celtic group with another, and that it was further increased when the coalesced Britons were in turn harassed by the Danes ?

Another curious superstition, known as the ' First foot ', prevails chiefly in the North of England and in Scotland. According to this belief, if the first person who enters a house after midnight of the dying year chances to be dark or swarthy, good fortune is boded for the coming twelvemonth. Not knowingly will the goodwife permit a light-complexioned man to cross the threshold. When we notice that among the objects which the dark man should bring into the house is a piece of iron, we are irresistibly thrown back to the Iron

Age descendants of our dark-haired Neolithic folk, carrying iron as they visit their taller masters, in token perchance of amity and the absence of malicious spells.

In a later section we shall see that a belief in fairies is, in a large measure, an obvious retention in folk-memory of a small, mysterious, magic-loving folk who were, in the mind of the Celtic peoples, the aborigines of the island.[25] Of course, fairy tales increase from age to age both in number and in artistic construction, but some of the simpler, ingenuous stories are very ancient.   Men of the Bronze Age and Iron Age first told these fairy tales of the dwarfish Neolithic people who were such a puzzle to their conquerors when mutual relationship sprang up.

The little folk of the Neolithic period lived often in underground chambers approached by passages, and more or less domical within.   Elsewhere they dug circular pits and roofed these with branches, bushes, turf, or reeds.   Hence the Iron Age folk peopled every mound with fairies.   As late as A.D. 862 there existed subterranean dwellings in co. Meath.   They are said to have been occupied by a people rich in gold and treasure, who were actually known as ' fairies '.   Although evidently people of the Neolithic race, they were at that time acquainted with bronze, which, alas! was of no avail against the iron swords of the Danes, who tore open and rifled the ' fairy hills '.[26]   This seems to be a good example of continuous tradition from the Stone Age.

Certain devious paths in philology have lately been explored, with valuable results.   Philological evidence, taken alone, is admittedly inadequate, and may indeed lead us astray.   But in certain directions, and under skilled leadership, it becomes a helpful guide.   Then we realize the truth of Archbishop Trench's epigram : ' Language is fossil poetry.'

Working on philological lines, and aided by fairy-lore, Sir John Rhŷs infers that the Neolithic folk counted by fives, being taught probably by Nature, who endowed them with five fingers on each hand.[27]   Among the fairies, events happen ' this day next year ', a form of speech which seems to be a non-Aryan survival.   If we wish to find a parallel to

Neolithic speech and habits, we must turn to the Basques, who speak an agglutinative tongue, comparable to the Chinese and other Asiatic languages.

In Basque, the first five numerals appear to be native, but the words for *six* and *seven* are probably loan-words from some Aryan (Gaulish or Latin) tongue. The Basque language has indeed words for *eight* and *nine*, but their length, and other peculiarities, betray external influences.[28]

With the Aryan Celts it was different. They were never without a decimal system of counting. Celtic nations of to-day go further, and number by scores, just as do the modern French. Yet it is curious that the Welsh, when counting between ten and twenty, have gone back to reckoning by fives, e.g. 16, 17, 18=1 on 15, 2 on 15, &c. So, in Old Irish, the expression for ' seven men ' is significant, *morfeser* (='a big-sixer ').[29]

Something more may be learned from the Basque tongue. L'Abbé Inchauspe has shown that, though picks, hatchets, and scissors are now made of steel, their Basque names, which are compound, have as their first member the word *aitz* (=stone, silex). *Knife*, again, is *aitztoa* (=little stone, little flint). The Abbé remarks that etymologists have searched in vain for the origin of the French *hache*, and suggests that this term, too, is derived from *atcha* (=*aitz*). He supplements these data by others which tend to justify the identification of the Basques with the Iberians or first inhabitants of Spain.[30]

Celtic philology naturally helps us still more. Without entering into the whole subject, which is discussed in good modern textbooks, two peculiar survivals may be noticed. One is the old ' rhyming score ' in which shepherds of the North of England still ' tell their tale', and with which schoolboys of the past generation were familiar. This jingle consists simply of the Celtic numerals degraded. It is said that the Indians of Maine and Ohio use the same corrupt version, which must have been introduced there by Welsh or English settlers.[31] The other relic is the use, in counties ranging from Somerset to York, of the word *ceffyl* (*keffyl*, *kevil*, *kevel*, &c.) to denote an inferior horse, and also a blockhead.   Now the term is really the Welsh *ceffyl*, and the Cornish *cevil*, and points to a time when the Saxon and Celt had come to live side by side, and when the Saxon entertained a feeling of contempt for his neighbour, not wholly extinct in our own day.[32]

The vocal talent of Welsh people is known far and wide, and Sir John Rhŷs believes that it is not of Aryan (Celtic) origin.   He asserts that race has, beyond all question, not a little to do with the artistic feelings, and suggests that very few Welshmen of the tall, fair-haired, blue-eyed type are eminently musical or prominent in the aesthetic revivals among religious bodies.[33]

A few scattered cases of continuity may close this chapter. The modern lady who ornaments her person with beads, rings, and bracelets, is unconsciously following the custom of the prehistoric folk who buried their dead in barrows. But there are still earlier records, for periwinkle shells, bored for stringing, are found in Continental caves of the Mammoth period.[34]   A person who to-day dons a straw hat or a chip bonnet is simply doing the same as the South Sea Islanders, but both are copying an art first evolved in the reed-thatched huts of their Stone Age ancestors.   The modern sewing-needle has its prototype in the bone or ivory needle of the barrows or the still earlier bone-caves.

The sailor who tattoos his arms and chest with figures, the fashionable lady who paints her face, and the circus clown who bedizens himself in a grotesque manner, reproduce habits allied to those of the Picts or 'painted' people of the Stone Age.

Ruddle, or red ochre, associated with a hollowed piece of sandstone and abraded as by use, was found by Bateman in a Staffordshire barrow.   Nor does the instance stand alone. Ancient habitations at Holyhead yielded large stones, tinged with haematite, which had probably been used for grinding pigment.   A quantity of red colouring material and a bronze mirror were recovered from the Glastonbury pile-dwellings, and may now be seen in the museum of that town.   A small stone box, found in Orkney along with celts and other Stone Age relics, actually contained red pigment.[35]   The present writer has himself found ruddle associated with Neolithic remains in a tufaceous deposit in Dorset.

A link is supplied by the North American Indians, who, until recent times, interred war-paint with their dead.[36] The custom is referred to in Schiller's dirge, which is thus lightly translated by Lord Lytton :

> The paints that warriors love to use,
> Place here within his hand,
> That he may shine with ruddy hues
> Amidst the spirit band.

It should be stated that the painting habit is believed to be pre-Neolithic. French caves, at least, as early as the Transitional period represented by the shelters at Mas d'Azil, have yielded skeletons coloured by rouge, and M. Piette associates the remains with the race of men who painted the pebbles at the locality mentioned.[37]

With respect to tattooing, the original purpose, as distinct from the derivative idea of ornament, was probably to inspire terror. The modern artist thinks of decoration only, and we know to what extremes fashion will urge its devotees. A ludicrous instance may be permitted in illustration. When the Portuguese, in the mid-fifteenth century, discovered the West African river district known as Rio do Oura, they found that a good trade could be done in seal-skins and oil. And to this day, as Miss Mary Kingsley tells us, the ladies of Lisbon ' are very keen on sealskin jackets, which their climate can hardly call for imperatively '.[38]

As practised by the natives of New Zealand and Formosa at the present day, tattooing appears to have a signification partly of decoration and partly of defiance. With some African tribes, again, a scar on the thigh betokens valour in battle, and is the equivalent of our war-medals.[39]

Whence did the early Britons obtain their colouring material for tattooing ? From herbs and lichens, if we may credit the account given by Pliny (c. A.D. 70).[40] And surely no more astonishing case of persistence and unconscious folk-memory can be adduced than that of the Hebrideans and the Faroemen, who still use dyes made from sea-weed,[41] or of the Welsh, who still extract colours from lichens.[42]

We turn to a vastly different question. A French physician of the present generation astonished the world by stating that nurses in Normandy were still giving the children's heads a sugar-loaf shape by means of bandages and tight caps. In Brittany rounded heads were preferred.[43] We now learn that another settlement around Toulouse had a like custom.[44] One hears whisperings of the same habit in our English counties, whisperings which can win full acceptance but tardily.

Here we look down a strange abyss. For comparative custom and ethnology teach us the widespread prevalence of this and kindred habits. Readers of Catlin's travels will remember how common formerly was the custom of flattening heads among the Red Indians. It was not only the Chinooks who were addicted to the practice, in earlier days it was rife among the tribes of Mississippi and Alabama. Indeed those who retained the natural round head were despised, this feature being the special mark of a slave, whilst the flattened head denoted freedom.[45] Other analogous deformities are seen in the cramped foot of the Chinese, the distorted leg of the female Carib, and the ' wasp waist of the European belle '.

The gipsy habit illustrates another trick played by unconscious folk-memory, an aberrant custom which is generally called atavistic. Apart from the hunting instinct, from the desire to camp out or hold a picnic, the fascination of the open-air life is strong, and many folk need little incentive to adopt such a mode. Some groups are gipsies by heredity. The real gipsy, as some one has observed with witty penetration, abhors houses : the passages, staircases, cellars, and cupboards give him the feeling that he is being trapped. A touch of the old instinct often shows itself in the literary man and the naturalist. It was pronounced in such men as Thoreau and Jefferies, Robert Dick and Thomas Edward, George Borrow and De Quincey. Then there are men who are born hunters, travellers, or sailors.

Mr. F. J. Bennett has drawn attention to an apparent survival of the nomad habit in Jewish history. At the Feast of Tabernacles, the Jews lived for a week in structures made of boughs of trees. Sacrifices were abundantly offered, and the laws were daily read in public.[46]   This last proceeding is suggestive of an earlier tribal moot.

The cave habit, now usually pathological rather than economic, is sometimes re-assumed by men in times of nervous distress and morbid foreboding.   The newspapers constantly report cases of such 'throw-backs'.   But modern cave-dwellers are more numerous than would appear from this statement.   At Dieppe there is a small colony of people who live in caves in the chalk.   Remarkable instances are also recorded from Yorkshire and the West of Scotland. Down to the last generation a considerable number of people lived in rocky caves near the Castle at Nottingham, and it was only of late years that the leases of these sub-terranean dwellings fell in.[47]

Repeatedly, during the last few years, the daily newspapers have contained descriptions of gipsy funerals, when articles of dress and ornament have been buried with the deceased 'king' or 'queen'.   Whether such a group as that of a primitive gipsy stock exists without intermixture may be questioned, but this funeral custom is far too prevalent to be accounted for as a freak due to individual caprice. Stranger than even the gipsy custom is the sporadic occurrence of kindred behaviour on the part of educated men and women.   For instance, in describing the funeral of Lord Palmerston in Westminster Abbey, Mr. Moncure D. Conway, an eye-witness, casually adds that gold rings fell on the coffin along with the dust.[48]

Having now touched upon a number of modern survivals, we shall go back and apply the ' continuity ' theory to that period which represents the dawn of history.

CHAPTER IV

FURTHER LINKS BETWEEN THE PREHISTORIC AND PROTOHISTORIC AGES

HOARY and lichened by age, grim and fretted by a thousand storms, our ancient megalithic monuments are still numerous, massive, and full of mystery. The matter-of-fact mason and the prosaic husbandman have indeed wrought grievous havoc upon them. Many have gone for ever ; some may still be detected in the walls of farm-houses and churches ; a few remnants still stand as of old. Inscriptions may, of course, be looked for in vain, and tool-marks are rare, for the stones are prehistoric. But though there is neither speech nor language, yet are their voices heard.

The story told by the megaliths—' big stone ' monuments—runs thus : A few thousands of years before the Christian era, a branch of the human family, accustomed to the use of stone tools only, and akin by necessity and culture to those races who at one time or another have reared stone monuments from the Himalayas to Peru, and from Scandinavia to the Southern Pacific, reached our shores and raised like memorials in Britain. These Neolithic people were followed by others who were acquainted with the use of bronze, and who continued, and to some extent perhaps copied, the works of their forerunners. After the Bronze Age, the raising of megaliths became so modified by outside influences that only the archaeologist can now trace their subsequent descent, though the underlying motive which first caused their erection was ever present.

What was this motive ? Originally the megaliths were probably funereal and commemorative in character. After-wards, subsidiary ideas of ancestor-worship were grafted on the primitive intention. A few stones, peradventure, are boundary marks. Some are obviously the stone framework of those burial mounds known as barrows. The exact determination of each kind may perhaps never be quite completed.

For the sake of convenience, we will glance at the principal kinds of these monuments, but some previous knowledge of them will be assumed.

The simplest kind is the menhir (Welsh, *maen* = stone, *hir* = long) or vertical standing stone, to which the provincial names of long-, hoar-, and tingle-stone are also given. Menhirs have had a long sojourn, and, under disguise, are with us to-day.

The stone-row, or alignment, which in this country usually

Fig. 4.   Fernworthy Circle, or Cromlech, near Chagford, Dartmoor.   The outline is somewhat oval and the long diameter is about 60 feet.   In the neighbourhood are several cairns and mutilated alignments.   Sittaford Tor stands in the background.

belongs to the Bronze period, consists of a number of menhirs arranged in lines.   In certain cases the menhir may be merely the survivor of a stone-row of which the other members have disappeared.   English stone-rows are best seen on Dartmoor, where they are of the Bronze Age.   At Carnac, in Brittany, the huge alinements, supposed to commemorate the burials of tribal chieftains, apparently continued to be raised until the Christian era was fairly advanced.[1]

Next in order of complexity, but not necessarily in that of chronology, are those circles of upright stones known as cromlechs (' curved stones ').   Examples may be found at Penmaenmawr, Fernworthy, in Devon (Fig. 4), Portisham

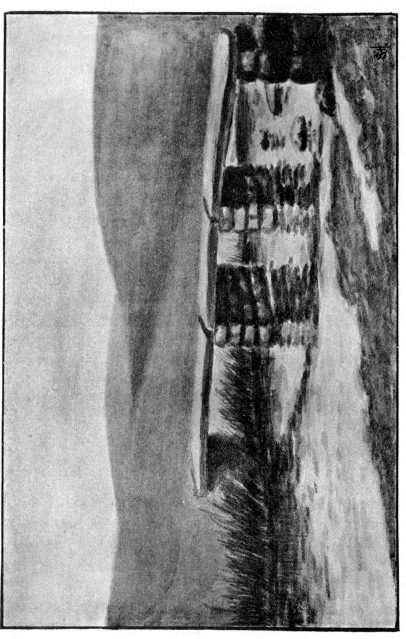

FIG. 5. 'Clapper Bridge,' at Postbridge, Dartmoor: a megalith, by some considered to belong to the Bronze Age. It is more probably Mediaeval, though it may date from the Early Iron period. The two larger slabs are 15 feet long and $6\frac{1}{2}$ feet wide.

(Dorset), Rollright, near the borders of Oxford and Warwick, and in many other places.[2] Then there are the dolmens, or ' table-stones ', consisting of a few upright slabs or pillars surmounted by a capstone. Throughout these pages the word ' dolmen ' will be employed in its modern, or Breton signification, as distinct from the Welsh usage, which inverts the meanings of ' dolmen ' and ' cromlech ', so that the former word is made to mean the circle, and the latter the stone-table. Philologists dispute whether the Breton etymology of ' table-stone ' is sound, and whether the word ' dolmen ' is not copied from Borlase's Cornish term *tolmên* (' hole of stone '), which is said to be little more than a century old.[3] Deplorable as this confusion may be, ' dolmen ' is now in France, and, to a less degree, in England, so distinctly the authoritative term for the stone-table, that it is best to restrict the meaning, although the guide-books, and a few of the older authorities, employ ' cromlech ' in this sense.

Most of the monuments of the dolmen group, some writers would say all, are merely the sepulchral chambers of barrows, the soil which once concealed the dolmens having been removed for agricultural purposes. There are also long, chambered varieties of dolmens, like the one at New Grange, co. Meath ; they are evidently the framework of long barrows. A few kist-vaens (='tombstones '), or closed chambers of stone, are found on Dartmoor ; galgals, cairns, or piles of rock are met with on the mountains of Wales and Scotland. Certain ' clapper ' bridges, crossing the streams of Exmoor and Dartmoor, are often assigned to the Bronze Age, but they are more probably relics of pack-horse days (Fig. 5).

The various megaliths just enumerated cover, then, a period extending from the Neolithic Age to that of Bronze. Individual examples may even be as recent as the introduction of iron. Our best-known megalith, Stonehenge, which may be roughly described as a kind of compound cromlech, is now generally considered, as the result of Professor W. Gowland's excavations, to be of rather late Neolithic age.[4] Lord Avebury thinks that it falls in the Bronze period, since on one stone a small incrustation of carbonate of copper was discovered. This crust, or rather stain, was, however, of extreme thinness, and the circumstances of its position were so peculiar as to demand cautious conclusions. Perhaps here would the value of the term Æneolithic be proved. The stone-pillars at Avebury, Wilts., being unhewn, are looked upon as falling entirely within the Stone period.

As the Iron Age came in there occurred a break, or more properly, a diversion, of the continuity of these monuments. It cannot be claimed that there were in the Iron Age structures analogous in every respect to the real megaliths. How the people of the later Bronze period disposed of their dead, and to what extent they reared megaliths, are indeed questions a little in dispute. With the Romans came modified methods of burial and worship. The Romano-Britons, having, as a body, left behind the bondage of stone tools, began to impute magic to their Neolithic predecessors, and to allot the barrows to these as fairy dwellings. Not only chieftains, but wizards and fairies, were located in the mounds and under the megaliths. Any descendants of the Neolithic race who chanced to be ' islanded ' on the downs or wolds in the midst of Gaels and Brythons would also have a reputation for sorcery.

A stage beyond the fairy legend would represent the barrows and megaliths as the work of giants. This seeming contradiction is not inexplicable, and will be again noticed. Meanwhile, we must expect to encounter many like contradictions and inconsistencies, which oftentimes are not very illogical, after all. To look for any high degree of consistency in barbaric philosophy is to disqualify oneself from understanding it. There can be no symmetrical theories which do not bring their own condemnation.[5]

Seeing that the stone monuments are generally associated with giants, rather than with small folk, there is a possibility that these structures were for the most part set up in the Bronze period, when the taller Celtic races were predominant; but it is more likely that the people of the Iron Age told the legends with respect to the earlier peoples indifferently.

We may now inspect some names which throw light on our

subject. Kits Coty House, near Aylesford, in Kent (Fig. 6),
is a dolmen which still bears a Celtic name, though the
Teutonic word 'house' is a reduplication (cf. River *Ouse*,
Hamble*don* Hill). Arthur's Stone, in the Dore Valley,
Herefordshire, the Whispering Knights of Rollright, Oxford-

FIG. 6.   Kits Coty House, near Aylesford, Kent : a dolmen composed of
sarsen stones. The large uprights are 7–8 feet high, the capstone measures
$12 \times 9\frac{1}{4}$ feet. This monument is now railed in.

shire, and their neighbour, the King's Stone, across the
Warwick border, and a few other examples, tell of the deeds
of heroes who were connected with the earliest days of Iron
Age romance.   Somewhat allied to this nomenclature is
King Arthur's Hall, a name given to old galleries, repre-

senting Roman workings for iron ore, at Doward Hill, Hereford.[6] Wherever, in fact, the retreating Britons made a bold stand against new-comers, whether in Cornwall, Wales, or Scotland, there the name of Arthur is freely applied.

Then we have Giants' Graves in Cumberland, a Giant's Staff in Cornwall, and the Hurlstone, a Northumberland menhir, all suggestive of champions and their feats. Wayland Smith's, that is, Wayland the Smith's Forge, not far from the Icknield Way in Berkshire, gives us an echo of the momentous struggle between the unwarlike Neolithic folk and the puissant warriors of the days of Bronze and Iron. Thus are commemorated the deft fabricators in metal, and their dark, uncanny craftsmanship. The ' bones of the wise Weyland ' are referred to by King Alfred in his translation of Boethius, and Alfred, it will be remembered, was born hard by, at Wantage. The Teutonic ' Smith ' was doubtless the representative of an earlier worthy who had been enrolled by the Britons before the Saxon invasion. The story, as we now have it, and as it is cleverly adapted in ' Kenilworth ', relates how the traveller, by placing a coin on the capstone of the dolmen, may have his horse shod by an invisible smith.[7]

The magical aspect of the megaliths shows itself in such nicknames as the Nine Maidens (Devon and Cornwall), the Nine Ladies (Derbyshire), Meg and her Daughters (Cumberland), and the Bridestones (Yorkshire and Cheshire). The circle near Lamorna Cove, Cornwall, is variously known as the Merry Maidens, the Stone Dance, and the Dawns Mên. There is a strong probability that the word ' mên ' here represents the Welsh *maen* = stone. The Wolf's Fold (Yorkshire), and the Pipers (Cornwall), seem also to be early names.

A further diversion of tradition was caused by the introduction of Christianity, when diabolism was freely invoked to explain the megaliths. Wherever the folk-memory became confused or modified, devils and demons were made responsible for natural and artificial objects alike. The new theory conveniently harmonized conflicting traditions.

Of Nature's handiworks, a list compiled by the writer

includes the Devil's Bridge, Jumps, and Highway ; the Devil's Chimney, Dairy, Cheesewring, and Punchbowl ; the Devil's Elbow, Throat, and Nightcap. Among the megaliths are the Devil's Arrows, comprising three standing stones near Boroughbridge, Yorkshire ; the Devil's Quoits, at Beckhampton, Wilts. ; and the Devil's Door, near Marlborough. These names, as well as those which follow, are but a selection out of many. Professor Windle's ' triallists ' will supply further examples.[8]

From the megaliths we turn to the barrows. The long barrow, usually deemed Neolithic, was often of colossal dimensions. Its plan of construction is believed to have been based on the dwelling of the deceased occupant. The galleried entrance and the encircling ring of stones may stand for the stockaded settlement. The squatting posture of the skeleton corresponds with a favourite attitude of the living man. So, too, the round barrow, with its girdling trench, forming a broken circle, its cist or urn, and its general outline, gives a simulacrum of the hut-dwelling.[9] Professor Flinders Petrie has described an analogous idea in the placing of the clay model of a house near Egyptian tombs, to supply the departed spirit with a dwelling similar to that which it occupied on earth. Mummy-cases are also found in the human form, and sarcophagi occur which mimic the woodcarved house.[10]

A less-accepted interpretation of the long barrow makes it correspond in shape to the buried human corpse and the chambered hut by which it is enclosed. By like symbolism, the round barrow answers to the urn containing the calcined bones of the body.[11]

Just pausing to note that generally the people of the Newer Stone Age practised inhumation, and that the Bronze Age folk cremated, or partially cremated their dead, we must ask whether there is any great breach of continuity. Both the Romans and the Saxons included burial in ' tumuli '— it is better to reserve the word ' barrows ' for the prehistoric period—among their various modes of entombing the dead. Roman burial customs may not have deeply affected the groundwork of British usage, but the Saxons, with half-conscious belief, recognized the sanctity of the early barrows and often interred their own dead therein. These later burials are distinguishable by the relative depth of the interment, by the posture and build of the skeleton, and by the nature of the associated objects.

As Christianity began to make headway the practice of cremation died out. Already in Rome the pyre and urn and columbarium of the pagans had begun to give place to the cerements and crypts and catacombs of the Christian community.[12] Taking for a test the presence or absence of dated coins as an anterior limit, it has been said that cremation did not occur among the Gallo-Romans later than the reign of Constantine (died A.D. 337).[13] A coin, however, does not mark a posterior limit, for obviously it may be placed in a grave years after it has been struck. In Britain, also, except among remote fastnesses, and in spots where heathenism lingered, the custom, according to Mr. W. M. Wylie, became extinct in the fourth century. It was a slow struggle, but at last the plains of the dead received into joint occupancy the remains both of those who had, and those who had not, ' passed through the fire.' [14] We find the poet Macrobius, who wrote at the beginning of the fifth century, declaring that burning had been discontinued so long that it was only from books that he could gain information regarding it.[15]

Mr. J. R. Green, the historian, has well summarized the changes wrought by the Christian permeation of the old society so far as funerals were concerned. ' The burial-fire was abolished ; and instead of resting beneath his mound, like Beowulf, on some wind-swept headland or hill, the Christian warrior slept with his fellows in his lowly grave beneath the shade of the village church.' [16]

Here we must emphasize very distinctly the fact that with respect to none of the periods previously considered do we know how the bulk of the dead were disposed of. Barrow burial accounts for but a small proportion of the total interments at any given time, so that the survival of even trivial customs may be eloquent as to the mode in which the poorer folk were formerly buried.

The tyro may here be warned that all mounds are not barrows. Some may be boundary marks. Others enclose Roman ' indicia ' placed there by ancient land surveyors ; still others are the earthwork bases of mediaeval or modern structures, defensive or industrial, such as keeps, towers, and windmills, while a few are nothing more than heaps of soil formed by the removal of material in making ponds. If we remember Labiche's delightful comedy we shall not be too ready to follow old Poitrinas in finding shields, swords, and lachrymatories amongst the rusty Dutch ovens, the broken spits and crocks of the garden rubbish-heap.

As is the case with megaliths, the nicknames given to barrows imply a slackening of folk-memory, and are indicative of a modification of custom produced by new agencies. The earliest names, indeed, fully preserve the ideas of dwarfs and giants. A long barrow in Staffordshire is known as the Fairy's Toot. This word ' toot ' (A.S. *totian*=to project, to stick out, to peep) is very common in such names as Toot Hill and Tot Hill (the ' look-out ' hill), but to discuss this question fully is here impossible. In the East Riding there is a round barrow called the Elf Howe (Old Norse, *haug-r*= mound, cairn). A stone cairn, which was found to enclose a burial urn, was known by the people of Hetton (Durham) as the Fairy's Cradle.

In Wiltshire the term Giant's Grave is attached to a particular long barrow ; in Kent a round burial mound has the same name. Near Bisley (Gloucester), there is a Giant's Stone Barrow. After this group we may rank the King's Barrow of Wilts, the King's Oven of Gloucester, and Arthur's Round Table, a name which occurs both in Westmoreland and the North Riding. These belong evidently to the Arthurian period of nomenclature.

Julaber's Grave, near Chilham, in Kent, and Hetty Pagler's Jump at Uley, Gloucestershire, may represent corruptions of Celtic words, denoting eponymous heroes, but they may, again, be perversions of more modern personal or place-names. Julaber, in particular, may be a shortened form, Jul-Aber, of Julian's Bower. (See *postea*, chap. xv.) ' Boadicea's Tomb ', the barrow in Parliament Hill Fields,

Hampstead—when so christened no one knows—is believed, from Dr. C. H. Read's examination, to belong to the Bronze Age.[17]

The Devil's Spadeful, near Kidderminster, and the five barrows known as the Devil's Jumps, at Treyford, Sussex, mark the influence of Christianity. This introduction of diabolism to explain forgotten origins was noticed in Germany by Jacob Grimm, who found that Roman fortifications were called Devil's Ditches. He says that the ' Roman castella ' were connected with idolatry.[18] At home, the Devil's Ditch, near Newmarket, represents fortifications made by the Iceni to keep back the Romans under Ostorius, A.D. 50.[19]

The Danish incursions also left traces in the names of barrows. Thus, we find Danes' Graves, at Kilham, in Yorkshire, and Hubba's Lowe (A.S. *hlœw*=hill, mound) in Wilts., applied to barrows which belong really to the earlier Iron Age. Danesbury Camp, near Northampton, showed, by the weapons and implements revealed to the excavators, that it was an ancient British cemetery, probably of the first century before Christ.[20]

Subsequent events in history gave us Robin Hood's Butts, a name occurring twice in Salop, and once in Staffordshire. Later, again, one suspects, are Old Adam, or Adam's Grave, at Luckington, Wilts., and the Five Marys at East Chaldon, Dorset. Still more recent as a barrow-name is Oliver's Mound, Richmond Park. This mound, now rased in the course of excavations for gravel, was traditionally said to be the spot whereon Cromwell stood to watch a skirmish, but it was most likely a British barrow.[21]

Prehistoric dwellings now claim attention. Else shall we be open to the accusation of General Pitt-Rivers that archaeologists often treat primitive peoples as if these did nothing but die and leave tombstones : ' mementos of mortality unto living passengers,' as Sir Thomas Browne finely phrases it.

Of the caves, whether on the seashore or in the hill-side, there is not strong British evidence of continuous occupation from Neolithic times onwards. Temporary residence at various periods, closely or remotely connected, may be deduced from the relics entombed in the cavern floor. The Kirkhead Cave, in the promontory of Cartmell, has what Dawkins calls a ' Brit-Welsh ' stratum of relics,[22] and Thor's Cave, near Ashbourne, Derbyshire, yielded remains of Brit-Welsh, Bronze and probably Neolithic days.[23] Gildas says that the Britons of the fifth century fled to mountains, forests, and caverns to shelter themselves from the Picts and Scots.[24] Victoria Cave, near Settle, though originally inhabited by Neolithic man, is one example of these refuges,[25] and other cases might be cited. The cave-dwellers of East Fife, who, during the period of the Scandinavian raids, incised their cave-walls with drawings of horses and men, as well as with lines and symbols, had the true Perigordian spirit of their French prototypes.[26] But the modern cave-habit, alluded to in Chapter III, must perhaps be looked upon as atavistic.

From the scarcity of caves suitable for habitation, such abodes cannot ever have been in general use, even in the Neolithic Age. The same may be said of the rock-shelters, an allied form of dwelling. Except as a temporary haunt, the rock-shelter did not long retain favour. In one instance, however, namely, at Castle Hill, near Hastings, the relics extended from Neolithic to post-Roman times.[27]

Our conceptions are vastly cleared if we realize the fact that dwellings of various kinds may have been contemporaneous. The choice of an abode varied with natural circumstances, rather than with race or period. People of the same cultural stage, or even race, may have inhabited caves in Pembroke, pit-dwellings in Surrey, and pile-dwellings in Suffolk. The Bronze and Iron Ages exhibit similar kinds of habitations. Overlapping of custom was manifested. Personal preference, outside influence, climatic and geological conditions may account for local retention or disuse of particular modes of housing. At no time was there uniformity in British civilization or general development.

The pile- or lake-dwellings, consisting of rude huts built on a platform supported by piles, were situated in, or near, a stream, mere, or swamp. The huts themselves were of wattle and daub, and were roofed with thatch or reeds.

An analogous kind of settlement was the crannog (Goidelic, *crannag*=structure of timber), of which remains are largely found in Ireland. The crannog was an artificial island, composed of logs, brushwood, or stones, sometimes staked round for compactness and strength. On this mound superstructures of wicker or hurdle-work were erected. Habitations of the crannog type, rich in relics, have been under exploration since 1892 in the marshes near Glastonbury ; they are assigned to the later Iron Age, previous to the Roman invasion.

The age of a lake settlement is determined by the nature of the remains found buried when the site chances to be drained and excavated. Swiss lake-dwellings are thus proved to have been successively occupied, in some cases, by men of the Stone, Bronze, and Iron periods. The nature of the evidence is fully detailed in the standard works of Munro and Keller.[28]

Most of our British lake-dwellings, so far as at present examined, belong to the Metallic period, and indeed to the Iron stage of that period.[29] In Holderness and a few other places, however, stone and iron relics have been found in association. Barton Mere, Suffolk, yielded bronze spearheads, and various Irish crannogs were found to contain bronze celts and daggers, with stone moulds for casting these weapons. A late Neolithic origin of some pile-houses may perhaps be assumed, but as a class the British examples are, as just stated, of the Iron Age. Mr. F. W. Reader has investigated remains of pile-dwellings of probable Roman date near London Wall.[30] Twenty years previously, General Pitt-Rivers examined and described similar structures at Southwark, on the Surrey side of the Thames.[31]

How far into the historic period pile-houses continued to be erected is, as Pepys said of Stonehenge, ' hard to tell, but may yet be told.' In river-bed or reclaimed swamp, now here, now yonder, rotted piles, marking the sites of former buildings, are constantly being dug up. But one would hesitate before asserting that there has been no ' solution of continuity ' since the Bronze Age, or that our wharves and docks, our pile-based granaries and shipment sheds, centuries old though they be, are genuine claimants to the succession. We may have here a case of imperceptible diversion of purpose, for it is of the first importance to remember that the original pile-structures were intended for abodes, not warehouses.

Switzerland, the land of ancient lake-dwellings, seems to furnish more certain survivals. It must have struck other ramblers besides myself that the Swiss chalets and cow-byres bear unmistakable traces of the prehistoric pile-house. Yet for centuries the cottager and the cow-herd have chosen, for their buildings, spots high and dry, frequently thousands of feet above the old lake-level.

In Venice there is a closer analogy, for the palaces of the city are built on trunks of trees driven into the soil beneath the water. Holland also is notably a pile-using country.

The shores of our own estuaries occasionally furnish examples of pile-built houses. Near Bradwell-on-Sea, Essex, at the mouth of a tidal creek, there is a rather modern pile-structure, a replica of those ideal restorations seen in archaeological works on this subject (Fig. 7).

Among other slight survivals, one notices that garden summer-houses are nowadays often reared on posts. Dependent upon a similar principle, cottages may still be seen which exhibit wattle-and-daub construction, and cow-houses are frequently built of ' cob ', that is, clay mixed with straw.[32]

In Ireland, that land of archaeological vestiges, we have better indications of continuity. As late as A.D. 1567, the O'Neils still dwelt in fortified islands, evidently crannogs, situated in ' sartin ffreshwater loghes '.[33] There is, indeed, a literary reference to crannogs in Ireland dated 1603; while still later, in 1608, there is a similar allusion to the Scotch isles : ' haill houssis of defence, strongholdis and cranokis in the Yllis.' Interesting, too, is the record, stating that a crannog in the Loch of Forfar was repaired in 1508, for this structure, partly natural and partly artificial, bears the name of St. Margaret, Queen of Malcolm Canmore, who died in 1097.[34] Thus there seems a strong case for occupation during the Middle Ages.

FIG. 7. Modern pile-structure, Bradwell-on-Sea, Essex. This building illustrates the unconscious survival of ideas betrayed when modern folk are confronted by problems similar to those which early man had to encounter. [Drawn by F. W. Reader.]

Stringent investigation, it is scarcely necessary to say, must be made before accepting any pile-building as pre-historic. About ten years ago, certain structures which appeared to be of the crannog type were discovered near Dumbarton Castle, in the estuary of the Clyde. After a fierce controversy, extending over some years, Dr. Robert Munro proved, conclusively, as most authorities believe, that the piles were not of Neolithic age, having been cut with a metal tool. Dr. Munro supposed that the structure represented the foundations of a beacon erected for mariners during the Middle Ages. Most, if not all, of the relics were of modern manufacture. Some one, who never thought fit to acknowledge the mischievous joke, had fabricated spear-heads and amulets of slate and shale. Professor Boyd Dawkins showed that in two cases the material employed was the American oyster-shell known as the ' blue point ', and imported for the first time some thirty years ago. Again, Dr. Munro contended that primitive folk would not be foolish enough to build a dwelling on the shore between high-and low-water marks. Nor would they use spears that would neither stab nor cut. Scarcely would they eat American oysters.[35]

Yet sides have been taken on the matter, and it is only right to add that Mr. Andrew Lang holds a view opposite to that just given. In his volume, ' The Clyde Mystery,' he traverses Dr. Munro's main contentions. Mr. Lang must be heard with great respect; nevertheless, the problem recalls other historical frauds. For when the Dousterswivels of fiction and the Flint Jacks of real life are upheld by antiquaries of the Oldbuck and Pickwick temperament, and reinforced by literary men of real ability, the way of safety is hard to find. As John Earle remarked of the perfervid antiquary, ' Beggers coozen him with musty things which they have rak't from dunghills.' [36]

We next come to the old British pit-dwelling, which is found both within and without the area of early fortifica-tions. What may now be seen of this kind of habitation is simply a round pit, a few yards wide, and a yard or two in depth. Such depressions are known as hut-circles. If we excavate the partially blocked up hollow, removing the peat and gravel, we reach the original floor of the dwelling, whereon may be found flint flakes, calcined flints, a few shards, and numerous pellets of charcoal. Smaller hollows apparently represent cooking-places.

The pits were doubtless once roofed over with a thatch of reeds, grass, bracken, furze, or heather, or mayhap they were rudely covered with branches of trees. Where the diameter was not too great, the branches would perhaps be overlaid with turf. The circles are found in groups, and each group represents a primitive village.

Districts like North Wales and Dartmoor, abounding in stone ready to hand, present ruins of huts rudely walled with dry masonry. To lessen the amount of artificial walling, advantage was also taken of the natural rocks of the hill-side. Some Welsh dwellings are known as ' Irishmen's huts ', that is, ' huts of the aborigines.'

In Ireland and Scotland the covering was sometimes formed by horizontal courses of stones, overlapping inwards and thus converging towards the top, forming, in fact, a corbelled dome. Of this kind are the celebrated ' beehive huts ', ' weems ', or ' Picts' Houses '. In Scotland, weems are known to have been inhabited down to the year 1823.[37]

Sometimes the beehive huts were but slightly, if at all, sunk beneath the surface of the ground. Being usually covered with earth, they were scarcely distinguishable externally from round barrows,[38] a fact of great significance, as will be seen later. Generally speaking, the depth of the hut is found to diminish as we approach historic times.

Like the pile-dwellings, the huts carry us from the Stone Age to that of Early Iron at least. Some of the ' late-Celtic ' examples have yielded fragments of Samian ware and querns, as well as cinerary urns, and Roman coins, thus betokening occupation subsequent to the Roman invasion. The low-walled huts of Anglesey, for example, are deemed by Professor Edward Anwyl to have been used continuously until Roman days, and perhaps later. The Rev. R. Ashington Bullen has described a late-Celtic ' potter's hut ' which was excavated in 1900 at Constantine Island, Cornwall.[39] This example was probably of earlier origin than those of Dartmoor, which have been explored from 1880 onwards. Other huts of an allied nature have been discovered in the Isle of Portland.[40]

There is little room for doubting that habitations analogous to hut-dwellings persisted for centuries after the Roman Conquest. The mediaeval houses of the peasantry in the Border district of Cumberland were mere huts of clay, thatched with straw,—just shelters against the weather and no more. The floors were scooped out like those of the beehive huts,[41] and the beds were simply litters of straw. Down to the beginning of the eighteenth century the buildings of Carlisle were mostly of wood and clay, with thatched roofs, and rarely of more than one story in height. Neither within nor without was there any paint.[42]

In the round huts of the charcoal burners of the New Forest the late Mr. T. W. Shore thought that there was a true Celtic survival. Thin poles are laid together to form a cone, and are interlaced with brushwood. A fire, often of charcoal, is lighted near the threshold.[43] Similar huts are often constructed by woodmen, but turf replaces the brushwood.

How the rectangular house was evolved from the circular one is not quite clear. Dr. Lange supposes that a transition is displayed in the oval huts which he believes to have developed from the round kind. Mr. S. O. Addy, after long and close study of the question, considers that this intermediate stage was not general, although it is possible that it happened occasionally. Mr. Addy admits that the beehive huts, which had a tendency to a rectangular form within, may represent the true transition, but on the whole he thinks that the straight-sided house was derived independently of the round hut. It was most likely elaborated from the booth, or shepherd's hut. This structure had a roof-tree which united two pairs of wooden forks or 'crutches', one pair at each end. The trestle-like framework was covered with any suitable material.[44] Against this opinion is the fact that some hut-circles, visible on Rough Tor, Cornwall, are distinctly oval, and some of the houses of the

Glastonbury lake-village were rectangular. Hence, the transition was at any rate made very early, and, in these examples, from predecessors of the walled type. One Surrey hut-circle had a rectangular side-apartment.

Another ancient method of roofing is seen in the Manor House at Knaresborough, which retains an original roof-tree. A forest oak rises through the kitchen up to a bedroom, where it is cut short to form a small table, being no longer required to support the roof.[45] This example illustrates the conjectural methods of covering the pit-houses in prehistoric days.

Some further light is shed by certain ancient earthenware urns, or ossuaries, which exhibit in their mouldings traces of primitive hut-designs. One Etruscan specimen shows the gables of a primitive house, with the boughs crossing at the ridge.[46] Other examples from Northern Italy reproduce the wicker huts of the period to which they belong. One foreign urn, which was dug up in Essex, has neck-mouldings which represent the ribs of a roof.

Persistence in design, not to say construction, is well seen in the bell-tent of the soldier,[47] the bothy of the Highland shepherd, and the tent of the gipsy in all lands.

Folk-lore and superstition often mislead one as to so-called ancient huts. The name of ' Shrieking Pits ' at Aylmerton, Norfolk, does not help much, while the ' Killing Pits ' at Goathland, Yorkshire, are believed to be disused kilns— ' kiln-pits '. Canon Atkinson found that ' British villages ' in the Cleveland district were really a collection of ' reef- ' or ' hole-pits ', formerly used for the extraction of iron ore.[48] The Rev. T. Longley submits that groups of so-called ' hut-circles ',—low mounds with saucer-like depressions, occurring on the Lincolnshire coast, when critically excavated, and examined in the light of documentary evidence, prove to be salternes, or salt-pans, in which sea-water was evaporated to obtain salt. Testimony is adduced from Holinshed's Chronicle, 1571, from various terriers, charters, and annals of religious houses, from Domesday Book itself. That some of the saltcotes are of Roman origin is most likely, since various parts of the Roman road leading from Lincoln city to the sea-coast are still known as Saltway, Saltergate, and Salter's Lane [49] (cf. remarks on ' Red Hills ', *postea*, Chapter IX).

' Pit-dwellings ' at Barmby Common, in the East Riding, are shown by inquiry to have been simply pits for the preparation of flax.[50] Plainly, every saucer-shaped depression is not a hut-circle.

Earthwork forts and camps, which are calculated to cause endless discussion as to date and purpose, need a similar reservation. Monkbarns, who had formed a pleasant theory about a supposed camp of Agricola, was, it will be remembered, rudely borne down by Edie Ochiltree, the gaberlunzie man, ' Prætorian here, Prætorian there, I mind the biggin' o't.' [51] A like disillusion, conveyed in very similar words, was once experienced by a friend of the present writer.

Especially must we be on guard with respect to the embankments which often surround strips of woodland. When the trees have been felled, these banks, with their trenches, have frequently a pristine appearance. Before declaring for antiquity, additional evidence must be sought. Are the trenches duplicated or triplicated ? Are there ' gateways ', ' wells ', dew-ponds, or dene-holes present ? What is the situation, considered pastorally or strategically ? Are there relics of human craft in the vicinity ? The danger is the more subtle in that ancient earthworks are frequently coterminous with belts of woodland of long continuance.

Modern examination of earthworks, a pursuit worthy of all encouragement, proves that numerous camps have been continuously occupied from the days of Stone to those of Iron. We may for the moment dismiss such questions as whether circular earthworks are always pre-Roman, and rectangular ones of Roman date, or whether the enclosures were intended for occupation, defence, or refuge, or for all these purposes in turn. Problems of this kind may be easier of solution when the investigations begun by the late Mr. Chalkley Gould have been carried further. Interesting as these topics may be, we pass to matters of a more verifiable nature.

The principle of continuity soon shows itself at work. Old Sarum, with its deep ditches and elevated position, was probably pre-Roman in its inception. It was certainly a Roman fortress, a Saxon 'burh', a Norman stronghold, and a Mediaeval city.[52] The earthworks at Boley Hill, Rochester, probably of British origin, were afterwards used by Saxons and Danes.[53] Merdon Camp, Hants, a British work, was occupied as a Norman fortress.[54]

On an irregular plateau, rising perpendicularly some 400 feet above the Dorsetshire Stour, is the ancient stronghold of Hod Hill. A Bronze Age, or probably Neolithic earthwork, with deep fosses on two sides, it covers an area of fifty acres. But in one corner, a few acres are taken up by a Roman encampment, whose defences are of moderate strength only. Dotted over the larger camp, and scattered outside the enclosures, are depressions marking ancient huts, clear indications of occupation previous to the Iron Age.[55] Hambledon Hill, a neighbour of Hod Hill, has a similar record, but here there is a further history, for the Royalists used it during the Civil War, and were driven from it by Cromwell and Desborough in 1645.[56] The same year saw Winklebury Camp, near Basingstoke, occupied by the Parliamentary troops, who were besieging Basing House.[57] By some it is believed that this camp was the scene of the fight between the Saxons and Danes in A.D. 871. We note, in passing, that ancient tumuli near York were raised in height and utilized as fortifications during the siege of that city in 1644.[58]

Woodbury Hill, a British stronghold in Worcestershire, is said to have been occupied by Owen Glendower and his allies, who were here encountered by Henry IV and his son.[59] Time alone can tell whether these old earthworks have yet rendered their last services to our country.

One astonishing case of folk-memory is connected with ramparts and trenches enclosed, on the open down, in Bourne Park, Kent. The spot is known as 'Old England's Hole', and is vaguely associated with some patriot defeat. It has been supposed that here the Britons made their last stand at the close of the second Julian invasion, 54 B.C.[60]

This example leads us to the nomenclature of earth-works.

In Maiden Castle (Celtic, ' the flat-topped fort '), Dorset-shire, and in Maiden Bower, a name applied to ancient camps in Cheshire, Oxford, Durham, and Northumberland, we have plainly the Goidelic suffix *dun* (Welsh, *dīn*), a hill-fortress, and thus we are carried back to the Bronze Age. Arthur's Round Table, a term used in Northumberland and West-moreland, is especially interesting. Sir John Rhŷs, while admitting that many developments of the Arthurian legend are of a comparatively late date, asserts that the materials existed from time immemorial, wherever there was a Celt who spoke a Brythonic language, either in Great Britain or in the Lesser Britain (=Brittany) on the other side of the Channel. More than this : besides the historic Arthur, there was a Brythonic divinity of the same name—a kind of Celtic Zeus—so that an early origin is demanded.[61]

We cannot get far without being arrested by the name Grim. There is the primitive settlement of Grimspound, on Dartmoor. We find also Grimes Hill near Kirkby Lonsdale, and Grimsbury Castle, in Berkshire, and Grim's Grave, a kist-vaen on Dartmoor. Grim's Dykes, applied to ditches and entrenchments, occurs in Bucks., Herts., Dorset, South Wiltshire, and three times in Berkshire. These names, given to earthworks, are paralleled by Grimes Graves in the hundred of Grimeshoe, or -how, the site of Neolithic flint mines, and by Grimstone, a Dorset village which has a barrow within its limits. To these we may add such place-names as Grimstead (Wilts.), Grimley (Worcester), Grimston (in four counties), and Grimsthorpe, Grimblethorpe, Grimoldby, and Grimsby, all in Lincolnshire. The last-mentioned place boasts a Mediaeval legend, supported by the device on the former Corporation seal, ascribing the foundation of the town to one Grim, a kindly Scandinavian jarl or viking. Thoughtful students will not accept this tale too readily. Nor need we believe the story of the Norfolk villagers, as told to the writer, that the flint-works at Grimes Graves once belonged to ' a Mr. Grim ' !

What, then, is the word Grim ? A comparatively modern

writer, speaking of Grimes Graves, makes the daring but ludicrous assumption that the pits represent the settlement of a Danish leader, Gryme or Grime. The statement is boldly made that the pits are arranged in the ' form of a quincunx ', and that the largest is the general's or commander's ' tent '.[62]   The ' Century Dictionary of Names ' (1895) simply has a quotation which gives no help. Isaac Taylor just mentions Grimes Dyke, and passes on.[63]   An etymology, once widely accepted, makes the word come from A.S. *grime*=witch, hence ' witches' work ', but Dr. Guest disputes this. Taking correlative words in German, Swedish, and Welsh, he decides that the term means a boundary, and considers that it indicates a long period during which Englishman and Briton dwelt side by side. According to Guest, the Scotch Graeme's or Graham's Dyke, that is the Wall of Antoninus between the Forth and Clyde, is a mere variant : John of the Graeme is the equivalent for John Grimes.[64]

Now, Grim or Grîme, a giant, is an outstanding figure in Northern mythology,[65] and we might be disposed to accept Guest's explanation. But when we notice that in most instances ' Grim ' occurs in connexion with old earthworks, ridgeways, or barrows, we shall, unless we accept the word as a later nickname, rather look back beyond the Danish invasion, the more so because the term is often applied to known British and Roman remains.

That a brook in Cheshire, named Grimesditch, runs by a hamlet which was granted in A.D. 1226 to Hugo de Grimesditch,[66] and that another Grimesditch, near Ewelme, Oxford, is mentioned in a charter of the reign of the first Richard, must not be allowed to obscure the question.[67]   Indeed, the first-mentioned place has a curious scrap of folk-lore attached to it, for an ancestor of the present Grimesditch family is said to have fought and killed a dragon in a *ditch*. Afterthoughts count little ; surnames copied from older designations and place-names are of scarcely greater weight. Nor do such names as Offandic and Wodensdic, with their restricted, definite localization, affect the question. The names occur in Saxon charters,[68] and probably relate to real or mythical personages. The vexed word Grim is rooted everywhere, but its origin must stand over until further facts are discovered.

Earthworks are, by popular vote, sometimes laid to the credit of the Danes. Danesborough occurs in Bucks. and Somerset, and Danesbank in Warwick. Yet the famous Danes Dyke, a double entrenchment, fortifying Flamborough Head, is supposed to belong to the Bronze Age ; the name was evidently a guess put forward at a later date. On the contrary, Danes Castle, near Exeter, may be the genuine work of the invading pirates, so that here the name may give the actual history.

Ambresbury Banks, a British camp in Epping Forest, has long been associated with the name of Boadicea. ' Alfred's Castle ', near Ashdown, in Berkshire, and ' Ethelbert's Camp ', at Dormington, Herefordshire, may speak the truth, or may be later nicknames. Another Ethelbert's Camp, near Folkestone, was, so far back as the time of Lambarde, about the close of the sixteenth century, attributed to Ethelbert, ' the first godly king of this shyre,' yet it is now said to be almost certainly Norman work.[69] Invented origins, consequent on weak folk-memory, are common, and each case must be considered on its merits.

Peasant folk often vaguely connect earthworks with some great battle, as in the case of Cardinal's Cap, at War Coppice, Caterham (Surrey). Or, again, the camp is believed to be a burial-ground, like ' La Cité des Morts ', near Dieppe, or our own ' Dead Men's Graves ', in Northumberland.

We know, by the way, that some of the earliest battles recorded in history were fought around earthworks or on hill-tops. The elevated fort where Vercingetorix defeated Caesar exists almost unaltered near Clermont-Ferrand, in the department of Puy-de-Dôme. And it was on a mountain near Shrewsbury, probably Caer Caradoc, that brave old Caradoc made such a stout resistance to Ostorius.

The multitude of ' Caesar's Camps ' must not be quite overlooked. We have them at Wimbledon and Aldershot, at Keston (Kent), and Crondall (Hants), at East Hampstead

(Berks.) and Sandy (Beds.). A few of these camps may actually have been used in Roman times.

'Castle Hills' and 'Galley Hills' occur in many counties, and with considerable frequency. Almost always they exhibit early work, though occasionally they represent the sites of Mediaeval castles. 'Robin Hood's Bower', near Warminster, embodies a sheer guess. Strangely enough, camps said to have been utilized by Cromwell are rarely christened after that general.

The reader may now desire to know whether there has been continuity in village sites, as distinct from ancient camp settlements.

More than twenty years ago, J. R. Green noticed that Roman towns undoubtedly often occupied British sites, though the earlier settlements could have been little more than a collection of huts.[70] Having admitted this continuity with respect to the Roman conquest, which did not fundamentally modify the mass of the British population, Green yet contended that the later Teutonic settlement vastly affected the country in this matter of sites, as in other ways. Not that he postulates a general slaughter of the Celts. He only argues that after a stubborn resistance there was a great Celtic retreat towards the West and South-West of the country.

This historian bases his conclusions upon the number of Teutonic names, seen in the traces of human life itself, in the vanishing of the *vill* and the *city*, and the appearance in their stead of the *tun* and *ham* and *thorpe*, and in the restriction of the Celtic *pens*, *duns*, *combes*, and *ocks* to natural features. Further he argues for the extinction of the Latin language, and the obliteration of the British (Celtic) tongue save in the Westerly districts. Finally he lays stress upon what he believes to be the essentially German character of the political institutions, the social customs, and the legal practices, which came in the train of the Teutonic settlement.[71]

It must be noted that Kemble, Freeman, Stubbs, and Gneist, a goodly array, belonged to the 'Germanist' School. But a wider outlook has been taken in recent years, and we may therefore briefly reconsider Green's contentions.

Language, a good servant, but a capricious and fickle mistress, does not help the Teutonic school so much as might be hastily supposed. To begin with, experience shows that the very numerous suffixes, *don*, *combe* (Welsh, *cwm*, a cup-shaped depression), *llan* (church), *caer* (fort), and others, frequently indicate a series of settlements on the selfsame site extending from the Bronze Age to the present time. Again, with the exception of a few places, such as Silchester, Anderida, and Uriconium, almost every one of the Romano-British cities has been continuously occupied. The Roman towns, often built on Celtic sites, were known by names Latinized from the Celtic ones, hence the continuity may be masked. We have Londinium, Lunden, London ; Eburacum, Eoforwic, Eurewic, York ; Lindum Colonia, Lincolne, Lincoln. In other cases the added word *ceaster* = *castrum*) conceals the root-term, as in Gwent = Venta Belgarum = Wintan-ceaster = Winchester ; Isca = Exan-ceaster = Exeter ; Corinium = Cyren-ceaster = Cirencester.[72]

' Almost every place,' says Grant Allen, ' which is known to have had a name at the English Conquest retained that name afterwards in a more or less clipped and altered form.' [73] Even where the Roman name, which, we have seen, was often based on a Celtic one, is now lost, the old term was kept in Early English. We call Anderida, Pevensey, but the Anglo-Saxon Chronicle speaks of Andredes-ceaster. The true English settlements grew up in the richest agricultural lowlands—not on the hills as in primitive days,—by fords of rivers, at the mouths of good harbours, in wastes and wealds. As a whole, during the entire early English period, the names of villages and country towns were English, the names of cities Roman.[74]

The *tuns*, *hams*, and *thorpes* of Green are largely explained when we realize that the Saxons abhorred city life. The unwarlike burghers were probably left, as Professor Rolleston puts it, in ' a condition of taxed submissiveness '.

Place-names, then, are not decisive witnesses for the Teutonic theory. What of the common folk-speech ? A larger number of Celtic words survives than is usually believed. Garnett and other writers put it as high as 200.[75]

Some of these words are in common use, and seem to show that the humbler classes of Celts, at any rate, were not exterminated. *Basket, cudgel, pail* are particularly the words of labouring folk ; *lad* and *tall* are types of words not so confined ; terms like *bag* and *whip* are common to Teutonic and Celtic, so that it is difficult to assign priority.[76]

These points need not be emphasized, for the linguistic argument is faulty. The imposition of a language by conquest, or the imitation engendered by political unity, does not by any means imply the extermination or banishment of the people who spoke the earlier tongue.

Language is independent of race. Else would France be a Latin nation, whereas it is Celtic, Iberian, and Teutonic ; [77] and the Swiss peasant would be a German at Andermatt, a Frenchman at Sion, and an Italian at Brigue.

Usually a language is not adopted by halves, it is taken wholly or it is let alone. Romance Latin displaced Bulgarian in Roumania, but is now said to be perishing before Slavonic, and Castilian is giving way to Portuguese.

The Romano-Britons, who spoke Latin and Celtic, are by some supposed to have been superior in culture to their Saxon conquerors.[78] Yet the language of the defeated and disorganized Britons was overwhelmed by that of the Saxons. Centuries of contact over a wide linguistic frontier has since transferred but a few Celtic words to the English speech. The Normans arbitrarily imposed their language as the official tongue in England, but could not dispossess the Saxon speech. True, as Dr. Beddoe estimates, the Normans were only some 20 per cent. of the total population.[79] But if the Normans, the dominant race, could not succeed, how came it to pass that the Saxons were able to accomplish the feat ? Probably, in no small degree, because their conquest was of a colonizing nature. They found the English village community already fairly developed. The bonds of that community might be loosened to admit new cultivators and new over-lords, but they could not be altogether rent in pieces. At all events, there remains the notable fact, that the Northmen, having adopted a Romance tongue after conquering Normandy, crossed to England and re-Germanized their language.

Replying to those who think that the Celts and Latinized populations in Lower Britain were cut clean off the ground by the Teutons, Sir John Rhŷs uses a striking argument. First, he recalls the probability that the first *Wealas*, or Welshmen, as they were called by the Saxon invaders, were not the Brythons, whom the Saxons termed Brettas, but rather the provincial Romans, or ' Latinizing peoples '. Now, at the time of the Saxon invasion the language of a considerable portion of the South and East of England had become Latin. The tables might therefore be turned on the holders of the extermination theory by asking, not, Where are the Celtic words to support the argument for the survival of the Celts ? but rather, How many Latin words remain in the earliest known specimens of English ? [80]

Let us turn to other corroborative facts, showing that not only Romano-British, but even Roman influences were not destroyed. Mr. H. C. Coote brings forward a good case for the existence of Roman influence in our modern institutions, in gardening and agriculture, in literature and art. The bequest of the Roman alphabet is incontestable.[81] Mr. Coote, indeed, in his illuminating volume makes a strong presentation generally. It is right to say that there are contrary voices with regard to certain departments of British life. Thus, Mr. G. L. Gomme, an opponent of the extermination theory, argues that Roman influence on agricultural methods was not very deep.[82] But by other writers the mediaeval guilds, for example, are believed to have originated in the *collegia*, or associations formed in Roman times for the worship of some particular divinity, or for burial purposes.[83] From the guilds, such writers as Mr. George Howell and Mr. Sidney Webb derive the modern benefit societies.

We must now hear the decision of the ethnologist. Anthropology says that Celtic, and indeed Neolithic types abound even in the Anglo-Danish counties of Lincoln, Norfolk, and Suffolk. In Jutish Kent and Saxon Sussex Celts are not uncommon, and a considerable leaven of the British element is found in Romney Marsh. Dr. Beddoe has calculated that over the greater part of England the Celtic strain amounts to one-half.[84]

When such authorities as Beddoe, Rolleston, and Haddon speak in favour of Celtic persistence, the matter is worth examination.

It must be noted that the terms Celtic, British, and Briton are used in the following paragraphs in the wide sense of pre-Teutonic. Celtic and pre-Celtic peoples may have been preserved in the midst of the victorious Teutons by the enslaving of some of the men, by the sparing of the women, and by allowing some of the conquered to rise to the status of citizenship.[85] To this list must be added those Celts who successfully resisted dislodgement. Sir F. Palgrave has collected historical passages tending to prove that at the end of the sixth century there were inaccessible places like the Fens where the older inhabitants managed to hold out.[86] This conclusion, accepted by Freeman, is probably correct.

A late charter of Cambridge mentions penalties for killing ' Welshmen ' (=Britons). Signatures appended to early charters, collected by Thorpe and Kemble, supply names demonstrably Celtic, and others assuredly not Teutonic.[87] On the Wolds of Lincoln, in the marshes of Somerset, in the Midland forest of Arden, on many a wooded height, and by many a morass, the Britons held their own.

Professor F. York Powell, writing of the Old English village, gives a most interesting and exhaustive classification of the inhabitants. So valuable is the list that I venture to give an epitome :

i. *Gentry*	Thegen (squire or landlord) Priest (parson)	Of gentle blood or rank.
ii. *Farmers*	Yeoman or Geneat (tenant-farmer)	Freemen.
iii. *Peasants*	Cotsetla (cottager) Gebur (copyholder)	Unfree.
iv. *Labourers*	Bee-keepers, cheese-wrights, barn-keepers, swine-herds, ox-herds, shepherds, bea- dle, woodward, hayward	Serfs.

| v. *Village* *tradesmen* | Fisher, keeper, fowler, smith, carpenter, leather-worker, potter, merchant-pedlar, &c. | Freemen. |

And this is Professor York Powell's noteworthy comment : ' It is probable that *thegen* and *geneat* and village tradesmen, save perhaps the smith, were mostly of English blood, with such mixture as marriage or concubinage with the British women caused ; the other classes, over most of the island, were probably largely of Celtic or pre-Celtic blood.' [88] If this table be accepted, one sees how large a proportion the old British stock formed.

Mr. Coote claims that the Romano-British folk continued to exist, not only as serfs, but as landed proprietors. Roman *cognomina* (=family names) were not unfrequent in Saxon times, and were held by landowners as late as A.D. 710–15. Even in the reign of Edward the Confessor, there were still, in Lincolnshire and Yorkshire, country squires of the gens Artoria.[89]

The testimony of charters and folk-names is borne out by that of the skulls unearthed from Saxon burial grounds. Professor Rolleston, after examining a large number of specimens, found strong evidence of Celtic survivals,—even the long-skulled Neolithic people were well represented.[90]

Upon whom do the supporters of the extermination hypothesis rely for their evidence ? Mainly upon Gildas, Bede, and the ' English Chronicle '. Gildas, who was a British monk, writing from the Celtic point of view, gives the exaggerated and pessimistic account of a member of the beaten race. Yet even Gildas admits that many of the British yielded themselves up as slaves, whilst others remained as isolated outlaws. Bede, or Bæda, a more simple and straightforward writer (*c.* A.D. 730), quotes the accounts of Gildas almost word for word, with respect to the earlier settlements. In later subjugations, he implies that the natives were, to some extent, spared. The value of the ' English Chronicle ' is impaired by the fact that it was chiefly compiled centuries after the events which it relates. When further fragments of traditional information are given, curiously they refer to Kent, Sussex, and the older parts of Wessex, where the Teutonic colonization was exceptionally thorough. Of the people of Yorkshire, Lincolnshire, and East Anglia, with their strong Celtic physique, we are told nothing. Nevertheless, the ' Chronicle' nowhere speaks of extermination.[91]

If, as Professor Rolleston supposes, the skulls teach that wholesale importations of Saxon women were unfrequent,[92] we may safely infer considerable intermarriage between Teuton and Celt.

On the positive side, we know that there existed ' double cities ' where the two races lived as neighbours. The Southern part of Exeter was English; the Northern, as shown by the dedication of churches to Celtic saints, was British. At Shrewsbury, the two communities, each having its own laws and customs, were separated by the Severn.[93]

In other instances, there was continuous occupancy, and, doubtless for some considerable period, Teuton and Briton dwelt side by side. The British town lying beneath Maiden Castle, Dorsetshire, became the Roman Durnovaria, the Saxon Dornwara-ceaster, and then Dorchester.[94] Places like Lincoln city represent British, Roman, and Saxon occupation in unbroken descent.

Professor Frederic Seebohm, who has submitted this continuity problem to a searching examination, claims that the test ultimately lies in the rural district. This seems like a direct challenge to the advocates of criterion by language. Professor Seebohm traces the primitive village community to Roman and pre-Roman influences.[95] Mr. Gomme, indeed, sees the beginnings of that community in times more distinctly prehistoric.[96] With this view we may fitly compare that of Professor P. Vinogradoff, a savant of cosmopolitan learning. He considers that the absorption of the early British by the Roman culture was by no means complete, and had not proceeded far when the Saxons broke in and Roman rule collapsed.[97]

We start, then, with an admitted British system of settlement. Was that system abolished, and were the old settlements desolated ? It is useless to cite cases like Anderida,

where we are told every Briton was slaughtered, and where
the two Saxon villages of Pevensey grew up outside the
Roman walls.   The answer returned, reasonably enough, is
that it was easier to rebuild outside the city than to clear
away the ruins after sacking and fire had done their work.

Seebohm reviews, as already stated, the case of the
country districts, and, by way of example, the area around
Hitchin, in Hertfordshire, especially.[98]   Hitchin was formerly
a part of the township of Walsworth.   The latter place-
name has a Saxon signification, though the word Hitchin
itself comes from the Celtic for ' streams '.   Two or three
pure chalk streams embrace Walsworth township, and one
actually passes through it.   It is not likely that the Romans
or Saxons gave the town a Celtic designation.   Again, it is
more probable that the retention of such a name should
prove the survival of some of the British occupants, than
that a new and Teutonic name should imply extermination.
On the hill towards the East of the town, British sepulchral
urns have been found, and on the opposite side a Roman
cemetery has been discovered.   The Icknield Way, an old
British track, dotted with barrows, is near at hand, lazily
winding up and down the edge of the Chilterns.   Every
commanding bluff of chalk has its traces of a hill-fort.
Roman roads and dikes are common, and driftways are
discernible on the close turf of the Downs.   The spade
frequently turns up Roman coins and pottery.   All these
remains suggest continuity.

Next there is the probability indicated by historic fact.
Most likely the Hitchin district fell under Roman sway after
the campaigns of Aulus Plautius and Claudius about A.D. 43.
The Saxon conquest of this region is fixed with reasonable
definiteness at A.D. 571.   For four hundred years, then,
the district was subject to Roman rule, and for rather more
than another hundred years, in fact until within some
quarter of a century of the arrival of St. Augustine, it was
under the management of the Romano-Britons.   There is
local evidence to show, so Seebohm contends, that in this
part of Britain at any rate, the Saxons succeeded to a long
settled system of agriculture.   He thinks that the Saxons

assumed the lordship vacated by the owners of villas, and that they adopted the village sites. This done, they continued, on the old three-field system, and by the aid of the old rural population—this addition is noteworthy—that method of cultivation which had been improved and matured under Roman rule, and which had supported three generations during the interval separating the departure of the Roman governors from the arrival of the West Saxon conquerors.[99]

At Ashwell, at Litlington, at Great Chesterford, and nearly half a score of places within the Hitchin ' sphere of influence ', the same story may be read : Teutonic sites coinciding with those of the Roman and pre-Roman periods. An old map of Much Wymondley, near Hitchin, proves that as late as 1803, the ancient open-fields, with their strips and balks, and their concomitant system of scattered ownership, still remained.[100] Waiving the question whether this open-field system of co-tillage was of British or of Roman origin, we here see a remarkable instance of pre-Teutonic continuity in what many would deem essentially an original Teutonic settlement. Other parts of the country would doubtless corroborate this evidence, were a proper examination instituted. In the North and West of England, where the Teutonic influence on state organization and local custom was not so complete, Celtic vitality would be still more marked.

Archbishop Whately somewhere lays down as an important rule that where there exists a large body of positive testimony in favour of any conclusion, such testimony is not to be set aside the moment we meet with an objection which does not seem easy to surmount. The difficulty, if carefully examined, may vanish with fuller knowledge. This has been the case with the extermination controversy ; the objections raised by the Teutonists are not unanswerable. The whole of the facts have recently been re-marshalled and balanced by Mr. T. Hodgkin, who is of opinion that the opposing schools approach each other more nearly than they themselves think.

The sites occupied by our parish churches would afford further testimony in support of continuity. A fair case can also be put for the abiding character of the Romano-British

Christian organization, which no massacres or fires could wholly destroy.   The old Neolithic and Bronze Age track-ways, too, will be found to keep company with other ancient remains.   All these reveal a comparatively steady, not an intermittent, custom and tradition.   The advent of metals caused modifications, marking an advance which could never thereafter be converted into a retrogression. If we would view, in the living instant, the events of a distant past of which the historian knows but little, we must turn to the barrows, the megaliths, the ruined dwellings, the earthworks, on the one hand, and to physical features, language, customs, and folk-memory on the other.   Better method there is none, other method there is none.   For, to use an old word, now unfortunately nearly obsolete, the past is ' irremeable ',—it cannot be gone over again.

CHAPTER V

TRACES OF THE AGES OF STONE AND BRONZE SHOWN BY LATER IMPLEMENTS

WE have next to consider how far the employment of stone implements survived into the Iron Age. For though the new material produced great economic changes, there was no real break. There was, at first, a steady decline in the industrial use of stone, then, save for minor purposes, a general cessation. The prevailing principle of folk-memory is here well illustrated. Disuse brings lack of interest, and ultimately a blank is left in the tradition of the common people. As we shall shortly see, the memories of the learned ultimately become almost as remiss as those of the ignorant.

Last to die out is the ceremonial or superstitious use of an object, of which the original purpose was secular and material. Actually before the new economy has become well established, superstitions arise concerning the old system, and to these the flow of time brings increasing vigour.

I have a recollection of having somewhere read of the discovery of an early Palæolithic implement in a Neolithic barrow. The precise record cannot now be traced, but whether trustworthy or not, it illustrates what may well have been a real occurrence. A Neolithic man finds an ancient pear-shaped implement, and dimly recognizes it as belonging to an earlier period. He himself indeed employs stone weapons, but this particular pattern, if not obsolete, is rarely used. The object belongs to a past which is far removed. Ignorance induces respect and reverence, the implement gains talismanic virtue. Had the implement been of a later Palæolithic or Mesolithic type, and therefore more recognizable, possibly he would have used it again, retouching it if necessary.

A man living in the Norman period picks up a polished

celt. For this man there can be no appeal to a bygone
economy. Books, if any be accessible, do not help him.
Coming down from his ancestors there is, mayhap, some
plausible tradition, but even those ancestors lived subse-
quently to the fabricators of the tool. The implement now
serves no industrial need, and the memory of its purpose
has died away.

A little later still, and the Mediaeval folk boldly claim for
the stone tool magical powers which would have astonished
its forgotten maker.

A reference to Mediaeval beliefs concerning stone implements will show how all tradition had then vanished.
Analogous ideas are met with in far-scattered countries where
a like relative stage of culture has been reached. We need
not search even so far back for an example, because the
Stone Age in several countries came down to the days of our
grandfathers.

About the middle of the nineteenth century, Erman
obtained in Kamtschatka a fluted prism of obsidian representing a core from which a succession of flakes had been
struck. Knowing that stone implements had been used in
the peninsula in recent times, Erman questioned the natives,
but to his surprise the persons who dug up the core did not
know what it was.[1]

There is a possibility that in some such instances tribes
have held back information through cunning or fear. In
Chapter I we saw that Dr. Roth could barely obtain information on this subject from the natives of Queensland.
Once a knowledge of metal is gained, that of stone is speedily
disavowed. A powerful chief may enforce reaction for a
time, but, on the whole, ' no step backward ' is the principle.

Bagehot claimed that primitive people, newly acquainted
with a particular material, agent, or contrivance, will at once
use it as well as, or better than, civilized man. The South
Americans manage the horse better than the Europeans who
introduced it, and many races use the rifle, a complicated
weapon, with more skill than its own inventors. In the
matter of tools, Bagehot compared the savage to a child, who
is quick to learn, rather than to an old man, who has once

forgotten, and cannot acquire again.[2] Aye, cannot and will not acquire again !

How far these observations may apply to the instructed members of a community is a matter for discussion, in which the existence of written records would have to be considered. It were a nice inquiry to ascertain to what extent the old schoolmen and ecclesiastics were actually victims of ignorance or forgetfulness, and whether at any period of our history traditions of the Stone Age had everywhere fallen into oblivion. To make this investigation one would perforce have to ransack our English literature from the earliest times to the seventeenth century.

Lucretius, the Latin poet who flourished just before the Christian era, anticipated the modern classification of stages of culture when he wrote : ' Arms of old were hands, nails, and teeth, and stones, and boughs broken off from the forests. . . . Afterwards the force of iron and copper was discovered, and the use of copper was known before that of iron, as its nature is easier to work and it is found in greater quantity.'[3] And at least one Mediaeval Englishman, Bartholomew the Franciscan, who wrote about A.D. 1260, knew that the Iron Age was preceded by that of Bronze. ' In old time,' says he, ' or (= ere) the use of iron was known, men eared (= ploughed) land with brass, and fought there-with in war and battle.'[4] It is highly probable that Bartholomew did but repeat written tradition, for his editors have compiled a long list of earlier English authors from whom he borrowed, making historically an unbroken chain for his assertions.

After Bartholomew's time, I know no further allusion in our literature for three or four centuries. Michael Drayton, in his ' Poly-olbion ' (1613), tells how the Welsh or ' Cymbri ' fought long and stoutly with brazen swords against the ' Gaules ' and ' German powers ', that is at the time of the Saxon invasion (Sixth Song). In a long note, he tells how the ancients made spears, swords, scythes, and ' Priests' Rasours' of brass (= bronze). On the Continent, Mercati, physician to Clement VIII, appears to have recognized, at the end of the sixteenth century, that the ' thunderbolts ' of

the ignorant were really the arms of men who were unacquainted with metal. A little later, Olaus Wormius, the
Danish collector, discussed stone arrow-heads, and somewhat favoured the view that they were artificial.

At home, in 1684, Sir Robert Sibbald, in his ' Scotia
Illustrata ', held a like opinion. Two years later Dr. Robert
Plot declared that either the Romans or the Britons used
stone axes with cutting edges, like the hatchets of the Indians.
He also recognized, and gave illustrations of, stone arrow-
heads and bronze celts.[5]

These views, it must be said, were not popular at the time.
But about this period—the exact date is uncertain—there was
found in London the now famous pear-shaped Palæolithic
implement still to be seen in the Prehistoric Department of
the British Museum. This implement was described in the
Sloane Catalogue as 'A British weapon, found, with elephant's
tooth, opposite to Black Mary's, near Grayes Inn Lane '.

The Palæolithic weapons had to go through a long period
of storm and stress before they were accepted as works of
man. John Frere, of Hoxne, in Suffolk, realized in 1797
that the implements were of human origin, and of pre-
metallic age. He stood among a select company, however,
for after the discovery of similar implements by M. Boucher
de Perthes in 1839, twenty years of scepticism had to be
encountered. The opposition to Mr. Benjamin Harrison's
Eoliths in our own generation was, and in certain quarters is,
quite as pronounced.

Now we must turn on our track, and, beginning with the
early Iron Age, try to catch the departing echoes of voices
from the Stone period.

On the industrial side, we shall find that stone tools and
weapons gradually fell into desuetude. But the employment
of stone implements ceremonially and in superstitious
observances outlived their economic use. So numerous are
these survivals that a separate chapter must be set aside
to discuss them.

First, Dr. E. B. Tylor's dictum may be recalled. Wherever we find stone instruments used as they were used in the
Stone Age proper, there the Stone Age has not entirely

passed away.[6] Accepted in the same spirit that one interprets Huxley's epigram, ' We are still living in the Cretaceous epoch,' this maxim will prove a good guide.

Beginning with the stone celt, which may be roughly defined as a tool or weapon of the axe type, we note that a German poem of the fifth century speaks of the heroes contending with stone axes. Dr. Much argued that these hatchets were not really made of stone, but that the word survived the thing. In like manner it has been urged that the words *stan-œx, stan-bil*, in Ælfric's Saxon glossary, refer, not to the material of which the tools were made, but to that on which they were used.[7] But this reasoning does not apply very forcibly respecting a language in its semi-developed form, when transfers of meaning would be more restricted. Again, Dr. Otto Schrader avers that the various Northern words for ' sword ' are derived from the cognate terms for a stone-knife ; for example, A.S. *sax, seax*, which, in turn, is etymologically connected with Latin *saxum*, a rock or stone.[8]

Another debatable passage, taken from the writings of William of Poitiers, tells us that weapons of stone were used by the Saxons at the Battle of Hastings. The precise meaning turns partly on the word *jactare*. Professor S. Nilsson argued for ' brandishing ' rather than ' throwing ', but Sir John Evans leans to the opinion that missiles, rather than celts, are referred to.[9] I notice, however, that *jacto* is used by Lucretius to describe the gestures of an orator, and by Cicero to indicate wavering or fluctuation of opinion.

Rude celts, or ' batlets ', are said to be still used as batting-staffs by the washerwomen of the Northern counties.[10] Neolithic or Æneolithic folk doubtless employed stone ' bats ' for the preparation of fibre, so here may be a case of unconscious survival.

Celts were probably often hafted simply by passing around them a withy or ash sapling. The modern blacksmith sometimes binds his chisel or swage in the same way, but instead of twisting the osier he secures it by means of a ring. Richard Jefferies, a close observer, says that the blacksmiths of Wiltshire used a sapling because, while tough

and pliant, it yet ' gives ' a little, and consequently the chisel
does not jar when struck.[11]

The stone maul, or hammer-stone, was also probably
wielded by means of twisted osiers.   These primitive implements long remained common.   In old copper mines near
Llandudno, dating apparently from the early historic period,
large mauls, varying from two to forty pounds in weight,
were found in association with bronze picks and a broken
stag-horn.   Lead mines in Montgomeryshire have yielded
a similar hoard, but here a pickaxe of iron was also found.
In Staffordshire, Cheshire, co. Cork, and other districts, these
' miners' hammers ' have likewise been recorded.[12]   Some
of the mauls were oval pebbles or boulders, grooved as if to
receive a withy.

Travelling tinkers in Ireland used stone hammers until
within the last generation.[13]   Sir John Evans relates that he
has seen London hawkers cracking Brazil nuts with a stone,[14]
and the custom is, to my knowledge, not yet extinct.   So,
in France, the women shell almonds with a smooth pebble
(*couède*, or *couèdon*).   The Icelander uses huge stone mallets
with wooden handles.   The Kaffir actually employs a stone
hammer in forging iron.[15]

The very word ' hammer ' tells a tale, for the term has
outlived the first concept.   The Old Norse word *hamarr*
meant ' crag '.   Possible cognate terms are the Slavonic
kamy, and the Russian *kamen'*, both meaning ' stone ', as if
the original word implied a ' stone-hammer ' (cf. with *stan-
œx*, page 102).[16]

The pounder of the Neolithic tribesman, diversely used
to crush grain or roots, and to detach flint flakes for the
manufacture of implements, had a persistent hold for many
centuries.   Fynes Moryson, journeying through Cork in the
early seventeenth century, observed ' young maides, starke
naked, grinding corne with certaine stones to make cakes
thereof '.[17]   Now, as querns or handmills were still in use
in England at that period, despite the old charter decrees,
the traveller can scarcely be referring to those contrivances,
since they would excite no wonder.   As late as 1772 Pennant
noticed the use of the quern in the Hebrides.[18]   The employ-

ment of stone in flour-mills extends to our own day. Advertisements boast of the superiority of stone for milling, and the words ' millstone grit ' tell of the former popularity of the well-known Carboniferous sandstone.

In Scotland, water-worn stones, having the appearance of celts, are used by the housewife for pounding salt, and by weavers as ' rubbing stones '. The polishing is unintentional, but many of the stones have been rudely chipped into their present shape. The warning, constantly repeated in Sir A. Mitchell's ' The Past in the Present ', that rudeness of itself is not a proof of great age,[19] is worthy of close attention. Especially is this necessary when examining crude stone objects which superficially have a Neolithic cast.

In the English Midlands the plates of iron on which crumpets are prepared are still called ' pikelet-stones ' (=crumpet stones).[20]　But in Scotland, not more than two centuries ago, oatmeal cakes were cooked on actual stones before a peat fire, just as to-day the natives of Guiana use stone slabs in baking cassava bread. The Scotch stones are often ornamented, and even dated. Sir A. Mitchell figures two interesting examples, bearing the dates 1674 and 1701 respectively.[21]　Could we but make the necessary search, we might still find these stones in use in some sequestered Highland glen. Yet what a distance has been traversed since the occupants of the Picts' Houses in Caithness and Orkney used flat stone discs, roughly chipped, for cooking purposes, or since the inhabitants of the Wigtownshire crannog baked their oatmeal cakes or bannocks on square slabs of stone.[22]

In the matter of grindstones, hones, and whetstones, we are still, according to Tylor's test, decidedly in the Stone Age. Only let it be noted that the Neolithic craftsman rubbed stone on stone ; there was no metal instrument to be sharpened. Perhaps, too, we should take note of the heavy stones which are employed as weights in the old-fashioned farm-house mangle.

Burnishing or smoothing stones present a closer kinship with the past. The currier still calls his smoothing tool a ' stone ', even when it is made of iron ; it is also affirmed that

he occasionally employs stone hafted in wood.[23]   Personal
inquiries do not enable the writer to vouch for the accuracy
of this assertion, but it is obviously made in good faith.
Canon Greenwell saw a Yorkshire shoemaker smoothing
down his leather seams with a celt, picked up, no doubt,
by chance.[24]   Weavers in the North of Ireland used to rub
the cloth, bit by bit, with a polished celt where this was
obtainable ; so the threads were closed, and a gloss was
imparted to the surface.[25]   Mr. E. T. Stevens says that in
producing the brilliantly coloured surface on ' flint-glazed '
papers, a polished flint was (1870) still employed.[26]

Pebbles of granite serve as ironing stones in the Orkneys
and the North of Scotland generally.[27]   Flat, pear-shaped
pieces of sandstone, rounded and polished, found at Culter
(Lanarkshire), and Alcester (Oxon.), are deemed by experts
to have been used for ' tawing ' or softening hides by
friction.[28]

These smoothing stones were formerly called sleekstones.
John Lyly, whose ' Euphues ' was first published in 1580,
writes, ' Shee that wanteth a sleeke-stone to smooth her
linnen, will take a pebble.'[29]   Milton, in his ' Smectymnuus ',
says that a certain proceeding is ' as improper as a toothed
sleekstone '.   Sleekstones are mentioned in the Customs
House Rates of Imports (2 James I, 1605).

Sir John Evans says that sleekstones were occasionally
inscribed with texts of Scripture.   One wonders whether
the ' rolling pins ' of pottery-ware, similarly decorated, and
commonly suspended as household ornaments until mid-
Victorian times, were whimsical ' sports ' from inscribed
sleekstones.   The conjecture is strengthened when we
notice that Cotgrave, in his French Dictionary (1611),
affirms that the sleekstones employed by curriers were made
of glass.   From glass to earthenware is an easy transition.
Evans considers that Sir Thomas Browne also implies that
sleekers were made of glass.   But if the reader will turn to
the passage in ' Vulgar Errors ', he will see that the old
philosopher, who is discussing the electrical attraction of
bodies, really says that ' some slick stones and thick glasses
[attract] indifferently '.[30]   It seems as if he simply uses the

adjective ' slick ' in its Old English sense of ' smooth '.
(Cf. Icelandic *slike-steinn*=whetstone.) [31]

Further light on the word is afforded by a fifteenth-
century vocabulary, the ' Promptorium Parvulorum ', where
we meet the spellings *sleykston* and *slekenstone*, with the
variations *slyke-*, *sleght-*, *sleeke-*, &c. The sense is the same
in all cases—a smooth stone. The object so named is
described as being of the form of a muller, and is said to have
been used for calendering linen and paper, for making
buckram and starching cloth—' *cum slycstone levifaca* '. [32]

It would appear that the sleeker has an unbroken pedigree.
Sleekers have been found associated with horse-trappings
of enamelled bronze, belonging to the late-Celtic period. [33]
And the archaeologist needs not to be told that ' polishers '
are common in collections representing the Neolithic period
proper.

Stones chipped into a roundish shape, and known to the
archaeologist conveniently, but somewhat conjecturally, as
' sling-stones ', long outlasted the Stone Age. In Iceland
they were still used in the tenth century. [34] Their modern
representatives, untooled, of course, are the pebbles of
schoolboy skirmishes.

An interesting analogue is the stone cannon-ball of real
warfare, very common in the Middle Ages. Stone shot was
used in English ' ordennce and artilery ' as late as A.D. 1515,
but in Rome such projectiles, thrown from coarse mortars,
are recorded in the year 1833. [35] Oftentimes one sees these
stone balls in the grounds of ancient castles, or built into the
adjacent walls, or anon they are dug up in the moat. [36] Von
Cotta has noted a curious survival in the fact that definitions
of weight connected with the calibre of guns have, in part,
been derived from the days of stone cannon-balls. [37]

Associated with Neolithic and Bronze Age relics there are
found small perforated discs of stone or bone, known as
spindle-whorls. These objects were employed in spinning
wool or flax. As a result of the momentum imparted to
the whorl by the hand, the rotatory motion of the spindle
was maintained. Similar little fly-wheels, made of bone,
lead, ivory, or earthenware, have been found among Roman

remains, and others, fashioned out of ivory, have turned up
during the excavation of Saxon sites.[38] Probably one
might still find, in the island of Lewis and Harris, tiny
specimens of lead, stone, or earthenware, for the inhabitants
were wont to use them in connexion with the distaff and
spindle, for twisting fishing-lines of hair. Yet it must be
noted that the modern Hebrideans appear to be unaware of
the original purpose of the true Neolithic spindle-whorl.
Genuine antiques of this class are in Gaelic called ' adder-
stones ' or ' snake-stones ', and are used in preparing a wash
for snake-bitten cattle.[39]   Thus they fall into line with the
stone which is holed naturally.   Mitchell, however, states
that in North Scotland socketed stones are still used as
spindles, as well as for the vertical axles of mill-stones, and
for the sockets of gate-posts.[40]

Certain flint implements, known to the collector simply
as ' scrapers ', have frequently shapes so specialized that it
has been supposed that the production of fire by percussion
was the prime purpose.   The matter hangs in doubt, but
arguments for a contrary conclusion, based on the misdirected
energy of chipping such flints, might be applied with equal
force to many other stone implements, and to modern
strike-a-lights.   The undoubted occurrence, in Yorkshire
barrows, of flint ' scrapers ', associated with nodules of iron
pyrites, may suggest a working theory that by the aid of
these flint objects prehistoric folk obtained fire, if not
always, at least when circumstances permitted.   For general
use, an unworked flint would no doubt suffice.

A moral is attached to this dispute : we have hitherto
erred in our hasty efforts at nomenclature.   To allot an
arbitrary purpose to every stone implement is folly.   In
the Museum at Frankfort, I once saw, attached to a collection
of Neoliths of abnormal facies, a label inscribed, ' *Instrumente
unbekannten Gebrauchs* ' (' Instruments of unknown use ').
English museums do not always display such a reticence.
He is wise who is not afraid to imitate the honest spirit of
the Frankfort confession.

In Chapter II we noticed the occurrence of stone arrow-
heads throughout the Bronze Age.   In Ireland, so plentiful

are these pretty little instruments, that Evans has mooted
the possibility of their having come down to much later
times.[41]   Against this theory, but only as a partially satisfactory rejoinder, it is argued that Irish arrow-heads have,
for the most part, lain hidden in bogs until recent days,
while in England, where they are commonly found on hard
or stony soil, they have been either largely destroyed or
picked up. This statement involves too wide a generalization. Moreover, as flint is far more widely distributed in
England, there should remain, in spite of the zeal of past
collectors, a correspondingly greater abundance of implements.

One outstanding fact bears on this particular question.
So well did the bow-and-arrow serve mankind that only
thoroughly proven superiority and the increasing cheapness
of iron permitted the substitution of newer weapons. The
ancient Egyptians, at the height of their civilization, retained
arrow-heads for hunting.[42]   In England, the bow did not
become extinct as a weapon until early Stuart times. We
take a leap into still more modern times, and find that at
Leipsic, in 1813, when Napoleon was so disastrously defeated,
the Cossacks were equipped with the bow-and-arrow.[43]   In
the following year, the world looked on in amazement,
while the Cossacks, still so armed, marched through the
streets of Paris.[44]

Our modern method of securing precision of gun-fire by
grooving the barrel of the weapon has been claimed as the
representative of the feathered arrow and of the slightly
twisted spear-head. In each case, rotation, with the
consequent steadiness of flight, was the purpose. Dr. Tylor
points out that our conical shot shows a partial return to the
ancient bolt or arrow, and finally, the breech-loading gun
is a repetition of the plan of placing the arrow in the butt-
end of a blow-tube.[45]

Certain Neolithic and Palæolithic weapons of the spear-
head type, as well as the ' winger ' arrow-head, are occasionally found to have a decided bias, or spiral quarter-turn,
and it has been urged that this feature was artificially produced, and was designed to ensure rotation. I have several

such specimens in my collection, but one hesitates to declare definitely for the theory. Right-handedness and left-handedness may have come into the question. But, on any view, the examples are too numerous to be accounted for by chance.

The hand-celts of stone, doubtless often used as missiles, have their correlative in modern rural England, where the fowler's throwing cudgel of wood is used, and is known as a *squoyle* (*squail, squailer, or swaile*). Other variants of the word occur, for the missile is found not only in Somersetshire, Bedfordshire, and Wilts., but also in New England, where it was taken by the early settlers. Writers such as Heath and Jefferies, who know the English peasant well, occasionally allude to the squail. Jefferies tells how the boys of his county made this effective weapon. Melted lead, and a tea-cup in which to mould it, were the chief accessories. The knobbed stick so made was terribly destructive to birds and squirrels. We may observe in passing that the counters used in a certain indoor game are also called ' squails ', the transfer of the term involving a slight difference of meaning.[46]

Tylor notes that the boy's pea-shooter, a hollow stick through which a pea is smartly blown, is the representative of the blowing tube of the South American Indian, who kills birds by discharging poisoned arrows in a similar manner.[47] We have no evidence, however, that prehistoric Britons used such a weapon.

The catapult, although a tiny replica of the ponderous military engine used by the Greeks and Romans, and by nations of the Middle Ages, seems yet an offshoot, genealogically, from the primitive bow-and-arrow. In both weapons, as in the bent bough which was their common ancestor, the property of elasticity is employed to produce the rebound.

The sharp-edged Neolithic flint knife is the very counterpart of the Sheffield steel blade. Any collection of even moderate size will exemplify this statement. Again, the ' combination tool ' of the Stone Age, comprising knife, awl, smoother, and scraper in one implement, reaches its highest development in the modern sailor's knife, which is a miniature tool-chest. The ordinary claw-hammer, the slater's pick, and the lady's manicure instruments, are additional examples. The principle is also illustrated in the combination tool, formerly used in Hampshire for dressing pigs. This implement comprised a scraper for the removal of hair, and a hook for tearing off the animal's ' claws '. Good specimens may be seen in the Horniman Museum at Forest Hill, London. The curious halberd-like knives attached to long poles, used by the country-folk of Central France in pruning the wayside trees, are veritable combination tools, comprising a hook, a piercer, and two or three blade edges in one piece of steel (Fig. 8).

In the ' Picts' Houses ' of Scotland, explorers have unearthed flat, broad knives made of a hard rock having a slaty cleavage. Only a century ago the natives of Shetland and of Lewis used knives of this kind for cutting kail.[48] Economical advantage may clearly outlive tradition.

Darwin and Haeckel have taught us that the life-history of the individual is not only a complete epitome of the development of the parent, but also an incomplete recapitulation of the life-history of the race. The record, as Dr. G. A. Reid observes, is ' written over and defaced ', but the method of growth may be made out. Hence no one is astonished to see a boy make use of a piece of hoop-iron, a shell, or a fragment of glass, as a cutting tool. Nor was I surprised when Mr. G. E. Dibley told me that he recently caught a schoolboy sharpening his slate pencil with a flint flake. So are the days of hand-made pottery revealed in the child's mud-pies, the early attempts at domesticating animals in his ' playing at horses ', the fierce clan fights in his games of attack and defence.

Undoubtedly, flint knives are good substitutes for those of metal. Leonora Christina, who in 1663 was imprisoned in Copenhagen, having been deprived of her scissors, used pieces of sharp flint instead. With these she could ' cut fine linen by the thread ', and she thus ' executed various things '.[49]

One curious case of the obstinacy of custom has been noticed among the Eskimos. Having become acquainted

with the steel knives bartered by the traders, they began to
make iron knives for themselves, retaining the pattern of
the old stone instrument. With this case of arrest may be
compared those given in Chapter II.

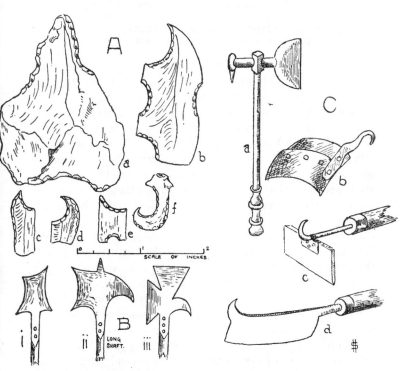

FIG. 8.   A. a. Palæolithic 'combination implement' (Thames gravels,
Hanwell).   b. Neolithic borer and hollow scraper (Surrey).   c, d. Neolithic
'multiple tools' (Surrey).   e. Neolithic 'multiple tool' (Suffolk).   f. Neolithic 'multiple tool' (Frankfort Museum).   [a, b, c, d, e, are from the
author's collection.]   B. i. ii. iii. Cutting tools, which, mounted on long
shafts, are used for pruning wayside trees in Central France. Scale about $\frac{1}{12}$.
c. Old English 'Combination tools.'   a. Eighteenth-century iron tool : axe
and hammer (Horniman Museum, Forest Hill).   b. Hampshire tool used in
dressing pigs. The scraper is used for removing the hair, and the hook for
turning over the pig and pulling off the hoofs. A more common form is also
shown, c (Horniman Museum).   d. Hedger's bill-hook: the recurved edge
is used for dragging down and cutting away overhanging briars and brambles
(Kent). Scale about $\frac{1}{8}$.

When we turn to household appliances and fittings we
discover more links with the past. In a turf hut in Caith-

ness, Sir A. Mitchell found a dinner-table formed by laying a stone slab on two rude blocks of stone.[50]   Again, in such outlying districts as Ross, Inverness, Orkney, and Shetland, chipped circular stones are used as lids for casks, pails, jars, and basins.   Truly, as a modern humorist puts it,

> Their furniture was made of stone,
> And every man rough-hew'd his own.

Sir A. Mitchell asks why stone should be used where wood is abundant.[51]   Folk-memory is latent and cannot respond, but the reply is that stone has there, perhaps, been continuously employed since the Stone Age.   Domestic vessels in Cornwall are often made of stone, but here, probably, convenience has been the chief factor.   In the Hebrides, where, along with vessels of stone, earthen cups and bowls made without a potter's wheel, and ornamented by a pointed stick, are still to be observed,[52] it is another matter.   Examples of such pottery have recently (1906) been placed in the British Museum.

Our word ' bottle ' preserves the memory of ancestral customs.   The word is derived from the late Latin *buticula*, the diminutive of *butis*, or *buttis*, which means not only a cask, but a wine-skin.[53]   As this word takes us back to primitive ways, so does the French *gourde* (=water-bottle) tell of the time when the water-bottle, if not so durable as ours, was more easily made.[54]

While still in the house, let us notice Tylor's theory that the candle may have come from the torch, which was originally a mere pine-splint dipped in pitch or wax.[55]   Hereafter, too, we shall notice a primitive chalk lamp which the Brandon flint workers formerly employed.

The hearth fire has handed down one relic of antiquity, the ' pot-boiler '.   The pot-boiler was a roughly rounded stone, usually flint, which was made red hot and then flung into the water contained in the primitive cauldron or in a puddled hollow in the soil.   By this means flesh was boiled, however inefficiently.   Or, again, the meat was grilled or baked over the heated stones.   The use of the pot-boiler for heating water was continued until late in the historic period.

Linnaeus, whilst making his Northern tour, saw the inhabitants of Bothland brewing beer in this way. At the present time, the Austrian peasant drinks such beer, which he calls ' stone beer '.[56] The English labourer, according to my experience, prefers to warm his supper ale with a red-hot poker. The rival methods have had a domestic struggle which has continued since the time when the seventh-century monks and nuns used iron balls to heat their water.[57] Iron seemed to conquer, but the stone ' pot-boiler ' was not quite beaten off the field.

Of the coracle, which the ancient tribesman carried on his back from stream to stream, pages might be written. The fishermen of the Severn and the Shannon still use this simple craft, though the cover is of tarred canvas, not of hide. But a friend tells me that the natives of Arran Island, Donegal, employ skin-covered boats to-day. As Lucan sings :

The bending willow into barks they twine,
Then line the work with skins of slaughtered kine.[58]

There is a good case for continuity. Pytheas, who is believed to have visited South-East Britain about 330 B.C., says that tin was carried to a tidal island Ictis (possibly the Isle of Wight or Thanet) in boats made of framework covered with hides.[59] In Saxon times, when the unhappy Britons were harassed by invaders, and were driven to hire pirate ' keels ' to protect the coast, coracles were in common use. Sidonius Apollinaris (A.D. 455), speaking of this chartered fleet, uses the expression ' *pelle assuta* ', as if the covering skins were sewn together.[60]

Dr. Tylor, whose works have already been freely quoted, notes that our words *ship*, *skiff*, are related to the Latin *scapha*, and the Greek σκάφη, the last of which corresponds so exactly in meaning to the term ' dug-out ', as to be an evident relic of the time when boats were really scooped out of hollow trunks.[61] Another link may be mentioned. Mr. J. Russell Larkby says that the fishermen of Chale (Isle of Wight) take from the beach blocks of the Lower Greensand to weight their nets, first carefully grooving the stones in the middle to prevent the rope from slipping off.

One observes, too, how closely the rude punts of our inland waters resemble the channelled trunk of oak or other forest tree used when 'first on streams the hollowed alder swam'[62] (Figs. 9, 10, 11).　The word 'punt' has an Anglo-Saxon equivalent with exactly the same spelling, and the earlier term doubtless represented some kind of flat-bottomed,

FIG. 9.　Prehistoric 'dug-out' boat (Sussex). Now placed under the portico of the British Museum, Bloomsbury. The length (35 feet) should really be shown about twice that of the punt figured below.

square-ended vessel.　Skeat further considers the Anglo-Saxon word to be an abbreviation of the Latin *ponto* (= a boat), a word used by Caesar.　*Pontones* seem to have been of huge size, and to have been adapted for transporting horses and chariots, but the shape was perhaps similar to that of the modern punt.[63]

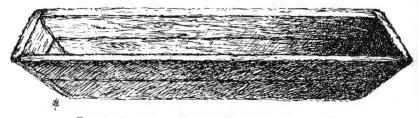

FIG. 10.　Rude punt still used on the river Arun, in Sussex.

Canoes dug out of the silt of the Clyde have been ranged in sequence according to workmanship, since they are found to exhibit examples from the days of Stone to those of Bronze and Iron.　From the fire-hollowed oak stem to the complicated structures of planks secured by oaken pins and nails of metal, there is a steady development.[64]　In Sussex there has actually been discovered a wooden anchor (Fig. 12).

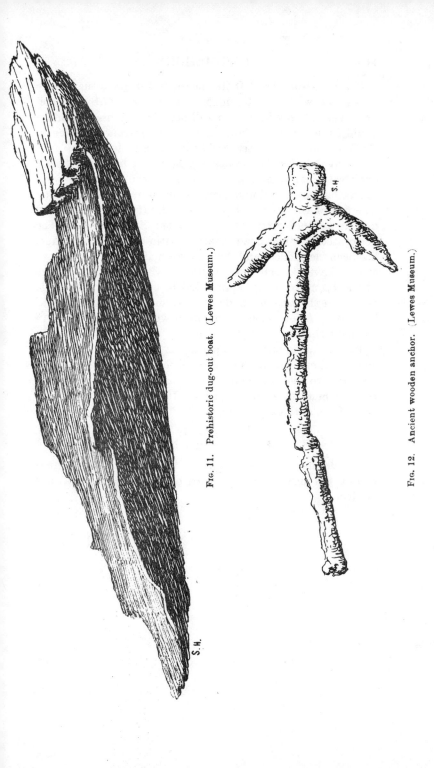

Fig. 11.   Prehistoric dug-out boat.   (Lewes Museum.)

Fig. 12.   Ancient wooden anchor.   (Lewes Museum.)

If the dug-out has left its successors, so have the bronze fish-hooks, which are familiar to the student of Swiss lake-dwellings. Essex fishermen still occasionally use fish-hooks made from the whitethorn, and specimens may be seen in the Museum of the Essex Field Club at Stratford.[65]

Survivals from the Bronze Age have not been specifically dealt with, partly because they fall into the general list, and partly because the domination of the alloy was incomplete. The age of Bronze was but of brief duration, if its rise and decline be compared with that of the Stone period. The perforated hammer head, characteristic of the Bronze Age, has been mentioned, and this shape remains to-day. Bronze shields have also left their impress. The overlapping flange of the bronze celt, as represented in one of its transitions, is seen in the present mode of attaching a rake or a hoe to its shaft. A few survivals in ritual will be touched upon in the next chapter.

To the antiquary, no apology is offered for this long enumeration. He loves to unravel the twisted skein of folk-memory, to discover one genuine case of survival, and to tell the news to kindred spirits. If, on the one hand, it is true of the antiquary,

> Till his ghastly tale is told
> His heart within him burns,

the reader has this advantage over the listener, who ' cannot choose but hear ',—he can turn over the pages to a new subject.

CHAPTER VI

STONE AND BRONZE IN CEREMONIES AND SUPERSTITIONS

WHENEVER the use of stone implements is kept up merely for ceremonial purposes, folk-memory has arrived at what may be called the exclusive and esoteric stage. A particular act must be performed in such and such a manner, and in no other. Our forefathers followed this custom, and bade us observe it ; this we know. We ask no reason, nor strive to remember why the charge was given. So speaks the voice of the people, and if we further seek the key to time-worn routine and custom, we find it in prescription, antiquity, and caste.

Now it is not to be supposed that the ceremonial use, of which we are about to speak, became in one moment sharply cut off from the industrial. There were lingering gradations. As economic considerations grew to be of little import, those pertaining to ritual became more weighty. Ultimately the ceremonial aspect alone had significance, for, in the words of Schiller,

Time doth consecrate,
And whatsoever is grey with age becomes religion.

And this religion, rude and material in its early days, was destined to become what Spencer described as ' the weft which everywhere crosses the warp of history '.[1]

The middle stage, when the borderland of social economy had not been definitely crossed, is occasionally traceable. Stone axes, much too small for use as implements, were recently employed in West Africa as currency, a plain relic of the times when real stone axes were bartered for the necessities of life.[2] As late as July, 1890, Professor A. C. Haddon found stone hatchets in vogue as a money standard for great transactions in Deboyne Island, near the extremity of British New Guinea. Yet the stone tool, as a tool, was obsolete, and, indeed, tomahawks of steel were accepted in payment for a canoe.[3]

The next example is a relic from the Bronze Age. It has been shown that the sapec, which is the only native Chinese coin, and which contains a square hole in the centre, is a survival from the period when bronze knives, some five or six inches long, were used as currency. In those days a ring was made at the end of the handle for stringing the knives. By and by the handle disappeared, and the ring was attached directly to the blade. At the same time, the thickness of the bronze was increased, so as to preserve the full weight of metal. The ring then became simply a round plate with a hole for stringing. Lastly, the blade was got rid of, and the conventional currency was thus evolved.[4]

It will be seen that a further step, such as the possible introduction of a new currency, might leave the miniature celts as ornaments or amulets with which were connected strong superstitions. In some such way the ceremonial respect may have been developed.

Another solution may be suggested to account for the sanctity of sacrificial instruments of stone. These would be at first almost purely of a utilitarian character. But during the transition to the Metallic period, the select priestly body, conservative by birth and calling, would hold to the ancient usage. Thus, when metals had distinctly gained the mastery, the priests, by direct transmission to the initiated, would keep alive the memory of a bygone Stone Age, even when, among the vulgar, all recollection of it had died away.

The theory of direct transmission is not based on surmise alone. Caesar has left on record the statement that probationers for the Druidical caste had to learn their secrets orally, although their teachers were not unacquainted with letters. The knowledge was too sacred to be made public by being committed to writing, and learning from characters was deemed likely to weaken the memory of the pupil. A period of twenty years was sometimes required to learn the complicated system of Druidical doctrine.[5] Little wonder that belief persisted when handed down by disciples so trained.

By whatever process the superstitious or ' standing-over '
stage be attained, all races which emerge from the Stone
Age seem to reach it in due order.   Herodotus says that
when the old Arabians made pledges of faith, the contracting
parties cut open with a stone knife the vein of their middle
fingers.[6]   Livy describes how, when the Romans consecrated
solemn treaties, a hog was killed at the temple of Jupiter
Feretrius. The ' pater patratus ', or chief of the four heralds,
brought out a sacred flint and with it struck the victim—
a plain proof of old custom.[7]   Curiously enough, however,
the brain was removed by means of a crooked iron, so that
the ceremony involved legacies from two early periods of
culture.[8]

Other peoples have like proofs of continuity of ideas.
Long after the ancient Mexicans had begun to employ
bronze for secular purposes, their priests kept up the practice
of tearing out the hearts of sacrificial victims with blades of
stone, usually obsidian.[9]   With sharp knives of stone, too,
the Guanches of Teneriffe cut open the bodies of their
deceased chiefs.[10]   In the most advanced times, stone played
an important part in the human sacrifices of Central America.
The victim was laid on a stone slab, his neck was placed in
a stone collar, his limbs were held down by chased fetters
of the same material, while the death-wound was given by
a stone knife.[11]

When the Egyptians embalmed their dead, the first incision
in the body was made with a stone knife.[12]   This proceeding
is usually admitted to be a clear instance of survival.   Yet
it should be noted that the industrial use of flint in Egypt
at a comparatively late period is said, on good authority,
to be due to expediency alone.   Stone sickles were imitated
from the metallic forms simply for rough work and for
common use.[13]   The ceremonial use, however, seems to stand
apart.

The Jewish rite of circumcision was, in Scriptural times,
performed with knives of flint.[14]   A most luminous fact is
connected with the modern practice.   For, though a steel
knife has now replaced that of flint, there is a remarkable
exception, authoritatively given to Dr. Tylor by one con-

versant with the facts. ' When a male child dies before the eighth day, it is nevertheless circumcised before burial, but this is done, not with the ordinary instrument, but with a fragment of flint or glass.' [15]

Here we may profitably halt a moment to observe that, just as the Druids and medicine-men of the Stone Age had a prejudice against the intruding bronze, so the peoples bred under the ascendancy of bronze were strongly biased against iron. Aeschylus speaks of iron as ' the stranger from across the sea '.[16] And before bronze had quite gone out of use, Achilles offered a mass of pig-iron for a prize.

Among the Greeks bronze had acquired a sanctity from its connexions with the literature and the worship of gods and heroes. In ancient Rome, again, the beard of the priest might be shaved with a bronze knife only. Before a new town was built by the Romans, its site was marked out with a plough having a bronze ploughshare.[17]

The Hebrew Scriptures abound with allusions to the prejudice against iron. Moses commands Israel to raise an altar of unhewn boulders—' whole stones, over which no man hath lift up any iron '.[18] Again, when Joshua builds an altar on Mount Ebal he refers to the injunction of Moses, which he carefully obeys.[19] So when the Temple was built, there was ' neither hammer, nor axe, nor any tool of iron, heard in the house while it was in building '.[20] In the Pentateuch, iron is mentioned thirteen times and brass (that is, $\chi\alpha\lambda\kappa\acute{o}s$, bronze) forty-four times. Rarely does the translation ' brass ' cover the meaning ' copper '. It is an instructive commentary that many of our own megalithic monuments, some of which were reared in the days of Bronze, are untouched by any tool.[21]

The earliest bridge across the Tiber was made entirely of wood. No iron was permitted to be employed, and whenever repairs were necessary, religious tradition, down to the very fall of the Empire, was sufficiently operative to secure the rejection of bolts made of this metal.[22] In recent times an enlightened Hindoo prince endeavoured to ward off small-pox and other epidemics by allowing no iron to be used in the buildings in his territory.[23] At home the

visitor to Exeter Cathedral will be shown, with some pride on
the part of the official, the bishop's throne, sixty feet high,
reputed to contain neither nail nor iron in any form.[24]

The prestige of stone was not confined to religious ceremonies alone. In surgery, stone instruments have been
specially valued. Those old formalists before mentioned,
the Mexican Indians, bleed themselves with lancets of
obsidian, as their forefathers did before the Spanish Conquest.[25] Émile Souvestre, in his delightful ' Chevrier de
Lorraine ', a story dealing with the days of Joan of Arc,
deftly utilizes the prevailing superstition. The wounded
soldier, Richard, comes to have his injured leg attended to by
Père Cyrille. Says the priest, ' *Je parie que vous vous êtes
adressé à des barbiers, ou à quelques drameurs* (= quacks) *à
couteau de pierre.*' [26] The suggestion is that the old surgeon-
barbers and quacks deemed that metal might poison a wound;
the priest claims to be superior to this superstitious fancy.

From the sovereign virtues of stone, real or supposed,
employed in the operations of the leech or farrier, there is
but a slight transition to its properties as a talisman, and
thence to its claims to secondary worship. This kind of
inferior worship, or *dulia*, is widespread, and is everywhere
given up tardily and with reluctance.

Present-day Arabs wear around their necks miniature
arrow-heads of cornelian, which they hold to be good for
the blood, and a protection against evils in general.[27] In
some Indian temples ancient stone implements are jealously
preserved, and Dr. Jannsen affirms that in Japanese chapels
like objects were treated with religious veneration.[28]

We come down the scale to superstition in the ordinary
sense of the word—that gross superstition which appropriates
to a family, or even to a particular person, the virtues of
the specific. In Brittany, home of Stone Age continuity,
the stone celt is dropped into wells to purify the water and
to ensure a full supply. There, the travelling umbrella-
mender will cheerfully accept celts—*pierres de tonnerre*,
as he calls them—as payment for repairs. In the English
Brittany which contains the duplicate St. Michael's Mount,
namely Cornwall, the celt was boiled in water and used

as a remedy for rheumatism.   The Savoyard rolls up the hatchet in wool or hair, and feels that good luck is assured.[29] Such old beliefs were held in Spain as far back as the times of the Romans,[30] so that there has doubtless been complete continuity from industrial use to foolish superstition.

Among the Scotch there was a grand list of ailments for which the arrow-head was efficacious.   The water in which it had been boiled was good for eye diseases and for the pangs of childbirth ; it was also popular with the cattle doctor.[31]   This belief continued till the present generation, and may still persist, for the Rev. J. G. Campbell, who was for thirty years minister of Tiree, and who died so recently as 1901, artlessly describes the mysterious object.   This was dug up as a ' smooth, slippery, black stone ', shaped like the sole of a shoe, and called a ' fairy spade '. Obviously this stone, with its magic properties, is our familiar celt.[32]

As Campbell's observations will again be drawn upon, let us note their inestimable value.   His information was derived wholly from oral sources.   Printed matter he ignored, and he chronicled nothing which had been previously recorded unless the fact had also been noticed by himself. He claimed, and so far as one may judge, justly claimed, to enter, as only a native can, into the spirit of Celtic thought, and to interpret its message as literally as might be possible.

A further example or two, out of scores, will show that the stone-axe superstition has sprung up on other soils. Natives of the Gold Coast take the disentombed celt, scrape off the dust, mix it with water, and drink the mixture as a medicine ; they also lay the hatchet in places sacred to the gods.[33]   In Borneo, the celt is enclosed in a cane-woven bag and suspended in dwellings as an amulet.[34]

Formerly celts were sent as presents from emperors to the great ones of the earth.   Or, again, the owner carved mottoes or texts upon the relic ; one such celt, probably of Alexandrian origin, was decorated with a gnostic inscription.[35] Perforated axes and hammers, incised with early runes, appear to have been treasured as family heirlooms in Sweden and Denmark.[36]

In the preceding chapter, mention was made of the

cylinders of pottery which were hung in houses in the days
of one's childhood.   On these ' rolling-pins ', which were
neatly kept in place by coloured ribbons, texts or didactic
verses were inscribed.   It was conjectured that these objects
were of the nature of ornamental ' sleekers ' ; they seem also
collaterally to represent the inscribed celt.   If that be so,
we have a kind of shadowy simulacrum of a superstition,
confusing the already complicated story.   A Neolithic
hatchet—the talisman of an Early Iron Age barbarian—
a treasured relic in the house of a cultured Mediaeval Father
of the Church—a charm in a peasant's hut.   Having run
through these stages, the implement, whose genesis and
very use had become completely forgotten, is conventionally
imitated in earthenware by a craftsman to whom the significance of the charm is, if that were possible, still less.

The celt, however, ran along its own lines of superstition.
A stone celt was sometimes made to serve as the tongue of
a sheep-bell, in order to ward off the evil eye from the flock.
Each successive leader of the flock, a ram, of course, had the
charm hung round his neck.[37]   But in these matter-of-fact
days, when sheep-bells are turned out of the factory by the
dozen, and when each bell is exactly like its neighbour, one
would scarcely expect to find the practice still extant.   For
my part, the closest observation and questioning, as cultivated by a ' snapper up of unconsidered trifles ', have produced no such discovery.   Nevertheless, as late as 1865 the
Irish continued to put celts in their cattle-troughs,[38] and but
a few years ago, the country-folk of the Hautes-Alpes used
to search the pastures with minute care to find these precious
talismans for the flock.[39]

A friend of the writer's once found a fine celt in an English
labourer's cottage, where it served as a weight for the clock.
Another celt was used as a whetstone by a sturdy mower.
Here, the superstition was lost, and practical motives alone
ruled.

Throughout the ages, stone arrow-heads have been known
to the vulgar, and to some not commonly deemed vulgar,
as fairy-arrows or elf-shot.   It was thought that these
objects had been shot by fairies at men and cattle.   Strange

circumstantial evidence was adduced respecting these elfish performances. A Scotch gentleman of great accomplishments, writing in 1664, tells how a lady, while riding, found one of these elf-bolts in the breast of her habit, and how a horseman had one placed in the top of his boot by the fairies.[40] Robert Kirk, in his ' Secret Commonwealth ' (1691), speaks of these ' Armes '—' solid earthly Bodies '— ' cut by Airt and Tools it seems beyond humane ', as ' having something of the Nature of Thunderbolt subtilty '. They are flung like a dart, with great force, and they mortally wound the vital parts without breaking the skin. Again, Dr. Hickes, in a letter to Pepys (1700), carefully describes the elf-arrows, and evidently believes that they were driven by invisible beings straight to the hearts of cattle.[41]

If for fairies and elves we read Neolithic men and women, we shall the better understand how these little people created, by the aid of real or supposed magic, such respect and fear in the minds of their taller conquerors as could never have been produced by physical force or arms of metal. The earlier race became veritable elves, and their arrow-tips belonged to the realms of magic and mystery.

The letter of Hickes brings us almost to the date when Plot and Sibbald recognized, as we have seen, the true nature of arrow-heads. The crowd, nevertheless, continued to believe in the supernatural origin of the tiny weapons. Mounted in frames, the little amulets were still worn around the necks of Scottish ladies. Here, again, the belief is found to be general. Bosnian peasants place much reliance in the efficacy of the charm. The Arabs suppose that their miniature arrow-heads of cornelian keep the blood healthy and fend off all evil.[42] The early Etruscans, Greeks, and Romans were permeated by a similar idea, for arrow-heads, forming the central pendants of necklaces, are found in the tombs of these peoples.

One special function of the arrow-head in Scottish witchcraft may be added. Images of clay or wax, representing the person whom the witch desired to injure, were pierced or cut with stone arrow-heads, which were preferred to instruments of metal.[43]

The best-known stone superstition, that the celt was a thunderbolt, has once or twice been touched upon. The notion appears to be common to all the continents. Our French neighbours, to go no farther afield, speak of *pierres de foudre* or *céraunies*.

Nowhere, however, is the belief more fixed than in our own country, where indeed it seems ' mortised in adamant '. That the various kinds of fossil belemnites, as well as the rounded concretions of iron pyrites from the Lower Chalk, are also called thunderbolts, matters little. Gods, fairies, witches, and other like beings, have divers weapons for afflicting the ignorant peasant, bowed low in his fear.

The thunderbolt myth meets us throughout our literature. One of the verses of the funeral dirge in ' Cymbeline ' thus begins,

> Fear no more the lightning flash,
> Nor the all-dreaded thunder-stone.[44]

And Brutus, speaking of hypothetical meanness towards Cassius, cries,

> Be ready, gods, with all your thunderbolts,
> Dash him to pieces.[45]

Among the Teutonic peoples, among the Germans and Scandinavians of to-day as well as our Saxon forefathers, the thunder-stone was the weapon of the ' sky-god '. The celt was Thor's hammer, hurled from storm-clouds by the angry god at his erring children. And as Thor, who was a kind of Northern Zeus, controlled the thunderstorm, the celt was indifferently a hammer or a thunderbolt.

The superstition is perpetuated in our place-names. Grant Allen has distinguished two systems of nomenclature according as the compound is formed from the A.S. *Thunor*, or the Norse and Danish *Thor*. The Thunor type probably represents the later influence due to the Danish invasion.

Of the first group we have not only our week-day Thursday (=Thunor's Day), but Thundersfield and Thursley (Surrey), and Thundersley (Essex). The Danish class is represented by Thurleigh (Bedford), Thurlow (Essex), Thursfield (Staffs.), Thursley (Cumberland), Thursford

(Norfolk), and Thoresby (Lincs. and Notts.).[46] Many of these names preserve sites sacred to the god of thunder.

Dr. Daniel Wilson states that until the close of the eighteenth century, stone celts dug up in Scotland were supposed to be the hammers with which the dead were to knock at the gates of Purgatory.[47] Here is a manifest Christian adaptation.

In old Teutonic laws the hammer figures constantly. It played a part at weddings and at settlements of property, it hallowed the funeral pyre, it was carved on gravestones.[48] Tell-tale facts these last, viewed in the light of barrow-burial : from them we learn how the later peoples accounted for the celts entombed in the early grave-mounds.

In fine, few beliefs have more stoutly resisted eradication than that which declared the lightning flash to be followed by the fall of a heavy body. Extremes meet, and in the recoil from the thunderbolt theory, there are found disputants who deny that the meteorites in our National Museum have ever fallen to the earth.[49]

Besides the celt, other stone implements, which are sufficiently characteristic to catch the eye of the uninitiated, have given rise to superstition. We have seen that the country leech brought spindle-whorls, under the name of snake-stones, into his daily practice. In some parts of England the same implement becomes a ' pixy's grindstone ' or a ' fairy millstone '.

We will now glance at a different kind of object, the calcined flint or ' pot-boiler '. What appears to be a real case of continuity is recorded by Sir John Rhŷs from the village of Four Crosses, near Pwllheli. In the year 1882, Sir John talked with the village saddler, an old man over eighty, who related stories handed down by his grandmother. This woman, who had frequently ' been with the fairies ' when a child, told how, on the eve of the Winter Calends, a bonfire was always kindled on a farm known as ' the Cromlech '—the name is very significant. Each person present used to throw into the fire a small stone, marked so as to be again recognizable. If the stone could be picked out by its owner on the morrow, a lucky year would follow, but a twelve-

month of mishap was in store if the search failed.[50]   When
we consider the season at which the fire was lighted, and the
place where the ceremony was observed—evidently the site
of an old megalith—we may conclude that this divination by
calcined stones is a case of subconscious folk-memory, rather
than an example of vulgar perversion.   The conclusion is
strengthened by the information that the custom was kept
up in other places.

Virtues imputed to ancient stone implements are likewise
attributed to stones having natural perforations.   Here,
again, we seem to have a direct bequest from primitive
times, for dolmens, funeral urns, and Roman tombs are
frequently found with little openings, which are usually
thought to have been designed for the egress and ingress of
the ghost.[51]

A similar idea prevails in the rural districts of civilized
countries, for the window of the death-chamber is opened
in order to release the spirit of the dying man.

An opposing series of facts must be considered.   A huge
pile of stones raised over the grave, a ponderous dolmen,
with its load of earth, the stake ofttimes thrust through the
corpse,[52] food and weapons placed with the dead—what
mean such facts, if a hole must be made to allow the spirit
to return ?

Frankly, the answer seems to be that the conflicting
practices point to wavering beliefs.   Not only among
barbaric peoples do we look for such contradictions ;   the
student has like inconsistencies thrust upon him when
dealing with enlightened races.   We laugh at such a
superstition as ' thirteen to dinner ', but seek a subter-
fuge to avoid being one of the thirteen.

These pierced megaliths deserve another paragraph or
two, before we pass to perforated stones in general.

Near the cromlech at Stennis, in the Orkneys, there
formerly stood a perforated pillar, through the aperture of
which lovers clasped hands and took a binding oath.[53]
A later stage of folk-belief shows that the stone need not
always be a prehistoric megalith.   Hughes, in his ' Scouring
of the White Horse ', gives a print of a stone, pierced with

several holes, which was padlocked to an oak-tree in front of the little inn at Uffington (Berkshire). These holes were kept plugged up, but sweethearts, visiting the stone, would remove the wooden pegs and blow into the holes for good fortune.[54] Other such stones are recorded elsewhere under the name of swearing-stones. Considerable interest attaches to the subject, for some writers contend that the wedding ring, which was once only a perforated piece of metal, was the materialization of an idea carried over from the earliest times.

Children were formerly passed through holed stones to be cured of various complaints. Near Lanyon, in Cornwall, scrofulous children were thrust naked three times through a holed stone, and were then drawn on the grass three times against the sun.[55] The last condition is important ; the sun superstition will be found to recur in other connexions.

In Arran Island, Galway, there was a holed stone, cross-inscribed, through which were drawn the linen clothes of sick women. Sometimes a stone was selected with a hole large enough to permit the invalid to crawl through.[56] Ireland, as Mr. Wood-Martin has shown, is indeed especially rich in traditions and practices connected with holed megaliths.[57]

A relic of the old belief underlies the custom of pushing ruptured children through a cleft ash-tree, the parts of which were kept asunder by wedges. The operation was attended with much ceremony, as was also that of immuring a shrew-mouse in a pollard ash, which had been bored with an auger for the purpose. References to these and kindred practices abound,[58] but whether the idea of tree-spirits does not enter into the custom is a disturbing factor—the hole may have been an incidental condition. We may therefore consider stones only.

Now, since a megalith cannot be carried in one's pocket, any naturally-perforated stone acquires an imputed virtue. Hollow flints are not uncommon, for the sponges or other organisms may fall out of, or be dissolved from, the surrounding silica. These hollow flints, then, were generally prized.

In East Anglia and Yorkshire a flint possessing a hole is suspended in the horse-stable or cow-byre, to prevent witches and hags from riding the horses or injuring the cows. After such hag-riding, horses would be found in the morning covered with sweat and foam.[59] The ' hag-stone ' prevented this calamity.   No ' Pharisees ' (= fairies), as a native of Hadleigh (Suffolk) remarked, could pass beyond such a flint.   In co. Antrim the hollow stones are hung around the necks of cows.   Professor A. C. Haddon saw, in Berlin, specimens of stones which, having been blessed in the churches, are still hung under the eaves of stables in Tyrol and Bavaria.[60]   Italy and other countries afford like records.[61]

Nowadays, this stage of the history of the ' lucky stone ' is represented by the degenerate cotton-reel attached to the bunch of church or farm keys.   Or a rude wooden peg, bored by the knife of sexton or garthman, is strung on the cord or chain.   Among educated folk, the bit of wood has further dwindled to a utilitarian plate of bone, and even this, in turn, is giving way to the more practical ' security label ' of metal.

Yet one doubts whether the vicarious virtues of the holed stone are quite discarded.   The fishermen of Rügen and Heligoland use such stones for lowering their nets.[62]   Mitchell states that they are still so employed in Scotland.[63]   Weymouth boatmen place them inside their boats to assist in anchorage.[64]   Perhaps the practical here dominates the superstitious—a somewhat anomalous sequence.

Sometimes holed stones were worn on the person ; again, they formed part of the stock-in-trade of the wizard and magician.   Sidrophel, in ' Hudibras ', knew how to

> Charm evil spirits away, by dint
> Of sickle, horseshoe, hollow flint.[65]

But as Aubrey, in his ' Miscellanies ', remarks naïvely—or is it ironically ?—' and a flint will do that hath not a hole in it '.[66]   From our modern, prosaic point of view, this seems to embody the truth of the matter.

If we wish to see a remnant of the old superstition to-day, we must turn to the schoolboy, and watch him proudly

take his 'lucky stone' from his pocket. Or we must go
to the gipsies, those nondescript 'vagrom men', full of
all cunning and folk-wisdom.   Mr. W. H. Hudson, in his
'Nature in Downland' (1900), tells how, while he was
looking for flint flakes on the South Downs, a tramp came
up and offered to find him some flints with holes in them,
and would with difficulty take a rebuff.

Perhaps quite as crude as the faith in the remedial powers
of holed flints is the belief in showers of stones.   Pliny
credited such stories.[67]   Their credibility, however, is about
as reasonable as that of tales of showers of blood and frogs,
although an explanation of the origin of the belief is not
so easy to find as in those cases.

A shower of stones was said to have fallen in 1803, at
L'Aigle, in Normandy.   In 1809, Cuvier reported that such
precipitations of stones from the atmosphere, both in
antiquity and during the Middle Ages, had been established
as truths in physical science.[68]   Not unnaturally, the
populace hold to the error a little longer than the sage.

Last comes the obstinate and unreasoning superstition
that stones grow.   Here, again, Pliny mentions the belief,
and also declares that certain stones bring forth other stones.[69]
By some strange chance, or by that insight which sometimes
follows in the train of actual observation, he recognized
the dissolvent action of natural agencies on rocks : 'Stones
we know disappear, and new kinds are discovered.'[70]   From
this sound premiss, Pliny perhaps deduced, or at any rate
was led to endorse, the theory of growing stones.

In Kent, Essex, and Herts., the lumps of Tertiary con-
glomerate, relics of pebbly beds, known to geologists as
'pudding-stones', are locally called 'breeding-stones'.[71]
In one form or another the idea is very general.   The natives
of certain parts of India think that 'Iceland moss', growing
on the face of a precipice, is the 'seed of the mountain'.[72]
One wonders whether the expression 'living rock' has been
caught up from the ranks below by writers and rhetoricians.

Did we say, a moment ago, that the unreasoning stage
has been reached ?   That is not quite a fair presentment.
The peasant is ofttimes 'baffle-headed', yet he has his own

rough scheme of philosophy. When the clergyman in the story attempted to prove to his bucolic parishioner that stones cannot grow, he thought that the matter was thus clinched : ' But if you put a stone on that mantelpiece, and look at it in five years, you will find that it has not grown.' Slowly came the dogged response, ' Noa, and I hreckon if you put a 'tater there, it would not grow, either.'

CHAPTER VII

THE LATER HISTORY OF THE MEGALITHS

WE have seen that the ascription to stones of healing powers is closely connected with the ancient sanctity of megalithic monuments and stone weapons. We now turn back to the megaliths themselves, and, following the direct line of descent, find that there has been a continuous tradition of veneration and mystery, debased nevertheless in later days by grossly perverted observances.

Viewed from the structural aspect, there is in the megaliths an orderly development, which would satisfy all but the very exacting archaeologist, perhaps even him also. The antiquary may find great delight in tracing the rise and decline of the stone monuments, nor will he, good easy man, afterwards resent old John Earle's dry description of those who revel amid ancient stones. ' A great admirer hee is of the rust of old Monuments, and reades onely those Characters, where time hath eaten out the letters. Hee will go you forty miles to see a Saint's Well, or ruin'd Abbey ; and if there be but a Crosse or stone footstoole in the way, hee'l be considering it so long till he forget his journey.' [1]

The menhir, or standing stone, which, it must be remembered, marked not only graves, but also boundaries and trysting-places, is seen developing itself from the rude stone pillar to the idol and the Christian cross on the one hand, and to the Roman milestone and the Mediaeval landmark on the other (Fig. 13). Mr. Baring-Gould has traced an interesting evolution of the churchyard headstone from the menhir, and has illustrated the process by examples from the Dartmoor plateau.[2] Moreover, he states that many of the churchyards of Dartmoor contain monuments which come down ' from the cromlech and kist-vaen as certainly as does the modern tombstone from the menhir '.[3] The present writer has particularly noted table tombstones

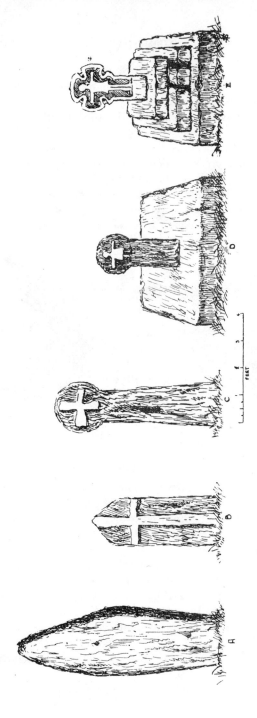

Fig. 18. The change from the Menhir to the Cross. A. Menhir at Boscawen-un, near St. Buryan, Cornwall. B. Early Christian cross, Tregwinow Down, near St. Buryan. (A and B are in the same locality as the Dawns Mên cromlech.) C. Round-headed cross, Trevalga churchyard, Cornwall. D. Figured cross near St. Buryan churchyard. E. More highly developed cross from St. Buryan churchyard (the bases are on a smaller scale than the cross).

in the churchyards of Throwleigh, South Tawton, and the neighbourhood, which are good modern representatives of the dolmen and kist-vaen (Fig. 14).

Stone coffins have been dug up in the churchyard of Worth Matravers (Dorset), almost identical with those from barrows in the surrounding Isle of Purbeck.

The churchyard cross, which was once more common than at present, replaced the menhir, and in many instances sprang from it. Not fewer than 5,000 Christian crosses existed in England alone before the Reformation.[4]

In Brittany, as I can vouch from personal investigation,

Fig. 14. Tombstone, Throwleigh, Devon. Monuments of this type, but usually bearing inscriptions, are common in various counties.

the adapted menhir is common. The great menhir at Dol is a good example, but that of Tregastel probably most impresses the traveller. Sculptured over this latter stone are the Cross and the instruments of the Passion. An obelisk at Pouancé has a hole cut in its face, wherein is placed an image of the Virgin. Oblations are still offered, not indeed to the rude stone, but to the image.[5] At Plumen, a gigantic monolith, topped by an insignificant cross, is resorted to for worship by peasants and children.[6]

But we can cite examples at home. A wayside cross, situated near the stone circle called the Dawns Mên, Cornwall, in the close vicinity of other British remains, evidently belongs to the transitional period. The round head of the cross is adorned with rude incisions, which seem to mark the change-over.[7] St. Samson, we are told, found the Cornish natives dancing round a tall stone : he merely inscribed a cross on it and let it stand.[8] The earliest Cornish crosses, recognizable as such, go back as far as the seventh century. Prehistoric monuments at Narvia, in the Isle of Man, have been similarly christianized by the carving of crosses on them.[9]

The normal stages may be thus outlined. The rude unhewn pillar gives way to a monolith coarsely shaped by artificial means. This monolith, becoming broad in proportion to its thickness, is treated decoratively. At the advent of Christianity the sacred symbol is carved on its face, and it becomes a ' cross-slab '. Gradually the relief of the cross grows more pronounced.

From this point the course of development, in one direction at least, may be summarized from Mr. J. Romilly Allen's ' Celtic Art '. One after another, portions of the background whereon is cut the symbol are removed from the ' cross-slab '. Then the top of the slab becomes rounded to suit the curve of the circle which encloses the head of the cross. Soon from the original ' cross-slab ' springs the cross proper, of the disc or wheel variety, wherein the width of the shaft is less than the diameter of the head. This result is obtained by dispensing with a part of the background on each side of the column. The arms of the cross project beyond the ring, and henceforth the development is rapid. The ' blind ' spaces between the arms and the quadrants of the circle are pierced right through, and we get the four-holed crosses of Cornwall. Finally, there comes the ' free-standing ' cross, which generally has two or more separate pieces connected by mortise-and-tenon joints.[10]

Tracing the descent along another branch, a series may be formed from the rude figures, carved in relief on the cross, to the well-wrought statue of the modern sculptor. Another line carries us to the Trajan column and the Nelson monument.[11]

In one particular custom we seem to be still closer to

primitive usage.   Mr. Grant Allen has shown that, while
deceased chiefs were frequently honoured by megaliths,
less important folk were commemorated by simple stakes.[12]
One recalls Milton's phrase, contemptuous but truthfully
descriptive, about the ' stocks and stones ' of our rude
forefathers.   These stocks are well represented to-day
by wooden wayside crosses and by the humble wooden
monuments in our crowded cemeteries.   In Bohemia and
Bavaria the ' death-boards ' grotesquely resemble the human
form.

As with the menhir, so with the dolmen.   The prehistoric
dolmen has its successor in the Christian altar, in the
mediaeval altar tomb, in the huge stone sarcophagi of
' enchanted halls ' like St. Paul's Cathedral and Westminster
Abbey.   Elsewhere the cairn gave rise to the Buddhist tope
and to that tumulus in masonry—the Egyptian pyramid.
The cromlech is replaced by the temple and the round
church.[13]   If it be urged that in England we have but four
circular churches, with probable indications of one or two
others, we need only point out that just as we have more
than one type of church, so our ancestors had more than
one kind of megalith.

Mr. Clodd has a sentence as instructive as it is concise :
' Between Stonehenge and the fair cathedral whose spire
we see as we return to Salisbury, the chain of continuity is
complete.'[14]

If we inquire what were the ceremonies connected with
the megaliths before the dawn of history, we find that the
conclusions of the authorities are diverse and unsatisfactory.
The minute astronomical investigations now being carried
on by Sir Norman Lockyer may eventually lead to a working theory.   Whether this proves to be the case or not, it is
clear that only by study of the monuments themselves—their
shape and position, their natural roughness or their artificial
tooling, their orientation, the relics which they yield to the
excavator—can we get a little guidance.   Much may also
be learned from the revelations of comparative custom.
Thus from the obscurity emerges the truth that, whatever
the original purpose of a particular megalith—be it funereal,

tribal, or commemorative—worship and ceremonial of some sort were afterwards associated with it.

We are here not concerned with the sources of religion, except to crave a suspension of judgement.   Mr. E. Crawley gives important reasons against ancestor-worship as an origin.   Not the departed man, not death, says he, was worshipped, but rather did our ancestors stand in awe of those phenomena connected with birth and reproduction and fertility.   Neither does fetishism, nor totemism, nor taboo represent the ultimate origin, though each in its place may have been a concomitant and perhaps a secondary development.

What precise form of worship obtained in prehistoric Britain is a secret of the past.   The speculations of eighteenth, and even nineteenth-century antiquaries must be swept away like cobwebs.   Some of these whimsical notions are illustrated in the old print which forms the frontispiece. We know not with what authority the prehistoric Druids, those early magicians and medicine-men whose fame is in every one's mouth, but about whom we really know very little, are so plausibly associated with the old megaliths. What the older writers imagined is interesting, but of slight value.   Of the Druidism of historical times more may be learned.

It appears that we are able to fix the date of the introduction of the Druidical myth.   The error must be charged against that industrious antiquary, John Aubrey, whose claims on our gratitude are otherwise clear and numerous. Yet he did posterity the disservice of taking too seriously the letter of a Scotch gentleman, Professor Garden, of Aberdeen, who in 1662 described stone circles as places of pagan worship.   Garden suggests that the circles may have been Druidical, but admits that there is no tradition among the people to corroborate that opinion.[15]   Thus the notion was started, and soon became current.   In the second 'General Index' of *Archaeologia*, there is attached to the item, 'Stones, Circles of,' a foot-note directing the reader to ' see under " Druids " ', a scrap of information which was not given in the first ' General Index '.

It may be assumed provisionally that many of the megaliths were connected with sacrifice, and that the victims
offered were sometimes human beings. This is indicated by
survivals and by comparative customs, to say nothing of
the assertions of early writers. The orientation of the
monuments points to the importance attached to the
position of the sun during the performance of the rites;
it may possibly imply some form of sun-worship as a separate system. It is well to remember that some megaliths
would mark burial-places in the first instance; others,
like Stonehenge, appear to have been reared near early
cemeteries, but were perhaps not themselves tombs.

That the early Christians encountered some cult, associated by the Britons with these monuments, is certain.
Generally, though the policy was not undeviatingly consistent, the new apostles wisely treated the older observances
with gentleness, diverting, wherever possible, the underlying
motive towards a worthier end. But the ancient errors
creep forth.

At first, under Constantine and Valentinian (c. A.D. 312–70),
the practice was to demolish pagan temples. In the time of
Theodosius (c. A.D. 370 onwards), however, the heathen shrines
were dedicated as Christian churches, and Honorius actually
forbade (A.D. 408) any further destruction. Gregory the
Great, in the early seventh century, gave detailed instructions for the adaptation of the temples to Christian worship,
and recommended the retention of the old observances
wherever these could be sufficiently purified to harmonize
with the new doctrines.[16] There is every reason to believe
that the ancient 'temples' were megaliths. It is also
practically established that the Christian cross was set up
as a meeting-place for hearing the Gospel, and that the
cross preceded the church. Bearing this in mind, facts
begin to explain themselves.

We have seen that the Christian policy was not uniform.
Pagans outnumbered proselytes, and 'mountainous error'
soon became too 'highly heaped for truth to overpeer'.
Hence at the Council of Tours (A.D. 657), priests were admon-
ished to shut the doors of their churches against all wor-

shippers of upright stones.[17]   Again, the Council of Nantes
(A.D. 658) exhorted ' bishops and their servants ' to dig up
and hide those stones which were worshipped in remote
places, and to which vows were still made.   Some centuries later, a statute of Canute forbade the ' barbarous
worship of Stones, Trees, Fountains, and of the heavenly
bodies '.[18]

Whence came these practices, persisting so obstinately
in the days when the rule of Iron was well established ?
Attenuated as the observances were, the Iron Age men did
not invent them ; they merely respected some canon faintly
held by folk-memory.

Analogy is clear on this point.   Councils of the Gaulish
Church issued edicts against the anointing of menhirs with
oil, with what success one may understand when he is told
that even to-day the Breton peasants in remote localities
smear these stones with wax, oil, and honey.[19]

Consider, too, the case of the Samoyads of the North.
So long as all goes well, the Samoyad follows Christianity,
but should his reindeer die, he returns immediately to his
old god Num or Chaddi.   Heathen services are conducted
by night within old stone-circles, and all images of Chaddi
are carefully screened from view.[20]   Mr. F. G. Jackson thinks
that within these cromlechs were formerly offered up those
human sacrifices with which the native used to propitiate
Chaddi.   Only a few years ago, a Samoyad of Novaia
Zemlia thus sacrificed a young girl.[21]

St. Boniface (b. A.D. 680 ; d. A.D. 755) found the natives
of Friesland using the capstones of dolmens as altars for the
slaughter of human beings.   A stranger was made to pass
through the openings between the upright stones, and then,
as it was euphemistically expressed, he was ' sent to Odin '.
The influence of the Saint secured the cessation of the actual
sacrifices, but down to the Middle Ages strangers were
compelled to creep through the dolmen.[22]

Irish superstitions concerning stone rings are numerous,
and may be found in the works given in the list of references.[23]   In the Isle of Man it was believed that to pasture
sheep on ground which was marked by a stone circle would

surely bring disease to the flock.[24]   We call these ideas survivals, and thus hide their true character ; in their totality
they indicate not spasmodic survivals, but continuity of
development.

In Cornwall the actual worship of stone monuments was
carried on down to the seventh century, the ceremonies
being conducted by torchlight.[25]

The stones venerated in later historical times were not
necessarily megaliths, for the original idea was widened.
At Kenmare, co. Kerry, there existed, in 1847, a water-worn
piece of clay slate, which bore a rough resemblance to the
human form, and which, under the name of ' Eevan ', was
adored as the image of a saint who lived ' in the ould auncient
times '.[26]   At the base of the tower of St. Audoen's Church,
Dublin, might have been seen, until about 1828, a rude stone
let into the wall which abutted on the street.   A cross in
low relief had been cut in the upper part, but the greater
portion of the surface was quite polished by the kisses of
hawkers and vendors, who visited it to ensure success.[27]
With this practice may be compared the silly custom once
in vogue at Billingsgate Market, London.   A new-comer
was compelled to kiss a certain stake, and pay sixpence for
the privilege of having one of the porters elected as his
' godfather '.   Taken apart from similar instances, this
folly would appear to be mere horseplay ; judged by analogy,
it has more significance.

A stone of dumb-bell shape, situated at St. Conall's Well,
Donegal, was reputed to have healing virtues, and at Killery,
Sligo, certain oval stones were believed to cure aches and
sprains.   Over an altar of ' speckled stones ' in the latter
county, oaths were sworn, and enemies anathematized.[28]
In a garden at Altagore, co. Antrim, a stone known as
' The Old Woman ' was fed with oatmeal cakes and butter,
which were said to be duly fetched by the *grogan* or fairy.[29]
Nor could this stone be successfully placed elsewhere.
When it was afterwards built into a gate-pier, it was under
a spell, and, like the fabled churches rebuilt on new sites,
was always carried back to its original position.

Fishermen in the south of the island of Inniskea, off the

coast of Mayo, whose inhabitants half a century ago spoke
the Irish language and acknowledged the rule of a chieftain,
invoked calm weather of a stone idol.   A sacred stone was
also used to procure shipwrecks.[30]

Stones wrapped in flannel, and kept under the custody
of a family or clan, have been treasured as charms for
securing favourable breezes.   One such ' bowing stone ',
a menhir eight feet high, near St. Columba's Church, on
the small island of Eriskea, north of Barra, used to be
swathed in flannel.   The natives, making obeisance to the
menhir, would recite the Lord's Prayer—a strange jumble
of ceremonies,[31] for such clan-stones most likely came from
the Aryan Celts, if not from their non-Aryan predecessors.[32]

A menhir of granite situated at Holne, a village on one
of the spurs of Dartmoor, was formerly the pivot of a May
festival known as the Ram Feast.   Before daybreak the
young men of the village would assemble at the pillar, and
having run down a young ram from the moor, fastened
it to the stone, slew it, and roasted it whole and undressed.
At midday, struggles took place for slices of the animal,
and these were esteemed as mascots for the ensuing year.
Dancing, wrestling, and drinking prolonged the festival,
which did not cease till midnight.   These ceremonies were
probably the degenerate relics of a real act of sacrifice.[33]

We have now made good the case for continuity, ceremonially considered, among Northern nations.   To show
that such continuity is no isolated phenomenon, other races
might be studied.   Let us content ourselves with a few
observations respecting the ancient Jews, as familiarized to
us by the Bible.

The Biblical examples portray a race well advanced into
the Age of Iron, but still tinged, even permeated, with the
traditions of the Stone Age.   In the preceding chapter
we saw how common was the early prejudice against tools
of metal when sacred buildings were erected.   The rude,
unhewn megaliths also continued to be popular.

Jacob set up a stone pillar at Bethel, and anointed it
with oil, making solemn promises the while.[34]   Generations
afterwards, Samuel met the Hebrew people there at a kind

of folk-moot.[35] When Jacob made the covenant with Laban,
a pillar and a cairn were raised.[36] Lot's wife was turned
into a pillar of rock-salt or gypsum.[37] Joshua set up twelve
stones, one for each tribe, at Gilgal,[38] and this spot was
one of Samuel's trysting-places when he wished to ' renew
the kingdom '.[39] To mark a victory over the Philistines,
an assembly gathered under Samuel's leadership at Mizpeh
reared the celebrated Eben-ezer, or Stone of Help.[40] Other
instances will occur to the reader.[41]

Along with these ritual customs we meet, just as in our
own history, denunciations of stone-worship. The people
were evolving towards a more subjective religion. In the
Mosaic law stone-worship is expressly forbidden.[42] Yet we
get a glimpse of the cult in the account of Saul's meeting
with the three men who were going to Rachel's pillar at
Bethel. Sacrifice was evidently the intention of these
wayfarers, for they carried kids as well as loaves and wine.[43]
The prophets thundered against the stone-worshippers.
And as the first Christians strove to attach the old objects
to a new faith, so, if Dr. Cheyne be right, the mono-
theistic Jews tried to convert the megaliths into memorials
of patriarchal history.[44] Yet the old fetish stones lingered
unexpelled in secluded places. Isaiah has a fine outburst
of mocking irony against the older worship :—

> Among the smooth stones of the stream (R.V., *valley*)
>   is thy portion :
> They, they are thy lot :
> Even to them hast thou poured a drink offering :
> Thou hast offered a meat offering.[45]

This dogged adherence to stone worship among the old
Jewish community must have left later traces ; we cannot
believe that the Fathers overlooked the tradition. They
probably knew, from personal observation, the vagaries of
folk-memory with respect to stone superstitions. Hence
the earliest advocates of Christianity in Northern Europe
must have been prepared in some degree for the customs
which they there witnessed.

While discussing the religious phase we must not forget
the political, for the megaliths afterwards gained this dual

interest, though the division was unknown in primitive times. The political customs were doubtless offshoots from the religious rites, shorn of a portion of their significance.

Among Northern peoples, princes and leaders were once commonly elected by assemblies gathered in and around stone circles. Eric, King of Sweden, was so chosen at Upsala in 1396.[46] In Norway, each of the electors sat on a stone during the formal proceedings.[47] Norwegian tradition also associates the stone rings with judicial courts. Michelet states that the French cromlechs served as open-air tribunals.[48]

Mr. G. L. Gomme, who has made a special study of primitive village communities, tells us that when the village was first established a stone was set up. To this stone the head man of the village made an offering once a year.[49]

Mr. Gomme's researches show that early folk-moots were held both at menhirs and at Christian crosses, as well as at tumuli. Hence it is more natural to assume continuity of custom, involving transmission by folk-memory, than to imagine an arbitrary border between the Christian and pagan systems.

A few instances will make this clear. The hundred court of Stone (Somerset) was held in the early morning at a standing stone on a hill. The stone was hollow, and the practice was to pour into the cavity a bottle of port wine.[50] We may be sure that the liquid originally employed in prehistoric days was of a more sinister nature. The court which met at the Hill of Conan (Forfar) was held at a large sepulchral cairn.[51] At Knightlow, near Coventry, there stands, on a tumulus, an old wayside cross of about the time of Edward the Third. From time immemorial it has been the custom for the steward of the Duke of Buccleuch to collect here the wroth or ward money for the parishes of the hundred. The time of the year, Martinmas (Nov. 11), and the hour, that of sunrise, are noteworthy, as they seem to point to solar rites. The custom was still kept up in 1879.[52]

A tradition which came under my own notice will show the difficulty of tracing origins in these days of vanishing folk-lore. An old lady, born in 1819, told me that in her childhood the village fair of North Thoresby (Lincs.) was held near the church, in a field which had a large blue stone in the middle. Around this stone games were played. Villagers born a little later, say 1830–40, could tell nothing of the custom. At last, in an old work by an unknown author, I read that the jury of the manorial courts formerly met at this stone, within ' an old enclosure ', called Bound-croft. Another ' blue stone,' a glacial boulder, once formed the boundary between Grimsby and Cleethorpes, and a third specimen divided Newcastle from Gateshead.

The hundred court of Brothercross, near Coventry, used to meet at a cross placed near a ford over the river.[53] At Shepway, courts were held at an old roadside cross, and it was ' att ye crosse ' where the manor court of Aston Boges assembled.[54] At Folkestone the mayor was formerly elected at the churchyard cross,[55] and at similar crosses tolls were often collected.

Mottistone, Isle of Wight, is generally supposed to derive its name from its menhir (*mote-stone*).

Further illustrations will be given when we discuss barrows in the next chapter, but at present some interesting London examples may be given.   Opposite the Bishop of Worcester's mansion in the Strand there was once a cross, at which, in the reign of Edward the First, the justices itinerant used to meet.   The citizens of London formerly held folk-moots at St. Paul's.[56] At the north-east angle of Hyde Park stood a ' geometric stone ', placed there by the Romans, and from this obelisk the hundred of Ossulstone (Middlesex) took its name (cf. Ossulston Street, St. Pancras).[57]

Shakespearean scholars will recollect that when Cade, in 1450, forces his way into London, he is represented as striking his sword on London Stone, exclaiming as he does so :—

Now is Mortimer [i.e. Cade] lord of this city.[58]

Mr. Gomme, upon whose excellent volumes we are now freely levying toll, supposes that this ceremony was not meaningless.   Once it entered largely into the municipal procedure of the City.   Proclamations were read at this stone, and from this spot defendants who were cited to the Lord Mayor's court had to be summoned.[59]   The stone, whose probable origin we cannot now discuss,[60] is still to be seen, built into the street wall, opposite the entrance to Cannon Street Station.

A link between Cade's action and early custom is seen at Bovey Tracey (Devon), where the authority of the new mayor is proclaimed by his riding round the local stone cross and striking it with a stick.   As Mr. Gomme puts it, ' at Bovey the custom has almost the force of a municipal law, while in London it was rescued from obscurity by the record of the acts of a rebel.'   Either the cross at Bovey, or some other upright stone in the village—it does not appear certain which—was formerly kissed by the young men, who thereby pledged their allegiance in upholding ancient rights and privileges.

London Stone is but one example of stones of immemorial sanctity, famous in the history of the British Isles.   The Coronation Stone in Westminster Abbey, known also variously as the Stone of Scone and the Stone of Destiny, is of great antiquity.   One need not believe any of the numerous fables which have gathered round this relic, and about which many futile pages have been written.   Suffice it here to give the conclusion reached by Professor Ramsay, Sir Herbert Maxwell, and the late Mr. W. F. Skene, that the stone was at first an ordinary Scotch boulder, which acquired exoteric dignity from its having been used at the inauguration of early Pictish kinglets.[61]

The King's Stone at Kingston-on-Thames, another coronation relic, goes back to the Heptarchy, if not much further.[62]   Then there are the Charter Stone of Inverness, the Leper's Stone of Ayr, the Black Stone of Iona, the Blue Stone of Carrick, and the Lia Fail of Tara, and even these represent only the best of known examples.[63]

It has already been seen that holed stones and perforated megaliths were deemed pre-eminently precious.   In like manner stones bearing the depressions and ornaments known to archaeologists as ' cup-and-ring ' marks were early set apart as tutelary objects.   Two of these stones, situated on the slopes of Cairngorm, were considered effica-

cious in preventing barrenness,[64] and other examples might
be given.

Sir A. Mitchell, who refers to the Cairngorm stone, utters
a timely caution to the enthusiastic searcher, and illustrates the warning by the following instance. At Burghead
(Elgin) one may see a cup-like hollow, four inches wide
and two-and-a-quarter inches deep, sunk in a slab which
is fixed in the wall of the burial ground. Upon inquiry,
the depression was shown to have been produced by children,
who were accustomed to strike the slab with beach pebbles
to conjure forth the sound of the ' rocking cradle and crying
child '. Sir Arthur suggests that, should the superstition
die out, it would be difficult to prove that the slab was not
a real cup-stone.[65] This is quite true, but what is the history
of the relic ? Sir Arthur says that the stone was visited
in the eighteenth century by women about to become
mothers. The modern ' cradle ' of the school-children of
Burghead is plainly a fading memory of the older belief,
but as it is scarcely likely that the eighteenth-century superstition was created outright, the slab may have a much
earlier significance. How came the stone to be built into
the churchyard wall ? The instance selected as a caution
is, one thinks, not of the best.

A more apposite warning is afforded by the story of the
undressed megalith which the same author saw in Caithness
in the year 1867. The stone, which stood five feet out of
the ground, had been erected only six years before to commemorate the marriage of a man who was unpopular in
the district. A spurious case of folk-memory might thus
be erroneously assumed. Yet even here there peeps forth
a fact which shows within what narrow limits the human
mind works. On each anniversary the stone was white-
washed by the inhabitants.[66] By this apparently stupid
practice, folk-memory, sometime latent, was kept alive.

In Southern England, and especially in London, knobby
flints, with rounded protuberances, are much in favour for
making the borders of flower-beds. These flint nodules
are decorative as well as useful. But was ornament the
original aim of those who set the example of periodically

whitewashing the stones ?   The whitened stones along the
coast-guard's cliff path prove nothing either way, for they
are simply guides.   Let us cast around for further instances.

The custom of whitewashing tombstones has often been
recorded.   Brand noticed that, as late as 1804, gravestones
in Glamorganshire were whitened with lime every year at
Easter, Whitsuntide, and Christmas.[67]   I have discovered no
later record, but one fancies the practice is not yet obsolete.

The fisher-folk of Inverary have an old custom, for which
they can give no reason but long tradition and observance,
of placing little white pebbles on the graves of their friends.[68]
Smooth white pebbles, sometimes five or seven in number,
but never more, arranged crosswise, have been found
in graves under the fallen ramparts of Burghead, the place
already noticed.[69]   A Scotch cairn, opened by Dr. Angus Smith,
displayed, on the ledge of a granite block, a row of quartz
pebbles, each larger than a walnut.[70]   Shield-shaped masses
of quartz, believed to be of symbolic or superstitious significance, were found in the Celtic cemetery explored in 1901
by Mr. Reddie Mallett at Harlyn Bay, Cornwall.[71]   Other
examples, going back to the barrow period, might be adduced.

One supplementary fact is instructive.   Manx boatmen
have a strong prejudice against having a white stone in a
fisher-boat, even as ballast.   Since Sir J. Rhŷs thinks it probable that the Manx folk once decorated their graves with
white stones, the feeling of repugnance is so far accounted
for.[72]   He asks whether we may connect the superstition
with the white stones mentioned in the Apocalypse.[73]   The
stones therein alluded to are symbolical of justification,
and may help us to interpret the prevailing Christian
custom at the turn-over from paganism, but I deferentially
suggest that they cannot, except by way of parallel
development, explain the prehistoric usage.   That usage
is surrounded by mystery, but the instances with which
we started represent, on one view, derivative practices.

Having now discussed lucky stones, perforated megaliths,
and stones naturally or artificially white, we may make a
short digression to the attractive subject of ancient superstitions regarding fossils.   ' Fossils,' the reader exclaims,

'are not megaliths'; nevertheless, the ideas connected with both are hard to separate. When we hear of the good or bad luck which is assumed to go with St. Cuthbert's beads (joints of fossil encrinites), St. Peter's fingers and thunderbolts (belemnites), Devil's toe-nails (gryphaeas), and snakestones (ammonites), we might hastily conclude that the picturesque name has originated the belief. But fossils as charms or mascots form an ancient chapter in history and an unwritten chapter in pre-history.

Pliny tells a strange story of a certain stone called by the Druids a 'snake's egg'. One of these stones incidentally proved fatal to an unfortunate Roman knight of Gallic birth, who was put to death by Claudius for having the object in his possession. Pliny gives a description of the egg, which he declares he had himself seen. It was as large as a medium-sized apple, and had a cartilaginous shell covered with disk-like processes.[74] Cornish accounts tell of a creature which, after ejecting its egg, pursued people with great fury. The egg itself brought good luck.[75] Some commentators think that the egg was a fossil echinoderm, but Conybeare argues for the probability of its being a Greensand 'fossil covered with *Ostrea sigillina*'. He compares the object with the 'gem' known as 'adder's glass', thick green rings of which have been found in British barrows.[76]

Conspicuous fossils must have attracted the notice of primitive men. For the moment, we will refer to occurrences recorded from British settlements, leaving the consideration of graveyard fossils to a subsequent volume. During the excavations carried out in the most methodical manner by General Pitt-Rivers at the Romano-British villages at Rotherly (Wilts.), and Woodcuts (Dorset), flint echinoderms (Fig. 26, p. 296), primarily derived from the Chalk, were found in quantities far beyond what could be explained by natural agencies. The surface soil yielded great numbers during trenching, thirty-three having been discovered in the south-east 'quarter' of Rotherly and ten in the east quarter.[77] They were also found in the pit-dwellings.[78] The constructors of these early villages had evidently observed the fossil urchins in the ' residual drift ' near the surface, and had collected specimens with considerable industry.   General Pitt-Rivers, as a provisional solution, suggested that the fossils may have served the purposes of coinage.   The Glastonbury lake-village, of pre-Roman age, has yielded several ammonites pierced as spindle-whorls.

But the fossils had probably a deeper import.   We know that the various species of the genus of the Chalk fossil known as *Micraster*, and popularly called ' fairy loaves ', are still prized.   The Essex labourer believes that while one of these fossil sea-urchins is kept in his home, he and his family will never lack bread.   And away in North-West India, a species of black ammonite, named by the priests *Salagrama*, is regarded as the embodiment of Vishnu, and figures in the religious ceremonies of the Brahmans.[79]

The field has now been surveyed.   Such superstitions as still survive are destined to disappear sooner or later. And, alas ! many of the megaliths are gone for ever.   The present duty is to record the legends and to preserve the monuments.   Of Stonehenge we hear much, but there exists a multitude of other more or less perfect remains, comprising stone circles, dolmens, menhirs, hut-circles, and barrows.   In future ages these will be of inestimable value to the archaeologist.

When the question of the purchase of Stonehenge by the nation was being debated some years ago, a distinguished parliamentarian, from whom better sentiments might have been expected, declared that he ' would not give one brass farthing of the nation's money for those old stones '.

But money is not everything.   In that world of legitimate imagination in which the plain man as well as the antiquary can dwell in hours of leisure, these monuments are not appraised in measures of gold or silver.   By the aid of these old megaliths the past may be visualized as in a pageant.   And as the teachings of the antiquary and ethnologist become more widely spread, the people at large, entering into this heritage, may be found to object to the wilful destruction of such priceless relics.

CHAPTER VIII

FAIRIES: MOUND TREASURE: BARROW SUPERSTITIONS

ALREADY, in considering the names by which barrows
are known in rural England, it has been briefly stated that
the more important graves were surmounted by elliptical
or circular mounds of earth, to which the term ' barrow '
is applied by the archaeologist.

For the most part, the true nature of a barrow has passed
beyond the range of folk-memory. Only the instructed
observer realizes that underneath the hillock rests some old
chieftain,

> Upon whose mound the single sheep
> Browses and tinkles in the sun,
> Within the narrow vale alone.

Direct knowledge, then, having been lost, around these
barrows there have grown up many curious superstitions.
There are, first, beliefs which connect the barrows with
fairies, or it may be giants; these beliefs associate punish-
ment with the desecration of the mounds, and conversely,
prosperity with their protection. Then there are superstitions arising, to some extent, from the fairyland myth.
Then follows that darling tradition of the common folk—
the story of treasure buried in the mounds. Finally, there
remain a few vestigial observances, shadows doubtless,
of far-off tribal and territorial institutions.

A preliminary note about fairies and fairy tales will prevent misconception. No writer of eminence claims that
all fairy tales are as old as the era of barrows, or even
that they are all ancient as the folk-lorist counts antiquity.
Legends must indeed have an origin, but they change with
the years. They gather accretions, or they lose substance
by attrition, or they become transmuted by the imaginations
of intermingled races. New tales, or at least, tales retold

and amplified in such a way that they would not be recognized by their authors, emerge from the conflict of versions, and all that can be wisely done is to plod backwards to find the theme which furnished the first inspiration. The task is rendered none the easier by reason of the downright inventions of the makers of modern picture-books.

Again, there are diversities of fairies. Professor A. C. Haddon, in a lecture delivered at Cardiff in 1904, distinguished five chief kinds of beliefs about fairies, resulting in the strange medley known collectively as ' fairy tales '. In its entirety, spirit-lore presents us with a queer mixture of the possible and the impossible. There are stories of the spirits of plants and animals ; of local, household, or domestic spirits ; and of witches and wizards. We are mainly concerned with the two last-named. Cutting away many of the extravagances of hereditary fairy tales, there remains ' a large residuum of occurrences ; these point to a clash of races, and we may regard many of these fairy sagas as stories told by men of the Iron Age of events which happened to men of the Bronze Age in their conflicts with men of the Neolithic Age. Possibly these, too, handed on traditions of the Palæolithic Age '.[1]

This explanation is the best yet put forward, especially as it suggests that the Bronze and Neolithic folk themselves had fairy tales. Till a theory be found which fits the facts better, this explanation may well stand.

One difficulty, as it has always appeared to the writer, must be fairly faced. The fairies, according to the legends, live in mounds. These mounds, that is, barrows, are now known to contain remains of the dead, and conjecturally they are copies of actual dwellings. The fairies are, of course, little people ; the story-tellers are, by comparison, of great stature. So far, so good. But if the writer's observations are typical, the mounds, ' tumps,' ' lowes,' and knolls to which superstitions are attached, are most generally those of the round or Bronze Age type—the more abundant kind of barrow. In other words, the barrows which should, according to the theory, entomb Neolithic folk, actually contain the skeletons of a larger race. The long barrows, on the whole, seem to be associated with giants (Giants' Graves), but the rules, ' fairies for round barrows, giants for long barrows,' intercept and cross each other.

It was provisionally stated in Chapter IV that the long barrows are of Neolithic Age, whilst the round kinds contain remains of Bronze Age folk. Dr. Thurnam's maxims, ' Long heads, long barrows ; round heads, round barrows,' were temporarily accepted as agreeing with the normal facts. Thus much might be conceded as the result of the painstaking diggings of Greenwell, Bateman, Cunnington, Jewitt, Atkinson, Pitt-Rivers, and many other workers, and of the scientific determinations made by Thurnam, Garson, and Rolleston, after much careful study of skeletons.

But now reservations must be made. Let us first recall the series usually accepted :—

 i. Eolithic and Palæolithic races—no relics of burials.

 ii. 'Non-Aryan' { Neolithic race (or races ?) also called Iberian, Ugrian, Euskarian, Basque, &c. } Long barrows— dolichocephalic (long) skulls : usually inhumation.

 iii. 'Aryan' { Goidels or Gaels Brythons Belgae } Round barrows—brachycephalic (broad) skulls : inhumation and cremation. Methods of burial during later stage doubtful.

The long barrows are generally said to contain burials by inhumation only. This is mostly true for the South of England, but the long barrows of Westmoreland and Yorkshire have yielded evidence of cremation. Since the barrows of both regions contain long skulls, the difference in custom was perhaps one of locality, not of date, and the exception to this extent weakens the generalization.[2]

The next fact, frequently overlooked, cannot be so lightly neglected. Canon Greenwell found that the round barrows of Yorkshire contained more skeletons of long-headed than of broad-headed people. He suggested, and others have since contended. that these burials attest a fusion of races, or at least a friendly partnership.[3] Other writers have thought that the conquered Neolithic race reasserted its prepotency of breed. In any case, the long skull is here no proof of age or culture, and Thurnam's maxim is faulty.

Within the last year or two the Yorkshire problem has been again attacked. Dr. William Wright, reviewing the evidence, concludes that the intermixture of skulls does not necessarily imply a peaceful intermixture of two races. Similar finds are recorded from the Continent. In Yorkshire, too, the presence of bronze articles and the practice of incineration cannot be ascribed to one race exclusively, and the ' round head, round barrow ' epigram does not hold true. Dr. Wright believes that at the dawn of the Bronze Age a mixed race came over to our shores. This race embraced people of the Neolithic and Transitional (or Æneolithic, i. e. Bronze-Stone) Age. He dismisses as unwarrantable and incredible the assumption that a pure round-headed race could have made its tardy progress across Europe unmixed.[4]

Still dealing with the Yorkshire barrows, recent observations, while tending to upset previous theories, may help to solve our difficulty about the fairy traditions. We say recent, but the conclusions now to be stated were anticipated many years ago by the Rev. W. C. Lukis when examining the grave mounds of Brittany. Mr. J. R. Mortimer, who has spent forty years in investigating the barrows of East Yorkshire, and who therefore speaks with high authority, now comes forward and dissents from the theory that the long barrow is necessarily the older kind of monument. The disregarded suggestion of Lukis is revived with greater force.

Mr. Mortimer supposes that in many cases the long barrow has been formed by subsequent lengthenings of what was originally a round barrow, operations rendered necessary by successive burials. The encircling trench which characterizes the round barrow was never found to girdle the long barrow entirely ; it had been obliterated at the ends by the added portions. Mr. Mortimer also lays stress upon the fact just noted, that cremation of a kind, however imperfect, is a concomitant of long-barrow burials

in the North of England, while it is the rule in the unchambered barrows of the South.   The chambered long barrows,
it is urged, differ no more in form from the unchambered
ones than does the round barrow with a cist differ in shape
from its counterpart which contains no cist.   Neither is
there any evidence that the Yorkshire Wolds were ever
inhabited by one race exclusively.   Absence of relics in
the long barrows proves little, since so many of the round
kind are similarly barren.   On the whole, then, Mr. Mortimer
concludes that though there is little evidence of the age
of the long barrows, yet they are probably of slightly later
date than the round ones.   He has also surmised that the
Neolithic folk were taller than their successors; but even
if we admit a second Neolithic immigration composed of
taller members, we can hardly agree with this opinion.
It is true that Mr. Mortimer has personally excavated only
two long barrows, but he has had under observation others
outside his own district.[5]   The reader need scarcely be
again reminded that throughout England the long barrow
is by far the rarer kind.

The revolutionary theory thus stated may, if accepted,
help in unravelling the riddle why the fairies are located
in the round barrows.   Several suggestions may be offered.
For, while both Neolithic and Bronze Age folk may thus
be assumed to have raised round barrows, or shall we say
long and round barrows, the Stone Age people proper
would be the first to adopt the custom of mound burial.
This lies in the nature of the case, and is attested by barrows
which contain stone relics only, with no trace of metal.
Hence the primary tradition would connect the mounds
with the first builders, especially as the practice of mound
burial began to wane.

It is conceivable, too, that where, as in East Yorkshire, the
tradition was confused by contemporary burials of varying
races, the fairy tales were of later origin, and embodied only
those legends which appealed to the mind by reason of their
antiquity.   This is far more likely than that the 'round
barrow tradition' of fairies should start from Yorkshire
as a centre.

If Mr. Mortimer be right in supposing the long barrows to be the more recent, the fairies may indeed have first been associated only with the round kind. Afterwards, the idea would be transferred to the long barrow, and indifferently to any domical hillock. A time would come when all traditions of ' long ' and ' short ' would be lost—when a mound was a mound, and that was enough. The dome-shaped dwelling and the beehive hut lasted, as has been shown, until the historic period had well set in. And though the Iron and the Bronze Age peoples, men and women of good stature, continued to occupy the domical house, yet they probably saw survivors of the Neolithic race, living in isolated groups and using the same kind of dwelling. These Stone Age folk, ' islanded ' in separate settlements, for the most part self-contained, would be recognized doubtless as aborigines, and as pre-eminently the round-house people. Save on casual visits, there might be little intercourse between the races, and the mystery and uncanniness pertaining to the little folk would be thus emphasized. The lineage of the fairy tale, then, though far from pure, extends as far as the first builders of mounds.

There is always the possibility, however, that the second race of mound builders, whether Æneolithic or Bronze Age folk, turned the tables, so to speak, and gave rise to Bronze Age superstitions among the survivors of the Neolithic community. This reversal of ordinary events seems to be indicated in Cornwall, where Giants' Castles and Giants' Graves are common, and where tales are current concerning Blunderbore and little Jack the Giant-killer. In other words, the Stone Age folk lived in fear of their stalwart conquerors, and further fancies may have been added to the abundant stores of legend. We may put forward this hypothesis in spite of the primitive ease of converting any enemy into giant or fairy indifferently. Else we must assume the tales to be of much later development, when the earlier races and their doings had become utterly confused in popular lore. An alternative theory, which may have some validity, teaches that the presence of unexplained megaliths gave rise to the stories of giants.

The question whether there were one or two pre-Aryan races in Britain, exclusive of the older Palæolithic people, increases the difficulty. But such difficulties are inherent in a science where deductions must be made from numerous converging fragments of evidence, each, perchance, decipherable in more than one way.

The study of skulls and skeletons seems as a whole to favour but one purely Neolithic race. Sir John Rhŷs and Mr. Brynmor-Jones, employing the data of philology and folk-lore, claim that there were two 'pre-Aryan' races. The first were the 'mound-folk' proper, an unwarlike, swarthy little race, perhaps of Lappish affinities ; these are the people caricatured in the fairy tales. The second, or conquering race, consisted of a taller, blonder, blue-eyed folk, who tattooed themselves and fought battles.[6] The language of the conquerors may be supposed to have been modified by idioms taken from the mound-builders whom they enslaved. From the Celtic Goidels, who in their turn had conquered all previous settlers with whom they had waged battle, this second race received the name of Picts, that is 'painted' or tattooed people. This term distinguished its possessors from other 'aborigines' already met on the Continent by the powerful Goidels.[7] Baring-Gould calls the dark people Silurian, and the taller, fair people, Neolithic. With this idea of Neolithic folk we may compare that of Mr. Mortimer. Roughly, we might then class both the mound-folk and the Picts as Neolithic, and the earlier Goidels as Æneolithic, but it is very doubtful whether these race-divisions coincided so clearly with stages of culture.

In the end, the Picts found a home in the East and North-East of Scotland. Meanwhile, the mound-folk became their slaves and drudges. Amalgamation of races may have taken place, but this is uncertain. Yet there was doubtless much intercourse, and even companionship. The little people would act as nurses to the children of the Pictish lords. Something of this kind was repeated later, when the Picts were beaten by the Goidels, whose speech and syntax were broken up by contact with those whom they defeated,[8] only in this case there was probably race-fusion.

So far the erudition of Sir John Rhŷs gracefully carries us. But some writers like Skene have considered the Picts to be Celts, that is, members of the Aryan group. It is, however, noteworthy that the Pictish custom was to transmit kingdoms through the female line—a non-Celtic idea—and Zimmer deems the race of pre-Celtic origin.[9]

Mr. W. C. Mackenzie, again, has argued that under the title ' Picts ' two distinct peoples have been confused, the short, dark Pets, Peti, or Pechts of peasant tradition, the true mound-people, and secondly, a taller, painted people, the Picts of the history-book.[10] This conclusion is substantially in agreement with that of Rhŷs, the Peti plainly being here correlated with the Neolithic mound-folk.

Conformably to this theory, it is admitted that some of the underground dwellings, which were roofed with stones, earth, or grass, and which were accessible by low and inconspicuous openings, may be ascribed to the Picts, while others were occupied by the preceding dwarf race.[11] In the Orkneys and Shetlands, where the Picts are colloquially called Pechts, they have partly taken the place of the real fairies.[12]

Constantly bearing in mind that the pre-Aryan people, or peoples, had at first a much greater extension over our islands, we may leave this vexed topic, to deal with some conclusions which have been reached respecting the little fairy-folk. The writings of Sir John Rhŷs will be liberally consulted. The conclusions stated therein will be found to be strongly corroborated by the simple annals compiled afresh from Highland tradition by that careful observer and sure-footed guide, the Rev. J. G. Campbell, to whose charming narrative we have previously referred.

The original fairy-folk were unwarlike and poorly armed. They likèd milk, and kept domestic animals, including the pig. They hunted and fished. Thieves by nature, they frequently stole such articles as they required, the object most coveted being the quern or handmill, which, according to the general belief, was originally got from themselves—a curious little tangle of tradition.[13] Nor were the visits of the pilferers much resented, for they were followed by good luck and prosperity.

It was otherwise with a second sort of raid. Living secluded in their ' weems ', reluctant even to disclose their names, the ' Little Folk ' would leave their settlement by night or at early dawn, creep down to the Celtic villages, and kidnap babies. Secrecy and wariness marked every action. In the words which Falstaff applied to fairies, ' No man their works must eye.' [14] Instead of stealing out-right, sometimes an exchange was made. For the pretty blonde babies of the Bronze folk there were left behind ' ugly brats, with short legs, sallow skins, and squeaky voices '.[15]

Later versions not only speak of changelings, misshapen, peevish creatures, but they make the fairies substitute for the mother herself a stock of wood.[16] The mound-folk of modern superstition are thus weird and uncanny. Yet Campbell tells us that they are firmly held to be counterparts of mankind, a fact which seems to stamp the Neolithic theory of their origin as sound. Among the fairies are women and children. All require food and clothing. They sleep like other mortals, they are subject to disease and death. Their occupations are spinning and weaving, churning and cooking, grinding meal and baking bread. Oftentimes the belated peasant hears within the hillock the sound of the fairy mill, and the songs of the fairy women.[17] Plough-ing in the field, he picks up an ' elf-bolt ' (arrow-head) or an ' adder-stone ' (spindle-whorl). Mystery is followed by vaguer mystery.

Everywhere in the Highlands the red-deer are associated with the fairies, and the superstition possesses a strange ring as of underlying truth. Although the horns of these animals are constantly shed, they are not found, because they are hidden by the little folk.[18]

Tales about the mating of fairies with mortals are sup-posed to point to some exogamous tendencies among the Pechts,[19] which encouraged occasional alliances with the taller Celts.

Contradictory notions are prevalent as to the size of the

mound-folk. At times the little people can go through
a keyhole. Again, they can just carry a single potato.
In Cleveland they are tiny green men, wearing queer little
caps, and they live in hummocks like of those of moudiwarps
(= mould-warps = moles).[20] Here we touch the confines
of literature, and get a glimpse of the quaint beings depicted
in the fanciful poems of William Blake.

Anon, by the licence of the untrained imagination of
primitive man, the mound-dwellers become giants. In
some fairy tales, the dwarf swells out into a giant, all, as it
were, in a parenthesis. For the huge man, of herculean
powers, was also needed to round off the story. So Finmac
Coul was big and strong enough to thrash the devil ; so
Og, the King of Bashan, was represented in the fables of
the Rabbis as having his head in perpetual snow, whilst
his feet were parched in the Arabian desert.[21]

The ' true belief ', the genuine tradition, seems to have
been that the mound-folk were a small race, ' about four
feet or so,' ' the size of a little girl.' [22] To reconcile the two
estimates, a theory was evolved that the little people could
change their stature at will. It is of this stage that the poetic
Eddas of Northern Europe appear to speak. Relying on
the evidence derived from this source, Professor Friedrich
Kauffmann states that among the old Germans and Scandinavians, ' giants and dwarfs were originally identical
phenomena.' [23]

In Britain, amid all the welter of opinions, the orthodox
belief is the more clearly heard. This would be the natural
and primitive creed to those who were once actually
acquainted with the slight figures and the domical, underground abodes of the Stone Age folk.

As the centuries rolled by, other origins were assigned
to the fairies. Distinctions of class were made, and Christian
doctrines permeated the traditional fables.

Thus, in Jutland we find a genealogy which traces the
fairies back to the story of the fallen angels. Some of these
deposed beings fell on mounds, and settled there as berg-
men or hill-folk. Others alighted on moors and became
the ancestors of the elf-folk, while a third group dropped

into dwellings, and from them descend the domestic sprites or brownies.[24] The reader will not fail to notice that the Christian setting of these beliefs supposes the pre-existence of the mounds, an important point to the ethnologist.

Like many other products, then, of the evolutionary process, fairy tales of to-day are often complex, being blended of diverse elements. There are elves and sprites ; witches and wizards and warlocks ; demons and kobolds ; and blear-eyed midnight hags, garbed in ' the remnants of a tattered hanging '. The printless feet of pigmy kings and queens dancing on the dewy grass paradoxically leave permanent traces in the form of fairy rings, ' whereof the ewe not bites.'[25] The swart ' demi-puppets ' throw elfin darts (Neolithic arrow-heads), and bake fairy loaves (the fossil *Micraster*), which, as already noted, whosoever shall keep will never want bread. From the delightful word-picture in ' L'Allegro', true, doubtless, to the rural England of Milton's day, we gather that the nocturnal visitants took toll for assistance given to men, for ' faery Mab the junkets eat '.[26] And the same poem

> Tells how the drudging goblin sweat
> To earn his cream-bowl duly set ;
> When, in one night, ere glimpse of morn,
> His shadowy flail hath thresh'd the corn
> That ten day labourers could not end.[26]

But there are also witches who turn the beer sour in the brewing vat, retard the butter in the churn, or throw over the villager a spell or a sickness, only to be warded off by the aid of iron, silver coins, or a twig of the rowan-tree (= mountain ash, *Pyrus aucuparia*). The list of fairies likewise includes Titania and Oberon, Puck and Robin Goodfellow, fairies black, grey, green, white, and

> Fairies small, two foot tall,
> With caps red on their head.

From all this medley throng we cannot fail to sort out Tom Thumb and Jack the Giant-killer, allegorical personages as old as the Neolithic and Bronze days.

Nor does this fairy-lore all end in mere sentimental superstition. Even in this prosaic twentieth century, the reality of the belief is constantly converted into action. The daily newspapers frequently record cases wherein the most ludicrous methods are adopted to break the spells of witchcraft. In some instances, indeed, the results border on tragedy rather than folly. Nevertheless, there is a sentimental phase of the matter—people believe because they wish to believe, and because folk-memory, however blurred and defective, retains somewhat of its pristine love of the unknown and the marvellous :—

> The odour of the wine which first shall stain
> The virgin vessel, it will long retain.

Dr. Arthur Evans has talked with a woman, still living, who showed him a fairy's hole in a bank near the Rollright Stones, on the boundary of Oxford and Warwick. This hole she used to close with a flat stone, ' to keep the fairies in.' When a girl, the woman had been to hear the Whispering Knights—really stones representing a collapsed dolmen—murmur their fateful prophecies.[27]

One consequence of the belief in the power of fairies for good or ill was a precept that barrows and howes must never be destroyed. Level a fairy mound, and ill luck was inevitable. Craigie, in his ' Scandinavian Folklore ', tells the story of a farmer who began to dig through a mound, the grave of a giantess, in order to drain a pool on the opposite side. When he had got as ' far as where the giantess' knees would lie ', all his cows died, and he had to give up his task.[28] Another farmer, who dug some of the greensward from a barrow for manure, had his house besieged and blocked up by mound people. Only when he had promised to repair the mischief did they retire. The mound having been restored, the visitors came no more. Blessing and plenty fell on the farm, and its owners are ' rich folk to this day '.[29]

Borlase, the Cornish antiquary, who flourished in the middle of the eighteenth century, learned of this superstition by narrowly escaping personal danger. He had been investigating one of the many barrows or barrow-kistvaens locally known as Giants' Graves, with which the Scilly Isles then abounded. Unfortunately, during the night following the excavation, a hurricane blasted the crops of corn and potatoes in the district, and the islanders were very much concerned, believing that Borlase had offended the giants, and thus raised the storm. At the same time, they were curious to know how much money he had found in the Giant's Grave.[30]

The folk-lore of Wales, Ireland, and the Isle of Man extends this barrow superstition to other ancient remains, and even to old burial grounds and churches, thus bridging over the pagan and Christian systems. A Manxman of South Barrule, having carted away the earth from an ancient graveyard to dress his fields, first suffered the loss of his cattle, and then died himself. Sir John Rhŷs, to whom the story was told in good faith, asserts that seldom is a ruined Manx house pulled down or its material again used.[31] Elsewhere labourers are very loath to be among the first to commence the dismantling of an old church.

The other side of the superstition teaches that the protector of the barrow received positive benefits. Farmers who were careful of the ' roof ' of the mound, not breaking the turf with spade or tether-pin, had their horses and cattle driven round by fairies to the lee side on stormy nights.[32]

Irish literature teaches that fairy-mounds were once actually worshipped.[33] Almost down to the present time the Norwegian peasant would, on the eve of a holiday, visit the ' bœttir ' mounds of the invisible folk, and make offerings of cakes and porridge, with libations of wort or buttermilk.[34] In 1859, a Manx farmer, who had allowed a tumulus on his farm to be excavated, sacrificed a heifer to avert evil consequences.[35]

Where education lags, the peasantry even to-day hold to the barrow belief in grim earnest. The English newspapers of August 18, 1905, contained a circumstantial account from St. Petersburg, of the investigation of a strange story. A tumulus in the Russian province of Oroff was said to be haunted by a white woman. A landed proprietor and a company of friends set out one moonlight night to examine the mound. The ghost was seen, and one of the party attempted to close with it, with the result that he afterwards became dangerously ill. The story was seriously given to the person by whom it was transmitted, and was evidently believed by the credulous natives.[36]

In the record of Borlase's adventure in the Scillies, a subsidiary superstition was hinted at—the belief that barrows contain hoards of treasure. This cherished delusion would appear to be a product of the late Bronze or the early Iron Age. The people of the late Bronze Age, at least, had not altogether forgotten that the mounds were graves. Doubtless, too, they had been told, even if they did not know from personal experience, that objects were often buried with the dead. With the bodies of the entombed men there were often placed, though by no means in the majority of cases, implements of stone or bronze, with ornaments of gold, jet, or amber. This custom was the nucleus of a goodly heritage of myth.

After-events favoured the treasure legend, and accretions grew with the passing of the centuries. Dr. A. Jessopp has unearthed a mass of evidence showing that in Norfolk, a county not really rich in barrows to-day, hill-digging for the sake of treasure was a favourite pastime with the Mediaeval dabblers in magic. ' The lust of gain in the spirit of Cain ', backed by a vague but ever-present curiosity, produced a veritable mania for opening mounds.[37] We may be sure that many of the barrows which show signs of having been mutilated, but not properly examined, have been hastily dug open by senseless treasure-seekers from the fifteenth to the nineteenth centuries.

A most astounding instance of the endurance of folk-memory is related by Professor Boyd Dawkins. Near the town of Mold there was a cairn known as Bryn-yr-Ellyllon, ' the hill of the fairy or goblin.' Country people averred that the spot was haunted by a ghost clad in golden armour, and that from time to time they had seen him enter his abode. A day came when the tomb was opened by the antiquary. Within was the skeleton of a tall man equipped with a corselet of bronze, overlaid with gold. The corselet, which was of Etruscan design, probably belonged to the Romano-

British period.[38] Unless, as some one has naïvely remarked, the ghost did walk, the tradition must have been handed down for at least fourteen hundred years.

Somewhat akin to this story is one that comes from Fife. Norrie's Law (A.S. *hlœw* = hill, mound), a barrow in that county, was reputed to be so rich in gold that when sheep had lain on the mound their fleeces became yellow. In 1819, whilst sand was being dug out of the Law, the labourers lighted upon a cist, which contained a coat of armour, a shield, a sword-handle, and a silver scabbard.[39] Popular tradition had accomplished what the monkish philosophers had attempted in vain—the transmutation of a baser metal into gold.

Welsh folk-lore abounds in like stories. On the top of a mountain in the south-west of Anglesey was a dolmen surrounded by a circle of stones, within which, people said, lay an iron chest full of ancient gold. Supernatural guardians, by the aid of terrifying portents, scared away all who attempted to dig for the treasure. Near the same place is Arthur's Cave, where the British (Brythonic) hero took refuge during his wars with the Goidels. Various treasures were said to be hidden there. A limestone cavern in Carmarthenshire enjoys two traditions. The first says that King Arthur and his warriors lie asleep inside, clasping with their right hands drawn swords with which to repel disturbers. The other story asserts that ' Owen of the Red Hand ' once lived in the cave, and that he and his men were shut up therein and starved to death. The sequel is curious but not unexpected : in the year 1813, ten or more human skeletons of unusual size were discovered in this ogof (= cave).[40]

Sir John Rhŷs, starting with the axiom that the legends of hidden treasure in mounds and caves are very ancient, traces the genealogy of these old stories somewhat as follows. The piles of gold and silver were at first very great. The warriors were a host, and they guarded their treasure for unnumbered years. As ages rolled by, the story-tellers felt that these items of the story were disproportionate to the visible relics ; the narrative also made the sentinels appear too niggardly. Later accounts, therefore, allowed the intruders to take away a reasonable quantity of gold. Then the treasure sank into a mere accessory of the armed men who, in reality, are ' not guarding any such thing, so much as waiting for the destined hour when they are to sally forth to make lost causes win '.[41]

The course of the tradition has thus diverged widely from the fairy superstition. But one would gather from the context that Sir John Rhŷs's explanation applies only to certain localities, and is not intended to be universal. The latest gloss, moreover, will be seen to be tinctured with ideas of resurrection.

A degradation, or if that word be not allowable, a development in another direction, appears in the Scandinavian version, in which a ghoul or ' grav-so ' inhabits the mound, and watches over it. At night a weird light burns, and seldom does the tutelary monster allow the treasure-digger to escape alive.[42]

Not precisely in the same category, but still enlightening, is the story of the Swedish barrow which was opened in Smaland a century and a half ago. People had long prattled about Odin's having been buried there. The oncoming of Christianity transformed the idea, and the place became known as Hell's Mount. On opening the mound a vault containing a coffin of flints was revealed to the workers.[43]

To our Teutonic forefathers the barrows appealed with great force as places of sanctity, which gave a binding character to covenants sealed on such spots. The low barrows which they themselves occasionally reared were perhaps recognized as belonging to the same generic group of objects as the earlier ones. Mr. Gomme mentions many cases in which barrows served as Saxon meeting-places. In one instance, that of Coleshill (Warwick), a charter fortunately exists which carries the custom back to A.D. 799. The Hundred Court of Grimeshow, or -hoe (Norfolk), used to be held at a tumulus not far from the famous prehistoric flint mines known as Grimes Graves.[44] At Forehoe, in the same county, the trysting-place was at a spot where there were four barrows.

The Rev. R. W. Eyton analysed the localities where the

thirty-nine pre-Domesday hundreds of Dorset were wont
to meet. He found that fifteen of these hundreds assembled
in the open air remote from houses, and twenty-three in
inhabited places : the locality of the remaining court was
unknown. Of the fifteen open-air assemblies,

8 met at barrows on hills ;

1 met at a tree on a barrow ;

2 met on *duns* (sites now lost) ;

2 met near monoliths ;

1 met in a combe or valley ;

1 met on the line of a fosse.[45]

Barrows, I have noticed, frequently mark the boundary
of a parish. A round barrow stands at the intersection
of the boundaries of the three Cornish parishes of Trevena,
Boscastle, and Camelford ; similarly, Grim's Grave, near
Fisherton-de-la-Mere (Wilts.), touches three parishes.

It would be instructive, did space permit, to discuss the
juxtaposition of churches and barrows, or it may be, pseudo-
barrows, i.e. simple mounds containing no funeral relics.
For the present, we will only observe that Mr. Addy has
collected a mass of evidence to show that the old moots,
or open-air courts, were often held on barrows, the judge
sitting on the raised summit. Afterwards the moots were
held in ' municipal buildings ' and churchyards, while in
very many cases the church and the court-house were one.[46]
The lines of proof are numerous and interesting.

Mr. J. R. Mortimer has recently published facts bearing
on this section. He found that on the Yorkshire Wolds
the Teutonic settlers were accustomed to select a British
barrow and to excavate, in the substance of the mound,
trenches from five to seven feet deep. These cuttings formed
a cross whose arms were always towards the four points of
the compass. Anglo-Saxon remains were found in many
of the trenches. The mounds, which locally go by the name
of Moot, Mall, Hanging, or Gallows Hills, had evidently
an imputed sanctity, so that the assemblies derived prestige
from the association. The traditional Yorkshire name
for these sunken crosses is *bields* (= shelters), the popular
idea, quite erroneous, being that they were first dug as

cattle shelters, and were made crosswise so as to afford protection from all quarters of the heavens. Mr. Mortimer also describes and illustrates crosses in relief, found on ancient sites, and composed of ridges of earth and stones.[47]

One other matter must be lightly touched. To keep the fairies from stealing querns and handmills, the owners used to turn these articles *deiseal*, or from right to left, i.e. sunwise. The deiseal turn was in common use, and much could be written on the subject. A sick woman, incited by a dream, so the Highland story goes, begged her husband to draw a furrow thrice round a fairy hillock, sunwise, believing that this would save her life. The husband, over-persuaded by sceptical neighbours, neglected the charm, and the wife consequently died.[48] One notices the collocation—the fairy mound, the sacred circle, the power of an iron ploughshare over stone-using people, the right-hand turn, and the mystic number three.

The liking for the right-hand turn may possibly be explained by supposing that the Aryans (Bronze Age folk) were sun-worshippers, and paid great attention to the sun's apparent motion day after day across the sky.

Another aspect of the question should, however, be examined. A close study of stone implements gives reason for the belief that the Stone Age folk were ambidextrous. To such people a left-handed helix is as easy to describe as a right-handed. One can hardly say whether the tools of the Bronze Age tell a like tale.

Is it not possible that the Bronze man learned from his predecessor the wonder-working power of the deiseal ? Various clues seem to lead to the belief that Neolithic man also observed the sun and its motions. If he really were ambidextrous the use of the deiseal turn would prove direct selection. Then the Bronze Age man, unconsciously obeying that deep-seated tendency among all races, whereby the victors readily assimilate the beliefs and practices of those whom they have vanquished, would imitate the deiseal turn, apart from any preference or personal aptitude. He would also be quick to use the left-handed circle—the ' widdershins ' movement, as a counter-charm, so as to beat the Neolithic wizard on his own ground, and undo what had been accomplished by cunning.

To conclude, mound-lore seems to have developed in three directions, giving birth respectively to ideas about fairies, sanctity of sites, and buried treasure. Wholesome respect or ever-enduring fear kept alive the first and second beliefs; the third needed little stimulus, so long as human nature remained as we know that it still continues to remain.

CHAPTER IX

THE REPUTED VIRTUES OF IRON

EVER since written history was ushered in at the dawn of the Iron Age, the man who stands at the forge has been a personage whose services to his fellows were not to be lightly disregarded. As the comparatively brief reign of Bronze drew near its close, and the founder's mould began to give place to the smith's hammer, there arose a race of craftsmen to whom respectful recognition was speedily accorded.

These primitive Vulcans and Tubal-cains, men of might, gained by their skill in reducing and shaping the intractable metal a reputation that could never have been obtained by the aid of the more ornamental alloy, or of the massive flint-stone, eternally inert and prosaic.

But for some time after its introduction the use of iron was not at all common. Bronze tools, though subsidiary, still held their ground, and even a few stone implements lingered on. Prejudice against the new metal counted for something, difficulty of working proved a still greater hindrance.

It is true that iron-slag is found on sites which we have every reason to believe are prehistoric, that is, sites occupied probably a few centuries anterior to the Roman invasion. Such discoveries have led some writers superficially to suppose that iron has been known from the remotest ages, and that there is no support for the theory of the progressive stages of Stone, Bronze, and Iron,[1] whereas all that such a discovery indicates is a pushing back of the introduction of iron and supersession of bronze.

Egypt and other parts of Africa may have been exceptional in their history, for the evidence seems to show that in the Nile district iron was known as early as bronze or copper. A lump of iron rust was found wrapped up in a fabric along with articles of copper, belonging to the sixth dynasty (B.C. 3300–3100)[2]. Even such facts are not of course conclusive.

In Caesar's day, iron was sufficiently scarce in Britain to be coined, like bronze, into bars or rings for the purposes of currency.[3] Each portion of iron so used had a standard weight.

With the Roman settlement came an impetus to the employment of the metal. The conquerors began to reduce the ore in the Forest of Dean, in the Wye Valley, at Alcester, in the Midlands, and in the Forest of Anderida, which covered the Weald of Sussex and stretched into Kent. Then the triumph of iron became assured. Warrior and workman alike proved its superiority over bronze and stone. Henceforward, though there might be slight checks, and perchance even trivial retrogressions—as was once the case with Polish farmers, who, after a bad harvest gave up iron ploughs and returned to wooden ones—the new metal could never be wholly cast aside.

The Wealden ironworks, above mentioned, were justly renowned till Mediaeval times, and even later, nor was it until the Midlands and the North became joint competitors that the industrial centre of gravity shifted, and the Southern trade began to dwindle and ultimately to die out. The last furnace at Ashburnham was closed down less than a century ago (1828).[4] It may be noted that splendid examples of the Wealden smith's art are to be seen in the Museum at Lewes, and in many a country mansion of South-Eastern England. Some of the artistic door-knockers of old London, and the antique link-extinguishers, once so much in vogue, are products of the Wealden furnaces, as are the railings around St. Paul's Cathedral.

And here we may observe a striking commentary on the theory that the death of an industry is soon followed by forgetfulness of its former existence. Canon Atkinson states that the ' reef-holes ' of Cleveland, alluded to in Chapter IV, were dug undoubtedly for iron ore as late as the reign of Henry the Seventh.[5] Credulous antiquaries have hastily called these ' reef-holes ' hut-circles. Only careful exami-

nation revealed their true character.   In the same neighbourhood are ' cinder hills ', made up of slag resulting from
the incomplete reduction of the ore.   ' But all tradition,
all trace indeed, of any survival of recollection as to the
time when, or the way in which, they had been accumulated,
had ceased to be, and to all appearance, had so ceased for
a long time past.' [6]

On the opposite side may be urged the vitality of the tradition that the Jews once farmed the tin mines of Cornwall.
The precise time, namely the reign of King John, is even
assigned.   Old smelting-houses are certainly called ' Jews'
Houses '.   Marazion is alternatively known as Market Jew.
But Max Müller and other authorities have declared that
the word ' Jew ' is a disguise, and has no connexion with the
Hebrew race.[7]   The tradition is clearly an afterthought,
based on this deceptive word.   Even if we admit the correct-
ness of the legend, the implication tells rather in favour
of the theory of disuse, for tin-mining has never fallen
into abeyance since the time of John.

We shall have to return to this subject again and again.
Concerning the Wealden iron industry, ancestral memories
are, to say the least, faint.   The Roman and Romano-
British works are kept in mind by the aid of book-lore,
supplemented by refuse-heaps of slag.   In Surrey the
oblivion is perhaps deeper still.   The first Surrey ' iron-mill '
was not set up till the middle of the sixteenth century.
There are notices of the industry as late as 1764.   By the
year 1814 the craft was extinct, though about a decade
previously iron ' hammers ' were to be seen at Witley and
Thursley.[8]   The tradition is kept alive for the tourist by
the guide-book, and for the philologist by such names as
' Abinger Hammer ' and the ' Hammer Pond '.   Yet despite
these encouragements, there is little doubt that, were it
not for the spread of reading amongst the poor, the former
existence of the old works would soon be ' clean forgotten,
as a dead man out of mind.'

Incited by the mention of Surrey, some one may claim
as an exception to the theory the case of the famous chalk-
quarry at Sutton, in that county.   This venerable pit,

long since abandoned in its main portion, is much worn and fretted, its surfaces are clad with green and grey lichens and bright wild flowers, and its margin is overhung with trailing shrubs. Books assert, and tradition is charged with the onus of proof—though I have never heard that the tradition was general—that here Sir Christopher Wren obtained the lime which he required for the building of St. Paul's Cathedral.[9] Granting that the legend were indeed much in the mouths of the common people, the fact would not be surprising. For, without prejudging the question of discontinuity in the practice of quarrying chalk, one may safely say that since the time of Wren the getting of this material, for one purpose or another, has never been altogether suspended. The proprietor of the Dorking Lime-works, for example, tells me that the ledgers of the successive firms which have quarried chalk there go back over 170 years. Folk-memory, then, has not been dependent on the chain of verbal testimony alone.

Contrast this case with that of the rude earthenware which has been found in large quantities at the ' Red Hills ', near East Mersea, in Essex, and of which specimens may be seen in the County Museum at Stratford. The ' Red Hills ' are low mounds, covering, in some instances, an area of several acres. That there were primitive potteries near the site seems plain. Probably the finished articles were coarse evaporating vessels for salt-pans. Yet respecting the workers not one whit of tradition has come down to us. Farmers inaptly call the mounds ' red hills ', because the soil, when upturned by the plough, is of a red colour—that is all.

To return : we saw that iron-working was carried on in the Romano-British period, and we believe that there was never afterwards any general extinction of the smith's trade. Local works died out and were forgotten, but somewhere or other the craft flourished, and projected to later folk-lore traditions which assimilated with the general stock. The horseshoes, consisting of thin, broad bands of iron, fastened to the hoof by three nails, as found in ashpits at Dorchester and in the valley of the Cam, as well as in ancient grave-

mounds, are admittedly of Romano-British date. The earlier
' slippers' were sometimes made of iron, sometimes of rope.[10]

Horseshoes have also been found in Anglo-Saxon graves
in Berkshire.[11]   Domesday Book contains several references
to smiths.   There were six of these artificers in the city
of Hereford, each of whom paid a penny rent for his forge,
and was liable to be called upon to make horseshoes at
a fixed rate for the king.[12]

In Mediaeval times, the blacksmith and his raw material
were the cause of much solicitude.   Thorold Rogers, extracting his information from such invaluable records as
Walter de Henley's essay on Husbandry (*circ*. A.D. 1250),
gives a vivid account of the scarcity of our most useful
metal at that period.   On a manorial farm, it appears that
the most formidable item of expenditure in the necessary
renewal of dead stock was the annual cost of iron.   Relatively
speaking, iron was considerably dearer than lead, and frequently nearly as costly as tin, copper, or brass.

The representative of the lord of the manor yearly
attended one of the great fairs, such as that of Stourbridge,
and bought a supply of iron which might be either of home
or of foreign origin.   The iron, which was sold in bars of
about four pounds each, was jealously preserved by the
bailiff, and doled out as required to the local smith, to whom
the amounts were carefully debited.   Over and over again
the smith is found apologizing for the large consumption
of iron, pleading that the drought, by hardening the soil,
had caused unusual wear and tear.

At this time, cart-wheels were often unprotected by tires.
Harrows had only oaken teeth ;   indeed, three centuries
later we find oaken pegs still used on stony soils.   These
old harrows remind the student of the Roman tribulum,
with its rows of flint flakes, as described by Varro.   The
Mediaeval ploughshare was merely a wooden frame with
an iron point, and the iron shoes of the horses or oxen by
which it was drawn were exceedingly light.[13]

It is interesting to note that ox-shoes were still used (1905)
on the South Downs, near Newhaven.   A comma-shaped
shoe, attached by four nails, was provided for each part of

the divided hoof. It appears that sometimes the fore-feet only were shod.[14] In England the custom of shoeing, and indeed of using, draught oxen is exceptional. On the Continent it is common. I have watched with much curiosity the shoeing of oxen in Central and Southern France. The British pedigree of the ox-shoe is ancient. General Pitt-Rivers describes and figures a Romano-British cow-shoe of iron, rectangular in shape ($3\frac{2}{5}'' \times 1\frac{1}{8}''$), and slightly concave on the upper side ; the specimen was dug up in the ancient settlement at Rushmore.[15]

Let us go back and pick up the threads of superstition, to see how tales and legends composing our iron-lore arose. We must always remember that, at the time of the introduction of iron, there doubtless lived people to whom the Stone Age was something more than a misty tradition, and that there existed remnants of two or three races of the pre-Iron Age.

Again, before the arrival of iron, the users of bronze must have gained credit for the possession of a cleverness, as useful to its owner as at first, perhaps, it was dangerous. The alchemist of the Middle Ages had in after days a like experience. But bronze soon obtained renown, and reached its highest development. Then came iron. Men gave up the use of bronze, and caught ' with its surcease, success '. Thenceforward the contest was not simply between bronze and stone, but between metal and stone.

The swart Neolithic men saw with fear—fear, however, curiously reciprocated in divers ways by those who were its cause, the growing power of the taller Bronze folk. While the Bronze men, puzzled by the mysterious customs and ceremonies of the unsociable little folk, deemed the Stone men clever wizards, whose ways were dark and subtle, the Stone men, in their turn, looked upon the skilful fabricators of ironwork as superior beings, whose deadly knowledge, obtained none knew where, merited righteous respect.

We saw in a previous chapter how Wayland Smith's Forge appealed to the imaginations of our Teutonic ancestors, who could not understand the true nature of that megalith.

It is conceivable that this name supplanted an earlier one
of similar purport, that before the Saxon inroads there
stood over, from past periods, communities of Stone Age
men, who, through the disuse of dolmen and barrow burial,
were equally ignorant, and who supposed the megalith to
be the home of some upstart Aryan blacksmith.

Wayland Smith has his counterparts in Roman mythology. Vulcan was a metal-worker among the gods. In the
dark caverns of Etna the Cyclops forged armour for brave
warriors. The Greeks, too, in the ' early dawn and dusk
of Time ', had a divinity of great majesty in ' dateless old
Hephaestus '.

It may be remembered that iron, though the representative of material power, was yet disliked for ceremonial
purposes, so that its use in religious observances was long
avoided.

The beaten races knew to their cost that iron gave supremacy, yet it must have caused a glow of triumph to behold
the conqueror, on the most solemn occasions, rushing back
to the use of stone. On the other hand, the dread of iron
on the part of the earlier peoples gave the usurpers a great
advantage. Naturally, then, we find iron accommodating
itself to the tradition that made the Neolithic folk fairies.

Iron, but preferably steel, in any form, is believed by
the Highlanders to be a protection against the elfin folk.
Campbell gives many examples of this superstition ; in one
instance the charm is a sword, in another a knife or a pair
of scissors, again it is a needle, a nail, a ring, a gun-barrel,
or a fish-hook.[16]   The occupation of tinker (Goidelic,
' tradesman ') is one of honour, and among the Gaels the smith
is credited with more virtue than other artisans.[17]   By what
curious turn of fortune, then, has the Breton tinker come to
take stone celts in return for his labour ?   What a crossing
of ideas !

When the Irish peasant wishes to keep the fairies from
a child till the baptismal day, an iron poker is laid across
the cradle.[18]

A North Wales story, conjectured by Sir J. Rhŷs to point
back to the Stone Age, makes a fairy wife run away from

her husband in consequence of his having unintentionally struck her with the iron part of his fetter, stirrup, or bridle.[19]

Norwegian lore teems with similar examples. Legends linger therein concerning huldres, beautiful women with long tails and brindled or light-coloured bodies. Huldres, by their music, enchant men whose calling takes them among the mountains, but no harm can happen if the traveller carries about his person a piece of steel or silver.[20] Here we get an enlargement of the earlier belief. At first it was bronze against stone ; then iron against both stone and bronze ; lastly, metal, any metal, was a prophylactic and a strong defence.

Another tale records that a smith captured a huldre in a wood, by holding over her the barrel of his rifle. He marries the huldre. They quarrel because the woman wishes to spit and roast their child for supper. The husband objects, the huldre throws round him a steel wire, and he has to give in—a literal turning of one's weapons against oneself.[21]

In the England of our days, it is a florin or a half-crown, cut into quarters if need be, which constitutes the best gun-charge for slaying witches. But whether it is a plough-share to raze a fairy mound, or an axe to fight the guardian of fairy treasure, or a weapon to take gold rings from a troll or giantess, or a spell to drive off witches, iron is the sovereign metal.

The supremacy of iron seems now to be almost world-wide. In India, the performer of certain funeral rites holds in his hand a piece of cold iron to guard against any evil spirits which may be liberated from the dead man.[22] One remark-able custom is recorded of such far-separated peoples as the Chinese, the Eskimos of Alaska, the natives of the Celebes, the Lithuanians, the Prussians, and the Scotch. As practised by the people last named in this list, the custom consists of thrusting a nail or needle into all meal, butter, cheese, flesh, or whisky, which chances to be in a house after a death has occurred, the purpose being to prevent death entering the provisions.[23]

More intelligible to the student is the practice of placing

articles of steel or iron beside the churn-stick to keep off the
fairies and allow the butter to ' come '. Should any provisions unfortunately be charmed by witch or fairy, they
should be put on an iron plate and heated before the fire,
so that the worker of spells may be burnt and rendered
unable to sit down for fourteen days.[24] Beliefs of this kind
are seen in their lowest form, though the stages of degradation are still traceable, when the peasant of Kent or
Hereford lays a bar of cold iron on the barrels of beer to
prevent the beverage being soured by thunder.[25] In the
Highlands, iron actually averts thunder and lightning.
Thus are Thor's stone bolts circumvented by metallic
charms.

Occasionally one is able to link isolated fragments of
folk-lore, which, though superficially disconnected, are seen
to be complementary when placed in juxtaposition. The
Irish peasant who supposes that whirlwinds are raised by
fairies has his fellow in the hinds of Kent just mentioned,
and each has his interpreter in the Arab of the desert, who,
on seeing a sand-pillar, cries ' Iron! iron! '[26] Light comes,
too, from Scotch fishermen at sea, who, hearing a com-
panion use blasphemous language, cry out ' Cauld iron ',
grasping as they do so some object made of that metal.[27]

In the Bermudas, should a witch enter the house, the
occupants thrust iron into the fire.[28] From Ashantee and
Morocco come similar methods of thwarting ghosts and evil
spirits. To seek the aid of such beings the reverse method
must be adopted. Hence the Gold Coast negroes, when
consulting their fetish, remove from their persons all articles
of metal, ' a practice,' remarks Mr. F. T. Elworthy, ' with
which all Freemasons will not fail to perceive reasons for
lively sympathy.'[29] Bearing the Gold Coast practice in mind,
we shall not, when we read of the former popularity of iron
bars and iron utensils as exports to Western Africa, deem
usefulness in material affairs the only incentive to the trade.
The reputed efficacy of iron against witchcraft must be
remembered.[30]

With regard to the shape which the metal amulet may
assume, there is one—the crescent or horseshoe—which is

so universal as to deserve separate mention. In this form there is involved not only the negative idea of warding off mischief by the expulsion of fairies, but the positive faith in good hap and prosperity to the possessor.

Who has not seen ' The horseshoe nail'd, each threshold's guard ' ? and who has not sought the origin of the symbol ?

Mr. Elworthy, who has written ably on this subject, avers that the horseshoe talisman is common not only among enlightened Englishmen, but among Jews, Turks, infidels, and heretics all the world over. This authority has himself seen horseshoes nailed up in Constantinople, Spain, Italy, Sicily, and Egypt. In Holland the charm has added virtue if it chances to be a stolen specimen.[31]

Our archaeologists often write as if the custom of nailing up horseshoes were becoming obsolete, and confined to provincial England. This is far from being the case; the habit is prevalent on the London fringe, and is observable in the metropolis itself. The educated lady who hangs up the symbol in her drawing-room carefully gilds the iron beforehand, but the underlying superstition, all unconfessed, is nevertheless present. Long discussions are waged as to whether horseshoes attached to walls and gables should be set up in threes, fives, or sevens, and whether the triangles so formed should have the apex above or below, and further, whether the gaping part of the shoe should be turned upwards or downwards.[32] Occasionally, as in Lincolnshire, the peasant polishes the horseshoe, and rears it against the fireplace.

English history and literature are intertwined and interwoven with the horseshoe legend. Nelson had one nailed to the mast of the *Victory*. Successful men of business have attributed their prosperity to the finding of a horseshoe, a rusty specimen by preference. To quote literary passages on the subject would be to ramble out of all bounds.

John Aubrey, that wandering purveyor of queer customs, saw a horseshoe in the porch of a Suffolk church, placed there to keep away witches. He was told that the practice was common. As if to parallel his own laconic remark about holed stones (Chapter VI), he dryly adds, ' One would imagine that holy water alone had been sufficient.'[33]   This last example exhibits an interesting case of Christian syncretism as it existed in rural England of the seventeenth century.

At the time when Aubrey wrote there was a popular sentimental greeting which ran, ' May the horseshoe never be pulled from your threshold ! '

In Somerset and some other counties the horseshoe supplements, if it does not supplant, the holed flint so often referred to previously. Hung up over the cow-house, the shoe keeps off pixies.   Herrick advises farmers to

> Hang up hooks and shears to scare
> Hence the hag that rides the mare.[34]

This precaution taken, horses will be free from night-sweats, and witch-knotted manes and tails. A scythe or sickle suspended from the rafters may be used as a substitute.

With the horseshoe must be coupled the iron crescent. Mr. Elworthy found specimens hung up in Cairo—' The crescent symbol of the Pagan Diana used as an amulet by the Mahomedan iconoclast ! '[35]   The same form is found among the amulets of the Ashantees ; ornamentally, it occurs on ancient Roman gems ; and emblematically, on the Turkish ensign.

In Europe generally, and—to be local—in the British Isles, we see the crescent used decoratively on the trappings and harness of horses (Fig. 15), a fact observed and commented upon by many writers. It is conjectured that Moorish influence has been at work, but that would hardly account for the general distribution of the custom.   Nowadays, the crescents and horseshoes seem in danger of being crowded out by shields, hearts, crowns, flowers, and monograms, which are also affixed to portions of the harness. The horse, whose cast shoe will become a valued charm, must itself be protected while the shoe is actually being worn ! The idler who rambles through French museums will see unwieldy ornaments of the horseshoe pattern which were once used by ladies in dressing the hair.

Mr. Elworthy, summing up the evidence, thinks that we

may assume the horseshoe to be the handy conventional sign of the crescent. His general conclusions are that the crescent was a powerful amulet, that the horseshoe became

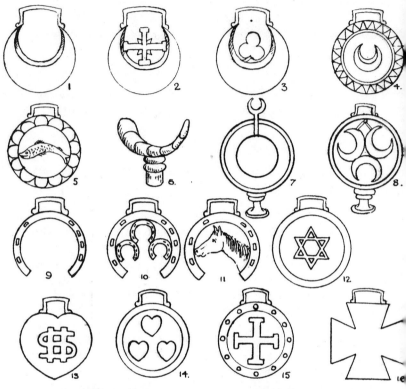

FIG. 15. Metal ornaments found on horse trappings (North Lincolnshire, 1907). Nos. 1–8 represent forms of the crescent amulet; Nos. 8–11, the horseshoe. No. 12 is a well-known mystic symbol. No. 15 shows the cross potencée, and No. 16 the cross patée: these seem to denote Christian influence. Nos. 13 and 14 indicate the decay of folk-memory concerning amulets, though the heart pattern was originally talismanic. Nos. 7 and 8 form bridle 'plumes', No. 6 is a hook for a bearing-rein; the remainder are either forehead medallions or breeching decorations. The patterns 1–4, 9, 11, 13, 14, and 16 are fairly common in London.

its representative, and that the virtues of the latter are reinforced by its being made of the witch-hated cold iron.

I would suggest, as a slightly better interpretation, that the crescent and the horseshoe are collaterals derived from

the same stock of primitive ideas ; that they are akin, but
not in lineal descent the one from the other.

It will be remembered that in prehistoric times the broken
circle was a popular symbol.   It was exhibited with some
degree of scrupulosity.   The circular trench of the round
barrow was left incomplete in one portion of its course.
Within the substance of the mound there was often a ring
of stones, broken in one place.   The ellipses of monoliths at
Stonehenge are again incomplete, indeed they are familiarly
known as the ' horseshoes '.   A favourite ornament of the
Bronze Age was the penannular bracelet.   On old rock faces
those artificial carvings termed ' cup and ring ' marks reveal
the same design.   Plainly, the idea of the interrupted circuit,
common to the horseshoe and the crescent, is very old.
Some have seen therein a trace of sun-worship, but this is
speculative.

That the employment of iron enhances the value of the
symbol is on all hands admitted.   When iron was newly
introduced, it would have a still greater significance, auspi-
cious or eldritch, according as it was viewed by the conqueror
or the conquered, the Bronze-Iron man or the Stone man.

Besides the belief in the protective powers of iron, we
have to reckon with a superstition involving secretiveness
and even fear.   North-country folk, in particular, consider
presents of pins, knives, and other sharp instruments as
unlucky.[36]   ' Knives,' says Gay in the ' Shepherd's Week ',
' always sever love.'   Similar aversions are recorded from
Denmark.

Take, again, the strange action of the rural labourer
who covers up his ploughshare or scythe with a sack, lest
the moon, shining on it, should cause it to rust.   In this
instance, the ill-concealed fear of being known as a trafficker
in the new metal has survived, but in such a trivial form
that it has become associated with that notorious disturber
of human affairs—the moon.

In the same category must be placed the practice of
biting off a child's nails, instead of cutting them, during the
first twelvemonth of its life.   A mass of nail-lore of this
type has accumulated in the course of centuries.

The Nazarites who made vows not to let any razors
come near their heads had successors in the Lombards who
refused to apply a cutting instrument to their beards. The
man might be defiled by the iron, and should his enemy gain
possession of the waste hair, evil could easily be wrought.[37]

Comparative custom yields further instances, as when
the blacksmiths of ancient Rome and Pompeii, in order
to counteract the ill effects of constantly handling iron,
wore a phallus, presumably of stone, as an amulet.[38]

All this superstition, the records of which might readily
be amplified, tells of the birth of the Iron Age, when the
new metal was used by stealth lest gods and fairies might
be offended. The credulous folk who began to use the
iron were painfully inconsistent. Iron would ward off the
spells of fairies, and keep away those who wished to kidnap
the young babe, yet, as we have just seen, the child's nails
must be trimmed without the use of iron, or at any rate
the metal must be used surreptitiously. To the spirit of
conservatism, which we now see illustrated in the Northern
Farmer's antipathy to the ' kettle of steam ' (steam cultivators and threshing-machines), there was added the gospel
of fear.

After all, however, it is the lucky or propitious virtue
which has prevailed, and which continues to prevail. Iron
is of good omen because it is strong, and strength in the
physical world is counted as superiority. Iron is victorious,
in peace and in war. ' Sir,' said the Grecian sage Solon
to the wealthy Croesus, who had been ostentatious with his
stores of money, ' if any other come who hath better iron
than you, he will be master of all this gold.'[39]

This chapter opened with a reference to the prestige and
prowess of the primitive blacksmith. The very word ' smith '
has been shown by Schrader to present many points of
interest,[40] and the calling which it denotes has always
been a fascinating theme to poets and novelists. Thus
literature and tradition have acted and interacted upon
each other. Elihu Burritt, Quentin Matsys, and the obliging
smith of Gretna Green, have all enriched the romance of
iron, and kept alive the spark of imaginative lore.

Apart from these worthies, however, there is an inherent charm in the smith and his shop. Longfellow's New England school-children are not fonder of loitering by the stithy than is the forlorn cottar of Connemara. The Italian peasant listens anew to the soughing of the goatskin bellows, and the ' rude Carinthian boor' warms himself at the smithy in the bleak mountain pass. To the genuine peasant the world is still young, and he beholds it with the wide eyes of a child.

So the smith remains popular. Patiently reducing the stubborn ore on the margin of a primeval forest, forging a shoe for the steed of a Roman patrician, shaping the bars for a trial by ordeal, riveting on a knight's armour for the tournament, casting bombards for the ever-memorable Agincourt, repairing an axle at an old posting-house, or welding plates for a twentieth-century battleship, the smith has always been at the front. He has given titles to such ancient families as the Ferrars (*ferrum*). He has perpetuated his renown in our most common English surname. He stands to-day in small fear of being superseded. And should the time ever arrive when the nations shall beat their swords into ploughshares and their spears into pruning-hooks, his arm will be as puissant as of old, and in no degree more idle.

CHAPTER X

OUR OLDEST INDUSTRY

OUR oldest industry is not, as many might casually suppose, the tillage of the soil. Agriculture is indeed of ancient descent. In very early days agriculture was of prime importance, and even in a manufacturing country like our own, it still finds employment for more labourers than any other occupation.

But there is a calling which is still more venerable, for it is co-eval with the hunting stage of man's existence. This is the fabrication of implements and appliances of flint.

As a hunter, man needed stone weapons, and when the chase afterwards became less attractive than the farm, stone was likewise required for his first tools. The stone which was most general and most easily worked was, in Britain, the well-known flint, in one or other of its forms : Tertiary pebbles, nodules fresh from the Chalk, and chert (impure flint), from other geological formations.

The matter may be put in another way. Palæolithic man, a hunter and fisherman, manipulated flint nodules to his special purposes. Neolithic man—hunter, fisher, shepherd, farmer—mined flint and elaborated tools manifold and diverse. Bronze and Iron Age men retained the use of flint ceremonially, and, to some extent, industrially. Flint is worked in our own day. If, therefore, it can be shown that flint-working has never ceased out of the land, the claim of this existing industry to ancient lineage will have been established.

It will make the claim more cogent if the familiar case of the Brandon flint-works be examined in detail. Brandon is a small town on the Northern border of Suffolk. It is built near the Little Ouse, which separates that county from Norfolk. Across the river, about a mile and a half distant, on the Norfolk side, are the prehistoric flint pits of Grimes Graves, to which we shall shortly revert.

To-day, the manufacture of gun-flints, ' strike-a-lights ', and ornamental flint blocks finds intermittent employment for some half-score of Brandon men, and steady work for half that number.

The making of gun-flints has in former times been carried on at Crayford, Chislehurst, and Greenhithe, in Kent, Purfleet in Essex, at Beer Head in Devonshire, at Norwich, in parts of Wilts. and Sussex, and in a few other districts.[1] But at Brandon the industry is a living one, and its continuity from prehistoric times is most likely perfect.

In the close neighbourhood of Brandon, among the ' drift ' gravels of the Ouse, typical implements of the Palæolithic age are met with. Grimes Graves, the renowned Neolithic flint mines, one of which was reopened and examined by Canon W. Greenwell thirty years ago, are, as already mentioned, but a short walk distant from Brandon. At Santon Warren, Lakenheath, and other spots in the district, Neolithic implements occur plentifully. Lastly, there is the modern flint industry. Can the stages be linked together ?—that is the absorbing problem.

For the sake of those to whom the subject is new, let us briefly summarize the conditions and methods which obtain to-day at Brandon, premising that the notes made during a special visit have been carefully checked and supplemented by the writings of Mr. J. Wyatt,[2] Mr. S. B. J. Skertchly, and other authorities to be hereafter mentioned. And above all, on every doubtful point, I have had the freely-rendered assistance of Mr. Fred Snare, the ' king of the knappers ' in modern Brandon.

The industry to-day is divided into two branches, involving the employment of two distinct sets of workers. One group raises the flint, the subsequent shaping, or ' knapping ', being performed in the town by special workmen.

The raw material is now mainly procured from Lingheath, about a mile SSE. of Brandon. Generations ago flint was mined a little more towards the West, on the ground known as Brandon Park, but these workings have long since been abandoned.

At Lingheath the Chalk area is honeycombed for a space of several acres with vertical shafts and horizontal galleries which have been made during the last 200 years. The particular zone of the Upper Chalk which yields the supply of flint is believed to be that of *Micraster cor-anguinum*.[3] During the period of my visit, I could not spare sufficient time for collecting fossils in order to verify this opinion, but the view is probably correct.

Most of the borings have been filled up with the waste material from the excavations, and are now grassed over, leaving the ground irregularly broken into hummocks and depressions. Other pits still show the white rubbly chalk and the surface soil with which they have been blocked up. A few others—those which are still being worked— are roughly covered in, between the periods of working, with trimmings of gorse or hawthorn bushes.

A typical shaft, approximating to a section which is given by Mr. Skertchly, is roughly rectangular (nine feet by five feet), and goes to a depth of about forty feet below the surface. Some three feet of sand and gravel is first dug through. This layer occasionally yields a few Palæo-lithic implements. Beneath this crust lies the more or less abrupt junction with the White Chalk, and below this, again, the worker soon reaches a thin, continuous layer of flint, only five inches thick. This flint is of little use, as it does not ' flake clean '. A little lower, a band of marly pipe-clay is cut through, and the scattered, or partially coalescing nodules of flint, forming the ' upper crust ' of the digger's scheme of rocks, are laid bare. These masses are used in building walls, and the layer was, in earlier days, sometimes burrowed into laterally to get material for filling up the shaft when no longer required. Of late years, however, Mr. Snare informs me, the digger has ceased to fill up the disused pits.

Neglecting these undesirable nodules, the worker keeps on till he touches a one-foot layer of flint, the ' wall-stone ', which has very uneven surfaces—' paps ' above, and ' legs ' below. This stratum yields good cores for builders. Next comes an irregular line of flints, known as ' horns ', though they are more finger-like in shape. Many feet below this lies a band of ovoid flints often united into a continuous mass. This layer is the ' floor-stone ', a layer of almost homogeneous flint, and though it is only eight inches thick, yet it is for this the workman has, with much labour, sunk the shaft. Most of the gun-flints, certainly the best kinds, are made from the flint of this layer.

Horizontal galleries are now bored in various directions, that the fullest advantage may be taken of this choice material. Hence the ground-plan of a flint mine is rather complex. In practice, the shaft is sunk a little lower than the floor-stone, in order to expose isolated flint nodules, the ' rough and smooth backs ' of the labourer. But these are not of uniform quality and cannot be depended upon.

Examining the pit, at once we note that the method of winning flint is very primitive. Nothing resembling a general excavation is to be seen. A shaft is bored and radiating tunnels are made. The available flint is exhausted, and another pipe is begun. The ramifications of each new shaft approach, but rarely intersect, those of an older one. The flint-miner will essay to prove, to his own satisfaction at least, that his methods could not be bettered.

The bottom of the shaft is reached with the aid of six or seven ' stagings ' or steps, which occur alternately at intervals of about five feet. The steps, formed of the projecting chalk on either side of the shaft, provide a rude kind of staircase. In addition, between the stagings, pieces of flint are left outstanding for footholds. Holes, cut alternately right and left, serve the same purpose. Pursuing an old method, the flint-miner bores in a zigzag manner, but yet preserves a practically vertical face to the descending shaft.

There is no windlass, or pulley, or rope, or pail, not even a ladder. Climbing upwards from step to step—no easy operation for a novice—the worker carries his hard-won treasure into the daylight. At most, a comrade standing midway may assist in hoisting up the blocks of flint.

The selected flint is taken to the workshops in Brandon,

and sold by the cart-load, or ' jag ', according to quality. A small royalty, payable to the Charity Commissioners, has to be included in the price.

The ' flint-knapper's ' labours now begin. Employing hammers of various weights, he ' quarters ' the unwieldy masses of flint, and proceeds to strip the blocks into ' flakes '. He wears on his left leg a tightly-strapped pad of leather, on which he rests the core or block which is to be flaked. The core is held inclined at a slight angle, and the knapper, using a specially-shaped hammer, by means of a series of slight blows, or more correctly taps, detaches flake after flake, which he dexterously sorts as he goes along.   Some flakes are long and even, and are suitable for making two, three, or even four gun-flints.   Others are adapted for strike-a-lights, others are waste, fit only for road metal. Into these operations it is unnecessary to enter fully, as they do not concern our discussion.

We may, however, add that the gun-flints are exported to Central and Western Africa, as well as to Spain, Austria, and other countries.   The sizes are dependent upon the kind of fire-arm for which they are needed, whether pocket pistol, carbine, Dane gun, musket, or cannon.   The strike-a-lights, or flints used for obtaining lights and fires, are in great demand.   The introduction of the lucifer match, three-quarters of a century ago, tended to injure this branch of the trade, but the old tinder-box has lately had a remarkable revival.

The ' Lovett tinder-box ', a specimen of which lies on a shelf hard by as these lines are written, contains a trimmed flint, a small bar of steel, and a woven fuse, all neatly packed in a metal box, secure from damp.   The War Office bought 14,000 of these boxes for shipment to South Africa during the Boer War.   Each box was considered to be as serviceable as 300 times its bulk of matches.   Not only soldiers on the veldt, but hunters in the South American forest, and peasants in the fastnesses of Spain and Italy, have a preference for this old-fashioned mode of obtaining fire.

Nor does this conclude all the uses of flint.   Beautifully squared blocks, arranged in ornamental patterns, are em-

ployed in large quantities for decorative work in the walls
cf churches and mansions. Skilfully devised to represent
crosses, chevrons, or lozenges, these squared flints are
exceedingly effective for the purpose.

These worked blocks have some bearing on the continuity
theory which will shortly be offered, for they were used
in Mediaeval days. The Bridewell, near St. Andrew's
Church, Norwich, has walls of elegantly dressed flint, dating
from the year A.D. 1403.[4] This is not our earliest record
of the art, for the Romans used faced flints at Caistor,
not far from the same city.[5] It is believed that this is the
only existing example of such early work, the reason for the
employment of flint in this case being apparently the local
scarcity of stone.

We now proceed to trace backwards the continuity of
the flint industry at Brandon. A few dates will assist us.
It was only in 1835 that the gun-flint was superseded by
the percussion cap. The flint-lock was in general use in the
British army throughout the eighteenth century, having
been introduced for purposes of warfare about the year
1686. Gun-flints in general were, during the intervening
period, properly flaked and retouched at the edges, but as
late as 1738, rough, home-made flints were occasionally
used by fowlers and sportsmen. The earliest mention of
the use of the true flint-lock anywhere is in the year 1588.
Before that date, a rude hand-lock was fired by means of
unshaped flints, and earlier still, it is supposed, by the aid
of iron pyrites. There appears to be no English record
of the use of pyrites, no specimen existing in the Tower of
London, but we know that in 1586 this medium was employed in Brunswick.[6]

Mr. Skertchly follows back the evolution of fire-arms
from the percussion cap to the wheel-and-hand-lock, thence
to the wheel-lock alone. Before this there was the hand-lock.
in which the cock fell away from the gunner, and earlier
still a similar weapon wherein the ignition was towards the
gunner. Finally, we get back to the old crude ' hand-fired '
hand-lock. In broad terms, this transports us, as we have
seen, to the last quarter of the sixteenth century.

During this period of evolution in the weapon, there was also a perfect gradation of the manufactured gun-flint. The fine modern gun-flint comes from a single-backed, or single-ribbed forerunner. This, in its turn, was derived from a ribless gun-flint, and this again, as Mr. Skertchly claims to have proved by means of close comparisons, was an offshoot from an Old English ribless strike-a-light.

The gun-flint, then, is ultimately developed from the strike-a-light, but not from the modern pattern of that object. There is a generic difference between the two articles : the gun-flint of to-day is ribbed crosswise, the strike-a-light longitudinally. According to Mr. Skertchly, the earliest gun-flints were similar to the old strike-a-lights, only smaller, and, like them, they were rounded at the heel. To put the matter another way, modern gun-flints and modern strike-a-lights are, on Mr. Skertchly's evidence, collateral descendants from Old English strike-a-lights.[7]

Mr. Snare insists upon a somewhat different genealogy. He says that the first strike-a-lights made in modern times, say four centuries ago, were rudely oval in shape (Fig. 16. 2), because the worker chipped away the bulb end of the flake. A more nearly circular type followed (Fig. 16. 3). Then came the ' Old English strike-a-light ' (Fig. 16. 5), which tended to become square in outline, though still preserving a slightly uneven curve at the sides. From this last were developed the various square gun-flints.

Mr. Snare asserts positively that the strike-a-light and gun-flint of horseshoe pattern, that is, the straight-heeled variety, were never manufactured in England. These articles represent a French type (Fig. 16. 7), and are made on the Continent at the present day, finding a ready sale in Valencia.

If this be the correct view, Mr. Skertchly's reliance on the horseshoe gun-flint and strike-a-light, as furnishing a transition between the historic and the prehistoric, is misplaced. The oval and circular strike-a-lights are the true links.

For these old oval and circular fire-kindlers, what are they in reality ? They are true representatives of Neolithic

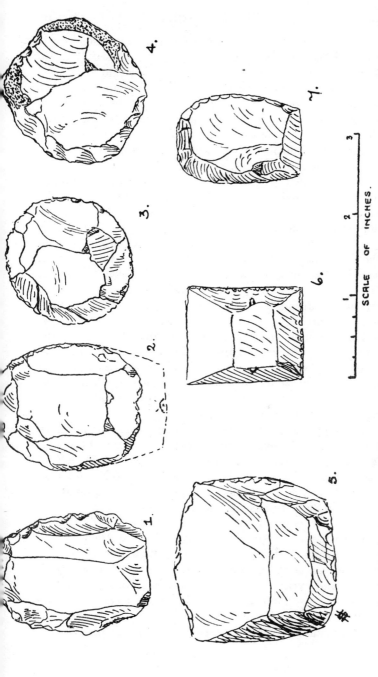

FIG. 16. The development of the gun-flint and the strike-a-light. 1. Neolithic 'scraper', horseshoe pattern (Suffolk). 2. Early English strike-a-light notice that the bulb end of the flake has been removed). 3. English circular strike-a-light. 4. Neolithic circular strike-a-light, or 'scraper' (Surrey). 5. 'Old English' strike-a-light. 6. Modern English gun-flint. 7. French gun-flint; straight-based. [All from author's collection.]

SCALE OF INCHES.

objects, which are usually called scrapers, but which probably were scrapers and ignition agents combined (Fig. 16.
1, 4). A series of well-arranged specimens would prove this
development almost conclusively. On the same day that
the writer found a finely patinated scraper on a Neolithic
site in Suffolk, he asked Mr. Snare to make a strike-a-light.
The one object was an almost exact replica of the other.

The only difficulty arises with the horseshoe ' scraper '
of the Stone Age (Fig. 16. 1), but the puzzle is soon solved.
Mr. Snare says that the older workers at Brandon chipped
off the bulb and so rounded the flint (Fig. 16. 2). We
may, then, piece the connexions thus : The Neolithic
horseshoe scraper, or fire-kindler, came first ; afterwards
the Neolithic craftsman and his successors began to trim
the flake to a circular or oval form. The two patterns then
lasted for some time as fellows, until the oval or circular
kind ousted the other, and it was at this stage that the
modern tradition takes up the account. There has thus
been no gap.

This development is the more credible if we trace the
' flint-match ' backwards till we find it used as both strike-
a-light and scraper, and thence, before the coalescence of
uses, to a time somewhere in the Stone Age, when it was
a scraper only. At that period, any raw, untrimmed flint
served to obtain sparks for a fire.

To emphasize further the transition is perhaps needless,
but once more it must be insisted that the birth of the gun-
flint does not carry us back to the birth of the strike-a-light
also. The strike-a-light is not an economic Melchisedek,
without father or mother. A portion of the evidence
comes part way to meet the other portion.

. It may be assumed, says Sir John Evans, that flints have
been in use as fire-producing agents about 2,000 years.[8]
In the works of Pliny, Virgil, and Claudian there are distinct references to striking fire by means of flint and steel,
or flint and pyrites. A piece of steel, supposed to be a fire-
producer, was found along with Roman pottery at a Swiss
lake-station.[9] A Saxon grave at High Down, Sussex,
yielded similar objects.[10] French graves of the Merovingian

period give like records.[11] A bronze dagger and a nodule of pyrites were found together in a Cornish barrow, flint and a grooved mass of pyrites were associated with an interment at Basingstoke, whilst in several barrows of Derbyshire and Wilts. flint and pyrites were present.[12]

We have seen that even in the heyday of the gun-flint in England, common fire-arms were often primed with rough flints picked off the surface of the field, or perhaps with genuine Neolithic flakes, slightly adapted. Be this generally true or not—and from the accounts of aged men it is certainly true in part—stray gun-flints, recognizable by the pattern as such, are seldom found in the fields. During many years I have picked up only a few stray specimens.

How can we account for this astonishing scarcity? The gun-flint, as a finely-finished production, probably reigned little more than 150 years in England, but, even so, the rarity of lost and discarded specimens is a mystery, quite as troublesome as the puzzle about the destiny of lost pins and needles. Mr. Snare thinks that fowling-pieces were fitted up with a new flint before the keeper or sportsman set out, and on the return home the old flint would be cast away near a gun-room or outhouse, and trodden out of sight. This may be so, but it is a nice problem, and I cannot think the answer satisfactory.

The identity of shape and design between the ancient and modern strike-a-lights frequently perplexes the archaeologist, and causes him to hesitate before assigning a period to an implement. He has learnt that neither shape nor working, neither polish nor patina, is alone a criterion of antiquity.[13] Situation counts for much, but, through the admixture of objects of various ages, even this may fail. A wise combination of all the tests and all the local circumstances, together with such accidental aids as dendritic markings or possible documentary evidence, must be striven for. I once picked up on Beer Head a circular scraper, and to this day dare not say whether it is ancient, or a comparatively recent fabrication from an old gun-flint station which is known to have existed a mile or two away,

The associated flints—borers, knives, and combination tools—pleaded for antiquity, but the mention of these raises that wide question as to the date of the discontinuance of such implements, and to attempt an answer would carry us too far afield.　One can merely refer to the flints found in Saxon graves, placed there perhaps as agents for obtaining fire, and to the numerous examples picked up from Roman sites.　Evans has suggested that some of the Roman ' finds ' represent carpenter's tools—spokeshaves, smoothers, and scrapers.　Recently, Mr. W. A. Dutt has endeavoured to discriminate Roman flints by their harsh, unpatinated surfaces.　There are two possible sources of error : the site may previously have been Neolithic ; and the two tests proposed are not, taken alone, altogether decisive.

Similarity in form and design persisting through many centuries is indeed, to the archaeologist, a trite commonplace. The tourist through Cornwall may perhaps see ingots of tin, whose peculiar shape agrees with that which Posidonius, visiting Britain in the first century B.C., compared to a knuckle-bone [14] ($\dot{\alpha}\sigma\tau\rho\dot{\alpha}\gamma\alpha\lambda os$).　One ingot of this kind was dredged up in Falmouth harbour a few years ago, and bronze ingots, some 2,000 years old, and of the knuckle-bone pattern, were discovered in Crete in 1900.[15]

More than this : the Greek and Latin words for knuckle-bone signify, in the plural, ' dice,' because these objects were first made from such bones, by the simple process of numbering the four sides.　The Roman gambler's dice, the mediaeval diviner's ' properties ', the modern school-boy's fluted ' huckle-bones '—the road is clear and well-beaten.[16]

How such transitions occur is seen in our own day.　The gauge of the first railways was taken from the breadth of the old stage-coaches.　The railway-carriages, even now occasionally termed coaches, at first had steps up the back. The luggage was put on the top and covered with tarpaulin. The names of famous old stage-coaches were often trans-ferred to the new carriages.　The guard is still so called, though he no longer guards the mails.[17]　Facts like these help us to understand how our slow-moving forefathers kept to one pattern for flint fire-producers.

Leaving the chronological and the teleological arguments, we may look around for corroborative testimony.

First, let us consider the excavations on the hill-top at Grimes Graves, and see what may be learned therefrom. At this somewhat elevated spot, a generation ago, Canon Greenwell made those astonishing discoveries which are nowadays described in every archaeological textbook, but which will remain for ever marvellously instructive.

Reopening a collapsed pit, the explorer found that from the vertical shaft there ran short side galleries from three to five feet in height.   When the Neolithic miners had burrowed as far outwards from the boring as was safe or convenient, they sank fresh shafts and proceeded as before.

At the flint works of Cissbury, near Worthing, pits and relics of an allied character, though differing in detail, have been explored and described.[18] In Denmark, that country from which we learn so much pre-history, no similar pits are found, the explanation doubtless being that extensive layers of flint were easily accessible near the surface.[19]

On the whole, the structure of the Grimes Graves pits is therefore unique.   Besides large numbers of flint celts and other tools, the excavators found great quantities of unworked flint flakes, with chisels of bone and horn, and rudely-hollowed stones, reasonably supposed to be primitive lamps, intended for holding grease.   A somewhat similar group of relics was found at Cissbury.

There also came to light at Grimes Graves pickaxes made from the antlers of the red-deer (*Cervus elaphus*).   All the tines, except those of the brow, had been removed.   Two of these simple tools were laid tine to tine, as if they had been used respectively by right-handed and left-handed workmen. The roof of the gallery having fallen in, these picks and other objects had been entombed for perhaps 3,000 years.   When the passage was reopened, the picks were found to retain an incrustation of chalk, and, wonderful to relate, this coating plainly exhibited the impression of the workman's fingers, and even the very skin-prints.   The reason for this preservation seemed to be that the chalk had been transferred from the miner's moist hands to the shaft of the pick.[20]

As we shall not be able to return to the subject of primitive pickaxes, we will here note that they are frequently found in ancient settlements and workings. They have been dug out of barrows,[21] and Mr. F. W. Reader informs me that he saw them turned up during the excavation of the Romano-British village at Woodcuts (Dorset). Mr. A. Bulleid found others while exploring the Glastonbury crannog. Mr. Reader has also described a specimen found in peat near Braintree (Essex), associated with relics of the late Bronze or early Iron period.[22] Old tin ' stream-works ' in Cornwall,[23] copper mines near Llandudno, and a lead mine in Montgomeryshire[24] have also furnished specimens. In the Montgomeryshire workings a pickaxe of iron was also found —an interesting collocation, indicative of the turn-over of methods.

This last-named discovery has important bearings. For if the reader will visit the Geological Museum at Jermyn Street, London, and will compare the iron pick of the Brandon flint-miner with its prototype of deer-horn, the derivation of the one pattern from the other will be obvious (Fig. 17). Throughout the ages the primitive model has been preserved. The London street paviour may at times be seen using a pick of similar pattern, only in this case the head is secured to the handle by means of an iron ring. It was doubtless with a one-headed pick that the dene-holes and other old excavations were made—but this is to anticipate.

Another strange instance of conservatism as displayed in ancient industries is seen in the flaking hammers used to-day at Brandon. The head of one of these hammers is rhomboidal in longitudinal section, and the tapering shaft enters a hole of such slight diameter as to prove immediately its unsuitability for delivering a heavy blow without breaking.

The fact is that the object of a flaking hammer is not heavy percussion, but the concentration of the greatest possible weight within the least possible volume. The

handle is wanted to obtain precision, not momentum.[25]   The
smallness of the ' eye ', then, presents no difficulty.

Compare this flaking hammer with the old stone tool
which reached its greatest perfection in the Bronze Age.
Instantly the likeness appears.   There is much the same
general shape, but what at once impresses the observer
is the orifice in the ancient celt-like tool.   Boring was evidently started from opposite sides of the stone, leaving the
aperture so small at the centre as to suggest that a thong

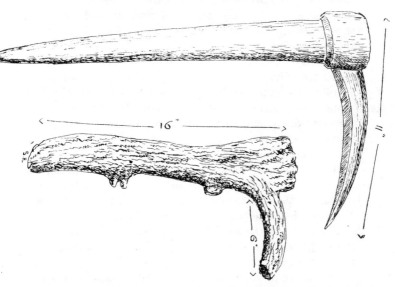

Fig. 17.   Prehistoric pick of deerhorn, and modern flint-miner's pick.
(From specimens in the Jermyn Street Museum, London.)

or sapling was used instead of a wooden handle.   Else the
shaft would snap on the least rough usage.

Now look at the iron tool, with its ridiculously small
aperture.   If we watch the knapper at work, the direct
reason is obvious.   The worker does not in reality strike
the flint core in the ordinary sense, he appears to let the
hammer fall, with a clean, smart tap, virtually by its own
weight :   *Tap, tap, tap !*   The knapper stops to pick up
a piece of flint, and the automatic action of his right hand

causes the hammer to make rhythmic beats and rebounds on the leather pad—*tup, tup, tup*—till presently the iron falls again on the flint—*tap, tap*—but no heavy thud, no ringing blow is ever heard.

Here, then, is the surface explanation. But we may be fairly certain that the weak handle is not a modern adaptation. At the back of the modern iron tool lies the tradition of the old broad, perforated celt, which, perchance, was a flaking-hammer in its day.

The pedigree may be followed further. The ancient bored hammers are not finely modelled and ground, they are coarse in design and workmanship. Earlier still the trimming is rougher, and beyond this again the perforation is rudimentary—there are only notches and depressions sufficient to give a grip to finger and thumb. Most primitive of all are the pebble hammer-stones of the Neolithic knapper, specimens of which, showing the battered ends, have been discovered in the Brandon district,[26] and in half a hundred other localities.

More comparisons remain. Mr. Skertchly has drawn up, in tabular form, a summary of the analogies between the primitive and the present industries. So illuminating is the analysis that the leading features will bear reproduction.

Suppose that a Neolithic flaker could be set to work beside the Brandon craftsman. The first man mines his flint at Grimes Graves, the second arranges for his material to be mined at Lingheath. The pits, abandoned, or in use, form a cluster in each case. Each miner goes directly to the ' floor ', to reach a particular stratum. Each burrows sideways from the central shaft, and fills up the passages with chalk waste. The shafts made by the men are both rectangular. The work is done with a one-sided pick ; that in the hand of one worker is of horn, the tool of the second is of iron.

The two men raise their flint to the surface without mechanical aid. They flake with peculiar hammers ; one hammer is of stone, the other is of iron. The centuried Neolith fabricates oval and horseshoe scrapers, his latest successor also makes the circular implements, but calls them strike-a-lights. Both men undercut the sides of the implements to give them finish.

Leaving the two men at work, we notice one or two other details. Though the Brandon knapper now uses a square-ended flaking hammer, yet the Old English tool was rounded at the end like its stone predecessor. This latter pattern was derived from the square-ended French type, which is found to be more serviceable for producing ' double-backed ' flints.

This French importation is instructive, for the French system of mining and working flint differs largely from the English in all the points just enumerated. There are also contrasts in the shape and workmanship of the implements. The reason is believed to be this : the French industry was started only in the year 1717, and had no old tradition to build upon, while at Brandon there was a long unbroken record of folk-memory. On the other hand, it must be confessed that the round-heeled gun-flint and strike-a-light of France seem to link up a little better with the horse-shoe scraper. Mr. Snare says that the retention of the rounded heel was the result of the use of a different kind of lock. Retention—notice the word : one naturally asks whether the French had not also some partial tradition of horseshoe scrapers which lingered from primitive times.

Some English flint-miners still occasionally use a rude candle-holder cut from a lump of chalk, much like those discovered at Grimes Graves and Cissbury;[27] and these, again, are suggestive of the soapstone lamps in which the Eskimo burns whale-blubber by means of a wick made of moss. One of the Irish bone-caves, too, has yielded a round stone lamp.[28]

We must now glance at a few dissimilarities of custom, which, however, are more apparent than real. The Grimes Graves pits are roughly funnel-shaped, and are nearly three times as wide at the top as those of Lingheath.[29] Experienced workmen, however, say that the funnel-shaped mouth is due to the action of frost and rain, with the subse-quent slipping of material. The modern rectangular pits tend to become rounded by obliteration of the angles. The burrows are also said to be somewhat different.

The ancient pits exhibit no stagings or ledges—at least, these are not now discernible. But Canon Greenwell thinks that they once existed. Indeed, a workman now living, one William Ashley, who helped in the exploration of Grimes Graves, asserts that in one pit a rude staircase, formed, not by steps cut vertically, but by a series running spirally round the shaft, was seen and noted by himself.

On the supposition that no steps existed, Mr. Skertchly suggests that the material was hauled to the top in baskets of skin or wickerwork, to which were attached ropes made of hide or vegetable fibre.[30] The point is not specially important—either plan is conceivable.

With these exceptions, the ground-plan of a Grimes Graves pit is ' not very unlike a shockingly bad drawing of a modern plan '.[31] Moreover, the ancient worker was accustomed to fill up his pits with waste material, and until recent years the modern miner acted likewise.

On the whole, Mr. Skertchly thinks that there has been an improvement in mining the flint, but a degeneration in the manufacture.[32] In passing, it may be observed that only celts and the larger implements seem to have been made at the Grimes Graves factory, arrow-heads and the smaller instruments being carried down to the banks of the Little Ouse and worked there.

There is good ground for concluding, from an expert workman's examination of the quality and texture of flint implements, that raw material was an object of barter, and found its way to districts in the South and South-East of England.

The analogies cited, which can scarcely be accidental, may now be supported by other considerations. The population of the Brandon district is said to contain a fair percentage of individuals of the short, dark-haired Neolithic type,[33] so frequently mentioned heretofore. Now we know that the knapping trade has descended from father to son for centuries. Mr. Snare himself can reckon six or seven generations of flint-workers in his ancestry. It is conjectured that the Neolithic originators of the industry tended to remain concentrated near Brandon, and that their children, though influenced by the successive inroads of later races, continued to practise the old art. It cannot be pretended, of course, that throughout the ages the flint trade has been confined to one unmixed people : the supposition is simply that a Neolithic type can still be distinguished.

If a parallel be sought, one might find it, haply, in the peculiar customs lingering among the coal-miners of the Forest of Dean. These customs are believed to date back to Roman, and perhaps even pre-Roman times. Physically, too, there are traces of persistence. The long heads, the dark hair, and the prominent cheek-bones of the inhabitants, have not, Dr. Beddoe thinks, appreciably altered since Neolithic times.[34]

Lastly, philology claims its word. Again and again has it been stated that some of the local terms employed by the Brandon workmen are possible relics of a non-Aryan (Neolithic) language—'outliers of the old pre-Aryan tongue'.[35] Would that this attractive theory could be upheld !

Not lightly to reject such a fascinating hypothesis, I have noted all the local words which seemed to be peculiar, and have, from time to time, asked Mr. Snare to supply all the dialect words bearing on the industry. We will now examine some of these words.

Groundage, for ' royalty ', is a good Teutonic word, and may be dismissed at once. The two terms *gain* and *fleet* represent varieties of meaning for which, as Mr. Skertchly observes, the language of the cultivated has one word only— ' near '. A *fleet* pit or layer (OE. *fléat*; cf. Dutch, *vloot* = shallow) signifies near the surface ; *gain,* a familiar Saxon word, means near in a horizontal direction. The *toe,* or bottom of the pit, has no recondite history. A layer of flint is called a *sase, saice,* or *sayce.* Nothing appears to be known of this word, which indeed has a very local restriction. Speaking under reserve, we doubt, however, whether the advocates of the Neolithic speech-theory would press its importance.

The words *paps* and *horns,* applied to flints with protuberances, present no difficulty. The whimsical word *gib,* given to flint ' when it is coloured like the Rock of

Gibraltar ', was coined by a knapper who had served as
a soldier and had ' seen the world '. How fortunate that
the origin of *gib* is known, else this word would be an alluring
pitfall to the philologist. The term *jarm*, meaning a massy
pillar of chalk left as a support between two ' burrows '
of a pit, has a curious look. A very little thought, however,
suggests that it is a provincial rendering of *jamb*. Turn
to the English Dialect Dictionary, and behold a corroboration of the belief. *Jarm* is actually cited as being used
for *jamb* in East Anglia, to denote vertical supports in pits
and quarries.

A heap of flint is called a *jag* or *jagg*, one and a half jags
making a horse-load. The etymology of *jag* is unknown,
but the word does not look mysterious. It may be ancient,
however, for some of these short words are from primitive
roots. *Jag* is used in the United States—carried thither,
one would conclude, by Suffolk immigrants to New England.
But alas, the word is recorded from a dozen other counties,
so that while the argument for a pre-Aryan origin might
conceivably hereafter be made good, the support for local
descent at Brandon is weakened. *Jag* has survived generally
just because it has survived, not because of any connexion
with the flint industry.

Knapper is considered by the best authorities to be of
onomatopoetic or echoic origin. It represents the sound
caused when an object is smartly struck. Echoic words
are usually very primitive, and *knap* might be of this group,
though, even then, not of necessity non-Aryan. We know
also that some words formed on this principle are comparatively modern. *Sosh*, a Brandon word used in the
sense of slanting or sloping, may perhaps be also imitative.

Strikers are used to draw flints from the counter, and
tellers are employed for counting—these words are self-
explanatory. A flint which breaks or curls or does not
' run clean ' during flaking is said to be *bruckly* (OE. *brucol*;
Scotch, *brukel*=fragile, uncertain, shaky). The word is
recorded from eight English counties, widely separated,
as well as from Scotland and Ireland.[36] *Dockey*, for meal-

time or ' leaving-off time ', looks like a word of modern
coinage, but I can glean no information respecting it.

In fine, the language test must be frankly abandoned.
Captivating as the idea may be at the outset, it is neither
honest nor useful to urge an unstable argument, even
should the story, through this omission, lose some of its
picturesqueness.

Having been compelled to reject the linguistic evidence,
a curious fact may be mentioned. The flint merchant and
the flint worker quote prices by the *mille* (1,000). This
fact seems to point to French influence, first felt, it may be,
a century and a half ago. In accordance with this system,
5 flints make a cast; 20 casts = 100; and 100 casts = 500.
The number 1,717, in the knapper's notation, reads one
thousand seven hundred, plus seventeen casts (or fives).

In adding columns of figures, a scale of fives is used until
the hundreds column is reached, when the ordinary decimal
notation is followed. One is almost tempted to connect this
notation by fives with the Neolithic folk, who, as we have seen,
are believed to have counted in this scale. The use of the
word *mille*, however, seems sufficient to banish the fancy on
the instant, unless indeed the custom were possibly grafted
on to prior usage. Some say that the term was introduced
by French workmen who came to Suffolk as prisoners of
war during Marlborough's campaigns.[37]

These trifles of antiquarianism, if not indeed illustrative
of the great age of flint-knapping, are entertaining to him
who loves the study of the shreds and vestiges of popular
custom. Such scraps often form the only evidence. To
most people the use of tally-sticks rests on hearsay only.
We know indeed that the ignition of a collection of tally-
sticks caused the destruction of the Houses of Parliament
in 1834. But that was not the last record of these ready-
reckoners. Less than forty years ago, the pound-keeper
at Withington, near Manchester, employed tallies. A split
stick was notched on each side, half being given to the
owner of the beast which was impounded, and half retained.[38] In 1905, I saw the tally-stick in daily use in
the shops of Bourges, a city of considerable bustle and

business.　Primitive methods are very obdurate in the more ancient callings.

I will conclude with a specimen of the flint-worker's book-keeping as an illustration.

This method of presenting a statement or bill is almost as crude as that of the tally-stick.　Mr. Snare avers that it has been in use for centuries.

It will be noticed that ○ stands for £; halving this, ⊖, we get 10*s*. ; a vertical stroke, |, is 1*s*. ; a horizontal stroke, —, is 1*d*.　A ' jag ' is ⌒ ; a half-jag, ⌒.　The knapper asserts that his oddly-formed 7 (seven), the only figure employed, is copied from the flint-winner's pick.　The X seems to be derived from ⫟⫟ repeated (although one would expect ⫟⫟⫟⫟ and then V for half X), as in counting at games, and as in the farmer's and publican's scores.

3 jags 'stone' ..	£1	1	0	would ap-	‖‖	or ⌒⌒⌒ .. ○·	
1½ jags	..	10	6	pear as		— or ⌒⌒ .... ⊖·≣
	£1	**11**	**6**		**○·⊖	·≣**

Flint-maker's tally :—

	s.	*d.*		
2,000 @	9	0	(or 2 mille at 4*s*. 6*d*.	XX .... ⫟⫟· ‖‖‖
1,500 @	6	6	per mille)	X⫟⫟ ... ⫟⫟· |·≣
3,000 @	9	3	would appear as	XXX ... ⫟⫟· ‖‖‖·≣
1,750 @	7	6		X7— .. ⫟⫟· ‖·≣
£1	**12**	**3**		**○·⊖‖·≡**

With the account of this primitive tally we finish the evidence—industrial, ethnological, and archaeological.　The facts virtually prove the proposition set out at the beginning of the chapter : that the manufacture of flint implements has gone on without any, or with but slight interruptions from prehistoric times to this moment.[39]

CHAPTER XI

ANOTHER ANCIENT INDUSTRY : THE VICISSI-TUDES OF MARLING

THOSE who are acquainted with the annals of agriculture need not to be told that scientific methods of restoring and renewing impoverished lands are quite of modern development. Writers of the Middle Ages, like Walter de Henley, give instructions for the physical improvement of the soil; but, did we not recognize the manifest earnestness of the authors, we should dismiss their recommendations as the dicta of schoolmen and charlatans.

There were indeed some exceptions. Occasionally the old essayists seemed to have garnered, from conversations with husbandmen, or to have stumbled upon by actual experiment, remedies both practical and sound.

Fitzherbert, in the sixteenth century (1523), was one of the heralds of the new ideas. Tusser, writing in 1562, embodied in sage apophthegms, duly and painstakingly rhymed, much of the tillage lore of his day.[1] About a century later (1649), Blith had advised a free use of such manures as chalk, lime, dung, marl, fish, woollen rags, seaweeds, ashes, and soot. Such advocacy, somewhat feeble and intermittent, was reciprocated by practice still more erring and casual.

Jethro Tull, in his ' Horse-Houghing Industry ' (1731), pleaded for systematic weeding of the field. Houghton, forty years later, speaks of folding sheep on turnips, and notices the spread of the potato. Soon followed Coke, with his conversations on tillage and stock-rearing, and Towns-hend, with his ' Norfolk ' or ' Four-course system ' of rotation of crops. Having once learned by actual experi-ment the value of extracting fractionally the soluble salts of the soil, and of giving the exhausted land an opportunity to recuperate, by other and more economical means than that of bare fallows, farmers were on the high road to success.

A long line of zealous students and experimenters now appeared, and on the farm itself practical workers developed the theories which were taught by these masters. Soon the labours of Liebig, Voelcker, Lawes, and Gilbert cast behind for ever the blundering half-truths of old time.

Having made this rapid survey, we now have to notice an astonishing fact. Athwart all the old errors and crudities, the ' accredited fallacies ', as a modern philosopher terms them, there run, from the earliest historical times to the present day, the strands of a cord which in places has been worn through. In plain words, primitive farmers discovered empirically the value of chalk as a corrective and fertilizer, but the knowledge was apparently afterwards lost, and then rediscovered.

A moment for preparation. What is the modern theory as to the services rendered by chalk ($CaCO_3$), and in a greater degree by quicklime (CaO) to various soils ? Briefly the theory is as follows : chemically, limestones, especially if pulverized, induce a reaction with the acids in the soil, and thus aid in decomposing organic manures, and in promoting the formation of nitrates. Sour, peaty soils, which by nature contain too much organic matter, are thus rendered sweet and harmless. Again, where the store of calcium carbonate, as an actual source of plant food, runs short, the chalk may supply the deficiency.

Physically, chalk and lime, added to a stiff soil, produce greater friability. For a hungry or sandy soil, impure chalk, represented by some form of marl, is to be preferred, as it encourages the adherence of the particles, and increases the water-absorbing capacity.[2] This end is secured by the clayey matter which the marl contains.

The earthy impurities in ordinary chalk—I am excluding the Chalk Marl—are but a small percentage of the whole. In the higher zones of the Upper Chalk, apart from the flints, which are siliceous, the insoluble residue of silicate of alumina and oxide of iron does not average more than two or three per cent. of the total.[3] The zone of *Marsupites testudinarius* is especially pure.[4] Analyses from lower zones of the Upper Chalk, from the Middle Chalk, and more particularly from the ' Grey ' or Lower Chalk, give much higher percentages of insoluble matter.[5]

With respect to the ' marl ' commonly so called—though the term is ambiguous and unscientific, very different results are found.   Thus, the Chalk Marl of Farnham contains 66 % of $CaCO_3$; the Clay Marl of Kimeridge, 34 % ; the Keuper Marl of Worcestershire, 8 %.[6]

On the other hand, take the Gault, which might casually be passed over as practically pure clay.   We get these results : The Gault of Surrey contains 10·5 % of $CaCO_3$; the Upper Gault of Bedfordshire contains 53·5.[7]

While, therefore, some deposits called marls are really clays, it will be seen that others, usually accounted clays, such as the Gault, are really marls.[8]

Obviously, the physical and chemical benefits accruing from the use of marl depend largely upon the particular kind of material chosen, as well as upon the soil to which it is applied.

Lest this introduction should be thought superfluous and discursive, its importance must be emphasized.   We shall find that agricultural writers rarely distinguish between chalk and the more impure limestones and chalky clays ; all are included under the term ' marl '.

Two distinct terms are therefore desirable, and I would suggest ' chalking ' and ' marling ' respectively.   This counsel is for the future; for the moment we must use discrimination in considering what the old authors mean by their one term, marling.

The ' Century ' Dictionary says that marl properly denotes an admixture of clay and carbonate of lime, but adds that the word is vaguely used.   The origin of ' marl ' is probably Celtic, but it is stated that the Welsh and the Irish Gaelic *marl* must be derived from the English term.[9]   The Welsh word seems to stand for alluvial earth.[10]   We are now prepared to meet with our word in company with a descriptive prefix, as rock, clay, chalk, white, or red marl.   Were the prefix always added, there would be less ambiguity.

The evidence available seems to show that marling and chalking have been to a large extent supplementary and contemporaneous, though not demonstrably coeval. Where chalk is locally absent, the farmer has employed some substitute most nearly allied. But the introduction of clayey marls is believed to be of later date than that of chalk.[11] Not only this, but the use of chalk has outlasted that of the numerous varieties of marl. The red-marl pits of Cheshire fell into disuse before the mid-nineteenth century. In that county the very practice is now forgotten, though a curious reminder exists in the custom of ' marling ' a man, that is, ' cheering him at dinners '—a relic of the days when gangs of marlers applauded the givers of largesse.[12]

The abandonment of marl in favour of chalk and lime was finally brought about because these were cheaper, and also more rapid and effective in their action.

I have mentioned the wide signification of the word ' marl '. When we come to look for either visible or documentary evidence of the extraction of chalk for a top-dressing, we are hampered by another doubt, caused by the careless use of the terms ' chalk pit ' and ' chalk quarry '.

It would be preferable to restrict ' chalk quarry ' to those places where chalk is obtained from the foot or the sloping sides of an escarpment, by means of large, open, vertical workings, in which crowbar and drill and gunpowder are employed, and in which advantage is taken of natural joints and bedding-planes. Then only can chalk be truly said to break up in blocks or squares (Fr. *carrière* ; Lat. *quadratus*).

Now, although no rigid rule can be drawn up, one commonly finds that ' chalk pits ', including both the old circular shafts to be shortly noticed, and the comparatively recent scoopings from the hill-side, were made to get material for ' marling ' (=chalking); while the huge, deep, straight-sided quarries have generally been worked for builders' lime and cement. Could we be always certain, therefore, that the terms ' pit ' and ' quarry ' were carefully used, we should have a clue to the age of particular workings, and to the probable practice or disuse of chalking and liming land.

It was my privilege, for many years, to be associated with Mr. G. W. Young in making the investigations preparatory to his masterly papers on the Surrey Chalk. Along with

Mr. W. Wright, the discoverer of *Marsupites* in Surrey, we visited some 400 chalk-pits and quarries. Many of these were disused and grassed over, or had large trees and undergrowth blocking up the hollows; others are still being worked. Besides visits to the Surrey pits, geological excursions, some of them extending to a week in length, were made to the Chalk in Dorset, Devon, Hants, the Isle of Wight, Kent, Sussex, and the North of Ireland.

In Surrey, one fact, apart from zonal and palæontological considerations, soon revealed itself. All around the sides of the Downs, in spots where the junction of the Chalk and the overlying Clay-with-flints forms tortuous, tongue-like projections on the geological map, the chalk had been excavated for spreading over the ploughed fields. The North Down farmers had discovered that near the line of junction the material could be most readily obtained. Where the chalk was needed chiefly for the uplands, which often have a tenacious capping of clay, there was no wisdom in digging for it at a lower level. Knowledge that had been lighted upon empirically had been handed down for generations, and was still sometimes put to the test. In one district, that of Coulsdon and Chipstead, by a remarkable coincidence—it was nothing more—out of a total of forty-eight pits, no fewer than thirty-five had been made within twenty feet of the 500-foot contour-line, which there runs along the clay-tipped shoulder of the hill. Out of a total of 179 chalk-pits visited in North-East Surrey, 109, disused or in working, lie on the upper slope of the clay-capped ridge, just below the Clay-with-flints.[13] This number has since been increased by a survey of the Guildford area.

Old Lincolnshire folk inform me that in their boyhood the arable lands of the Wolds, which have a good covering of clayey drift, were periodically ' caulked ' or ' limed ' (= chalked). The material was dug from surface pits, and laid in heaps on the fields before the frosts of winter. In the New Year, boys were employed to pick out the flints from the crumbling chalk before it was ploughed in. Doubtless this flinty chalk was obtained to a large extent, though not entirely, from the *Holaster planus* zone, which has recently been shown to run through the county from Louth to the Humber. The lower zones were also drawn upon. The pits or hollows, partially defaced by the plough, are still visible in the middle of many fields. Expense of cartage and bad roads prevented the application of chalk to those farms situated on the boulder clay and the alluvium of the plain below.

Everywhere field-names and road-names are found to connote the use subserved by the old pits, but we must interpret the map by our knowledge of the term ' marl '. I have noted only a few examples in Surrey : Marlpit Lane, near Stoats Nest, is one. Just above the village of Merstham are ' Marling Pit ' and ' Marling Glen '; these may refer to the true Chalk Marl, which was probably reached in that locality. Elsewhere, whether in Surrey, Dorset, or Kent, ' Marl Pits ' and ' Marl Pit Lanes ' most generally indicate pits of pure chalk.

Taking a big leap backwards, we will now discuss the history of marling and chalking.

The early Britons, as we learn from the elder Pliny, who wrote about A. D. 70, used marls as manures. He even credits the Britons and Gauls with the discovery of the art, but it is said by modern writers that the Greeks of Megara were also acquainted with marling.[14] Tacitus is thought to imply that the Rhine folk disdained to manure their fields,[15] but his words do not quite seem to bear that interpretation. Stand the fact as it may, Pliny is at some pains to describe the British system.

Clearly, too, this author speaks of both chalking and marling. He distinguishes six kinds of ' marl ' : (1) white (=chalk) ; (2) red ; (3) columbine (probably some white rock with glittering particles or crystals) ; (4) argillaceous ; (5) tufaceous ; (6) sandy.[16]

Chalk, which Pliny calls *creta argentaria*, is, he avers, greatly used in Britain, and is obtained from pits often a hundred feet deep. The passage, which is of prime importance in view of the subject of dene-holes, to be discussed in the next chapter, runs thus : '*Petitur ex alto, in centenos pedes actis plerumque puteis, ore angustatis* [alternatively,

ore angustis, or, apparently corrupt, *ore angustatur*] *intus,
ut in metallis, spatiante vena.'* [17] The readings vary a little in
different editions. It will be advantageous to carry this
description in the memory—wells narrow at the mouth,
frequently a hundred feet deep, spreading out within.

These various kinds of marls (*margae*) must be ploughed
into the soil—' *Omnis autem marga aratro iniicienda est* '.[18]
According to the old historian-naturalist, marl has a richness
and fatness because its particles are, as it were, condensed
into so many fatty kernels. This puzzle-headed, make-
believe theory shows how a practice may be rightly valued
before its explanation is understood. More to the point is
Pliny's note that British marls were so effective that no
person need marl twice in a lifetime, one dressing lasting
eighty years,[19] an over-estimate, as most authorities now
think.

In the British or Romano-British period, though precisely
during what length of time I cannot ascertain, British chalk
was an article of export, presumably for use as a manure.
Our information on the subject comes chiefly from Keysler,
who wrote in 1720, and De Montfaucon, who followed, in
1721.

It seems that about the year 1646 or 1647, a tempest
swept the coast of Zealand, in the Netherlands, and laid
bare a number of stone altars, which had previously been
buried in the sand. There were also exposed to view urns,
vases, and statues, the last representing the deity Nehalen-
nia or Nehelennia, the patroness of chalk-workers. This
goddess Nehelennia, the origin of whose name is disputed,
is usually sculptured with a dog by her side ; in her lap
is a basket of fruits symbolizing the fecundating power of
the earth.[20]

So far, the two old authors take us. A modern authority,
Kauffmann, asserts that Nehelennia is the goddess and pro-
tectress of sailors, and that her name means literally ' the
Seafarer ' (fem.). He adds that excavations on the island
of Walcheren, on the site of earlier finds, have indubitably
proved the existence of a temple of Nehelennia. There is
evidence that the temple was standing at the end of the

seventh century, when it was destroyed by Willibrord in the course of his missionary travels.[21]

One of the altars, Keysler relates, told how Secundus Silvanus, a British dealer in chalk, vowed an altar to the goddess after a successful voyage. This votive altar was in the form of a column, and the actual inscription ran :—

Deae Nehalenniae
Ob Merces Recte Conser
Vatas Secund. Silvanus
Nego + tor Cretarius
Britannicianus
V. S. L. M.

The authorities differ as to whether the + is merely a connecting link to form *negotiator*, or the Christian cross ; the + form, they say, was not uncommon instead of the т. We may read thus : To the goddess Nehelennia, for (his) goods well preserved, Silvanus Secundus, a British chalk merchant, willingly fulfilled (his) merited vow (*votum solvit libens merito*). The letters V. S. L. M. stand for the usual concluding formula. The chalk carried to Zealand, doubtless as marl, is thought to have been excavated in the Kentish districts of Dartford, Crayford, and Chislehurst ; indeed J. R. Green states this as a fact.[22] One fancies that reasonable inference regarding the matter is all that can be claimed. We know that these districts were important in Romano-British times. Not far away, at Upchurch, in the lower valley of the Medway, there was a factory where common pottery-ware was made. And incidentally, we note that Pennant, at the close of the eighteenth century, observed that Greenhithe exported vast quantities of chalk to China, for the manufacture, he supposed, of pottery.[23]

Pennant, too, had his conjecture about Nehelennia. The Roman name of Tadcaster, Yorkshire, was Calcaria. Quarries, if not of chalk, yet of a limestone adapted to the same purposes as chalk, which the name would imply, were worked there. A local place-name, Helen's Ford, might be, he supposes, a corruption of Nehelennia's Ford.[24]

Tracking the allusions from one writer to another, I find that Pennant's hypothesis is a repetition of, if not actually copied from, an idea put forward by Keysler, three-quarters of a century previously. Keysler, in his turn, manifestly made use of the earlier and well-known work of an Englishman, William Camden. There is in each case the reference to *Vadum fluminis Wherf* (the ford of the Wharfe), *infra Wetherbeiam oppidum* (below the town of Wetherby).[25] Camden gives the additional information that Roman coins and other relics had been dug up in the vicinity, and that traces of old entrenchments could be discerned.

There are thus grounds for supposing that the British tradition of marling lasted into Roman times, for it would be too fantastic a conclusion that husbandmen who traded in this kind of fertilizer knew not how to use it themselves.

In the letters of the German savant, Thomas Reinesius (b. 1587, d. 1667), there is an enlightening passage which seems to have been hitherto overlooked. Reinesius states that chalk was formerly dug from pits in Britain, and that this was especially the case at the hill which Sorbiodunum (= Sarum), or *vetus Sarisburia*, at first occupied. Great abundance of chalk existed there, and it was exported to other countries (*indeque in alias regiones exportabantur*). Examining Old Sarum to-day, I find that a vast amount of chalk must have once been dug below the camp towards the West and South, and even close to the stronghold, for the outer rampart has in one place been seriously mutilated. There is also a huge pit inside the fort. Apparently relying on Camden, Reinesius says that an English versifier of the twelfth century—the date is noteworthy—exercised his wit in this epigram concerning Sorbiodunum :—

> Est ibi defectus lymphae sed copia cretae ;
> Saevit ibi ventus sed philomela tacet (*or* silet).[26]

That is, 'The hill had plenty of chalk, but no pure spring water ; there the wind raged, but the nightingale was silent.' Who was this writer ? One suspects Alexander Neckham (A. D. 1157–1217), whom Camden is fond of quoting, but I cannot find the lines, nor do the multitudinous readers of *Notes and Queries* seem able to help.

These old accounts are obviously to be trusted, for Keysler,

after quoting Reinesius, volunteers the statement that, at
the coast, where the hills trend seaward, the chalk is diversified by distinct bands of black flint (*creta ipsa variis nigri
silicis distincta ordinibus*). This little touch stamps the
narrative as a true one.

These old authors repeat Camden's speculation that
Sarum owes its name to the dryness of its situation. Imbued
with the philological spirit then prevalent, Camden saw an
analogy between Sarum and ' Mount Seir, most desolate '
(Ezek. xxxv. 7), a piece of pure guesswork.[27] We smile
at Camden's crude philology, but the fact remains that
the new city of Salisbury had to be built because the old
site was endowed with far too much wind and far too little
water.

The name Calcaria, already noted, was derived by Pennant
from a British word, *calch*, chalk.[28] There appears to be
no proof of the existence of such a word, unless it were
a translation of the Latin *calx, calcis* (= lime). The earliest
known forms are the A.S. *calc, cealc*, &c. (cf. Yorks. and
Lincs. *cauk*). At an early period, *calc* (= lime) became the
equivalent of the Latin *creta* (= chalk). Thus in an Old-
English vocabulary, A.D. 1050, *cœlc-stone* is considered to
represent limestone.[29] In the South of England, where the
word perhaps arose, ' chalk ' is the most common form of
limestone, and may therefore be the rock first so indicated.

Was the practice of marling held in favour in Anglo-Saxon
times, say from the Roman departure till the ninth century ?
The answer is a little wavering. Comparisons with the
later history of marling would seem to show that folk-
memory was at fault, and that the practice temporarily
died out. The course of events runs probably thus : The
Britons practise the art, the Roman agriculturists look on it
with unfriendly criticism, anon they recognize it, and the
custom becomes popular. Under official guidance chalk
is exported, and at home, chalking the land is over-done
and carried to extremes. A revulsion sets in, chalking
falls under a ban, and tradition, valuable only while the
custom lasted, becomes quite forgotten by the common
people. Moreover, if it be true, as asserted by Tacitus,

that the Germanic peoples did not marl their fields, it is not likely that the Saxons would at first take very kindly to the British custom.

Against this view there are one or two claims to be weighed. Mr. H. B. Woodward says that marl-pits were opened in Saxon times, and were known as *cealc-seathas* and *cealc-grafan*.[30] In considering this statement, much would depend on the precise range attached to the phrase 'Saxon times'.

Next, there is possibly some evidence obtainable from charters. The 'Swallow-hole' in Camden Park, Chislehurst, a depression very doubtfully artificial, is supposed to be referred to as a local boundary in a charter of Ethelbert, A. D. 862. In describing a grant of land to ' Dryhtwald the theyn at Bromleag ' (Bromley), these words are used : *'fram swelgende cregsetna haga to sioxslihtre'* (from the Swallow, the Cray-settler's dwelling, to the gibbet mark). A slight variation occurs in what appears to be a confirmation of the grant, A. D. 987 : ' *from Swelgende crægsetenahaga to siox slihtre.*'[31] If the interpretation ' Swallow ' be correct, the allusion is not strictly germane to our subject, for a swallow-hole is essentially a natural feature. We may conclude that evidence is lacking to prove the practice of chalking from the sixth to the ninth centuries. By the time the Conquest is reached, however, we are again within earshot of talk about marling.

Old Norman leases contain covenants to ensure the marling of the land.[32] Certain letters written in A. D. 1222 to Ralph de Nevil, Bishop of Winchester, by his steward, contain frequent notices of marling, with repeated requests for additional ' mares to draw the carts '.[33] The monastic chronicles cited by Seebohm, containing references to marling, belong apparently to this period.[34] In A. D. 1225 a Statute of Henry the Third gave every man leave to sink a marl-pit in his own ground.[35] A ' Swellinde Pit ', situated either at Bickley or Chislehurst, comes into ken about the middle of the thirteenth century. In a grant dating some-where between A. D. 1252 and A. D. 1274, one Andreas assigns to the Bishop of Rochester and his successors a rent of eightpence out of the ' Marlera ', situated *'apud Swellinde pette in villa de Chiselherst.*'[36]   In this document, at any rate, a genuine pit seems to be denoted.   The *Statutum Walliae*, A. D. 1283, commands the sheriffs and coroners to inquire as to the existence and condition of marl-pits near the public way (*iuxta iter publicum*).[37]   Leases drawn up during the Edwardian period often make the use of marl compulsory.[38] The fashion of marling and chalking evidently reached its zenith at this era.

The custom thereafter began to fall in popular esteem. One reason assigned is the want of confidence between landlord and tenant.   Leases were short, and tenants-at-will feared to make improvements.[39]   One partly suspects, also, a period of over-marling followed by disgust and apathy ; for chalking, at least, may be either a boon or a bane.   The custom, says Gervase Markham, whose ' Inrichment of the Weald of Kent ' first appeared in 1625, became obsolete after the Wars of the Roses.[40]

Maister Fitzherbert, who flourished nearer the period (A. D. 1523) assigned, gives another cause for the failure—he says bluntly that it was ' ydleness '.   This quaint old writer does, indeed, furnish a subsidiary reason, but it was a reason which would apply in part to all the earlier periods, namely the cost of labour, material, and cartage.   He remarks, ' Also in Cheshiere, Lankishiere, and other Countreys, they use for manure a kind of blewe Marl-like earth which they call Marle ' ; this material, he adds, is excellent, but ' exceeding chargeable '.   An acre of land required one load of marl —not chalk, and this cost from three to eight shillings.[41] Lime was also used, and cost about 1*s.* 2*d.* per quarter, the owner supplying kilns, fuel, and raw material.[42]   ' Lime, even close to the kiln, was dearer than Oats '—an odd but telling comparison.

Except possibly by academic writers, chalking and marling were now for some time overlooked.   The memory of the people had failed again.   It may be, indeed, that the tradition was not everywhere and altogether extinct, for Lambarde, journeying through Kent in 1570, eighty-five years after the defeat of the last Yorkist sovereign at Bosworth Field, appears to have caught a faint echo of the

Mediaeval practice. The pits at Crayford, says he, ' in the opinion of the inhabitants were in former times digged, as well as for the use of chalke towards building, as for to marle (or amend) their arable lands therewith.' [43]

Where a chalk surface remained exposed, as in a quarry, we can well imagine the natives making a clever guess, even though ignorant of the actual tradition. Whether the pits at Crayford were of this type or not is not clear. It is, however, noteworthy, that Lambarde's own opinion, as will be seen in the next chapter, differed from that of the Kentish folk, and one rather supposes that the ' pits ' were vertical shafts leading to underground excavations. Were this the case, the country people could see no actual exposure of chalk, and to account for the local story we may conclude that a lingering tradition existed.

But it is to the wiser husbandmen of the seventeenth century, who had probably turned again to read the older writers, that we owe the revival of marling. Ready listeners were found ; farmers instinctively discovered that something was lacking in the soil. Markham (1625), in the work already quoted, definitely asserts that the use of marl, which word, with the capricious licence of his day, he variously spells *marl, marle, maile, mayle,* and *male,* had only been reintroduced some thirty years previous to the date of his writing. Yet he notices that some of the disused pits contained trees 200 to 300 years old. This manner of bettering the land was therefore, he maintains, not first discovered in his time, but was a relic of ancient ' gainage or husbandry ', which was ' given over and gone out of use ', during the Barons' War and the Wars of the Roses.[44] If we take thirty years off Markham's date, we are within a quarter of a century of Lambarde's ' Perambulation '—no great gap.

Walter Blith, in 1649, actually uses our term ' chalking '.[45] The practice, he says, was good for the father and bad for the son. This proverb was afterwards often reversed, in allusion to the initial expense. Blith distinguishes chalking from marling, for he says, ' Marle is also a very gallant thing,' and proceeds to enumerate several kinds.[46]

Two years later (1651), Hartlib also makes the distinction. There is in Kent, he tells us, a hard, strong, dry 'chalke', which is used for walls and in lime-burning, but ' helpeth little for the land '. But there is likewise a ' small, unctuous chalke', which 'killeth rushes and broome '.[47] Then there is lime simply. Next come several sorts of marl, and ' in Essex the scourings of their ditches they call Marle, because it looketh blew, like it '.[48]

Glancing over the landscape, the students of the Commonwealth era could see, as Markham had done previously, abandoned pits wherein grew huge oaks, the growth of centuries. In writing about that period, John Aubrey tells us that some labourers of Smallfield, in Surrey, looking for a convenient place for a lime-kiln, grubbed up a dead oak, and found such a structure ready to hand, with ' lime-stones ' in it, 'disused beyond the memory of man.' [49]

This type of pit, with descendants of the old trees, and mayhap, occasionally the original saplings, now represented as oaks and yews of immense girth, is still to be seen in abundance. The pits are often, I believe, as old as the fifteenth century. Morton speaks of ' unsightly ' pits in Kent, Surrey, and the Weald.[50]

About a quarter of a mile South-East of Chipstead, in Surrey, there is, for instance, a pit whose antiquity is well attested by half a score of old yews. Hoskyns, that prescient Herefordshire squire, writing over seventy years ago, describes marl-pits apparently as venerable in aspect at that date as they are now. From the details of Hoskyns's life as given in the ' Dictionary of National Biography ', it would seem that his ' Clay farm ' was in Warwickshire, but the account would apply equally well to Surrey. He speaks of great yawning cavities in every field of five or six acres, deep enough to drown the weathercock on the church steeple, and wide enough to accommodate the church as well. Loads of clay, piles of felled timber, and heaps of useless pollards were thrown into the ' voracious depths ' of one pit, but it was still unfilled.[51] Incidentally, we notice why pits are not even more common than they are ; we learn, too, why the soil sometimes gives way, and temporarily engulfs horse and plough together.

There is some suspicion that, even after the Caroline period of revival, marling again had a downfall.   Chalk continued to be extracted for other purposes, it is true.   Dutch writers, describing the expedition of their countrymen to the Thames and Medway in the reign of Charles the Second, mention lime-kilns, which they call *kalkovens*.[52]   The parish registers of Grays, on the Essex side of the Thames estuary, speak of one ' Smith, a Lym Burner ', who was buried at that place in 1691.[53]   There can be little question that the industry has been carried on in those districts at least ever since those days.   In Chapter IX we saw that the Dorking pits go back to about the same period.

The case for lime-burning since Stuart times is therefore sound.   But who was responsible for the ' restitution of decayed intelligence ' concerning marling, as Richard Verstegan finely would have it ?   Lord Townshend, who (*c.* 1728) reintroduced marling into Norfolk,[54] seems to be the true claimant, that is, if we understand marling to be a scientific practice.   Arthur Young says that Townshend thus turned three or four hundred thousand acres of waste into gardens.

The custom became popular again.   Cobbett, in his ' Rural Rides ' (a work representing notes collected in 1830, but written about a decade earlier), relates how the Hampshire farmers fetched chalk many miles, and spread it over their fields, often spending as much as £16 per acre.   ' Being free chalk,' he adds, ' [it] is reduced to powder by the frost.' [55]

From Vancouver, who wrote in 1813, we learn whence some of this Hampshire chalk was obtained.   It was fetched from the tunnel of the Basingstoke Canal, although a supply could often have been procured nearer home.   The theory was that chalk brought up from some depth powdered better and formed a more satisfactory manure.[56]   This idea also led to the sinking of vertical shafts into the chalk, from the bottom of which the material was hauled by the aid of a windlass and a pair of baskets.[57]   The reader is begged to pay close attention to this method, as it will have an important bearing hereafter. Vancouver, by the way, puts the duration of the benefits of marling (= chalking) at from twenty-five to thirty years ; [58] Pliny, it will be remembered, made it eighty years.

From the Georgian rebirth may perhaps date some of the saws about marling, others are probably earlier. The Cheshire proverb,

> He who buys marl,
> May buy the land,

while referring to the beneficial results, slyly indicates the seriousness of the outlay. A slight variant runs,

> If you marl sand, you may buy the land.

Further rhymes are :—

> If you marl moss,
> There is no loss ;
> If you marl clay,
> You fling all away.

The context will usually show whether chalking or clay marling is intended.

Yet in spite of all this folk-wisdom, here and there marling again became a lost art. It was costly ; lime was more effective ; foolish farmers, bettering their instructions, marled land that did not require such an alterative. Even to-day one sees fields, of which the chalk subsoil lies only two or three inches below the surface, treated with a liberal top-dressing of chalk. In some places, moreover, there is the old preference for chalk obtained from some depth, as being ' fatter ' or ' stronger '.

We will now pause to summarize the ups and downs of marling.

There is clear evidence that the early Britons, using that word in its wide sense of pre-Romans, were well acquainted with the use of marl. The material was at first probably applied on the open uplands. Various lines of evidence indicate that the downs and moorlands, such as the North and South Downs, the Cotswolds, the Yorkshire Wolds and Moors, were the tracts which were first tilled. The wood-lands below were haunted by wolves and bears ; often, too, they were marshy and unsuited for tillage. Stone axes, and even bronze celts, would make little headway against the forest primeval. The presence of old cultivation terraces, of ditches and earthworks and barrows, of scattered stone tools, considerable flint factories and of abundant calcined flints, point to the hill-tops as the sites of the earliest settlements, and the analogous customs of communities in a like comparative stage of development bear out the belief.[59] With a small population, fresh land could always be obtained.

The general lack of organization before and subsequent to the Roman withdrawal, together with the disturbance caused by the Teutonic invasion, may have broken the continuity of marling.   Whether the custom was generally discarded cannot be determined. Under the Teutonic method of settlement villages sprang up in the valleys. The woodlands, hitherto inaccessible and neglected, were partially cleared, and virgin soil was opened up by the plough.   For the time, artificial manures were not necessary, but whether they were used, and whether the exportation to Zealand still went on, are questions yet to be answered.

The newly-tilled soil became partially exhausted as the centuries passed, and in the late Saxon or Saxon-Norman times the art of marling was again pursued.   The industry flourished, fields were lavishly treated, expense was not spared.   But about the end of the fifteenth century, cost of digging and haulage, agrarian troubles, ' ydleness,' and civil war, produced a reaction equally pronounced.   Under Henry the Eighth, pasture began to supplant arable farming, and sheep took the place of men.   Once more marling became obsolete or obsolescent, and, except perhaps in isolated spots, all recollection of it perished.

Under the Commonwealth and the later Stuarts, writers tried to win back marling to the husbandman.   The breaking up of the pastures in the eighteenth and nineteenth centuries, and the introduction of high farming, based more and more on scientific principles, revived the application of chalk and marl, for the agriculturist was eager to secure the greatest yield of wheat, barley, and turnips. Thereafter marling has had many vicissitudes. There was perhaps local unpopularity, but no complete abandonment.

Were one concerned to prove the continuity of the custom, the evidence is enough to make a fair fight. But to take facts as they are, it seems more probable that the practice of marling has been discovered and given up more than once.[60] If it has never died out entirely, its foothold during one or two periods has been local and precarious, in the midst of a general arrest elsewhere.

Stoppage, followed by rediscovery, may be illustrated by the industry of coal-mining. There is great probability that coal was employed in Roman times, particularly near the line of the Great Wall extending from the Tyne to the Solway Firth, for coal, ready for use, has been found among the fortifications.[61] Recent researches at Warrington seem to be confirmatory. But from the Roman period to about the year A. D. 1200 there appears to have been a complete cessation of coal-mining. A well-known passage in the Anglo-Saxon Chronicle seems to refer to peat, not to coal, and the supposed allusions in the Norman period are meagre and ambiguous.[62] The reawakening of the industry was forced on the unconscious population by economic needs.

A second example of rediscovery is afforded by the history of canals. The first canal made in Britain is supposed to be the Fossdyke, which connects Lincoln with the Trent. Its great antiquity is accepted, and it is usually attributed to the Romans.[63] Yet it was not till the eighteenth century that anything worthy of note in canal construction was again mooted. The introduction of railways was detrimental to the canal system, which, though never altogether discarded, fell generally into abeyance. We are now witnessing a second revival of canals. The death of an industry, followed by rebirth, is not, therefore, unknown, but we must always leave room for the possibility that fresh facts may close up apparent industrial breaks.

In what way did our forefathers excavate chalk for manuring the soil ? The earliest method, if we accept Pliny's account as based on personal observation, or on the word of honest witnesses, was by means of shafts and subterranean chambers.

Now it is noteworthy that Vancouver found a similar mode in use in Hants a century ago. It even obtains to-day at Hemel Hempstead in Herts., where shafts from fifty to ninety feet deep, having lateral galleries at the base, are sunk to get chalk for lime-burning.[64] The practice is also recorded from the neighbourhood of West Wycombe, Bucks., and Cudham, Kent.[65]

In 1887, Mr. F. J. Bennett read before the Essex Field Club a paper on 'Chalk-Wells', in which he carefully described a similar method of obtaining chalk in the district around Newbury (Berks.). Roughly, the plan pursued is this : A shaft, about four or five feet in diameter, is sunk into the chalk to a depth varying from fifteen to forty feet, according to the thickness of the overlying clay or sand. A 'thin-skinned' soil, where the Chalk is only just covered by other deposits, would obviate deep boring ; fifteen to twenty feet would be the depth under these conditions. But where there is a capping of Tertiaries, the greater limit would be reached.

From the base of the shaft, headings are driven. These are, at first, level, but they soon incline upwards and form a sloping plane down which the chalk slides into boxes placed at the foot of the shaft. After sufficient chalk has been extracted, parts of the quoins or divisions between the headings are knocked away. The 'well' then falls in and leaves a 'dell' or hollow in the surface of the field above. These dells, often fifteen to twenty yards in diameter, are usually so shallow as not to interfere with the work of the plough (Fig. 18).[66]

In Surrey I have gleaned a goodly sheaf of traditions concerning chalk-wells or 'draw-pits', formerly in use, and now all but forgotten : not a single example appears to have been known for many years past.

It is of prime importance to see how far back this mode of extraction can be followed. The correspondent who reported the case from Hemel Hempstead said that the practice had been going on for centuries, and though he appended no proof of his statement, the assertion may ultimately be found to agree with other facts. But the question is provocative of much debate.

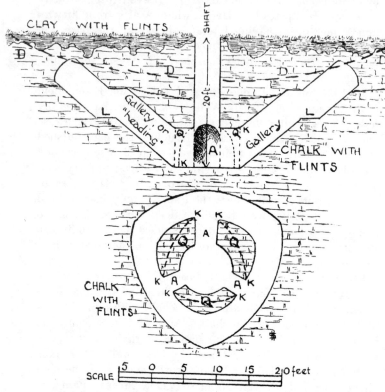

Fig. 18. Section and plan of a Chalk 'well' at Sevenacres, near Newbury. Q, quoins or piers. A, angles. L, landings. Three angles (A) were driven at the bottom, and the work was continued up the steep slope to the level or landing, L. Then the upward work was resumed till the 'headings' were united, forming a circular gallery which communicated with the shaft by means of the headings. Afterwards the quoins (Q) were cut away as far as safety allowed, viz. up to the dotted line, K. Ultimately, the workings collapse, leaving a dell or hollow (DD) at the surface. [From a drawing by F. J. Bennett and H. A. Cole: *Essex Naturalist,* I (1887), p. 262. By the courtesy of the Essex Field Club.]

On the one hand, so far back as 1782, Pennant noted that this was the mode of getting chalk at Redbourn, in the same county as Hemel Hempstead.[67]

Yet Mr. Bennett was told (1887) at Hampstead Norris (Berks.), that the method had been known in that neighbourhood for the previous sixty or seventy years only. Mr. Bennett himself thinks that it may date from the middle of the eighteenth century, and that it is decidedly more recent than the plan of taking chalk from open pits.[68] Daines Barrington, in 1785, discovered pits at Little Coxwell (Berks.), apparently disused chalk-wells. Similar reports and opinions concerning the age of the wells come from other localities. Should, however, the Hemel Hempstead, or any other, chalk-wells be definitely proved to go further back, these negative examples count for nothing ; a greater age must be admitted.

Granting the genuineness of Pliny's information, we must concede that the Britons obtained chalk by the sinking of shafts. A like method is partially in vogue to-day ; and yet the modern system does not appear to be a true descendant of the ancient one. It would be pleasant, from the point of view of folk-memory, to believe in the claim ; but it seems more likely that there has been a break, and that men have readopted an old practice after it had lain dormant perhaps for a dozen centuries.

Nor do chalk-wells seem to have been general over the whole chalk area, nor the periods when they were in fashion to have been altogether coincident during modern times. The system has died out in one neighbourhood, to be started in another not far distant. If there ever existed itinerant ' well ' sinkers, we might easily account for such vagaries.

In one place, there is a tradition stretching back for generations, in another the practice falls within living memory. In a third locality, only dells or depressions, oftentimes tree-clad, remain to tell of vanished customs.

In Berkshire, the chalk-well and the open pit may sometimes be seen in the same field. Around Hungerford and Lambourne, the open pit is preferred.[69] Where there is a considerable quantity of superincumbent sand or Clay-with-flints, the shaft finds favour, since the shallow surface pit would involve the removal of much useless material before the chalk is reached.

Behind the draw-pits and chalk-wells of recent tradition there is evidence of earlier examples, which may possibly harmonize with the supposed antiquity of the custom at Hemel Hempstead. In North-East Surrey, which the writer has tramped almost field by field, there are to be seen round pits, with no entrance by cartway. Huge old trees, including such slow-growers as the yew, thrive in and around these dells. Similar pits may be seen on the Chilterns in Buckinghamshire. It seems conclusive that these depressions are the result of the sinking of the ground around old shafts and adits. Admitting this, I should estimate the draw-pit system to date back some four centuries, with probable local breaks. Nearer to Pliny's description one could scarcely arrive at present. The later downland farmers have used the hill-side quarry, or have roughly scooped out the chalk, leaving irregular trough-shaped hollows on the brow of the escarpment, or again, they have simply bought their material from one or other of our huge lime-pits.

A third method of working chalk has been followed in a few places. It consists in driving tunnels or galleries into the sides of chalk hills. Like the chalk-well system, the evident purpose is to avoid the removal of overlying beds of gravel or sand—the ' uncallow ' of the Norfolk labourer. Mr. H. B. Woodward says that the tunnel system is now less common than formerly.[70]

A variation of this plan is to be seen at brick-works at Wickham Lane, Plumstead, Kent. There the passages are reached by stairs descending one hundred feet from the surface, so that we get a combination of the draw-pit and the hillside gallery. At Welling, in the same locality, similar workings are approached by means of a deep shaft. These latter workings, the proprietor informs me, have been opened only fifty years, but occasionally subsidences betray the presence of older galleries. There are many points of correspondence between the Wickham Lane and Welling mines on the one hand, and those of Chislehurst, soon to be discussed, on the other. In certain details, such as the height of the roof and the absence of beehive terminations, there are variations from the Chislehurst plan, but in general

Fig. 20. The Chislehurst chalk mines, showing two chalk tables or 'bottom canches', popularly known as 'altars.' The flint band is again seen near the top. [From a photograph by G. J. Mansell, Jan. 1904.]

Fig. 19. The Chislehurst chalk mines, showing the junction of several galleries. A prominent band of flint is seen near the roof, on the right. [From a photograph by G. J. Mansell, Jan. 1904.]

the comparison holds good. Incidentally, one notices that the chalk at Wickham Lane and Welling is excavated for brick-making, not for marling.

At Yattendon, in Berkshire, similar subterranean chalk galleries of unknown age were rediscovered in 1822 by the accidental collapse of the roof. Inquiry showed that there was no eighteenth-century tradition respecting these galleries; nevertheless, on the walls dates were carved, proving that the tunnels were known in the early seventeenth century. Doubtless the workings themselves were much older.[71]

The most famous example of the tunnel system is to be seen in the disused workings at Chislehurst, Kent, to which allusion has just been made. As these mines have been the subject of prolonged controversy among archaeologists, something may be said concerning them.

The Chislehurst galleries have been bored laterally into the hill which is formed by the outcrop of the Chalk on the borders of Camden Park. At the main entrance to the workings there is, overhead, a capping of Thanet Sands, about six feet in depth. As one ascends the hill by the roadway to Chislehurst village, he is led to infer, rightly, that this Tertiary sand-bed becomes thicker and thicker. Hence, for whatever purpose the chalk was originally mined, it is manifest that the operators were anxious to attack the hill where the Tertiary layer would present little hindrance, and that position was at the foot of the ridge and immediately below the outcrop of sand.

The galleries are from ten to twelve feet high, and average about nine feet in width at the floor, but they taper to about seven feet towards the roof (Fig. 19). Near the roof there is a prominent band of flint, fairly persistent throughout the workings. The vault is, of course, formed of solid chalk, which has usually been left sufficiently thick to support the pressure of the overlying Thanet Sands. Additional support is afforded by the huge, irregular, trapezoidal piers of chalk which separate the intersecting passages. Occasionally the sandy mass has, in later times, burst through some weak portion of the roof, and has formed a cone of débris on the floor below. Here and there the explorer encounters sharp turnings in the passages. Short side corridors are followed, torch in hand, and are found frequently to end in semicircular recesses, having coved or domical roofs. Within these recesses are seen, now and again, ' tables ' of chalk, formed by allowing several feet of material nearest the floor to remain untouched (Fig. 20).

The workings, as a whole, form a series of labyrinthine underground arcades, whose walls exhibit various degrees of fineness of tooling. A single visit is apt to bewilder the beholder, and to give him exaggerated notions both of distance and complexity. It is as if he had been traversing vast catacombs of great age.

In one place there is a particularly deep ' well ', or boring, having the upper part ' steined ', or lined with squared flints. The mouth of the well is protected by a parapet of brick rising about a yard above the ground-level of the passages.

Certain parts of the excavations are said to represent mutilated dene-holes, cut into when the passages were made, and therefore anterior to those passages. With a few probable exceptions, I think the existence of these dene-holes a little doubtful. One shaft, apparently of true dene-hole type, is visible on the hill-side, but only a thorough exploration of the grounds of Camden Park would settle the question. Should many dene-holes be ultimately found in this area, their connexion is not inexplicable ; we should have what Mr. W. T. Vincent has called ' a con-geries of dene-holes worked into galleries '. The woodland in Camden Park is indeed full of depressions, some of which Mr. W. Whitaker believes to be natural ' swallow-holes ', whilst others may be old pits.[72]

The present writer must frankly confess that, having originally doubted whether the Chislehurst tunnels could have been excavated simply to obtain chalk, he was com-pelled after frequent visits and careful study to alter his opinion. Most of the lingering mysteries were dispelled when, in January, 1904, he assisted Mr. W. J. Maxton, of Richmond, to make an exploration of the galleries. By careful pacing and by use of the compass, a plan of the main passages was drawn to scale, and thus were scattered the fables which have grown up and confused successive parties of visitors.

Since that tracing was made, an accurate survey has been carried out by Mr. T. E. Forster, and the result, in plans and sections, has been submitted to the British Archaeological Association. In all, Mr. Forster surveyed about twenty acres ; the remaining area is undefined, some of the alleys being blocked by water, lying waist-deep.

The first fact which came out clearly was that the workings, though extensive, covered a smaller area than had been thought, considering the statements which were current, and the ideas which might have been formed from haphazard ramblings.

To call these galleries ' caves ', as is the popular habit, is to prejudice the whole question at the outset. To look about for probable events in the dim past of the pre-Roman period, and then to connect these happenings with the so-called caves is, in the absence of reasonable confirmatory facts, mere folly. To allege, as has been done, that the passages extend fifteen, or eight, or even five miles, that they run on to a point below Bexley Heath, is not simply toying with the shreds of folk-memory ; it is a wild attempt to fabricate a tradition : ' Thy wish is father, Harry, to that thought.'

The tables in the semicircular niches, which have been foolishly called ' altars ', and have been ludicrously associated with Druidical sacrifices, seem to have originated incidentally, or rather, as a natural result of the methods employed.

In the paper which Messrs. R. H. and T. E. Forster read when their plan was presented, the authors asserted that these tables, or ' bottom canches ', as they would be called if occurring in old Northumbrian coal-workings, are due simply to the fact that the topmost chalk was removed first, and then, for some reason, the bottom portions, in these particular recesses, though by no means in all, were not removed. The domical or beehive shape of the alcoves was the result of this system.[73]

If, as I suggest, a short single-headed pick, of the Brandon type (Fig. 17), was employed—and considerations of working space seem to justify the assumption—the beehive outline would almost necessarily follow.   The miner, beginning to work with limited room for his pick to swing, struck out towards all parts of the arc within reach.   As he removed the uppermost chalk his sweep widened, and the curvature being maintained, there resulted those finely shaped chambers which the fancy might turn into a succession of apses— the chevet of a subterranean cathedral.

It must be stated that an ordinary double-headed pick is used in the modern mines at Wickham Lane and Welling. In those mines, however, the tooling is coarser, and there are no beehive recesses, square ends taking their place.

The compass showed that the ' altars ' (=canches) are not orientated, thus upsetting another popular tale.   It is true that several of the canches stand almost due North-East ; but this appears to be a coincidence dependent upon the axes of the galleries.   In other cases the bearings were widely divergent.

Those students who are desirous of pursuing the subject should themselves visit Chislehurst.   In addition, the papers given in the reference should be studied ; that of Mr. W. J. Nichols supplies the more picturesque interpretation of the facts, while Messrs. Forster advocate a more practical and prosaic reading.   In face of the Wickham Lane galleries, in the same district, one need not hesitate which conclusion to adopt.

At Puttenham (Surrey) there are also excavations in the Lower Greensand, with beehive terminations comparable to those in the galleries of Chislehurst.   There are, however, no ' canches ', and the area covered by the passages is comparatively small.

So far as I am fitted to judge, the case stands thus : The galleries are of various ages, as indicated by the methods of working, and by the coarseness or fineness of the surface tooling.   Marks of iron tools, and those moreover of a square cross-section, are alone discernible.   The earliest excavations probably go back to the Roman period, even a little further. Chalk for the fields, lime for cement, ballast for North-country vessels, will indicate possible stages in the history.

One point must not be overlooked. Amazing to tell, disputants often forget that the innermost workings could not have been commenced first, unless, indeed, we assume the pre-existence of dene-holes, or at any rate of ' draw-pits '. How far the outer series resembled these inner passages cannot be determined, because the typical character of the former has been destroyed by modern excavations for lime-burning. Should it be true that a number of dene-holes were first sunk, then the innermost, or most finely-tooled passages, might be the oldest; but this is unproven.

At different ages the passages have probably served as refuges, and as retreats for Thames smugglers. ' Caves ' at Eltham, not many miles away, are said to have been used as hiding-places in the seventeenth century. One need not be careful to deny that the Chislehurst galleries may have sheltered successively fugitives from the wrath of Danes, Yorkists and Lancastrians, Cavaliers and Round-heads, persecuting zealots and government officers. Who shall say ? But that the hiding-place theory accounts for the original construction is beyond belief.

Heaps of refuse flints, and rough flakes, found in several parts of the ramifications, show conclusively that gun-flints were once made here ; rumour says, and perhaps correctly, that this was during the Peninsular War. But local tradi-tion, as one might expect, becomes, when direct economical interest has ceased, a jumble of contradictory stories, fostered and supplemented by speculative antiquaries.

The best living testimony yet advanced comes from an aged resident of New Eltham (Kent), whose father, born in 1780, used to fetch chalk from the mines. This informant asserts that the chalk was brought up in baskets, presumably by means of a draw-pit.

At all events, the folk-memory of the Chislehurst mines is of an unsound character, having been vitiated by outside influences. But the loss and rediscovery of underground passages and chambers is not unknown elsewhere. Lamb's

Lair, in Somerset, a fine natural cavern, was rediscovered in 1820, after having been completely forgotten for more than a century. The subterranean chambers at Royston, to which we shall allude in the next chapter, supply another instance.

It is proverbial that modern ideas of political economy are valueless in explaining primitive handiwork. The enormous labour involved in raising linchets, fortifications, and barrows is, as we shall see later, not to be gauged by modern standards. We know what could be done by a determined tribe, whether working under forced or free labour.

The famous rock-dwellings cut in the limestones of Southern France, and in the hard lavas of the Auvergne, opening on the faces of perpendicular cliffs, evince long and hazardous toil on the part of those by whom they were constructed. With their stables, churches, and staircases, however, they represent not refuges, but almost permanent homes of Mediaeval and perhaps Gaulish populations, downtrodden and persecuted.

The semi-barbarous Nervii, a people of Gaul, employing their swords for spades and their cloaks for baskets, raised in less than three hours a fortification ten miles in circuit.[74] At Brandon, our own Neolithic predecessors used great labour to obtain good flint. But primitive man was no fool, and it is incredible that he should have burrowed the chalk at Chislehurst for flint, of which mineral little is really exposed in the passages. Burning the house to roast the pig would be wisdom beside such a proceeding.

The deep ' well ' is indeed a perplexity. Mr. R. H. Forster suggests that it was either sunk to test the lower beds of chalk, or that it was an adjunct in the cultivation of mushrooms, for which purpose the galleries were used, so the story goes, a generation or two ago. Neither explanation is quite satisfactory, although the former has some support in the fact that the Eltham workings also contain a ' steined ' well. Some of the dene-holes, too, which we shall discuss in the next chapter, are steined at the mouth to prevent the collapse of the sandy upper portion. The New Eltham witness, cited above, avers that the well was sunk ' in the sixties ', to obtain a supply of pure water for a mansion in the neighbourhood. The whole debate tends to become endless, but by carrying it thus far the investigation of the dene-holes is considerably aided. Folk-memory is unfortunately, in both cases, a broken reed.

CHAPTER XII

DENE-HOLES

QUITE a literature on the subject of dene-holes has been accumulated during the last few years, so that we are now in full possession of the facts concerning their form, structure, and design. Unhappily, unanimity of opinion among experts as to the original purpose of these subterranean chambers seems as far off as ever.

For a synopsis of the facts we are most indebted to the writings of Mr. F. C. J. Spurrell,[1] and to the *Essex Naturalist*, the Journal of the Essex Field Club, a Society which for many years carried out a systematic investigation of the dene-holes at Hangman's Wood, near Grays, in Essex. The scholarly report of the exploration of this group of dene-holes was presented to the Society by Mr. T. V. Holmes and Mr. W. Cole in 1887.[2]

Numerous other contributions will be quoted as we go along, and a few more will be cited at the end of the special references.

Dene-holes, or Dane-holes, are underground chambers, excavated usually in the chalk. A typical dene-hole consists of a narrow shaft sunk to a depth of from seventy to one hundred feet, and ending in a chamber or chambers which may be very simple or somewhat complex in form.

The shaft, which is notched with foot-holes, may start from a surface where the chalk has but a thin covering of turf, or it may pierce layers of clay or sand before the chalk is reached. In this second case, as great a depth as sixty or seventy feet of overlying material, usually of Tertiary age, may be bored through before the chalk is reached.

The chamber at the base of the shaft may be of the plain beehive shape, and may average ten to fifteen yards in diameter, with a height of about sixteen or eighteen feet. The dimensions, of course, vary. Instead of this simple

bottle type, however, it is more usual to find dene-holes
with secondary lateral recesses (Figs. 21 and 22). Thus
we get a cavity with round-ended, rectangular passages

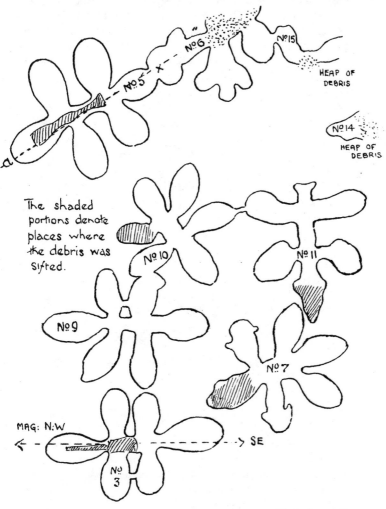

The shaded
portions denote
places where
the debris was
sifted.

FIG. 21. Plan of a portion of Hangman's Wood, Essex, to illustrate a portion
of the Dene-hole explorations. [Figs. 21 and 22 are reproduced from a
drawing by Mr. T. V. Holmes in the *Essex Naturalist*, I (1887), p. 248, by the
courtesy of the Essex Field Club.]

intersecting in the centre. Again, there may be four or five side-chambers, with curving outlines, so that the ground-plan assumes a stellate or petaloid form. The double trefoil, as it is conventionally termed, represents one type of ground-plan. The 'crypts' or lateral chambers will average twenty-five feet in length, and about fifteen feet in height and breadth. The chambers of adjacent dene-holes do not intersect, though the partitions are generally very thin.

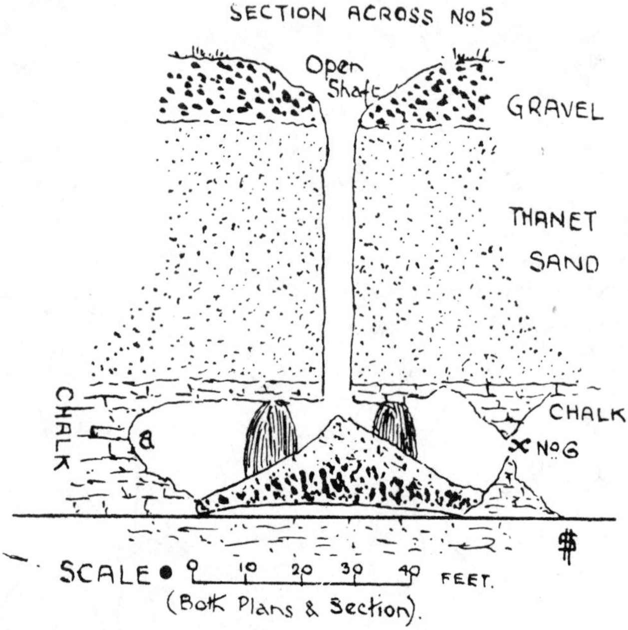

FIG. 22. Section across Dene-hole No. 5, along line a x. [*Essex Nat.* l. c.]

Dene-holes generally occur in clusters, which are frequently situated in woodlands, and in this event they are likely to be in association with old entrenchments or earthworks. The causal connexion between the two groups of remains must not, however, be hastily postulated. The pits at Hangman's Wood, Essex, some threescore in number, are all contained within a copse of a few acres.

Kent and Essex are the counties most noted for dene-holes, but there are records from several other localities. Fresh groups are constantly being recorded ; in 1907 an example was discovered at Stone Park, near Dartford. On the other side of the Channel also, in the valley of the Somme, pits which are true counterparts of our English examples are found in similar situations.

Subterranean caverns somewhat analogous to dene-holes were disclosed during the making of a sewer at Waddon, near Croydon, in June, 1902. In these, however, the chambers were entered from the side and not from above, and were scooped out of the Thanet Sands. The cavities were of the well-known beehive shape, but it is questionable whether they were of the same nature as dene-holes. The balance of evidence seemed to indicate that they had been used as habitations, though primarily intended for sepulchral chambers. Flint chips, cores, and scrapers, calcined flints, pieces of Romano-British pottery, and the bones of animals, pointed to an early origin.[3] As we shall see, the true dene-holes have hitherto been notorious for their poverty in relics.

A few moments spent on the consideration of the word ' dene-hole ' will not be unprofitable. The word is provincially pronounced *dane-hole*, and this indicates the popular and traditional explanation of the structures. (Old and Middle English *dene*.) The pronunciation which agrees with the spelling, *dene-hole*, seems rather to proceed from the study, and this word is not, Sir James A. H. Murray considers, a genuine popular form anywhere. If such a form does exist, it may possibly represent a Middle English word *Dene-hol*(*e*) and Old English *Dena-hol* (= Danes' hole), built up on the same principle as ME. *Dene-lawe*, OE. *Dena-lagu* (= Dane-law). As an alternative explanation, this academic pronunciation with the *ē* sound may represent some local form yet unrecorded.

On any hypothesis, the connexion with the word ' Dane ' seems to be fairly established. But the pronunciation *dēne* has suggested to recent writers *dene* = a (wooded) vale, ' and either on this account, or because it does not countenance any theory about the Danes, it has been generally adopted by archaeologists who have investigated these holes since c. 1880.' Sir James A. H. Murray adds that, to contract the term and to speak of ' a dene ', presumably to support the ' den ' theory, is reprehensible.[4] When we observe that Professor W. W. Skeat gives the origin *denn* (=a cave, sleeping-place),[5] we can understand how such an attractive etymology might soon gain currency.

The derivation of the word, then, supports the theory that these subterranean chambers were hiding-places from the Danes, and on a review of the evidence the student will be impelled to think that this was one of the uses of dene-holes, though not necessarily the original one.

Antecedent to the acceptance of any theory, however, there should be an attempt to discover the age of the pits. Owing to the scantiness of the remains yet found, a fact as general as it is surprising and disappointing, this is difficult work.

A dene-hole explored in 1857, at Camden Park, Chislehurst —not far from the ' Caves '—revealed a cone of sandy clay resting on the floor, and embedded in the lowest portion were the bones of the ox and deer, a deer-horn, and Roman and Romano-British pottery. All the bones were those of existing animals, except one, which was believed to belong to *Bos longifrons*. Above this layer was another containing shells of *Helix nemoralis*, whose unbroken condition attested that the gentle wash of a stream had covered the earlier remains. Overlying this band was a two-foot bed of pebbles, and, topping all, were bones, shells, the skeleton of a hog, and Samian ware, the last-named object belonging perhaps to the fifth century. If we assign the uppermost layer of refuse to the sixth century at the latest, we may conclude that this dene-hole belongs to the Early Iron Age.[6]

At Crayford (Kent) similar relics of pottery and animal bones were discovered, but along with these were numerous flint flakes and implements. These flints at first led Mr. Spurrell to think that the pits were early flint mines,[7] but further evidence coming to light elsewhere caused him

some years afterwards to renounce this opinion.[8] Pits
which were cut into during the making of a railway in
the Ebbsfleet Valley, in 1881, also contained Roman and
Romano-British objects.[9]

At Hangman's Wood, Essex, the tool-marks betrayed
the use of iron picks.[10] The pits there were unquestionably,
then, post-Neolithic.

One of the Hangman's Wood dene-holes yielded a fragment of early British ware, and another a piece of Nieder-
mendig lava, presumably part of a millstone. Millstones
of this rock, derived no doubt from Laacher See, in the
Eifel, were imported into this country by the Romans,
though not by them exclusively. Fragments of such
millstones are found, says Mr. F. W. Rudler, at most Roman
stations in this country. As, however, later peoples also
imported similar material, it is unsafe to base conclusions
on the Hangman's Wood specimen.[11] Other relics found
in this cluster of pits were portions of a yellow glazed vase,
probably of the fourteenth century; some pieces of sixteenth-
century pottery; and bones of the ox, horse, horned sheep,
dog, and badger, all of indeterminate date.

Briefly, then, the majority of the dene-holes belong to
the Iron Age, but the exact period in that Age cannot yet be
determined. A few of the simpler and shallower dene-
holes may be Neolithic.

The general disposition of these hypogeal chambers points
to a primitive condition of affairs, when boundaries of land
either did not exist or were of little account. Those dene-
holes which are sunk directly from a surface of bare chalk
are deemed the oldest.

A little information on the subject may be gleaned from
old writers. There seems little doubt that Dr. Robert Plot,
in his 'Natural History of Oxfordshire' (1705), refers to
some of the Essex dene-holes. He speaks of 'the gold
mine of Cunobeline, in Essex', which was rediscovered in
the reign of Henry the Fourth, and was then lost a second
time.[12] It is on record that a royal favourite, Walter Fitz-
Walter, worked the 'mines' (= dene-holes) at the beginning
of the fifteenth century, the 'gold' being doubtless the

bright yellow iron pyrites, which is, however, rare at Hangman's Wood. Foolish as such gold-searching may appear, we know that so late as the South Sea Bubble, 1720, there was a mad attempt to repeat the enterprise.[13]

A century earlier than Plot, in 1601, two dene-holes at Tilbury were described and figured by Camden[14] (Fig. 23). Joshua Childrey, in his 'Britannia Baconica' (1660) refers to examples both in Kent and Essex, and cites 'Cambden' as a former writer on the subject. A little before this, William Lambarde (1570), as we have seen, described pits at Crayford which were, I think, most likely dene-holes.

Fig. 23. Camden's sketch of a dene-hole, discovered at Tilbury, Essex. [Reproduced from William Camden's 'Britannia' (ed. 1610), p. 440.]

Messrs. Holmes and Cole pertinently emphasize the special interest of the gold legend. The significance of the story is this : as early as the time of Henry the Fourth, tradition traced back the dene-holes to the most powerful British king who flourished between the arrival of Julius Caesar and the Roman occupation in A. D. 43. Despite all the changes, ethnological, political, and social, despite the ' drums and tramplings of three conquests ', mediaeval country-folk held to the British tradition. They held to it during ages when folk-memory was not aided by books,

when most legends were transmitted orally. This fact
gives a slight presumption in favour of a British and pre-
Roman origin for the dene-holes. The supposition of
gold-mining perhaps indicates that the purpose of the dene-
holes was kept secret by their makers, so that to the men
of the Middle Ages the structures were as much a mystery
as they are at this day.[15]

Approaching this question of the purpose of the dene-
holes, we pick up the apple of discord. ' Give me theories,'
said a famous cynic, ' them I can understand; as for your
facts, they may not be facts at all.' Concerning dene-
holes there are theories in abundance, a round half-dozen
at least being worthy of a little consideration. Some of
the less tenable had better be dealt with first.

There is, to begin with, the conjecture that dene-holes
were permanent dwellings. For this there is no justification in the evidence. No kind of primitive house, known
certainly to be such, is of this class. Nor are there any
household remains forthcoming from the dene-holes to call
for the recognition of such a type. Temporary hiding-
places or lairs the chambers doubtless have been more than
once, but this matter will be discussed separately.

Certain circular pits, varying in depth and diameter,
from which no substance has been removed of the slightest
value to the inhabitants of the neighbourhood, are recorded
from Berkshire. From the description one is led to suppose
that the cavities represent some kind of pit-dwelling, not
at all of the dene-hole pattern.[16]

That the dene-holes were sunk to obtain water is a hypothesis too far-fetched for serious argument. The excavation
of one or two chambers alone would have been sufficient to
convince the workers of their error. Nor is it a much more
reasonable suggestion that the quest of iron pyrites was
the original or sole intention. Yet both hypotheses have
been mooted.[17]

Some people have hastily supposed the dene-holes to be
Roman rubbish-pits. The only evidence adduced is the
finding of Roman and Romano-British débris blocking up
the chambers already recorded. The Camden Park pit

might superficially be so interpreted ; but the agency of running water better meets the facts. One of our older antiquaries, Wright, speaks of large stones, lying flat on the ground, near the dolmen called Kits Coty House, in Kent ; these stones were found to be placed over round pits cut in the chalk and filled with flint.[18] The context seems to indicate that dene-holes or shafts for obtaining flint are referred to, but the language is obscure. Viewed in any light, the note does not support the cloacal or refuse-pit theory. Even should there be a genuine case or two of dene-holes having been used as shoots for Roman rubbish, we are as far off the primary purpose as ever.

Next, it has been surmised that the dene-holes are tombs. The celebrated cave at Royston (Herts.) is chiefly relied upon as a proof. Under the market-place of that town there was discovered, in 1742, a subterranean chamber of domical shape, to which access was gained by a vertical pipe. The chalk walls were covered with rude carvings, and niches had been cut here and there.[19] The carvings are supposed to have been the work of idle persons, but the chamber itself may well have been a columbarium, or urn-sepulchre, and may indeed have been excavated for that purpose. The country around is dotted with British barrows, and hard by is the junction of two Roman roads. King, who records the Royston cave, describes many analogous structures. Chambers of a similar type are reported from Ewell and Richborough (Kent).

In Rome itself a dome-like columbarium was discovered in 1692 ; it had recesses for the cinerary urns wherein were placed the ashes of the dead after cremation. The vault was reached by a shaft fifty-one feet deep, at the side of which were footholes strangely suggestive of those in the dene-holes of our own country.[20]

In the immediate neighbourhood of Hangman's Wood, namely at Grays Thurrock, a pit containing quantities of Roman burial-urns was opened in 1869, but there now exist no data to show whether the chamber was of the dene-hole kind.[21] At Hangman's Wood, as in the Kentish groups at Stankey Wood and Cavey Spring, neither niches, urns, nor human remains have been found. Fragments of ware might conceivably be buried in the trodden soil of the floor, but even then the niches would have remained. Hence the sepulchral theory cannot account for these groups of chambers.

Another assumption is that the dene-holes were sunk to get flint for the manufacture of Neolithic implements and strike-a-lights. This contention keeps coming to the front intermittently. It was seriously urged, at great length, by well-known writers, during the spring of 1905, when a local incident caused a correspondence on dene-holes to be started in many of the London newspapers. The argument is based on a false analogy with the pits of Grimes Graves and Cissbury. The excavations at those places certainly occur in clusters. That they were flint mines is now well established. The Grimes Graves group contains about 254 pits. Each shaft went directly to a particularly coveted band of flint, about forty feet below the surface, and there it stopped. The shafts varied from seven to twenty-two yards in diameter; those of the dene-holes are but a few feet wide. At Grimes Graves the flint layer was removed by driving lateral tunnels, significantly small as compared with the chambers and alcoves of the dene-holes. The Neolithic flint-workers filled up the exhausted pit, apparently with material taken from a new one. The dene-holes were evidently left open; the walls are as fresh and clean as when the hewers ceased working. Where dene-holes have become blocked up, it is mostly either through the collapse of the roof or the inwash of surface soil. A few may perhaps have been filled artificially.

When we consider the enormous labour required to bore through one hundred feet of rock, three-quarters of which does not bear flint at all, the scale turns against the theory. The dene-holes were not sunk to reach a special band of clean, homogeneous flint, for that does not exist, although there happens to be an unimportant layer two yards above the actual floor.

In general, Neolithic men and Bronze Age men were not cramped by any sentimental ideas of economy in the disposition of labour. Of this truth the earthworks and barrows testify. All the same, these folk, as was remarked in Chapter XI, were not stupid ; they would not wilfully persist in operations involving so great a disproportion between means and end as the flint theory demands. The Grimes Graves enterprise exhibits no such disproportion ; neither does that of Cissbury. At the latter site the surface soil is but a few inches thick.[22]

There is, of course, no *a priori* reason which is absolutely decisive against the flint theory, much less against the acquisition of flint as a by-product. But proof, even of this secondary purpose, depends on the discovery of refuse chips. The Essex dene-holes have furnished no implements or flakes or waste chips to justify the theory.

We have seen that the Crayford dene-holes, which from their stream-borne contents appeared to be Neolithic, were at first thought to be flint-works, yet even in this exceptional case the theory was afterwards abandoned.

Artificial caverns in the chalk at Hayes Down, near Lavant, Sussex, are believed to supply evidence of a flint factory. In the bottom layer of the floor, composed of loose fragments of chalk, a miscellaneous series of relics was found, ranging from Neolithic implements and cores to Roman pottery, with animal bones, human teeth, and charred wheat. Mingled with these objects, however, were leaden seals of the seventeenth century. The caverns must therefore have been open and known at that period. Altogether the evidence is unconvincing. The caves and galleries may have originally been formed to obtain chalk, and were doubtless afterwards used as hiding-places. Surface material, accompanied by the remains of various ages, would thus probably tend to crumble and slide into the pits.[23]

Should a Neolithic flint-heap ever be found in a dene-hole, discussion with respect to that particular pit will be almost closed. In our present state of knowledge, proof fails on all important counts.

We must next review the traditions, faint and fugacious though they be, in which the advocates of the hiding-place theory see their opportunity.

The popular name Dane-holes, spell it as one may, counts for something, for this pronunciation antedated any modern theories.   Three hundred years ago Camden found this name in vogue among the country-people around Tilbury.[24] Not only so, but the name and the idea are not restricted to the South-Eastern counties.

In parts of Durham, where the struggle with the sea-pirates seems to have been especially bitter, ' Danes' Holes ' were formerly common.   Caves so named occurred chiefly in the Magnesian Limestone formation, a noted locality being Embleton, a few miles West of Hartlepool.

Lincolnshire, the most Danish county of the Danelagh,[25] with its dense Celtic substratum, is a puzzling exception—it has, apparently, no Danes' Holes.   A county abounding with Scandinavian place-names, like -by and -thorp, a county where, as the writer can attest from personal knowledge, traditions of the sea-pirates lately lingered, seems to contain not a single dene-hole—name or object.   Different devices may serve a common purpose, and negative exceptions like Lincolnshire would not alone disprove the theory of concealment.   Possibly the Saxon churches, with their strong towers, were used as refuges ; to this day a number of these Saxon towers remain.   Their sole window, divided by the characteristic bulging baluster shaft, is very narrow, and is placed so high as to be attackable only by missiles, thrown by hand, sling, or catapult.   When these means failed, firing was resorted to ; traces of this are still visible.

Why dene-holes were not constructed in Lincolnshire seems inexplicable, yet not more so than why they should occur on the chalk hills of one division of a county when they are absent in the neighbouring division.   One thought presents itself : the dene-holes could scarcely have been made by the Danes, or surely Lincolnshire would possess examples.   They were most likely hiding-places during incursions of the Danes.   Hence they are presumably pre-Danish, and were not dug at short notice.

Even if we allow that refuge was the original purpose, there is no inherent necessity to admit that the dene-holes were not originated till the eighth or ninth century.

Rapine and slaughter long scar the records of folk-memory, as in the case of Cromwell and the Irish. Simply on the Danish theory, then, the date might be carried back to A. D. 787, but there had been other racial invasions previously.

The dene-holes, then, became associated with a people who probably had nothing to do with their excavation. Previously the chambers may have been British refuges from the Saxon hordes, and it is almost certain that they have been hiding-places since the Danish invasion, but memories of the fierce Northmen have blotted out those of all minor perils, whether early or late.

A partial parallel may be taken from the terms ' Dane Hills ' and ' Danes' Graves ', applied to barrows and earth-works, which are often demonstrably British in character.

There is a curious clue to the Mediaeval use of the dene-holes as refuges in the name Clapper-napper's Hole, a spot on the East side of Swanscombe Wood, Kent. Mr. M. Heys, who knew the place thirty or forty years ago, assures me that the now obliterated hollow was a true dene-hole, though, owing to the downfall of the roof, it could only be approached from the side, like a cavern. The wood and the district in general abound with blocked-up dene-holes; one near Milton Street Pit is still partially open. Local tradition said that this was a den once occupied by a robber, and connected with another retreat four miles distant. In Essex, too, there exists near Stifford a Clapper Field, which contains remains of caves.[26]

This old word *napper* or *nabber*, a robber (cf. slang word *nab*) survives in the term *kidnapper*. But what is a *clapper* ? Professor Skeat, to whom these place-names were submitted, while counselling caution in receiving an etymology rashly, stated that in Middle English, from Chaucer onwards, a rabbit-burrow was also known by the Anglo-French word *coney-clapper*.[27] Thus we read of ' Conies . . . that comen out of their claperes'.[28] If we take Clapper-napper's Hole to mean ' Robber's burrow '—the duplicated ' hole ' presents no difficulty—it would seem that the name was applied, facetiously perhaps, to a haunt of thieves and smugglers.

If the reader will carry back his thoughts to the preceding chapter, he will remember that Lambarde, in the latter part of the sixteenth century, noticed pits at Crayford which were said by the natives to be old excavations for chalk. One wonders, and may continue to wonder, whether the supposed Neolithic dene-hole was among this group, and whether there were more examples of this type. Lambarde himself did not accept the peasants' story ; he thought that the pits, which were presumably dene-holes, were ancient receptacles, or otherwise ' secret retraicts for families and goods '.[29]

Having thus got a foot in each camp, Lambarde unwittingly anticipates two of the three modern theories around which strife has been most severely waged : the refuge theory and the granary theory. Strong champions have appeared on each side, and the two claims must shortly receive our attention. We must also examine the peasants' story—the explanation which Lambarde himself rejected.

Does the refuge theory get any support from times anterior to the coming of the Danes ? There is, it is said in reply, one remarkable fact to be pondered. Dene-holes are frequently found in ancient woodlands, such as Jorden's Wood, near Dartford.[30] In the close vicinity, if not in the copse itself, one sees indications of hut-circles, ramparts, ditches, and early trackways.

Here we must pause a moment to mention, and to dismiss, the conjecture that the ditches, mounds, tracks, and woodlands were all accessories to the hunting of large animals, which were by these contrivances driven into the pits and there trapped or impaled. A host of objections at once arise, too many for consideration. The suggestion demands such an inversion of the observed facts that it needs but a passing allusion.

The signs of ancient occupation are probably not coincidences ; indeed, they might have been expected. But are they tokens of human habitation simply, or of defensive outworks ? Further observation is needed, because on the answer largely depends which of two prominent theories we may provisionally accept.

It happens that some of the rural parts of France contain similar groups of artificial structures to which the idea of hiding-places is attached.

Opposite the county of Kent, in the neighbourhood of Amiens, situated usually among the woodlands of a chalk district, excavations connected with the parish churches have been recorded from more than thirty localities. These excavations are known as *Les souterrains des guerres*, a name indicating that they were refuges in war time. There are also underground passages with semicircular recesses, and occasionally ' wells ' ; these structures evidently are comparable to the Chislehurst galleries rather than to dene-holes proper.

Again, in the forests around St. Omer, pits, both square and circular, are still called *Fosses sarrassines*, the word ' Sarrassines ' denoting invaders, whether English, Flemish, or Spanish. The word ' Saracen ' is of sufficient importance to merit attention later. The Saracens' Pits are clearly counterparts of our Dane-Holes.

On the Flemish borders are similar pits known as *Fosses as Inglais*.[31] Once more : Victor Hugo, in his ' Quatrevingt-treize ', writing within memory of the event, tells how, in Brittany, during the Vendéan War, woodland caves with small entrances and underground galleries, like funnels ending in dark chambers, were frequently used as dwellings and refuges. He asserts that they had been so employed intermittently for two thousand years.[32] French caves, too, of some kind or other, were employed as refuges in Caesar's time, for that warrior relates how he closed up the caves into which the Aquitanian Gauls had retreated.

These testimonies veer round again to the refuge theory, but the French excavations seemingly represent a jumble of various kinds of subterranean retreats, of which only some are dene-holes. It is but fair to record such examples, for they show that underground chambers have again and again been resorted to for safety. But nowhere are we told that refuge was the purpose for which the pits were dug ; the pre-existence of the hiding-places is assumed.

Our two remaining theories of origin stand out boldly

against each other, and much testimony can be adduced in favour of each. The first says that dene-holes were sunk to obtain chalk, mainly for marling purposes ; the second as stoutly teaches that they were designed for sub-terranean granaries. We notice that the original intention of the excavators is here in dispute. As will be seen shortly, the two doctrines may be correlated and harmonized, having once given the prime motive free play.

Several details which seem adverse to the marling theory may be examined. To obtain chalk by the method in question must have been troublesome and arduous work. Yet it has already been shown that a somewhat similar system is in use at the present day ; similar, but with important differences.

The ' chalk-wells ' or ' draw-pits ' of to-day, according to Mr. Bennett, are employed where the chalk does not lie more than fifteen feet from the surface. When the chalk is reached, the worker excavates it to a depth of some thirty feet, and then drives headings. When abandoned, the chalk-well eventually collapses, forming a saucer-like ' dell '. Contrast the dene-holes of Hangman's Wood. The makers of these pierced about sixty feet of sand, and then, passing through only about three feet of chalk, enough to form a moderately compact roof, began to carve out lateral chambers. If the dene-hole constructor, like our agricul-turists, wanted ' strong, fat ' material, which is found at great depths, he would, it is argued, have bored much further before scooping out his chambers. Actually, he left a roof so thin as to endanger stability, and at once began to hew out the material. He contented himself, too, with the uppermost layers of chalk. The plugging-up of the dene-holes was a process differing in nature from that of the collapsing of the chalk-well, being caused by a slowly accu-mulating cone of sand denuded from the sides of the shaft. Where the roof has fallen in, the pipe is still in many cases partially traceable. Sometimes, however, the shafts have been choked up artificially in modern days.[33]

In place of the rectangular ' headings ' inclining upwards, as seen in the chalk-well, the dene-hole has chambers of floriated or star-fish outline, with a common ground-level. The ' bell-tent' type is exceptional.

Chalk-wells are usually scattered, one being sunk here and another there as required. Dene-holes occur mostly in groups, so that a cluster of fifty or sixty is found within an area of six acres, the site being completely honeycombed.

Each dene-hole, while closely approaching the confines of its neighbour, has been carefully kept separate, though the partition may be very thin. It would have involved less labour to make the crypts communicate, and to extend the galleries both in depth and length. Against the argument that the dividing walls acted merely as supporting columns, it is contended that a somewhat thicker roof of chalk would have served equally well.

Less than a mile from Hangman's Wood, chalk is exposed at the surface, and much the same may be said concerning one of the Kentish groups. Would the early excavators cut through sixty feet of superincumbent sand unnecessarily, and by so doing render it imperative to use baskets or buckets for raising the chalk ? What General Pitt-Rivers said of the Pen Pits in Somerset applies here : ' The Britons, if such they were, who quarried here, probably conducted their operations much as we should do.' [34]

Expense of cartage can hardly count for much, when surface chalk and ' well ' chalk are separated by a mile only. Where the distance was considerably greater, the explanation would be reasonable. A few centuries ago, wheeled vehicles were uncommon, and roads were generally of the worst kind. Preference for deep, ' fat ' chalk is a more forcible plea, but did this preference anciently obtain ? The contention that private ownership accounts for the clustered dene-holes is met by the reply that these chambers seem to have been made in times when strict ideas of field boundaries and of individual property were little known. And in the case of Hangman's Wood, could the dene-hole chalk compete with that from the open quarries at Gravesend and Purfleet ?

The dene-holes exhibit marked unity of design and astonishing persistency of type. Messrs. Holmes and Cole

put the case thus : ' Each dene-hole may have taken as
long as a mediaeval cathedral to build '—surely there is
a little overstatement here—' but the dene-holes, unlike
most cathedrals, show no diversity of style.' [35] This uniformity would tell in favour of Messrs. Holmes and Cole's
theory—that the dene-holes were granaries. Were the
dene-holes simply chalk-pits, such close resemblances would
scarcely be expected, even allowing for human conservatism ;
nor is it probable that the tooling would be so fine. Against
this argument it may be said that agricultural methods
change slowly, and that the ground-plans of dene-holes
do indeed differ.

Although thousands of tons of chalk must have been
extracted, no traces of waste material remain. Chalk, it is
true, dissolves somewhat readily under atmospheric conditions, but it is fairly arguable that had the workers left
but a few waste heaps two or three feet high, some remnants
should still be seen. This point may be laboured too much,
for it is contended that not only the chalk, but also the
refuse sand and gravel were evenly spread out on the adjacent
land. The absence of refuse heaps is therefore held to be
the result of precaution, and to support the granary theory.

The ejected chalk has gone : that is plain. To dwell on
this fact may, however, give birth to a double-edged argument. It is conceivable, though not at all certain, that
the excavators, desirous of concealment, carried the conspicuous white chalk to a distance, and there scattered it
abroad. It is more likely—and the supposition does not
militate against the storehouse theory—that the chalk was
used for dressing the soil or for exportation, and again,
at a somewhat later period perhaps, for binding the constituent courses of Roman roads and laying the foundations
of buildings.

Slightly shifting round from the argument that the chalk
was evenly distributed, the granary advocates urge, with
some justice, that the material dug up could be utilized
for manuring, whether the excavation was, in the first place,
made for extracting chalk or for forming a storehouse.[36]
The admission, which to me seems inevitable after studying

Pliny's remarks on the subject, is a little damaging to the granary theory. Grant that the chalk had an economic value, and the objector to the theory may shrewdly ask whether the pits may not have been sunk simply to obtain that commodity.

Pliny's reference, noticed in Chapter XI, affects the controversy very closely indeed. Unfortunately his meaning is not altogether clear throughout. The phrase '*ut in metallis spatiante vena*' contains the kernel of his description. Roach Smith's translation, ' where they branch out like the veins of mines ',[37] does not seem satisfactory. Bostock and Riley have it thus : ' the shafts enlarge very considerably in the interior as is the case in mines.'[38] The Rev. E. Conybeare's interpretation is, ' but widening towards the bottom.'[39] But the reader will observe that *spatiante vena* is in the singular, therefore a more strict translation, I submit, would be, ' the vein spreading within, as in mines.'

This plea for exactitude is not a quibble. Pliny says that the Britons dressed the land with chalk. They got the chalk from certain pits. Supporters of the granary hypothesis do not deny Pliny's account, but they suggest that the natives would naturally deceive him about the dene-holes, saying that these were sunk to obtain chalk. Secret stores must be guarded.[40]

Now if Pliny actually saw the interior of a few dene-holes, his description would not hold, save on a very loose interpretation. The rather lofty, symmetrical dene-hole chambers, floriate in base outline, and clean-tooled, could not be compared to the veins of mines. At most, the account could only agree with the simple beehive or bottle-shaped excavation. Perhaps the expression should not be taken too literally, but on any view it is evident that Pliny knew of the existence of pits in the chalk. He may also have combined his information ; first, that chalk was used for manure ; second, that certain pits—dene-holes—were the sources whence that chalk came.

As it stands, the classical passage better fits the chalk-wells described by Mr. Bennett. These, it will be remembered, had a few ' headings ', sloping up towards the surface of the ground. How would this correlation harmonize with the statement that chalk-wells seem to date only from the middle of the eighteenth century? We have seen that the practice of marling has been dropped and afterwards revived, hence there may be draw-pits of more than one age.

Taking into consideration the difference between dene-holes and modern chalk-wells, and fully allowing that Pliny's account is puzzling, I am yet bound to say that the description agrees with the dene-holes more than the upholders of the storehouse contention care to allow. On the other hand, those defenders may argue that the gap between the ancient dene-hole and the modern draw-pit remains unbridged.

In reviewing the arguments against the marling school of writers, the storehouse theory has forced itself alongside the other. Further examination is, however, necessary. We turn, then, to inquire whether the dene-holes were storehouses for grain, and, inferentially, for fodder?

That Britain was a corn-growing country at the time of the Roman occupation is a well-established fact. Eumenius, who wrote early in the fourth century A. D., says that Britain supplied corn to the cities of the Rhine, and Zosimus, at the end of the same century, describes Britain as remarkable for the richness of its corn crops as well as for the multitude of its cattle.[41]

We can push the subject further. Pytheas, the famous Greek geographer of Massilia (Marseilles), who is believed to have visited Britain as early as the fourth century B. C., made notes of what he saw here. Unfortunately, his jottings have come down to us only in fragments which chance to have been quoted by other authors. The trustworthiness of Pytheas has been challenged, but his observations agree with known facts so far as to prove the genuine character of his statements. This question is well discussed in Sir E. H. Bunbury's ' History of Ancient Geography ', and the case against the old traveller may be considered to have broken down.

Pytheas, then, the ' Humboldt of antiquity ', as Mr. Elton called him, noticed abundance of wheat and barley in the British fields, but recorded that, owing to ' lack of clear sunshine ', the natives were obliged to thresh the corn in covered barns, not on open threshing-floors, as in the neighbourhood of his own city. Britain was a land of ' clouds and rain '.[42]

Connect these latter statements with those of Diodorus Siculus (B.C. 44), that the Britons gathered their harvest by cutting off the ears of corn, which they housed in underground repositories, and that daily the older stores were selected and dressed for food.[43] It is believed that the authority for these assertions was really Posidonius, the Greek tutor of Cicero, who visited our island about sixty years before the time of Diodorus Siculus.[44] The matter is unimportant, as the credibility of neither writer is disputed.

A curious confirmation of these narratives is supplied by a custom which obtained in the Hebrides till the end of the seventeenth century. Corn was, up to that time, threshed as it was daily required. The method, which quaint old Martin Martin calls *graddan*, is thus described : A woman would grasp a handful of corn in her left hand, and set fire to the ears. Whilst the husk was burning, she dexterously beat out the grain with a stick which she held in her right hand. Corn was thus dressed, winnowed, ground, and baked, within an hour of reaping.[45]

We may now compare what Diodorus Siculus says about subterranean granaries with Pliny's description of the chalk-pits. It is, with reason, urged that it is less likely that Diodorus Siculus—or Posidonius, it matters not which—should invent or be falsely told the tale about underground repositories, than that Pliny, seeing or hearing of pits (dene-holes), and knowing that chalk was used as marl, should erroneously connect the two series of facts. The account given by Diodorus Siculus seems to postulate an eye-witness, that of Pliny might be correct or incorrect, and might represent the writer's own collocation of facts, or an interpretation foisted on him by secretive Britons. The Britons, however, would scarcely assert that chalk-pits were granaries, since there was no motive for concealing chalk supplies.

Mr. Spurrell, the able advocate of the granary theory, believes that the use of chalk as a top-dressing was introduced from France not long prior to the coming of the Romans, and that Pliny's account was drawn up at a critical period of British history.[46] But the very point is that chalk was used as manure in Pliny's time. Mr. Roach Smith considers, moreover, that some chalk-pits probably existed many centuries before the days of Pliny.[47] The question of the introduction of ' chalking ' is therefore undecided.

The fact that the dene-holes do not communicate with each other was felt to be a weak link in presenting the marling theory. The partitions were more in consonance with the nature of a hiding-place. Fired from above, an untenable dene-hole could be quitted by breaking down the thin wall of chalk. The granary advocates claim that, the entrance hole being so narrow, it would be difficult to fire the contents. And of course, the strait aperture would also increase the value of the chamber as a place of refuge.

Ricks or heaps of corn would be easily seen by an enemy, and might be burnt or plundered at will. Hence the need for underground storage.

The enemy is supposed to have been a tribal one. Indications of inter-tribal defence are afforded, we are told, by the position of the pits on both banks of the Thames and Somme. The idea of nationality was yet unborn. Therefore if this view be correct, it at least proves that the dene-holes are of ancient date.

Estimates of the amount of grain requiring storage show that the accommodation afforded by the dene-holes was in excess. The explanation is that ears of corn, not threshed wheat and barley, were thus sheltered. Again, besides serving as barns, the dene-holes would also be covers for hay and straw fodder. Peradventure, too, we have here the earliest silos.

One asks to see the charred remains of the corn. No satisfactory answer is made. Any scattered grain may have been trodden under foot into the chalk floor by visitors

and refugees from Mediaeval days onwards. Some portion
may have rotted away. A part may also have been devoured
by small rodents, but to what extent such creatures find
their way into dene-holes does not appear to have been
noticed. I have heard of one authentic instance only : a
boy had fallen into a dene-hole, and had remained there
three days without food, save for a mouse which he caught
and ate. Most likely then, grain-eating animals do occasionally enter the chambers. The subject becomes mysterious ;
no underground warehouse of the true dene-hole type has
yielded material for its unravelling.

That corn hoarded underground will undergo partial
fermentation is not such a serious objection. We know,
in fact, that this kind of storage is widespread among the
nations. Professor Raphael Meldola has stated that the
carbon di-oxide produced in closed pits would form a gaseous
envelope which would effectually check fermentation and
preserve the grain.[48] Often, too, abortive germination
simply forms a pasty cake or crust which prevents further
access of oxygen and moisture to the mass, and the grain
is self-sealed. Quickly rises the comment, the less the
decomposition, the greater any accidental corn residue ; but
this remnant is not found.

In pre-Roman days our climate was probably more humid
and more continental. Storage below ground, shutting
out rain and frost, would be an advantage, if not a necessity.

It has just been said that many nations adopt cave and
pit storage of grain and fodder. This fact appears to be
the strongest evidence for British pit barns. Mr. Spurrell's
careful researches enable us to gather the extent of this
comparative custom ; the briefest summary is here given.

From all parts of the Old World underground grain-pits
are recorded. They are signalled from Central Asia,
from Northern Africa, and from most European countries.
The North American Indian employs an analogous ' bury '
in his hollow hiding-places known as *caches*.[49] During the
time of distress caused by a fire in a Russian district some
years ago, it was found that, owing to subterranean storage,
the corn had been saved.

Underground hoarding of grain is moreover an ancient custom. Tacitus observes that, in Germany, grain, covered with loose earth or compost, was stored in caverns, to which places the natives were wont to retire for refuge also.[50] Caesar mentions the use of the silo in Northern France and Belgium.[51] Hirtius describes similar receptacles on the Barbary Coast, in Syria, and elsewhere.[52] In the Old Testament we read of a field containing treasures ' of wheat, and of barley, and of oil, and of honey ', and the context refers to pits wherein the slain were cast.[53]

Souterrains, or ' subterranean ' chambers, both simple and complex, are found to-day in many parts of France. Some are proved, by documentary evidence, to have existed since the tenth century.[54]

In an article which appeared recently in the *Manchester Guardian*, it was stated that a reference to dene-holes is traceable in the ' Perceval ' or the ' Conte del Graal ', a poem written by Chrestien de Troyes (*circ.* A.D. 1180). The poet reproduced accurately various old Welsh legends. In one of these there is an allusion to certain damsels who conducted knights and other wayfarers to *puis*, or, as a later recension has it, ' caves ', situated in the forests of Britain. There food and drink were found. The *puis* (= *puits* ; cf. Lat. *puteum*) are supposed by the writer of the article to represent underground storehouses having the shape of wells or pits. During the Napoleonic wars, M. Jourdain and other writers, prompted by what they had witnessed in Spain, recommended the underground storage of grain and fodder. In Styria, Austria, Hungary, and Central Europe generally, pit granaries are the rule.[55] Near the *clusseaux*, or dene-holes, of Southern France, silos are often found cut in the Chalk; in some cases the covers have been found *in situ*. Whether the silos resemble the dene-holes in plan, Mr. Baring-Gould, who has written on the subject, does not inform us.

As Mr. Spurrell has admirably epitomized this branch of the subject once for all, there is no need to multiply instances. Store pits are best when cut in chalk or other limestone, or in tufa. Sand, which answers well for vertical shafts, is unsuited for the roofs of rapidly widening chambers. In formations of a loose character the pits are often lined with masonry or unbaked brick.

Two features seem constant : the deep, narrow, vertical approach, easily concealed, and the bulbous, conical, or domical recesses below.

Are there any undoubted English pit granaries which throw light on the problem ? Mr. Spurrell claims that some of the North Kent chambers, with their evenly chipped surfaces, are obvious examples of pre-Roman grain-pits.[56] Pending the production of relics, these examples may be left aside—it boots not to work round a circle. Real underground granaries have been detected at Winklebury Camp (Hants), in the Isle of Portland, and in Norfolk.[57] It must, however, be noted that all these chambers were of much smaller dimensions than the dene-holes. In Portland Isle the difference in size may perhaps be accounted for by the difficulty of excavating the hard Portland stone. Querns and blackened corn were there found mingled with the earth of the floor. The islanders may have stored grain only, not complete ears. In attempting to reconcile the smaller size of acknowledged granaries, the example of Winklebury, cut in the chalk, like a dene-hole, but not of great size, must be set alongside the Portland chambers.

At Rushmore, in Cranborne Chase, General Pitt-Rivers found cavities filled with grain, which he deemed to be post-holes for granaries—structures standing on four supports like some modern Wiltshire examples.[58] This would go to show that in the Romano-British period, at any rate, underground storage was not universal in England.

Side by side with this discovery, we must place the fact that the ancient inhabitants of Rushmore obtained chalk for top-dressing from shallow basin-shaped pits, and not from subterranean chambers of elaborate design. General Pitt-Rivers supposed that the Rushmore folk found the kind of chalk which they desired quite near the surface.[59] It may be suggested that the difference of method may be due to period and locality. The Rushmore remains are hypothetically much later than the chalk-pits of Pliny. The open pits and the above-ground barns seem to go together, as do the dene-holes and some sort of subterranean granaries.

Adverting to the dene-hole copses : are these primeval ? If the marling theory be correct, growing timber and brush-wood would be a hindrance to the excavation and removal of the chalk. The woods may have been planted sub-sequently, to enclose ground, dangerous and despoiled by the diggings. If the dene-holes were indeed refuges or granaries, a pre-existing wood might aid in concealment, but the disposal of the chalk would still be a difficult matter. The chances conflict, but the present woodlands are probably posterior to the dene-holes. We must, however, recall Caesar's statement ('De Bell. Gall.', V, c. 17) that a British town was a wood, fortified with an entrenchment and a rampart.

We are nearing our conclusion of the whole matter. Briefly it is this : Either the dene-holes were constructed as under-ground stores, and the chalk thrown out was disposed of in manuring the fields ; or the dene-holes were originally ' marl-pits ', which were afterwards utilized as subterranean barns. Each proposition is arguable, and the one purpose seems to be the corollary of the other. One idea doubtless followed the other without loss of time ; they may even have run parallel. The writer, feeling that Pliny's account cannot be set aside, is inclined to think that storage was generally, though perhaps not universally, the secondary purpose only.

Adaptations of this nature are before our eyes to-day. A small, disused chalk ' cave ' becomes an ice-house, a larger one is adapted as a cart-shed. Were all other chalk-pits non-existent, the antiquary might well puzzle his brains as to which was the primary object of the excavation.

As we have seen, folk-memory tells us nothing of value concerning the origin of dene-holes. Let the immediate, economic interest disappear, and the popular knowledge of industrial methods goes too. The percussion cap and the cartridge banish the flint fowling-piece, which thence-forward is known only to the collector of curios. Matches supersede flint and steel, and a hundred farm-houses may be searched in vain for a tinder-box. The horse tramway which once ran from London to Merstham was torn up only sixty years ago, but rarely can we find any one who can tell anything about its route. The spindle and distaff, yea, the candle-snuffers and the lucifer match, must soon be looked for in pictures and in museums only.

How soon an important event may pass completely into myth has been well shown by Mr. F. J. Bennett. The base of the first triangle made for the first ordnance map of Great Britain was measured on Salisbury Plain. The ends of this base line were marked by sinking two cannons in the ground until the muzzles alone stood out. One of these cannons is close to Old Sarum, and the other seven miles to the North, at Amesbury. Some twelve years ago, a native of the Old Sarum district told Mr. Bennett that the gun visible there was one of those abandoned at the autumn manœuvres in 1871, and a person at Amesbury affirmed that the gun hard by was one taken at Waterloo. Within a little more than a century all correct notions had vanished.

For the later periods, involving more romance and less rural economy, folk-memory, in the main, may probably be trusted concerning the dene-holes. Most likely the popular tradition is correct in connecting the name, as we have it, with the time of greatest stress and danger.

Meanwhile, reserved and mute throughout the ages, the dene-holes, like stoic philosophers, are ' equal to either fortune '. Call them storehouses or marl-pits indifferently, in either case they are not yet bereft of mystery or of human interest.

In lieu of an appendix proper, a rapid survey may be taken of the term ' Saracen ', already noticed as having been connected with Continental dene-holes. It was seen that the word denoted invaders of any nationality. There are equivalent terms in Old French, Spanish, Portuguese, Latin, Greek, and Arabic. The Romans and Greeks, up to the introduction of Mohammedanism, applied the term to all the nomadic tribes on the frontiers of the Roman Empire.[60] In English dialects, especially in the mining districts of Cornwall, the nickname has also been given to foreigners or to all who are not of British origin.[61]

Under the slightly disguised form ' sarsen ', the word

has been associated with megalithic monuments. It has also crept into geological nomenclature to signify the hard stones which have survived the denudation of the Woolwich and Reading Beds or of the Bagshot Sands.

A mere guess, thoughtlessly put forward by some irresponsible writer, derives the word from the village of Sarsden, near Andover (Hants). Mr. T. V. Holmes, who has written an excellent paper on ' Sarsen Stones ', says that they do not seem to have been common at that spot.[62] Moreover the old Wiltshire, and presumably Hampshire, pronunciation was, it would seem, indifferently *sarsen* or *sazzen*.[63]

Dr. Arthur J. Evans states that Sarcen (= Saracen) appears in the Anglo-Saxon Chronicle with reference to pre-Conquest days. As regards the megaliths, the common notion is that they represent heathen who have been turned to stone. The idea is found everywhere, but the term is of local application. The folk-speech of Eastern England does not seem to possess the word ' sarsen ', though it is reported from the Midlands. A piece of land near Birmingham was, in the sixteenth century, called ' the Sareson's ground '; this may represent a survival of the old meaning of ' Heathen's ground ', since, although the family name Sarson occurs in the city, it cannot be traced back more than a hundred years.[64] Cornish folk-speech calls the waste heaps from ancient tin-mines ' atall Sarazin '.[65]

In Guernsey the term is applied to a cromlech; in Brittany and in France generally a similar usage has a wide currency. Mr. Holmes cites many instances, and others could be added. The *blé noir*, or buckwheat, is also known as *sarrasin*, a word which indicates its Asiatic origin. We ourselves have sarcenet for a kind of silk, and Saracen's comfrey for a species of ragwort (*Senecio saracenicus*). In the Eastern counties, where the Danes take the place of the Saracens, we get such words as Dane's elder (*Sambucus ebulus*) and Dane's flower, or weed (*Anemone pulsatilla*), though the terms overlap into the sarsen area of Wiltshire. It is especially remarkable, also, that Gerard recorded *S. saracenicus* from Dunmow and Clare in Essex, under the name of ' Saracen's Consourd '.[66]

From Northumberland to Cornwall, and from East to West, the inn-sign ' Saracen's Head ' is very common. Mr. Holmes has collected many examples, and the present writer could increase the list. The reader will recall several that figure in literature. Larwood and Hotten state that few historical signs outlive the century that gave them birth ; ' once that stage past, they have a chance of lingering another century or two '.[67] Now John Selden was probably right in his suggestion that the name was first given after the wars with the Saracens.[68] How strong must have been the first impetus to cause the sign of ' Saracen's Head ' to be retained after all these centuries !

Consider another phase of the question. Dr. Arthur Evans has shown that there is a tendency to connect legendary heroes with ancient monuments, at the cost of earlier associations. This is markedly the case with the champions of Christianity against Islam. At some time not earlier than the tenth or eleventh century, the Rollright Stone (Warwick) was assigned to Roland the Brave, the legendary champion of Christendom, an earlier British hero being displaced in his favour.[69]

In the ninth and tenth centuries, every port of France and Spain sent forth sea-rovers, probably the scum of Saracenic peoples, on errands of conquest and plunder.[70]

We have obtained, then, this striking parallelism : at the time when the English folk were using the dene-holes as hiding-places from the Danes, and making us a bequest of the modern name ' Dane-hole', the natives of France were employing similar pits for refuge from Saracens and non-Saracens alike, handing down the nickname *Fosses sarrassines*.

The designation ' Dane-hole ' appears to mark out the last period at which the dene-holes were seriously used to harbour refugees. Hence we get a forward time-limit which will be useful as a starting-point backwards should new evidence be produced. For one can hardly believe that the pits were dug for shelter from the foe. As, moreover, the Danish period was not favourable to agriculture, we seem to be thrown back on the evidence of Pliny, after all.

CHAPTER XIII

LINCHETS

THE reader who has plodded through the two last chapters is prepared to meet many existing relics of ancient agricultural systems. Such remains, the precise age of which we shall have to consider, are exemplified in what are called linchets or lynchets. These are narrow terraces cut in hillsides, and known locally by numerous dialectal forms of the accepted word just given. For linchets have a wide distribution.

The terraces, or shelves, form tiny plateaus which may be anywhere from a few feet to a few yards in width, and have a rise from platform to platform, varying within about the same limits. These dimensions are, however, sometimes much exceeded, in which case it is probable we have linchets of a later age than the narrow kind. The linchets usually compose a number of tiers, two, three, and upwards to a score, and they may reach from the middle portion of a hill slope almost to the summit.

William Cobbett, in his ' Rural Rides ', speaks of the thousands and thousands of acres of ploughed land in shelves, in Wiltshire alone. ' The side of a steep hill [is] made into the shape of a *stairs* ; only the rising parts more sloping than those of a stairs, and deeper in proportion.'[1] Of course, the rising parts of stairs do not slope at all, but that is a trivial slip. More curious is Cobbett's faulty argument, based on the prevalence of linchets, that the gross population of the country has never varied. It is here sufficient to cite the homely illustration, and to note that, even to-day, Wiltshire has the greatest number of linchets to show us.

Variations of the word linchet were spoken of above. Of these, *lince*, and the West-country *linch*, or *lynch*, may be considered standard English, though the form *linchet* (*lynchet*) is preferable. An additional reason for discarding *linch* is, that Hampshire folk, as I can testify, call by that name the level balk or unploughed strip between two fields. As to etymology, the words come from the A.S. *hlinc*, a balk, or ridge of land. From the same root, though doubtless only mediately, come the surnames Linch and Lynch.[2] Professor F. Seebohm connects the word with the A.S. *hlinian*, to lean, and the Latin *inclinare*.[3] Dialectal forms, common from Gloucester to Hampshire, are *lanchet*, *linchard*, and *lytchet*.[4] The mere enumeration of such forms would show how widely dispersed are the terraces.

Sir James A. H. Murray gives two groups of meanings to the word *linchet* or *linch*. First, it is applied to a strip of land left unploughed between two ploughed portions. It refers also to a slope or terrace, especially on chalk downs, and for its employment in this sense Maton, an agricultural writer of the year 1797, is cited. Some of the other forms of the word are accounted for by Sir James A. H. Murray on the supposition that there has been confusion with *landshard*. Since this word has also the meaning of ' a grassy strip ', and since *linchet* itself was similarly used by Edward Lisle two centuries ago, the complexity need not trouble us. It is enough to note carefully that both *linch* and *linchet* may bear the additional interpretation of strips occurring on level ground, not on slopes, being thus the equivalent of the old Lincolnshire word *marfur* or *meerfurrow* (A.S., mere, or boundary furrow). The variant *link*, with the hard sound, seems to have been occasionally applied to terraces, but it is now practically confined to such a combination as ' golf links '.

These terms do not exhaust the nomenclature. In Wensleydale and Nidderdale *reins* and *reeans* are spoken of.[5] There is some doubt whether these reins represent true linchets, at least, generally. The correlative German word *rain* strictly means an unploughed strip of turf. Halliwell designates *rain* a Northern word, and defines it as a ridge.[6] The same meaning attaches to the word *balk*, or *baulk*, used in places as far apart as Wiltshire, Wales, and Scotland, yet it seems clear that this word is also used of the linchet proper. As we have seen, *linch* is the Hampshire equivalent of *balk*. I have recently discovered a reference

to *balk* in the 'Husbondrie' of Palladius, reprinted from
the unique manuscript of about the year A.D. 1420 : ' The
balke that thai calle unered lande ' (= unploughed land).

To note carefully these distinctions is not to be meticulous.
The real, grassy balks, which alternated with the tilled portions of land in the old open-field system of agriculture, are
fairly common throughout the country. We must, then,
remember that *linchet*—a Teutonic word—may be used in
old documents in reference to level fields. Misunderstand
the term, and there is a danger of prejudging the question.
The elevated linchets of our hill-sides might possibly be of the
same date as the flat grassy balks of the vales, but obviously
this must not be lightly assumed.

A few other local names may be mentioned. Some of
the Scotch dales have *bench-ends* or *daisses*.[7]   *Shelf* has
already appeared in the passage from Cobbett. This word
occurs in farm-names, just as homesteads are often called
' The Lynches ' (Herts. and Sussex).[8]   There are exceptions ;
I have noted a Lynch Farm at Kingston (Dorset), where no
terraces now exist—they may have been obliterated. In
Devon, where a dolmen is called a *shelf-stone*, there are
farms named Shilston.[9]

Before entering a general discussion concerning origins,
a possible error in observation must be guarded against.
River terraces, formed by deposition of material when the
river-bed was being eroded, occasionally simulate linchets.
The practised archaeologist can distinguish the genuine
from the false, but I have seen French river terraces, such
as those near Le Lioran (Cantal), which would mislead
others besides the tyro. Again, the ledges formed by the
well-known ' Chalk Rock ', which is conveniently, if not
quite correctly, taken to be the base of the Upper Chalk,
require a second or third inspection. Hard bands of flint,
turf-clad, likewise imitate the real terraces. Indeed, unless
such a keen observer and excellent antiquary as Mr. Thomas
Hardy has made a slip, the Wessex folk, arguing from
analogy, actually call such bands ' linchets '. Speaking of
Edward Springrove's cottages at Carriford, the novelist
says : ' Fifty years before this date, the spot upon which

the cottages afterwards stood was a bleak strip, along the side of the village street, difficult to cultivate, on account of the outcrop thereon of a large band of flints called locally a "lanch" or "lynchet".'[10] One fears that Mr. Hardy himself may be uncertain in the matter, for in ' Wessex Tales ' we are introduced to ' The " lynchets " or flint slopes, which belted the escarpment at intervals of a dozen yards'. If the reference be to slopes artificially faced with flints—quite another kind of object—the description is sound, but a series of naturally projecting flint bands running continuously at such short intervals would be most unusual.

There is an alternative. If Wessex folk have transferred the term to natural shelves, the change-over conveys its lesson. Folk-memory is moderately trustworthy respecting the belief that linchets were once cultivated, that is, the idea does not appear to have filtered down from the educated classes. An easy deduction leads the peasant to conclude that all terraces are of the same origin.

Now it is curious that, wherever one travels, two tales are current about the age of the linchets. The first explanation, commonly that of the peasant, who might thoughtlessly be expected to know, is that the terraces are modern : ' Oh, they were made in the days of our grandfathers '; or anon, more daringly, but followed by sturdy silence when pressed, ' I remember when they were made.' The second account comes from those of slightly higher rank, the tradesmen and large farmers : ' Oh, yes, they are very ancient, they are supposed to have been made by the Romans.' These answers, in practically the identical words, were given to the writer at Cormeilles, in Normandy, and again in Dorsetshire. The two responses, if applied to the same terraces, plainly cut away the ground from each other.

Two conclusions seem possible : either folk-memory is confused and not altogether to be depended upon, or there have been linchets raised at two or more periods. ' I mind the biggin o' 't ', is a sentiment that grows by repetition, and repetition may beget conviction. Viewed otherwise, the expression may represent a sound tradition of a practice not exceedingly remote. Linchets may conceivably have

Fig. 24. Linchets at Worth Matravers, Dorset. Situated on the beds of the Middle Purbecks, at an elevation of about 300 feet above sea-level.

been reared within living memory, though no exact records
are yet produced. Mr. G. Poulett Scrope averred that he
had himself witnessed the growth of these ' banks ', but as
these were at the foot of a steep slope, not near the top, there
is some doubt as to the exact kind of terraces alluded to.
Granting that there may have been modern constructions,
the tradition does not cover the whole history of the subject.
Older terraces existed. Thus there may have been a known
custom read into a custom entirely forgotten, a break having
been interposed.

Respecting the distribution of linchets, it would be as easy
to enumerate the counties where they are absent as to give
a list of those where they are found. The Chalk Downs of
the South of England are especially rich in examples.
Dorset and Wiltshire stand pre-eminent. The illustration
(Fig. 24) shows a group situated on the Middle Purbecks,
at Worth Matravers (Dorset). There is an even finer series
to the South-West, nearer St. Alban's Head. The ledges
are more numerous, and the drop is very steep. Though
cultivated within living memory, these linchets are known
to have been previously turfed over. There are also records
from the North-East, and from Carmarthen in the West.
Scotland abounds with well-preserved linchets, and on the
Continent they are met with in France, Spain, Germany,
Italy, and Hungary. Peru, Palestine, and India add to
the tale, and no doubt the seeing eye could detect terraces
in districts yet unrecorded. I have compiled, from personal
observation, and from the published writings of others,
a long catalogue, but it would serve no purpose to reproduce
it here.

It is becoming plain that linchets were once far more
common in Britain. As the area under tillage became
extended to support a growing population, many terraces
would be demolished. Improvements in the plough
and the introduction of cross-ploughing would aid in destroying others. Dr. Mackintosh long since wrote, ' Many
terraces are still cultivated, but every farmer I have met
with has assured me that there is now, and has been from
time immemorial, a general desire to plough down the

lynchets '.[11] The wars with France and America, during the eighteenth and early nineteenth centuries, caused many of our hilly lands to be broken up to supply food, and it was then probably that many interesting surface features were levelled down.[12]

Proceeding now to discuss the origin and purpose of the terraces, we shall scarcely be able to disentangle those questions from others which touch their age and mode of construction. These inquiries, again, involve the minor question—one dare call it minor, because the answer is so decisive—whether the linchets are of natural or of artificial origin. The writings of Professor Seebohm will be referred to, as well as the full, lucid, and masterly chapter in Mr. Gomme's 'Village Community', wherein that writer combats, in part, the arguments of Professor Seebohm and Mr. Poulett Scrope.

It will prepare the way if we realize that counsel is darkened by confusing two very different kinds of terraces—the comparatively broad, easily-cultivated shelves of the lowlands and undulating grounds, and the narrower, steeply-pitched linchets of the highlands and hills.

A generation ago, the subject of linchets was debated in *Notes and Queries*, when several correspondents, utterly mistaking the nature of the terraces under discussion, boldly stated that these were sheep-tracks, and that they could be seen in the course of formation.[13] The notion is not worth a moment's delay ; the writers were manifestly thinking of the narrow winding ledges, worn by the continual tramping of sheep, seen on every grassy hill.

Long before this, in 1798, a correspondent of the *Gentleman's Magazine*, signing himself ' Junius ', had observed the distinction between such ' minute terraces ', about half a foot wide, and the true linchets. Having seen the real linchets on the Chalk formation only, ' Junius ' was led to decide against their artificial origin.[14] In reality, linchets occur on various soils, Oolite, Chalk, Magnesian Limestone, Lias, the Purbecks, and on various sandstones. Tracts of country which lie along the slopes of the Middle Lias, particularly below the Marlstone Rock-bed, where the soil consists of micaceous sands and clays, seem to be much favoured.   Mr. H. B. Woodward has recorded many examples from Dorset, Oxford, and Warwick.[15]

Maton, writing in 1797, speaks of ' those singular natural terraces ', which ' owe their origin to subsidences of the ground in a state of solution '.   By this expression we gather that he means a sinking of the surface accompanied by mud-slides.

Dr. Mackintosh, who has already been quoted, submitted that linchets are mostly due to the erosive power of the sea waves, or to marine currents, ' at different levels, with or without floating ice.' [16]   In other words, he held that the terraces represent old coast-lines or raised beaches.   Even the famous linchets at Twyford, near Winchester, were placed in this category.   They are necessarily natural, ' unless we can conceive our ancestors having been endowed with so great a taste for the picturesque as to dig out chalk for burning in a series of ornamental steps or shelves.' [17]

Unlike such old beaches as the famous parallel roads of Glen Roy in the Highlands, the linchets, however, are not always parallel to the horizon.   They sweep obliquely round a hill at all angles ; some even run up and down the slopes, and have trenches between the balks.   Then consider how tremendous in time and how frequently repeated must have been the geological changes adequate to carve out an entire flight of terraces.   Mr. H. B. Woodward very decisively dismisses the raised beach theory : ' There is not the slightest evidence to support such a notion, which is indeed refuted by the varying inclination and distribution of the ridges.   They may occasionally be due to landslips, or to an accumulation of rain-wash.' [18]   This is the sum of the matter, and any possible exceptions have doubtless been ledges retouched by man.

Some examples supply unanswerable refutation of the raised-beach theory.   Chambers, in his ' History of Peeblesshire ', refers to linchets faced with masonry.[19]   In Islay, terraces were found supported by dwarf walls or by rough blocks of stone.   These examples are repeated in Rhineland. Some Wiltshire linchets were not only found to be so faced with flints that material for road-metal was dug therefrom, but the labourers engaged in the work sometimes came upon Roman coins, fibulae, and pottery.[20] Speaking of the Marlborough district, Mr. F. J. Bennett says that the retaining banks were faced with flint in the Chalk-with-flints area, and sometimes with sarsens in the sarsen area. Generally, vegetation and the wash of the soil obscure the facings, and the true nature of the supports can be seen only by cutting into the bank. Marlborough itself is partly built on old cultivation terraces, as shown by the peculiar level and pitch of some of the streets. Linchets have also influenced the direction of old coach-roads in the neighbourhood.[21]

In his summing-up, Mackintosh undermines his own position by admitting that the terraces have, in some cases, been partly formed by man. This conclusion would still leave the majority of the linchets as Nature's work. Like the assertion of Tate that the terraces are geological features 'levelled' and trimmed by art, Mackintosh's position is slightly more difficult to attack than the more wide-fronted statement that they are natural. Still the former objections apply none the less because the case is put in a weakened form.

It has been previously said that the linchets occasionally run up and down the slopes and are separated by trenches. Sometimes these trenches become swampy and harbour numerous water-plants, and in consequence it has been argued that linchets were constructed for drainage. That drainage was a secondary and undesigned result, due to the peculiar construction of such terraces, is probable. But a trench trodden by the feet of cattle, and waterlogged because of the slight inequalities of its gradient, would naturally support aquatic vegetation, and would allow surplus water to collect. Careful examination of a number of linchets soon disposes of the drainage hypothesis.

Though not correct, these last conjectures merge into the general opinion that linchets are indisputably artificial. Older writers usually left this question open. Baird thought that the linchets were used in Druidical ceremonies ; Pennant held that the terraces were employed by chieftains for inspecting their militia, 'rank above rank.' [22] These ingenious suggestions avoid the question of origin. Gordon, who wrote about 1730, is not so elusive. He decided that the terraces were Roman, and were thrown up as itinerary encampments. This hazard is interesting, for it seems to be the earliest date when an artificial origin, involving manual labour, was postulated by the antiquaries.[23]

The consensus of modern opinion teaches that linchets were constructed for agricultural purposes. What may be the age of the terraces, whether they were formed by the spade or the plough, and whether they were connected with the culture of some special crop or with tillage in general—are still points in dispute.

One of the latest opinions comes from Mr. Rider Haggard, who records linchets situated in large grass fields at Horley, near Banbury. These terraces are composed of red loam resting on oolite ; they are broad, and have a South or South-West aspect. Mr. Haggard believes that they are the result of spade work, and that they are the remains of old vineyards. The local name is Horley Vineyard or Horley Steps, and there is a tradition that a vineyard once existed there.[24] Anticipating the matter in an earlier work, Mr. Haggard said that there were vineyards at Ditchingham (Norfolk) in the thirteenth century, and that, judging from an old engraving, vines were grown there as late as 1750.[25]

With the Horley terraces Mr. Haggard compares others situated at Kirmond-le-Mire, near Market Rasen, Lincoln- shire (anciently Chevremont le Myrr, i.e. *Moor*). Recalling his previous notes, he again claims that the vine was culti- vated on the linchets in Roman or in later times.[26]

I have not seen the linchets at Horley, and therefore cannot say how far they conform to other well-known examples. In the winter of 1904, however, in company with Mr. J. T. Fieldsend, on whose farm the Kirmond-le- Mire terraces are situated, I carefully examined the Lincoln- shire terraces.

The Kirmond linchets form three groups. One series, near the farm-house, stands on the Chalk, which is there

obscured by loamy clay. This group consists of six or
eight rather low terraces, which could easily have been
raised by the plough, so far as turning-room and slope are
concerned. The second group is also on the Chalk, and the
third on sandstone (Tealby Beds) of Neocomian age. These
two last flights are near the tops of steep hills, and though
the use of the plough would not have been impossible, the
task of construction could not have been a light one. Near
the linchets runs the Roman road from Lincoln to the
Humber, and hard by is a large, round, pine-clad barrow,
belonging to the Bronze Age. Such a conjunction of linchets
and other ancient remains is not uncommon, as we shall
see in the sequel.

Of the Kirmond terraces, there is no ascertainable record,
either oral or documentary. As to their employment for
vine culture I am a little sceptical. One group alone faces
South, one looks North-East. Readily admitting the strife
which is waged concerning the climate of Britain in Mediaeval
and early historical periods, it must be observed that the
bulk of evidence points to the existence of greater rainfall,
more copious mists, and a lower temperature in former
times. Drainage, levelling of soil, the destruction of forests,
have combined to make the country warmer and drier.
Admittedly, Lincolnshire, on the whole, is a dry county.
The sunny chalk hills are often parched in summer time,
but the droughts and heats are too frequently followed by
blasts and blizzards. The Kirmond district of Lincolnshire
is indeed capitally suited for the ripening of corn. It is a

> Land of the grey and golden wold,
> Land of the glimmering seaward plain,

but both wold and marsh are terribly bleak and wind-swept
for many months, and crops are liable to suffer from late
spring frosts.

The former presence of vineyards in England must not,
however, be denied too rashly. Something turns on the
exact purport of the Domesday words, *vinea*, *vinum*. It
is argued by some that *vinea* implies an orchard as well as
a vineyard, since *vinum* and the correlative οἶνος had
a wider meaning than true grape-juice.

Cider has been suggested as an interpretation of the Domesday *vinum*, but it is affirmed that an ancient manuscript gives instructions for the manufacture of a beverage which could only have been wine.

Mr. de Gray Birch, however, asserts that there is no doubt of the existence of vineyards in the country at the time of the Great Survey. At Wilcote (Wilts.), there were ' *Ecclesia nova, et domus optima, et vinea bona* ' (a new church, an excellent house, and a good vineyard). Granting the restricted meaning of the term *vinea*, thirty-eight examples are recorded, chiefly from the Southern part of the realm.[27] Newly-planted vineyards are mentioned as existing in Middlesex, and, indeed, F. W. Maitland supposes that the vineyards of Domesday Book were mostly of the Normans' own planting.[28] Were this the case, and assuming that the linchets are vine-terraces, either the linchets date only from Norman times, or the Normans utilized terraces previously made for some other purpose. But we can scarcely imagine that a flat county like Middlesex ever possessed many true linchets, whether for corn or for vines. Either there were vineyards without terraces, or these latter were of very low elevation.

William of Malmesbury describes minutely the method of viticulture, as well as the flavour of the wine which was manufactured.[29] A statement of Giraldus Cambrensis makes it probable that there were a few vineyards in Ireland in the time of Bede.[30] Flavius Vopiscus (A.D. 300) tells us that vine-growing was attempted in his day,[31] and the Rev. R. W. Eyton has gone so far as to suppose that the Domesday examples were relics of the Celtic period.[32] This leaves a chance for the terrace-vineyard theory, but there are no old documents available to convert possibility into certainty.

Probably the case stands thus : There existed ancient vineyards in Britain, producing wine of inferior quality, but insufficient in quantity for home needs. Its price in Mediaeval times was not much less than that of ordinary Burgundy.[33] Soon after the dissolution of the monasteries, and perhaps partly in consequence, the vineyards

became uncultivated. The competition of the better
Continental wines no doubt hastened the ruin of the
industry.[34]

The existence of vineyards must be accepted, but this does
not imply either acceptance or rejection of the vine-terrace
theory. Superficially, there is a similitude between linchets
and Continental vine-terraces, but the likeness fades somewhat as we examine the two classes. Such vine-terraces
as I have seen in France and Germany do not present the
graceful curves of our linchets. They have not the same
curious little ' gores ' or crescent-shaped end-pieces. They
do not sweep half round a bold limestone bluff and then
disappear insensibly. Rather are they broken at intervals,
quite apart from boundary walls, and the adjacent sections
often stand at different levels. Where banked up with
masonry, the work is not crude, like the flint facings of the
linchets. The unevenness and interruptions of level may,
indeed, be due to the modern system of individual pro-
prietorship, while the long-sweeping linchets may go back
to the days of communal farming. None the less is it
probable that some of the German and Austrian records of
linchets refer actually to derelict vineyards.

But were the early Continental vineyards of the linchet
type ? It is of course possible, even probable, that the modern vineyard ledges are derivatives from the linchet ; yet
it is singular that the break-up of the open-field system
has left us no patchwork vine-terraces like those fringing the
river banks as well as the hill-tops of Germany, did such
terraces ever exist here. We have only linchets and linchets,
first and last, and no apparent off-shoots.

While, therefore, we cannot deny the possibility that
some of the broader terraces were utilized, or possibly formed,
for purposes of viticulture, the verdict at present must be
' not proven '. One may feel certain that the narrow
linchets perched on hill-tops must be excluded from the
vineyard theory, to say nothing of those on the loftiest
mountains of Argyle, or of those near St. Alban's Head,
where the glass-work of the ancient little chapel not far
distant has to be protected by wire screens from the fury

of the storms of the English Channel, which throw up fragments from the upper part of the cliff.

To summarize : If the linchets represent ancient vineyards,
we should expect to find greater uniformity of slope and
aspect in the sites chosen ; they ought also to occur in the
vicinity of Mediaeval settlements, especially those of a
monastic type.   On the contrary, we see great diversity in
steepness and size, the terraces face all points of the compass,
and they are frequently remote from Mediaeval villages,
abbeys, and monasteries.   In this connexion we must
remember that distance from the farmstead would be
a serious matter in the days of bad roads and insufficient
means of transport ; moreover, we have yet to learn that
the farmers of the Middle Ages were accustomed to till
the higher slopes of the hills.   Finally, there is the question
whether the vine would thrive on what is sometimes virtually
pure chalk—a chalk subsoil with a very thin covering of
top-earth.   As Canon Jackson once remarked, if it be true
that the linchets are old vine-terraces, then indeed must
Wiltshire have been a veritable Champagne or Burgundy
country, so numerous are the existing examples.

The advocates of the vineyard theory at any rate recognize that the linchets are artificial, and that they were used
for cultivation.   Put into its perspective, then, the exact
nature of the crop, vine or grain, is really a small matter.
Moreover, Mr. Haggard, as we shall see, is so far in line with
some modern conclusions as to suggest that the terraces
were worked by spade-culture.

This conclusion about spade-work is not everywhere
accepted.   Let us glance at the opinions of such a high
authority as Professor Seebohm.   In the old open- or common-
field system of cultivation, dating back at least to the Saxon
period, a considerable portion of the land was allotted
to the villagers in strips, each consisting of an acre or half
an acre.   These strips were known in England as 'balks',
and in Scotland as 'rigs'.   An arable strip alternated with
a turf strip or balk, the latter providing pasturage for the
cows of the temporary occupiers.[35]

Professor Seebohm continues :   'A less universal, but

equally peculiar feature of the open-field system in hilly districts is the "lynch".' Lynches, he proceeds to explain, arose through the old custom of ploughing horizontally along the hill-side, and of turning the sod of the furrow downhill, the plough having always to return one way idle. Were a whole hill-side to be ploughed as one field, there would thus be a gradual travelling of the soil from the top to the bottom of the slope, but there would be no external characters left to denote the method of cultivation employed. But let a hill-side be ploughed in strips, with grassy balks interposed between each pair, no sod could pass from one strip to the next, whilst within each individual strip the movement of the soil downwards would go on, age after age, just as in the first case. In other words, each year a furrow would be taken from the higher edge of the strip and transferred to the lower edge. Given sufficient time, the result would be that the strips would become long, level terraces, rising one above the other, and the balk would grow into steep rough banks covered with self-sown bushes and brambles.[36]

In this lucid description we have a definite claim made on behalf of the plough. Be the age of the linchets what it may, let the plough be introduced into Britain when we will, there is the postulate. Not to beat the air, it must be noticed that most, if not all, of our authorities agree that some of the broader linchets were originally plough-formed. Such terraces, comprising a few tiers only, are generally found in level districts, or on the lower slopes of hills. Consequently the pitch is slight, and the shelf low. The low terraces in the South of Portland Isle must, I think, have been so made. Others, at Hitchin, are, according to Seebohm, plough-made, and may be of Mediaeval date. The linchets at Abbotsbury (Dorset) are supposed by some to belong to the same period.[37] The date of the plough-linchets is thrown even further back by Thomas Wright, who thought it probable that the Roman plough was responsible for some of the terraces.[38]

A subsidiary argument has been advanced by Seebohm and Poulett Scrope. They contend that it was only by the linchet system that soil could be prevented from being washed down from one strip to another. In our own time, Wiltshire farmers have, in winter, carried up to the top of the hills soil which has been washed down during the previous autumn.[39] This practice, however, neither desiderates nor is productive of terraces. Allowing the argument of economic necessity for the moment, we notice that it does not touch the question of formation by spade or by plough ; so far the claim is pointless. If linchets were adopted to prevent loss of soil, they may nevertheless have been possibly raised by the spade, and they may be historic or prehistoric.

Again, did soil preservation come into play whether the hill-side belonged to one man or to many ? It is usually taught that a given strip did not permanently remain with an individual occupier. Seebohm's remarks are worth quoting somewhat fully on this point. ' Now this fact [the writer has been describing fields in the manor of Winslow, where the strips of the occupiers followed in a particular order] strongly suggests that originally the holdings had not always and permanently consisted of the same strips, but that once upon a time the strips were perhaps allotted each year in the ploughing according to a certain order of rotation. . . . This, and this alone, would give the requisite elasticity to the system, so as to allow, if necessary, of the admission of new-comers into the village community, and new virgates in the village fields '.[40] (*Virgate*=yard-land or bundle of strips.)

Professor P. Vinogradoff, after a close analysis of the opinions now current, concludes that traces of shifting ownership, or ' shifting severalty ', are found in England as scattered survivals of ' a condition which, if not general, was certainly more widely spread in earlier times '.[41]

As the common-field system has its roots in the far past, the loss-of-soil theory presumably relates to days when communal rights were paramount, when the transfer of fertilizing material from one strip to another might truly be one man's loss this year, but his own or his neighbour's gain during the succeeding twelvemonth. Thus, individual precaution would mainly be lacking. If the common-field system is pre-Saxon, or pre-Roman, the linchets might go back with it, and on this basis alone be very ancient, presupposing that terrace-cultivation was really a feature of the system, But there is serious doubt whether the word *lince*, occurring in old documents, refers to a terrace at all. If *lince* is employed in the sense of a grassy strip, the whole argument connecting the terraces with the common-field agriculture is impaired. Yet it must be admitted that the principle of soil-preservation might apply to later valley farmers who made low-lying linchets, so far as the upper-most terraces of their groups were affected.

The rotation of ownership, however, does not seem to be a settled question. First, Maitland states that, while there is evidence of early co-operation in agriculture, there is none of a communistic division of fruits. Next, he doubts whether the village folk, assembled in council, had power to allot the arable strips at regular or irregular intervals. The hold of the individual on his strip rapidly developed into a partial and inevitable ownership.[42] This contention granted, the economist's soil-theory might apply to the linchets, but it would make the terraces of a later age than would otherwise be the case. For it would be the establishment of individual ownership which most turned men's attention to loss of soil. Here the argument may be left ; prevention of soil-creep may have been a secondary motive at all times and under any system of ownership, but a more cogent reason for terrace-cultivation will be adduced presently.

It is now generally understood that there have been two modes of settlement in England. There was, first, the Neolithic, or pre-Aryan method, which mostly prevailed among the old hill-top communities, on sites now indicated by prehistoric remains ; and, secondly, there was the Aryan system. Even at the risk of ever ' laying fresh foundation-stones ', let us repeat the agricultural conditions of the Neolithic period. Forests in the valleys, marshy, undrained, and trackless, the haunt of wolves, bears, and wild boars ; even when not flooded, the valleys would be unsafe for half-naked Britons on foot. The stone tools of the settlers were unsuited to woodcraft, though a start would be made during the Bronze Age to clear the forests. Tribal defence and climatic conditions necessitated the spending of a part of the year, at least, on the uplands.

Now the usually thin-coated and exposed Chalk Downs have probably always been as bare as, or barer than, we see them to-day. On those Downs we find camps, hut-circles, barrows, and abundance of stone implements, infallible proofs of early settlements. Contrast the open downs of Wiltshire and Berks., thickly dotted with barrows and megaliths, with the better wooded Chilterns, which have little wealth of such monuments. May we not infer that in the one case the hills were bare in primitive times, but in the other there were, over large areas, thickly-timbered districts ? Only on the lower slopes of the downs, in hollows and gullies, there would be thickets of thorn, gorse, juniper, and yew, interlaced with trailing clematis and briars. Under physical conditions of this kind, the old ' wild-field grass husbandry ' might prevail. Tracts of grass could be successively cultivated, exhausted, and allowed to revert to pasture, fresh spaces of virgin soil being then broken up Such a method would, however, be sparingly adopted whenever linchets, at the cost of much labour, had been patiently raised.

Much of the downland area is thinly clad with close turf, but the surface is not uniformly destitute of a fair depth of workable soil. While on some of the slopes the turf rind is but two or three inches deep, the upper portions of the hills sometimes retain a crown of tenacious clay, perhaps a foot or two in depth, even more, if a Tertiary residue be present.

The captious, but observant, Cobbett noticed this apparent paradox. That the crown of the hill should be coated with rich brown earth, interspersed with rough, irregular flints, while the hungry coombe should have a floor consisting almost entirely of bare flints, was a bewildering fact.[43] The modern geologist, also, knows this ' Clay-with-flints ' as a source of controversy. Formerly, it was taught that this layer represented the insoluble portions, the 'vertical drift', of a considerable thickness of chalk, representing perhaps the dissolution of entire chalk zones. It has been recently shown that there must also be present the relics of other formations to account for the thickness of the deposit.[44] We now recognize, too, what Cobbett could not have been expected to perceive, that the layer of so-called 'Clay-with-flints' may actually prevent a hill-top from further denu·dation.[45] Where the summit of the hill is poorly covered with soil, either the Tertiaries have never existed or they have been denuded away.

We have outlined the Neolithic mode of settlement, which was connected with elevated grounds. In the course of the centuries, the common-field system came into vogue, with its co-tillage, its probable settled arrangements of soil-plots, and its collections of stiips, known later as 'shots' or 'furlongs'. Under this new system, grass land remained grass land, arable was kept arable. Whether this method was introduced by the Bronze Age Celts, or by later 'Aryans' like the Teutons, does not at present concern us, but it marks the farmer's invasion of the lower levels of the country. The Aryans were essentially farmers of the vale.

Not only were the bottoms now brought under tillage, but the cultivation of the hill-tops seems to have been almost altogether discarded for ages, until, indeed, pressure of population caused the abandoned tracts to be again encroached upon. Speaking of the Anglo-Saxon period, Grant Allen says that agriculture was confined to the alluvial bottoms, and had nowhere as yet invaded—he might have said, re-invaded—the uplands, or even the stiffer and drier lowland regions. Forests like those of Arden, Elmet, and the Weald remained almost untouched.[46] Parts of Salisbury Plain and of Sussex, which contain traces of ancient settlements of pre-Saxon age, were little more than a century ago unbroken and turf-clad. No plough had stirred the soil within the times covered by memory, nor, save 'a thief or twain', or an occasional shepherd, were there any signs of human life to dispel the feeling of desolation and loneliness. Yet such districts, Mr. Prothero considers,

' indelibly indicate the sites of the earliest settlements, and the nature of the soil first selected for tillage '.[47] But the sites were not Aryan, at least as regards original selection. Britons in the early Christian era—survivors from the old Neolithic stock—isolated from the main currents of life, may have sporadically cultivated these regions, but that is another matter.

The Aryan settlements were usually established near some stream. Here were rich meadows for pasturage, behind which was the homestead. At the back of the homestead, a patch of arable land stretched up the hill until the soil became too steep for the plough. Some of the broader terraces may possibly have been formed now. Above the cultivated plots there would either be the bare hill-top, or, where the soil was favourable, a tree-covered area which overreached the summit, to meet the woodlands of manors which extended upwards in an opposite direction from another river valley. In the first case—the more common one in the Chalk area—there was no need, and apparently no desire, to re-plough the old open crests and tablelands ; in the other, no necessity to clear the forests of the heights so long as clearances could be more conveniently made below. Metal weapons kept at bay the wild creatures which imperilled the lives of earlier folk. On the fringes of Windsor Forest and the Weald, village-names ending in -field (= feld, open country) are common. These places seem to represent the Teutons' first contact with the great primeval forests. Most of the survivors of old Neolithic tribes had doubtless long ere Saxon times become reconciled to new masters and new methods. The long-heads of General Pitt-Rivers's excavations indicate seeming exceptions, but even these would come into line at last.

To secure an equitable distribution of territory for each group under the Aryan settlement, great pains were taken. A good water-supply, conditioned aeons previously by the disposition of the geological strata ; a just partition of the various kinds of soil, whether chalk, clay, sand, or loam ; a fair apportionment of pasture for flocks and herds, and of woodland for pannage and fuel, fundamentally determined the boundaries of each settlement, and left traces which can be discerned in the curious outlines of parishes even in our own day. The parishes of the Evenlode valley in Oxfordshire, and of the Rother valley in Sussex, clearly show this principle of allocation. On the map of Surrey one notices long, whimsically arranged, narrow parishes, such as Godstone, Tandridge, and Burstow, which can be explained on no other theory, and I doubt not that such cases might be greatly multiplied.

Mr. W. Topley, in his classic paper on ' Parish Boundaries in the South-East of England ',[48] showed how the escarpment around the Weald was parcelled out into 125 parishes, of which 119 belong to villages situated at the foot of the slope, and only six to settlements on the Chalk higher up. Even these six parishes are not really exceptions, there being a perfectly satisfactory reason in each case. The cultivation adopted was from below upwards, but on the untenanted plateau all was bare turf, yielding abundant British remains. A large part of the Chalk area in Sussex was open land, quite unsuited for dense native woods. A like arrangement occurs in other Chalk districts of England. Mr. Topley thought that the hill-top sites were employed for refuge, and the valleys for common habitation. Other writers have suggested a seasonal migration from the heights to the plains, but this would hardly apply to the Neolithic folk, the earliest agriculturists of our country.

What was the fate of the old system of terrace cultivation, whether springing from the needs of the Stone Age or from that of the Metal Age ? It would appear that the linchets were abandoned in the face of better tools for tillage and woodcraft, and of more elaborate husbandry. The iron axe cleared the forests, virgin soil was broken up, and plateau cultivation became a lost industry. That there were certain ' linces ' under tillage in Anglo-Saxon times is well proved. They are mentioned in a charter granted by King Edward, the son of Alfred the Great, and in other old documents there is frequent allusion to ' hlincs ' and ' hlinces '.[49] To repeat : it is a moot point whether these linces were terraces or merely balks in the level fields. Some

' linces ' may have been low terraces, for, as already stated, there are linchets believed to be of Mediaeval date (see Addenda). No imperative necessity, no known incentive even, could have existed in Mediaeval times, to produce such a result as the cultivation of hill-tops. There was ample space at lower levels. Other shelves appear to have been under cultivation during the Georgian era, and the low terraces of Portland Isle are actually tilled to-day. One also encounters, now here, now yonder, traditions among country-folk as to the nature of linchets. Gerard Boate, writing in the year 1652, seems to have found traces of old terrace cultivation in Ireland.[50]

Nevertheless, there is no proof of complete continuity. The gently elevated terraces of the type understood by tradition are probably, at most, no older than the Teutonic settlement. They belong to that system of cultivation which commenced in the valley and left off some distance up the slope. The steep, strait terraces of the plateau and hill-top seem to represent that system which started from the heights and crept downwards as far as was considered safe and expedient.

Professor Seebohm observes that the country around Cambridge gives distinct evidence of almost all the features of the old open-field system, except ' lynches ', an absence which he accounts for by the flatness of the district.[51] The conclusion may scarcely be thus narrowed : no colonists, and no system of husbandry, could be expected to raise linchets on a large scale within a level area. There are no linchets because the country is flat, but whether the Cambridge area was under the plough at the time the linchets were in vogue—a doubtful question—is a quite separate problem.

Late linchets, it is true, like those of Portland, may lie on a very moderate slope. But at what period, within the domain of written history, could those terraces in Islay have been cultivated, terraces which Dr. Daniel Wilson found at great altitudes, in wastes for ages given up to the wild fox and the eagle ? A similar question might be asked concerning the ridges of which Alexander Campbell (1804) affirmed that they could be ' distinctly traced near the summits of some of our most elevated mountains ' (in Argyle). Or consider the terraces, on hills less lofty, at Newlands Kirk (Peebles), described and sketched by the late Robert Chambers. They must be extremely old (Fig. 25). Or what can be said of those shelves, in form almost square, which adorn Mere End Down (Berks.) like a terraced chessboard ? These are obviously not intended for defence, and they are too small for ploughing.[52]

Fortunately, the study of comparative customs has largely removed the question from the realm of surmise. Mr. Gomme, in his painstaking analysis, shows that the Scotch terraces, which he thinks belong to the tribal stage of man's development, are exactly paralleled by those of the Karem rice country in China. In India, again, where the races have not become so completely merged as in Europe, Aryan and pre-Aryan peoples exist side by side, each race retaining its own peculiar customs and ceremonies. The Aryans restrict themselves to the plains or ascend the slopes a very little. The older races occupy the hill-tops and cultivate the land for a short distance downwards. Their system of defensive earthworks, with trenches and covered ways, strongly resemble some of the British examples which are contiguous to our linchets.[53] The Indian evidence has been corroborated by Mr. R. B. Foote, of the Geological Survey of India. In the Bellary district, he found that the small terraces which had been raised on the hills of granitic gneiss were associated with traces of human habitations. Hard by were convenient rock-shelters, and the soil yielded abundance of flint flakes, celts, and stone implements generally.[54]

It will be an advantage to mention a few cases where British linchets are in juxtaposition with remains of unquestioned antiquity. The flint faces of certain Wiltshire linchets, which contained Roman relics, have already been alluded to. It has been suggested that the de-Romanized Britons reset the containing walls of their old terraces after the departure of the Romans. This supposition, if correct, would furnish an instance of late use, probably not common.

FIG. 25. Linchets at Newlands Kirk (Peebles-shire). These terraces begin at a height of about 40 feet above the Lyne stream, and ascend to 110 feet. The hill faces the spectator at an angle of 38°. [From a drawing by Robert Chambers in the *Proc. Soc. Antiq. Scot.* I (1855), p. 128.]

At Hambledon Hill, Hampshire, linchets are seen close to old habitations and fortified earthworks ; the terraces are, indeed, cut in the only cultivable soil in the vicinity.[55] Other Hampshire linchets are near earthen strongholds and pit dwellings ; the huts are dug in the chalk and have floors of chalk or flint. Querns, pottery, and flint flakes have fallen to the excavator, all pointing to a Neolithic origin, though there were signs of a later occupation. Blewburton Hill, Berkshire, has an ancient camp with cultivation terraces in close conjunction.[56] Stantonbury Camp, near Bath, may have served a double purpose ; the terraces are ' well adapted for slingers ', and in times of stress, the farmer doubtless became a soldier.[57] The terraces at Arthur's Seat, Edinburgh, judging from the relics dug up—skulls, deer-horns, and bronze implements—probably represent a Bronze Age settlement. To add more examples, or to labour the contention, is excess, especially if the reader is acquainted with linchets like those of Dorset and Wilts, oft-times far removed from modern or Mediaeval villages, and therefore unconnected with historical settlements. These facts must tell, yet, ' Grant we have mastered learning's crabbèd text, Still there's the comment.' And the comments themselves are also involved and hard to decipher.

With Mr. Gomme, the present writer thinks that recent knowledge of old systems of cultivation in the village community has coloured the view of those who hold that the hill-side linchets belong to Saxon or Norman times. Independent observers, not biased by modern controversies, have noticed that the comparatively inaccessible position of many linchets postulates cultivation other than that of the plough. Marshall, in 1798, supposed that the linchets of Wiltshire were made ' by hand ', because down to his time, the turnwrist, or turnwrest plough, with its reversible mould-board, never had ' a firm footing '.[58] This implement, also called the ' one-way plough ', because it turns all the furrows in one direction, can be used both going and returning along the field, and is pre-eminently the plough for hill-sides.[59] Its introduction was long posterior to the days when linchets were first made.

Messrs. Hornsby, of Grantham, and Messrs. Ransomes, of
Ipswich, inform me that the date of the introduction of
the turnwrest plough is unknown, but that the implement
has been developed from the old wooden-shared ' turnwrest '
of Kent.   This plough was first used in that county alone.
The ' one-way plough ' is of somewhat different design,
but the purpose is the same.   Marshall's point is that the
linchets might perhaps have been formed by a plough of this
kind, but that such an implement did not exist in earlier
times.   Professor Seebohm thinks that the turnwrest led
to a ' great saving of time ', but argues that it merely supplanted the earlier ' one-way-idle ' plough.

In this connexion, we must notice that old writers,
like Maton, observed that the steeper the ascent of a hill,
the narrower were the terraces, and the more abrupt the
ridges.   Could a plough, whether drawn by horses or oxen,
turn on such linchets, especially at the narrow ends ?
The villagers of Worth Matravers assert that the last time
the linchets near that village (Fig. 24) were ploughed,
both plough and team fell down the hill.   The difficulty
seems to be this : whichever kind of plough was adopted,
as the furrows gradually approached the vertical inland
bank, the team would be treading on the upturned earth,
and it would not be possible to plough close to the upright
face.   If, on the other hand, operations were begun near
the precipitous edge, away from the perpendicular face, the
team would be in danger.   These difficulties would be most
felt with the narrow linchets, but would always be present
where the terrace, once formed, had become very steep.

Professor L. C. Miall, in his charming chapter, ' The
Corn-rigs of Beamsley Fell,' looks from his study-window
across Wharfedale, and sees, in the lower valleys, old furrows
(corn-rigs) and drainage marks in pastures which have not
been cultivated within the memory of aged people.   This
is not all.   Higher up the valley are remains of more ancient
tillage, namely, ' terraces once cultivated by the spade.' [60]
Near ancient earthwork villages of Sussex and Wiltshire,
local tradition, according to Mr. Prothero, tells of a former
spade husbandry.[61]   Canon Greenwell, after stating that

some Yorkshire linchets are due to ploughing, adds that in many cases they have been undoubtedly cut in the hill-side.[62] Canon Jackson, again, thought the plough theory untenable where the hill falls precipitously, and the narrow terraces come closely together. There the pick and mattock would be used.[63] Most noteworthy of all, Professor Seebohm, in a footnote, allows that 'in some cases on the steep chalk downs, terraces for ploughing have evidently been artificially cut'. Even in these examples, however, he says there must always have been a gradual growth by annual accretions from the ploughing.[64] May it not be that the cultivators of modern England reopened and tilled with the plough wide terraces built up artificially in the long past ?

Going beyond the feeble testimony of absolute chronology, Mr. Gomme cites archaic customs which suggest that, not only were the linchets artificially cut, but that they were cut with the spade. That 'spade', too, in the first instance, was probably an implement of stone. Sir Arthur Mitchell figures a Highland caschrom (Gael. 'crooked-foot'), or footplough, which was simply a crooked piece of wood, obtusely bent and tipped with iron. This crude implement, driven into the earth by means of the foot, has been used within the present generation. No other plough, in Sir Arthur Mitchell's opinion, could take its place and do its work.[65] The Highland spade, round in the shaft, with a one-sided, iron-fronted head, fitted with a single notch to receive the digger's foot, is an even simpler tool, a mere development of the primitive digging stick.[66] Mr. Gomme has described several digging-sticks of savage races,[67] and more than one authority is of opinion that some of our flint 'celts' were agricultural tools.[68]

Opposed to spade-labour is the argument of the gigantic nature of the task involved. But, one repeats, we shall never appreciate prehistoric methods till we divest ourselves of the modern idea of economic adaptation of means to ends, allowing always for play of common sense. Witness the huge forts and earthworks, from Silbury Hill and Maiden Castle downwards ; witness the long-barrows, the soil of which was doubtless basket-borne, and which were raised

simply to satisfy an aspiration, an idea ; witness the megaliths, often dragged from afar, with an expenditure of labour
almost unaccountable.

Against the objection that primitive folk were not sufficiently skilled to raise linchets, swiftly there comes the
rejoinder that racial aptitude, as is now universally recognized, was remarkably developed along certain lines. The
scent and sight, for example, of the early hunter cannot
be understood by the modern civilized man. The workmanship displayed in some of the best flint weapons has
never, so far as I can judge from copied specimens, been
equalled by the cleverest modern fabricator. Nor could
man of to-day, supplied with like materials and appliances,
produce better pottery, better textiles, better boats, than
the ingeniously designed, though sometimes crude ' manu-
factures ' of prehistoric folk. Could not the men, who by
means of deer-horn pickaxes excavated the pits at Grimes
Graves, or who, later, hollowed out with an iron pick suites
of subterranean chambers, with partitions as it were of a
mere hand-breadth, have also grubbed up the soil with
flint-tipped mattocks and embanked it with their stone
spades ? Would the men who reared Stonehenge and
Avebury be beaten in the attempt to set up rude masonry
to support a cultivation terrace ? The questions need only
to be put in order to evoke a reply which will remove the
industrial objection.

It may now be possible to see how far the divergent
views about the age of the linchets can be reconciled.
Seebohm, we have noted, connects the terraces with the
open-field system of husbandry, and believes that they
were formed mainly by the plough. Now this same authority,
by careful methods, arrives at the conclusion that the open-
field system, with its three-course rotation of crops, as
followed in Britain, is of pre-Roman origin. First, by documentary evidence he traces the system back to the Anglo-
Saxon period. He next shows that the three-field allotment
of farms is absent from North Germany, and therefore could
not well have been introduced to Britain by Teutonic
invaders. Lastly, while granting that the Romans may

have introduced the three-course rotation of crops, he claims that this innovation was grafted on to an earlier open-field system, having its own land-divisions and its method of co-operative ploughing.[69]   In short, ' the open-field system in its simpler forms was almost certainly pre-Roman in Britain as elsewhere.' [70]   If we may fairly infer, though the assertion is not actually made, that the linchets are also assumed to belong to the earlier days of open-field husbandry, we are taken back to the domination of the Bronze Age, or at least early Iron Age, ' Aryans.'

This degree of antiquity is perhaps enough to claim on the strength of the evidence alleged.   But Professor Seebohm is insistent in showing that this open-field system was probably preceded by a tribal method of cultivation, which, like the modern ' run-dale ' or ' run-rig ' of Scotland and Ireland, was quite distinct from the settled three-field plan which ruled in England.[71]   Under the tribal system, portions of the unenclosed waste were alternately cultivated and suffered to lie lea for periods of years.[72]   In the West of Britain, vestiges of this tribal, ' and perhaps older system,' run parallel with the manorial, open-field system.   Moreover, ' neither the village nor the tribal community seems to have been introduced into Britain during an historical period reaching back 2,000 years at least.' [73]   If the tribal system, with its ' co-aration of the waste ', included linchets in its scheme, a goodly age is manifestly granted to these terraces.

Seebohm's conclusions have indeed been reviewed, and in some measure impugned, by other writers.   Maitland does not think it probable that our English fields were laid out in strips and manses (= landholders' residences) by the Britons of the pre-Roman period.[74]   Again, Vinogradoff, with his wide experience of comparative institutions, while admitting that the practice of run-rig or shifting occupation may, in the Highlands, go back to Celtic days, carefully points out that the system is found in operation among the Saxon communities of the Lowlands.[75] That fact, of course, allows for the contingency of borrowing of the custom by either people, but if it was the Highlander

of later times who copied from the Teuton, the limit of time
is lessened.

The question of how far the village community was composed of dependent serfs is keenly debated. To the serf
cultivator of Seebohm, Maitland and Vinogradoff oppose the
early freeman ; to the manorial system they reply with the
theory of ' free origins '. Maitland does not deny the
early existence of slavery, because he thinks that there
would always be sufficient inter-tribal warfare to supply
the ceorl with captives.[76] Mr. Gomme combats Professor
Seebohm's statement that ' there were manors everywhere ',
and, while allowing that the manor absorbed many of the
elements of primitive English institutions, considers that it
did not originate those institutions, and, as a governing
factor, has been antedated.[77] Instead of Seebohm's manor
with a village community in serfdom under it, Gomme sees
an Aryan tribal community with a village of non-Aryan serfs
under it : Aryan folk and Neolithic folk—' groups of kindred
occupying their several homesteads and the lands around ;
small villages of serfs occupying cottage homes massed
together and using the lands around them in intermixed or
run-rig occupation.' [78] These serfs were, at first, the hill-
top folk, who, being less accessible to the invader, did not
receive the first shock of any new conquest, and hence
retained primitive methods longer than the communities of
the valley or the plain.[79]

To pursue these conflicting technicalities will not help to
decide the age of the linchets. On all hands, a great age is
allowed for, though the terraces are assigned to periods
ranging from the Neolithic to the Teutonic. Does the
species of tool or implement employed help us ? Well, the
Aryans, as we learn from various classical writers, had the
ox-plough.[80] In addition there was the crude plough, little
more than the bent and pointed branch of a tree, which could
be drawn by men and women. Accepting the theory of
plough-construction, the linchets might still, then, be pre-
Roman. Contrariwise, it might be argued that the spade
has been used in all the ages. This drives us back on
reasonable probabilities, and we cannot do better than

recall the words of that shrewd observer and clear thinker, Grant Allen. He is speaking of the linchets near Ogbury Barrow (Wiltshire), where the soil-cap is very thin. The terracing, he thought, was a device for collecting enough soil to grow corn. But no one, he argued, has attempted to grow corn on the open Chalk Downs in any civilized period of history until the nineteenth century. The Downs are naturally so fitted for sheep-walks, that he who would endeavour to turn them into waving cornfields would be either a barbarian or an advanced agriculturist. Hence he concludes that the Downs were first terraced when a primitive system of tribal warfare existed universally in Britain.[81]

The linchets, archaeologically, occupy a peculiar position. Had no examples survived, we should not have known that they had ever existed. Some terraces have indeed been effaced by the plough, others have had their supporting-walls covered with close turf. Save, however, for a liability to a rounding of the contours, the linchet is all but indestructible under natural agencies. Hence, in lofty positions, terraces remain, and other terraces of less elevation have escaped demolition through their unsuitability for wheat-growing.

Dr. A. Jessopp humorously speaks of a time when, although every rood of land may perchance have maintained its man—he is referring to the old manors, the open-fields of which were allotted in patches of two or four roods—it was somewhat difficult for the man to maintain his rood. To some such indefinite, but pre-manorial period the linchets seem to belong, a period when individual ownership and private boundaries could not have been strictly defined.

Folk-memory tells us practically nothing on the subject. That the terraces of the lowlands should not be true survivors of the early ones, which we have supposed to be of Neolithic date, might appear curious did the case stand alone. The constant infusion of new races modified agricultural economy, and a practice once dropped would become forgotten. All the same, there is a possibility that somewhere or other the older examples were copied. Yet throughout the realm of archaeology occasional lack of continuity emphasizes the customary influence of dogged tradition. As with the dene-holes, there is occasionally a revival of methods, unintentionally imitative of others which have been lost. It is pleasant to record instances of true continuity, but with the linchets it does not seem allowable. Wherever the age and purport of the hill-top linchets are talked of by the peasantry, we may suspect that modern theories, fostered by later analogies, have supplied the clue.

Before dismissing the linchets, we must notice that Mr. J. R. Mortimer has distinguished two kinds of shelves in the East Riding, namely, cultivation terraces and habitation terraces. The cultivation terraces, presumably our linchets, possibly began, he considers, with the Romans, and continued until Mediaeval times. On the Yorkshire Wolds, these shelves are found near old villages, and they run parallel with the sides or bases of the hills. The terraces must at some time have been bounded by fences, because ash and other trees occur in places at irregular intervals along the margins. Mr. Mortimer believes that the plough was the agent of construction.[82]

The habitation terraces, or platforms, on the other hand, are classed with the Neolithic barrows as representing our oldest existing earthworks, though the two kinds of structures are not necessarily closely connected in time. These terraces may occur singly, or in groups of two or three, so far as they are still visible in East Yorkshire. Remarkably alike in appearance, they are from 15 to 21 feet broad, and 100 to 200 yards in length. One end of each terrace has the full width just given, but the other runs to a fine point. The terraces are situated at about one-third of the distance from the foot of the slope, and are quite remote from old village sites. Mr. Mortimer thinks that they were pleasant and secure spots for hunting villages.

As to the age of the ' habitation ' sites, there is more satisfactory evidence than is the case with the ' garden ' terraces. At Fimber, close to British earthworks, a terrace was trenched across, and yielded bones of animals and coarse pottery, such as are usually found in British barrows. At Leyburn, in terraces of limestone, there were discovered bones of deer and reindeer, flint implements, pot-boilers, and pottery. An exceptionally instructive terrace, lying between Fimber and Burdale, was seen to be obliquely cut through by an old, but filled-up hollow way. Sections were cut through this ancient trackway, and during the process the spade turned up fragments of Roman pottery. Nothing, however, was found lower than half the depth of the section. Hence the road itself must have been of pre-Roman date, whilst the terraces were obviously older still.[83]

The value of such testimony is very great, especially in view of scepticism as to the antiquity of ledges of earthwork. Mr. Mortimer's distinctions, nevertheless, further confuse the question. May it be that his cultivation terraces stand for our later linchets, and that his habitation terraces are the survivors of prehistoric linchets ? The hunting theory needs more support before it can gain assent.

A more fanciful distinction has recently been drawn. Messrs. A. J. and G. Hubbard, while recognizing true linchets, have described others, known in Wiltshire as ' Shepherd's Shelves ', which they suppose to have been ' wolf-platforms '. Here the tribesmen stood to keep off the wolves from the cattle compounds, situated on the hills above the terraces.[84] The hypothesis appears to rest mainly on the positions of the terraces with relation to camps and ponds of supposed ancient date. Adequate proofs are, however, quite wanting. The ponds themselves we shall at once proceed to consider, leaving the hill-top linchets provisionally explained as prehistoric cultivation terraces.

CHAPTER XIV

DEW-PONDS

A ' DEW-POND ' is an impervious or watertight hollow artificially excavated on a hill-top, deriving its main supply of water from dew, fog, and mist. It is obvious that every pond must receive a greater or less amount of rainfall, but a real dew-pond does not depend chiefly on that source. Neither is it largely fed by surface drainage, least of all by springs.

The name dew-pond is in common use, and is favoured by writers on the subject; nevertheless, it is partly a misnomer. Dew is an inadequate factor in keeping the ponds full, it is more or less universal throughout a given area, and it affects lowland ponds as well as those of the uplands. Correct notions on this point are desirable, especially if we accept the modern theory of the formation of dew.

Dr. John Aitken, in an address delivered before the Royal Society of Edinburgh in 1885, described a series of elaborate and careful experiments made by him in order to ascertain the origin and nature of dew. His conclusions were partially opposed, or at the least supplementary, to those of Wells, whose theory of dew,[1] propounded in 1814, had been accepted by all subsequent writers. Dr. Aitken claimed, with some reason, to have demonstrated that the greater part of a deposit of dew is formed of night vapour that has just risen from the ground, and has been trapped and condensed by grass and other objects in its course upwards.[2] This theory, supported by many careful experiments, is, at any rate, worthy of careful consideration, for, if correct, it would imply that a portion of the water of a dew-pond is derived from the pond itself by previous evaporation. To this extent the popular idea of the source of supply of dew-ponds is plainly erroneous.

Dew, as we shall shortly see, adds its quota to the supply

of the pond, but if this moisture first rises as vapour—a
vapour which from accidental circumstances, such as the
advent of a slight breeze, may not be laid down as dew—
a more comprehensive name must be sought for the ponds.
Dew is believed to be deposited without the aid of a cloudy
intermediary, the vapour from which it is condensed existing
in an invisible state. Again, dew and fog may occur together, and when there is fog hanging over the hills there is
generally dew on the grass. The heaviest dew, however,
would not deposit from one to two inches of water on the
grass, an amount which has been recorded as the rise in
level of a dew-pond in a single night.

Mr. G. Dines, as quoted by Mr. E. A. Martin, concluded, as
the result of observations, that the average *annual* deposit
of dew on the surface of the earth actually falls short of 1·5
inches (see footnote to Table of References, Chapter XIV).
Moreover, high downs are much exposed to wind, and
dew is with difficulty formed under windy conditions,
because the moving air does not remain long enough in one
place to allow condensation to take place.

In Wiltshire, I have observed that the peasants talk of
a ' mist-pond '. An old labourer of eighty, who, until five
or six years ago, lived near Worms Heath, Surrey, applied
the same term to the pond there. ' Mist-pond ' is also
reported from Kent.[3] Mr. F. J. Bennett has suggested
' mist-and-rain-pond ', which has the merit of preciseness,
but the demerit of length. Even then, ' mist ' must be held
to include ' fog ' also. In any event, while we continue to
use the name dew-pond, we should remember its draw-
backs.

As to geographical distribution, the dew-ponds occur
most generally on the Chalk Downs of the South and South-
East of England. They abound in Sussex and Hants, and
are not uncommon in Berks. and Wiltshire. The example
illustrated (Fig. 27) is from Surrey. No dew-ponds seem
to have been reported from Hertfordshire, but structures
by some considered quite analogous, have been noticed
on other geological formations in Warwick and Suffolk.
Records have been also garnered from the South of Portugal.[4]

Fig. 26. Types of fossils found in ancient graves and settlements. The fossils are flint 'casts' found in the Clay-with-flints, or in drift gravels and earths ; originally they were derived from the Chalk formation. On the top : *Conulus* (= *Echinoconus* = *Galerites*) *albo-galerus* : The 'Shepherd's Crown' or 'Helmet'. To the right : *Micraster praecursor*, Rowe. A typical 'Fairy loaf' or 'Fairy's heart'. To the left : *Echinocorys* (= *Ananchytes*) *scutatus*, Leske. A 'Fairy-' or 'Sugar loaf'. [Photograph by J. G. V. Dawson.]

Fig. 27. Dew-pond, Marden Park, Surrey ; 650 feet above sea-level. Beech trees overhang the Western side of the pond, the age of which is uncertain. [Photograph by W. Plomer Young.]

Marshall, in 1798, noticed Yorkshire ponds which had some likeness to our Southern ones.[5] The Lincolnshire wold farmer of to-day secures reserves for a dry season by the construction of a huge tank of galvanized iron. Much further information and more extensive records concerning distribution are desirable, but meanwhile it is essential to remember, especially when we discuss the question of age, that absence of dew-ponds in one district and presence in another tells neither way. Other places, other modes ; and this diversity may be as true of water-supply as the variety of contemporary dwellings, customs, and occupations.

The facts about the efficiency of these ponds may be simply stated. Dew-ponds preserve a supply of water on the hills when the ponds in the valley have failed. A dew-pond near Inkpen Beacon (Hants), 900 feet above the sea-level, is never dry, though it waters a large flock of sheep.[6] Another pond, situated near the celebrated Chanctonbury Ring, on the Sussex Downs, contained after the dry season of 1899 several thousand gallons of water, whilst the ponds on the plain below ran dry.[7]

Gilbert White, who was much interested in this subject, states that in May 1775, when ponds in the vale, which were of considerable size, dried up, the smaller ones on the hill-tops above Selborne were little affected. One pond, at an elevation of 300 feet above White's house, was only 30 feet in diameter, and at no time more than 3 feet deep in the middle ; yet it was never ' known to fail ', even during severe droughts. Yet that pond constantly afforded drink for three or four hundred sheep, besides twenty head of large cattle.[8]

To give a recent instance : four or five years ago, after a spell of dry weather, the strange sight could be witnessed, in a Southern county, of horses and carts climbing a dry chalk hill to fetch supplies of water.[9] Mr. E. A. Martin has humorously conjectured that such a proceeding may be the origin of the immortal Jack and Jill,[10] and there is no impossibility in the idea. Again, a small ' sedge ' of herons has been seen to desert the parched lowlands and live for some weeks near an upland dew-pond, finding therein frogs,

snails, and aquatic insects.   Thus the words of Rudyard
Kipling are scientifically correct—

> Only the dew-pond on the height,
> Unfed, that never fails—

if a little poetical licence be allowed for ' unfed ' (not visibly
fed).   At first thought, the replenishing of a pond during
a drought, and the actual diminution which sometimes occurs
during a moderately rainy season, are startling and para-
doxical facts.

Before going further, it must be stated that many dew-
ponds are known to be of modern date, and it is with the
construction of these that we shall next deal.   The method of
formation has been well described by Messrs. A. J. and G.
Hubbard in their interesting book, ' Neolithic Dew-Ponds
and Cattle-Ways.'

We are told that there still exists at least one wandering
gang of men who make the construction of dew-ponds their
special work, just as in Mediaeval times there were itinerant
bands of masons and bell-founders.   The writers inform us
that at Alfriston, Sussex, a family has been proficient as dew-
pond makers for three or four generations.   The pond-
makers select a dry soil, remote from the smallest rivulet,
which would be detrimental to the highest success.[11]

The site having been selected, earth is scooped out, much
in excess of the requirements.   A coating of dry straw is
laid over the bottom.   Then follows a layer of well-chosen,
finely-puddled clay, and over this, again, stones are closely
strewn.   Lastly, the margins are effectively protected by
well-beaten clay.[12]   The writers lay stress upon the dry
straw as an essential part of the structure.   Independent
inquiry, however, shows that the use of straw is far from
being general.   I have even heard its employment strenu-
ously denied, but, as with other sweeping statements, some
qualification must be made.   Where straw is used—if it
be still used, it doubtless assists the puddling process, by
toughening the clayey floor, and by permitting of expansion
and contraction without any cracking of the material.
Unhappily for theories, the premiss is not always clear.

Messrs. Hubbard make the straw to be the bottom layer ; other writers place it as a middle bed.

Mr. Clement Reid, who has made a careful study of the dew-ponds of South-Eastern England, says that he does not think that they are so scientifically made as is generally reported. Some dew-ponds do dry up during droughts. Farmers are continually making new ones, and sometimes, but only by accident, hit upon a satisfactory site.[13]　Mr. E. A. Martin has recorded that the famous Selborne pond, already mentioned, has been empty within late years.[14]

Mr. H. P. Slade, in a short treatise published in 1877, gave a number of practical hints on the construction of dew-ponds, which, however, for reasons to be afterwards given, he preferred to call ' Artificial Rain-Ponds '. A drawing, illustrating the author's recommendations, is given in the pamphlet. Mr. Slade insists that the slopes of the pond should be non-absorbent, else four-tenths of the supply will be lost.[15] All the weeds are not to be destroyed, as some are required to keep the pond pure. Incidentally, we are told that sheep, if left to themselves, prefer the water of dew-ponds to that of the colder springs.[16]　A well-made pond, according to Mr. Slade, remains effective for a long period ; one particular pond, made in 1836, lasted and was serviceable until 1876, when it had to be repaired.[17]

By all authorities it is agreed that worms, and the trampling of sheep and oxen, are the great enemies of dew-ponds, since these agencies tend to disintegrate the puddled floor. Richard Jefferies, describing a dew-pond—' a broad, circular, pan-like depression, partially filled with water '—says that when it was made a layer of soot was put down to repel worms and grubs.[18]

Much to our loss, White of Selborne gives no account of the making of a dew-pond, but Marshall, who wrote a little later (1798), speaks of the ' Drinking Ponds ' of the Surrey Downs and describes their construction. Each ' bason ', as he calls it, was lined with a coat of chalk, six or eight inches thick, beaten down with rammers. Next, a grout or batter, composed of pounded chalk and hot lime, was evenly spread

over the hollow, to a thickness of half an inch. Two or three
other coats were then usually applied, to ' glaze ' the bottom
and prevent the ravages of worms. Marshall adds that
these sheep ponds should be railed in so as to keep off cattle
and horses.[19] The method just described differs largely
from that given by Messrs. Hubbard, but a survival, or re-
currence, of this mode of construction is seen in the cemented
or concrete-faced ponds now becoming common. Mr. C. J.
Cornish records a dew-pond with a concrete bottom, situated
on the Brightstone Downs in the Isle of Wight, which has
never run dry for thirty years. Edward Lisle (d. 1722)
recommends that artificial ponds should have four equal
slopes, and should be ' covered with a gravel or a mortar
earth, four or five inches on the tops, which, cattle treading
in, will cement with the clay, and bind . . .' This idea of
the results of treading is erroneous, but Lisle also advised
that the pond should have ' shade ' to prevent the cracking
of the clay.

Among shepherds it is a very general maxim that the
pond should have one or two overhanging trees to aid in
condensing the fog. Mr. Clement Reid also says that the
pond should be shaded by a stunted thorn or oak, or a holly
bush. Failing these, the South bank should be cut sufficiently deep to screen off much of the sun's action.[20]

Another maxim is, that when a dew-pond is constructed
near the spur of a hill it should have the slope towards the
spur, so that a part of the rain-wash may be intercepted.
This device would, of course, put the pond outside the
strict definition, though Mr. Baldwin Latham has asserted
that there is no dew-pond which does not receive a certain
amount of surface drainage.[21] On the other hand, the
Rev. J. Clutterbuck, in his prize essay on ' Water-Supply ',
states that the highest elevations are usually selected so
that there shall be no accession of surface water.[22] This
advice was anticipated by Thomas Davis in his volume on
the agriculture of Wiltshire (1811). The supplementary
water, in any case, must not be allowed to make a forcible
inrush. Mr. Anthony Collett, writing evidently from personal
knowledge, says that even a rivulet entering the pond

renders it useless by destroying the virtues of the clay crust and the coating of straw.[23]

Just noticing, as we pass, the allusion to straw, one may observe that the supply from rain-flow would be ' wash ', that is, mud and water, and this, in time, would tend to choke up the hollow. The best dew-ponds are said to be those of the Sussex Downs, near the sea ; these ponds get the full benefit of sea-fogs, and the first draught of the moist South-West winds.

Let us next see if there is unanimity concerning the source of the bulk of the water of these ponds. In other words, are they Mist-ponds or Rain-ponds ? Mr. Slade, in the little treatise before quoted, boldly avers that ' Rain is the main, if not the whole source of the pond's supply '.[24] And again, ' Heavy rains increase the value of the rainfall '—a safe statement, surely—' while minor neither increase nor diminish it.' He appends numerous tables of observations upon which his conclusions were based, as well as some graphic representations of the fluctuating supply. In view of more recent experiments, one is driven to believe that there must have been some serious error which vitiated most of Mr. Slade's experiments. Indeed, at the end of his tractate he seems to reveal a little misgiving on his own part, for in a footnote this remark occurs, ' The annual condensation [presumably by the water of the pond] will be found to bear but a small ratio to the annual rainfall.' [25] Such a statement cannot be accepted as axiomatic. It does admit the agency of fog, but depreciates, on inconclusive evidence, as will be shown, its total effect. It should also be added that Mr. Slade's experiments appear to have been concerned chiefly, if not entirely, with one pond.

The more recent experiments, to which allusion has just been made, were carried out on the suggestion of the Rev. J. G. Cornish, at Lockinge, on the Berkshire Downs. When a heavy dew was predicted by the local shepherds, a notched stick was thrust into the pond overnight, care being taken that the notch was level with the surface of the water. The stick was removed next morning, and a fresh notch cut, to show the water-mark. On the night of January 18, 1901, a rise of $1\frac{1}{2}$ inches was recorded, on the following night 2 inches, and a little later, January 24, there was an increase of another inch. During one particular fog, occurring even in May, the level rose $1\frac{1}{2}$ inches. Five nights of winter fog gave a total accession of 8 inches. During five days of heavy spring dew, with no accompaniment of fog, occurring in April and May, an increase in the same pond of $3\frac{1}{2}$ inches only was registered. This amount, if truly produced by dew alone, is immensely greater than estimates would generally warrant. Though one of the dews was heavy, it seemed clear that the dew was a less important agent than mist.[26] It appears to be also a just inference that there must have been atmospheric movement to transfer the vapour to the dew-pond area, and since the old theory taught that a calm air is essential to the deposition of dew, Aitken's teaching about rising vapour seems here to get support.

The results obtained by Mr. Cornish, though at first sight startling, will not altogether astonish those who have had occasion to spend several hours in a fog-laden atmosphere on a moderately high hill. Tennyson had some insight touching this matter, though, with pardonable freedom, he ascribes the moisture to dew alone :—

> Calm and deep peace on this high wold,
>   And on these dews that drench the furze,
>   And all the silvery gossamers
> That twinkle into green and gold.[27]

Mr. J. H. Shorthouse, in ' John Inglesant ', brings out this phenomenon very aptly, writing as he does obviously from experience. And Gilbert White, to revert once more to the sage of Selborne, noticed that shepherds, and fishermen, and ' persons that are much abroad, and travel early and late ', have good reason to know these ' prodigious fogs '. Even in the hottest parts of summer, ' the surfaces of things are drenched by those swimming vapours, though, to the senses, all the while, little moisture seems to fall.' [28]

Mr. Clutterbuck gives calculations for ascertaining the volume of the unseen supplies of water, but as he assumes an average daily amount to be consumed by each member of the flock, his conclusions are necessarily faulty, and of vagrant interest only.

It will, however, be worth while to step outside the strict limits of our investigation, and ask what explanations of the principle of dew-ponds have been put forward. This done, we must return to our real inquiry, the age and origin of the ponds.

Dr. Stephen Hales, we are informed by White, settled the matter for himself promptly and decisively by asserting that ' more than a double quantity of dew falls on a surface of water than there does on an equal surface of moist earth '.[29] This dictum avoids the real difficulty, but even as it stands it cannot be accepted, since the rate of cooling, and consequently the amount of condensation, depends largely on local circumstances.[30]

Messrs. Hubbard's elucidation of what they call the ' thermodynamics ' of a dew-pond invokes the agency of the straw-lining already mentioned. During a warm summer's day the earth stores up a considerable amount of heat, ' while the pond, protected from this heat by the non-conductivity of the straw, is at the same time chilled by the process of evaporation from the puddled clay.' Consequently, during the warm night the moisture of the comparatively warm air is condensed on the surface of the colder clay. ' As the condensation during the night is in excess of the evaporation during the day, the pond becomes, night by night, gradually filled.'[31]

As I understand this explanation, it could only apply to the first filling of the pond. Afterwards there would be no ' cold clay ' exposed, save at the margin. The writers proceed thus : ' The dew-pond will cease to attract the dew if the layer of straw should get wet, as it then becomes of the same temperature as the surrounding earth, and ceases to act as a non-conductor of heat. This, practically, occurs if a spring is allowed to flow into the pond, or if the layer of clay (technically called the " crust ") is pierced.'[32]

Surely the straw must ultimately become wet under any conditions, be the clay rammed never so tightly. Springs may be neglected, as being unusual. Would it not be possible for the straw to get sodden by hydrostatic pressure from below ? We remember, too, that some authorities make the straw the middle layer, not the bottom, as in Messrs. Hubbard's plan. Moreover, as a fact, the tread of animals penetrates the clay crust, and the pond, though impaired in efficiency, yet continues to serve for years. What, too, of those ponds, evidently the majority, in which straw is not used ? Neither Marshall nor Jefferies mentions straw ; inquiry to-day traces it only doubtfully in most districts. Theories based on the non-conductivity of this material could therefore, at most, give only a partial solution ; where the straw is absent, they are worthless. Dry straw, indeed, as already noted, is said by Mr. Collett to be employed by the Berkshire craftsmen when lining the pond at the present day.[33] Clutterbuck also mentions straw, though he describes its purpose differently. Speaking of the making of a pond, he remarks, ' As the portions are finished, they are protected from the action of the sun and atmosphere by a covering of straw.' [34] This seems to refer to a temporary loose bed of straw placed over the crust until nightfall arrives and the pond is to start its history.

Clutterbuck tells us that when all is finished water is introduced by artificial means. If obtainable, he advises piled-up snow as the readiest and least expensive method of securing a start ; wattled hurdles should be erected to encourage, during a snowstorm, the requisite drifting.[35] A century ago, Davis recorded this filling with snow ; the after-supply, he asserted, is kept up by clouds and dew.

In the neighbourhood of Calcutta ice is obtained by placing porous earthenware pans of water in an earth cavity lined with rice straw. The straw seems here to have some value.

Another theory supposes that fog and mist collect around minute particles of dust, and these tiny spherules are more readily attracted by a sheet of water than by any other surface.[36]

A third hypothesis, propounded in 1900 by Mr. A. Marshall, teaches that there is a difference of electric potential, and therefore an attraction is set up between the innumerable

particles of fog-water and the summit of the hill on which
the pond is situated.   Mr. Marshall suspended two porcelain
basins, alike in all respects, by silk threads over a spot on
the South Downs.   An upright sheet of copper was placed
in each basin.   One basin was allowed to remain insulated
by the silk thread, but the other was earth-connected by
wire.   During the night of April 1, 1899, when a thick mist
prevailed, the basin with the insulated ' screen ' received
15·5 c.c. of water, the other, with the earth-connected screen,
collected 18·0 c.c.   The insulated apparatus tended to get
an electrical charge from the particles of moisture, therefore
the attraction was less than in the apparatus earth-connected.
The result was the more remarkable, as the silk soon became
saturated, rendering the insulation imperfect.[37]   I quote
Mr. Marshall's account, adding the simple comment that it
seems to furnish a probable, though only partial, explanation
of the phenomena.

Professor L. C. Miall gives an explanation which is here
summarized.   Moisture-laden winds, rising from lower levels,
become chilled by expansion, and the hitherto invisible
moisture is thrown down, either as clouds which gather
around the hill-top, or as dew.   Thus there is an excess of
condensation over evaporation owing to height.   This is
the first factor.   Then the pond itself acts as a powerful
ally in the following manner.   The surface-layer of the
water cools by radiation, becomes denser, and sinks.   Continual replacement of the surface-layer by the rise of the
warmer portions is set up, and this continues until the water
is cooler than the surrounding rocks and earth.   At this
stage the pond becomes an efficient condenser of vapour.
Professor Miall believes that a part, and probably a large
part, of the pond's supply is in this way derived from the
invisible moisture of the atmosphere.[38]

Some writers have argued that the presence of a tree
counts for nothing, because the increase of water is not
confined to ponds so shaded.   We note, however, that the
tree is planted as a supplementary agent only.   Mr. Reid
speaks of ponds which, on a hot summer's day, contain only
a few inches of water, insufficient, seemingly, to last a week.

Towards evening, or at early dawn, a sea-mist drifts in, and there is a continuous, steady fall of moisture from the smooth leaves of the overhanging tree. The dew-pond at Marden Park, as shown in Fig. 27, is well furnished in this respect. In town, also, one sometimes sees the pavement under an avenue of planes or poplars quite wet from the incessant drip of moisture, whilst elsewhere the dust lies like dry powder.[39]

To test the ' distilling ' power of trees, Mr. C. J. Cornish placed two vessels out of doors on a dewy evening. One was put under a cherry-tree in full leaf, and the other on stone flags away from trees. The latter vessel would be affected by dew and by the more limited condensation only, the former received the drippings from the cherry-tree. In the morning the vessel under the tree was found to contain twice as much water as the other.[40] In the Indian jungle, amid dews and mists, water patters from the trees like rain. Briefly, the predilection of the flock-master for a co-operating tree seems to be justified by results, and we may conclude that trees enhance the efficacy of the pond.

A few additional considerations are worth submitting. Wells cites experiments performed by Six, showing that there is a fall in temperature of 1° F. for an ascent of 250–300 feet.[41] Closely connected with this fact, no doubt, is the increase of rainfall in elevated regions, amounting to 3 or 4 per cent. for every 100 feet of rise.[42] Again, as noted by Miall, the evaporation on high grounds, owing to the diminished temperature, is less than on low lands.[43] There are times, too, as Baldwin Latham observes, when the water in a pond at great elevation seems to be in direct communication with the clouds, though the sky around is quite clear.[44]

The theoretical aspect of dew-ponds has now been treated with a fullness which may be pardoned in view of the scanty and little-known references to the subject in our scientific literature. We must now return to the high road of our mental journey.

We have seen that some of the dew-ponds are modern constructions. We now ask, Are all dew-ponds of recent date ? Mr. Slade, referring to examples in his own district of Wallingford, asserts that dew-ponds were not known there till about the year 1836.[45]   Thomas Davis notices them in Wiltshire thirty-five years earlier. Mr. Clutterbuck states that in one known instance the increase in the number of dew-ponds has been a matter of definite arrangement between landlord and tenant.[46]   This, of course, merely proves that dew-ponds are made at the present day.

The reverse evidence is stronger. A keen Wiltshire archaeologist, able to estimate the value of that befogged folk-memory which can always recall ' the beginning of things ', tells me that he considers the ponds on the Wiltshire Downs to be far older than the date 1836. Mr. Collett speaks with a like voice ; the Wiltshire ponds, he says, outrun all memory and tradition. In the eighteenth century they were used to water the huge flocks of sheep that were driven over the downs of Wiltshire, Hants, and Dorset on their way to the great fortnightly fairs.[47]   The tracks along which the flocks went may still be traced in our ' Drives ' and ' Drove Roads ' of the Southern counties. Vancouver speaks of dew-ponds in Hampshire in 1813. They were constructed at great labour and expense to catch the ' downfal (sic) waters ', retentive clay and flint facings being employed.[48]

Gilbert White, a careful writer, gives no hint that the dew-ponds were an innovation of his day. White was born in 1720, so we might reasonably surmise that dew-ponds were in existence during the first half of the eighteenth century. Indeed, we have a corroborative instance to hand. It is given in a curious work written by Dr. Christopher Packe, of which the following is a part only of the title : ' Explanation of a new Philosophico-Chorographical Chart of East Kent ' (1743). He describes a large pond, situated on the top of Collier's Hill, near Brabourne, in Kent, ' an hundred perpendicular feet ' above the springs below, with which it does not communicate ' except in a very flush time of water '. At such periods it overflows by an artificial cut in the lip of the pond. The pond is never empty, even after a dry spring and summer. Packe is puzzled by this phenomenon, but he gets very near the truth, for he believes that the pond is supplied by the ' condensation of elevated vapours '.[49] Whether the pond is a natural or an artificial one is not quite clear, although artificial provision has been made for an overflow. I find that the top of Collier's Hill belongs to the Hythe Beds of the Lower Greensand, underneath is the outcrop of Atherfield Clay, while the foundation is of Weald Clay. The springs referred to presumably emerge at the junction of the two first-named groups of strata. The perennial character of the pond's supply is said to be maintained to-day.[50]

Beyond the early eighteenth century, records do not seem to be available. Folk-memory is wanting, or is, at any rate, bemused by educated influence. If the dew-ponds actually existed at any period previous to the ' wool-growing ' centuries—the fifteenth and sixteenth—their introduction perhaps followed a disconnecting gap. Something of this kind, we have seen, appears to have occurred in connexion with linchets and chalk-wells. It is true that agricultural methods change slowly, and there is a possibility that a few of our extant dew-ponds are survivals from early times, and have been again and again repaired. Bearing in mind the shifting of the old population from the hills to the vales as the woodlands were cleared, I should nevertheless doubt whether the present ponds antedate the period of the Mediaeval sheep-masters. Valley pastures are usually well watered, but when the wolds and downs again came into use as sheep-walks, ponds would be essential accessories.

Yet there is a likelihood that dew-ponds of some kind were known to our ancestors of the Neolithic and the Bronze Ages. First, there is forced upon us an *a priori* probability, amounting almost to conviction, that excavations of this nature must have been known and utilized. Water was needed. Depressions are discoverable in the ground near old settlements, and are not always of the hut-circle type.

The primitive settlers of the hill-tops, who have bequeathed to us their camps, barrows, and cultivation terraces, had, above all things, an imperative need of a constant water-supply. To state an example : Within an area of 160 square miles on the South Downs, Mr. A. H. Allcroft has counted sixteen prehistoric forts, belonging to the

Neolithic and Bronze periods ; the number was doubtless
once greater. In the absence of direct and positive evidence,
we are justified in pursuing the exhaustive or eliminative
method of inquiry.

We will consider the case of Winklebury Camp, near
Basingstoke. Its age is rather uncertain, but there is a long
barrow on its boundary, and the relics already yielded seem
to indicate a late Neolithic origin. This opinion has lately
been expressed, as a result of careful exploration, by Dr.
C. H. Read, of the British Museum.[51]

Years ago, when General Pitt-Rivers was examining
Winklebury, he was struck by the absence of any visible signs
of a water-supply. The nearest place where water can be
obtained in modern times is at the foot of the hill, 850 yards
to the West of the camp.[52] A spring on the plain below is
traditionally said to have been used in the Middle Ages.
Could such sources have been satisfactory in Neolithic
times ?

We remark, first, that the interior division of the camp
was considered by Pitt-Rivers to have been reserved for cattle.
The theory that such forts as Winklebury were refuges for
men and their herds in times of strife may be indeed taken as
rightly well-trusted. But it must not be overlooked for an
instant that ancient herdsmen would require water for their
flock at all times, in peace or in war. Water must therefore
have been found for oxen and sheep as well as for tribesmen.

Setting aside the need of adequate supplies for grazing
animals, let us admit that a permanent investment of a
refuge-fort was an unlikely event. We still have to meet
the fact that neither man nor beast can live many days
without water, much less could warriors so deprived keep up
physical strength for defence. Nor would the quantity of
water required be small.

Did the inhabitants carry into the camp a supply sufficient for two or three days ? This is doubtful ; first, a hostile
inrush would permit little preparation, and secondly,
primitive skin bottles and earthenware pans would hardly
meet the demand. No ; rather is it a modern question
which says, Whence shall we bring water ? Primitive man

went where the water existed, or could be readily obtained. We may be sure that not even under the severest stress would he live on the hill-tops unless he could easily satisfy this first necessity.

Did wells, yet undiscovered, exist within the entrenchments ? We know that Normans, Saxons, and Romans were in the habit of sinking wells. Yet few Roman examples have been discovered on the Chalk Downs. I think that the reason is obvious. The requisite depth of bore would be almost prohibitive of attempts at this kind of work.

In his long and painstaking explorations at Cranborne Chase, General Pitt-Rivers discovered no wells on the high ground near the crest of the hills at Rotherly (Wilts.). On the lower levels, at Woodcuts, over the Dorset border, the spade exposed two wells, one of which was proved to be of Roman date by the finding of the remains of a Roman bucket at the bottom. This well was 188 feet in depth.[53] Holes or ' put-logs ', 12 inches apart, were cut into the sides of the shaft.[54] The shallower well, driven to a depth of 136 feet only, showed no sign that water had been reached.

A modern Woodcuts well, sunk from a level 77 feet below the site of the ancient borings, yielded no water until the rock had been drilled to a depth of 211 feet. And to-day, the only sources of water in the Chase, wherever there are no wells, are dew-ponds and the roofs of buildings. General Pitt-Rivers thought it probable that at Winklebury there may exist wells hitherto unrevealed to the investigator, but, on the whole, he inclined to settle the matter by postulating a much higher water-level in ancient times.

Should wells ever be discovered at Winklebury, they will most likely be of Romano-British date. The question is not, however, Did the Romans and Romano-Britons bore wells ? but, Did the earlier folk, equipped with rough spades of bronze and flint and mattocks of deer-horn, essay such a task ? Until we conceive this probable, and can assume that the tribesmen knew that water existed at great depths—until, in short, some Neolithic wells are produced in evidence—we may well hesitate to speak affirmatively. If the dene-holes should be cited as parallel constructions, we would answer that the true dene-hole is seldom even conjecturally Neolithic, or even of Bronze Age. While candour compels one to admit that the tasks of sinking a dene-hole and a well respectively are somewhat fairly equated, yet so long as a simple solution offers itself, we need not search for a complex one.

As to the ancient water-level of the chalk, was it sufficiently high to furnish springs close to the besieged camp ? By most writers it is agreed that the British climate of the Stone and Bronze periods was much more humid than at present. The felling of primeval forests, the introduction of artificial drainage, the rise in the mean winter temperature, have, since those days, diminished our annual rainfall. We have to remember the positive testimony of Pytheas concerning the dampness of our atmosphere in early times. Geologists believe that the intermittent ' bournes ' of the Chalk once ran more frequently. Unfortunately, adequate data on these points are not procurable, but the main argument stands. General Pitt-Rivers supposed that the well-level of the Chalk was from 30 to 50 feet higher during the Roman period, so that springs would burst out again at greater elevations.[55]

Remembering that the water-level of the Chalk, especially in the neighbourhood of large towns, is sinking year by year, owing to both natural and artificial causes,[56] the existence of a higher level in Roman times can scarcely be contested. Whether as great a difference as, say 40 feet, may be assumed, is debatable. Again, a conclusion based on the comparison of one modern well with one ancient well, without close knowledge of the dip of the Chalk, of possible faults, of the presence or absence of 'swallows' and large fissures, is not unassailable. But in the two cases given, it is not a difference in level of 40 feet, but of 100 feet, which has to be accounted for. (Woodcuts modern well, 211 feet + 77 feet = 288 feet ; Roman well, 188 feet.) Taking the greater limit actually asked for by Pitt-Rivers, namely 50 feet, such a rise in the water-level would not materially affect camps constructed at such elevations at Winklebury and Maiden Castle. Fifty feet will scarcely meet the difficulty, for Mr. Clutterbuck

states that the water-level of the Chalk varies from 100 to
400 feet beneath that of the ponds,[57] whose elevation generally corresponds with that of the camps. In the present
state of our knowledge, the well theory must be deemed
untenable. On the other hand, if we consider that General
Pitt-Rivers's reasoning is valid, it will, while removing
the necessity for dew-ponds, lend one more testimony to
the belief in the existence of ancient hill-top communities.

Once more ; a spring or bourne generally leaves some
trace in the form of a gully or dry water-course, and this
might actually be intensified after long subaerial denudation.
Some traces of this kind should remain, because turfed
ground is excellently adapted for the preservation of such
features.

Not to lose sight of the chief question, it must be repeated
that the camps are largely pre-Roman, and we have to
inquire how the inmates secured one of the prime necessities
of life. The query becomes more pertinent if we leave
Winklebury, and consider a ' contour fort ', like that of
Cissbury, where we know that there was a permanent settlement of men engaged in mining and working flint. Not
only was Cissbury, with a periphery of 1¼ miles, a settled
camp, but it was doubtless occupied continuously from
day to day, for we cannot suppose that the inhabitants
climbed up the hill every morning and down in the evening,
and that they carried with them a daily supply of water.
Yet this must be conceded, if we reject the presence of wells
or springs, unless indeed there is some fourth explanation
forthcoming.

There is such an explanation—the possibility that dew-
ponds, or hollows of a kindred nature, were utilized. The
evolution of the dew-pond, first suggested, I believe, by
Mr. F. J. Bennett, is worth considering.[58] The ditches of
the earthwork camps would be constantly trodden down,
first by the excavators, and afterwards by the members of
the garrison and their impounded cattle. We have only
to suppose a surface of Clay-with-flints, or any other retentive clay, and it is evident the fosses would soon contain
water. Additional defence would thus be provided, and,

during warfare, perhaps a supply of drinking water, in addition. Mists and dews would soon have free play, and the greater rainfall would keep up the reserve. In the course of time, the trenches might be closely rammed of set purpose. Finally, dew-ponds, imperfectly water-tight, no doubt, might be designed within or near the fort.

The accidental puddling of trenches came under the writer's notice in April 1905, when examining the series of round barrows on Povington Heath, Dorset. The weather had been dry for many days previously, and the thirsty heath, save for an occasional bog, was much parched. Where, however, the trenches encircling the barrows had a slightly clayey bottom, the water was held up. The trampling of moorland sheep and cattle may have helped in the puddling, though in the modern artificial dew-pond, where specially constructed layers or crusts are concerned, such action would have a reverse effect.

There have also probably always existed, here and there, a few natural dew-ponds, formed by depressions in the Clay-with-flints, or in Eocene clays.

It may be objected that prehistoric villagers could not have understood the principle of dew-ponds. The objection is sound, but we reply, ' Neither would they understand, except experimentally, why a clay-lined earth-cavity, or a crude pan, would retain the water in which primitive folk are accustomed to parboil their meat.' Puddling was resorted to in each case. Experience was the only light, as it is to the average flock-master of the twentieth century. One repeats, though it ought not to be necessary to say it at all, that practice does not always involve a knowledge of theory.

The theory of the development of dew-ponds above sketched may or may not be correct. But there is a coincident clue. Richard Jefferies, who shall be cited, not as possessing authority, but as one who had shrewd native insight in matters affecting agricultural economy, observed that two modern dew-ponds are situated near isolated camps in Wiltshire. He was led to infer that similar ponds could have furnished the only available supply to the ancient

communities.[59] It is necessary to state that in this and
other counties modern ponds are sometimes found near old
forts, but these instances of juxtaposition do not exhaust
all the evidence.

We may now reasonably ask whether some of the depressions in the vicinity of ancient earthworks were not dew-
ponds. The hollows may be dry, o. they may be choked
with rank vegetation. They may, again, still be subject to
swampiness, as in the depression which I have elsewhere
reported from Henley Wood, Chelsham (Surrey).[60] An oval
hollow, quite dry, occurs a little distance away. Mr. Bennett
records a small dew-pond at Ladle Hill Camp, Berkshire,
which is probably of recent construction, but he also mentions several hollows, seen by himself and Major Cooper King
at Perborough Camp (Berks.), which may represent ancient
ponds.[61] A pond situated towards the South of Chanctonbury Ring, Sussex, in a direct line between that earthwork
and Cissbury, is believed to be ancient, though it has probably been cleared more than once. Two modern ponds are
to be seen in the neighbourhood. At the Eastern angle of
the fort on Ditchling Beacon (800–50 feet) there is a dew-
pond, probably of ancient date. There is also, at the North-
west, what the historian calls a 'rain-water pond', now
dry, considered to be coeval with the earthwork, because
the ramparts have been modified in order to induce supplies
(Fig. 28).[62] Another example may also be traced hard by.
Other dew-ponds, of unknown age, lie to the West.

Mr. T. W. Shore noticed dew-ponds near Hampshire camps
of the Bronze Age, and believed that this mode of obtaining
water was known to the fortress-builders. He found that
the large camps were near wide, open, treeless areas, supposed to have been unafforested from the earliest times.
The hill-fortresses, he said, have, at the present day, either
within or near them, dew-ponds or 'cloud-ponds', or they
possess remains which attest the former existence of these
accessories. The smaller forts, found in the forests, are
supplied by streams or springs. The only instances of wells,
two in number, discovered by Mr. Shore, occurred in small
camps of this nature. He also particularizes St. Catherine's

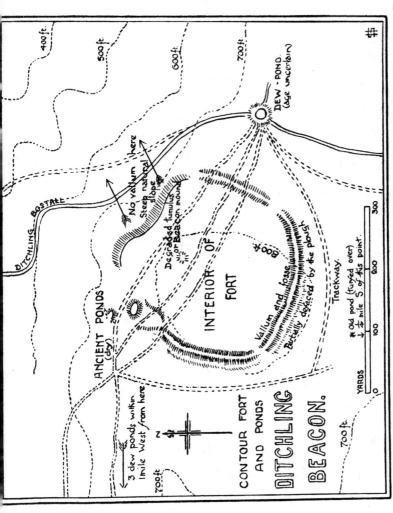

FIG. 28. Map showing ancient fort and ponds at Ditchling Beacon (Sussex). The fort is 800–50 feet above the sea-level

Hill, near Winchester, 327 feet in elevation, and requiring, according to General Pitt-Rivers's calculations, 3,300 men for its defence. This number does not take into account women and children. The water-supply, Mr. Shore thought, was afforded by a permanent dew-pond which lies at no great distance, and which to-day waters a large flock of sheep.[63]

Further examples can be given. Visitors to Maiden Castle, near Dorchester, may see, within the actual fort, what was probably an ancient pond. Messrs. Hubbard have described a dried-up dew-pond in St. Martinsell Camp, near Marlborough.[64] They give other instances, some of which must be received under reserve, until we know whether or not they are of modern construction.

Messrs. Hubbard also lay down several conclusions of vast importance should these ever be firmly established. Some dew-ponds, the writers assert, are fortified in a manner similar to that of Neolithic settlements. Signs of a dwelling, of a kind like those found within the camp, are not infrequently discovered in close proximity to the pond, and this kind of residence the writers believe to have been a guardhouse, where perhaps the cattle were counted as they passed in and out of the rings. Some Neolithic earthworks seem to have been built expressly to be in communication with the ponds.[65]

The only instance yet noted where the pond is within the camp is the already-cited case of the Dorsetshire Maiden Castle. It is suggested that, in the majority of cases, such a position would be shunned because of the trampling of cattle.

At least one failure on the part of our primitive fathers is recorded, for at Ogbury Camp (Wilts.) an unsuitable site was selected, with the result that the pond never held water. Cattle-tracks run down to it, to reappear on the farther side, as if the herds passed right through the hollow on their way to the river below.[66] The writers believe that the usual plan was to dig a pond in the very middle of cattle-tracks— that is, tracks formed by the tread of cattle, as distinguished from artificial cattle-ways—so as to intercept all paths but one. There was thus no alternative for the cattle but to drink at the dew-pond on the hills, and so keep away from the wolf-haunted lowlands. To this day the old danger from wolves is recalled by a peculiar instinct found among the half-wild cattle of Chillingham. The cows of this herd are said still to retain the habit of concealing their calves.[67]

I have tried to present Messrs. Hubbard's theories with all possible fairness, though I think that the writers go much farther than the data warrant. Before these speculations can be heartily accepted, more must be known. Meanwhile the ideas offered to us stimulate thought and encourage a search for further details.

Facts and opinions may now be gathered and allowed to converge. That many dew-ponds are of recent date admits of no question. Generally, the excavations have a recorded history of two centuries only. Probably, however, they existed from the fifteenth century onwards. They would not be needed in Norman and Saxon times. The old mound-builders required a good water-supply, and there is no available proof that the water-level of the Chalk was sufficiently high to feed the down-tops ; a definite verdict on this matter must nevertheless be suspended. Celtic farmers and their Neolithic predecessors cannot be proved on present testimony to have been well-sinkers. Lastly, hollows of the dew-pond kind would have served the purposes of the dwellers in the forts, though the ponds could not have been dug on scientific principles, being partially rain-fed, and occasionally failing of their purpose. And, indeed, all ponds situated at great heights must be to some extent fed by showers of rain and snow.

If we accept the prehistoric dew-pond, we need not rush to the extreme of thinking it the only possible mode of obtaining water. On a hill of moderate elevation, with a favourable concurrence of geological conditions, intermittent bournes or ' lavants ' might serve very well. Advantage might be taken of natural or artificial runnels whenever there was a downpour of rain, no unusual event. Temporary camps or earthworks constructed for special purposes might be intentionally planned near running streams. Thus, ancient pits, presumably for habitation, once existed near a constant spring at Coombe Hill, Croydon,[68] though no trace of either huts or spring is now to be found. Another most important consideration is that away from the Chalk Downs there were often alternative sources of supply. Hence, as with dwellings and settlements, there may have been contemporaneous diversities.

The desertion of the upland camps and settlements led to new requirements and new systems. The Teutons who tilled the valleys needed the dew-ponds little, if at all. Springs and rivulets sufficed, otherwise wells were bored. When the down-tops were once more required as sheep-walks, dew-ponds would again be a necessity. Guided by experiment and observation, the Mediaeval husbandmen and shepherds trod safely the path along which the ancients, with more or less success, patiently groped. The folk-memory of ponds was, for the time, rejuvenated. Once more tradition failed, and once more it was taken up in the nineteenth century.

Actual continuity of dew-pond construction has not been proved, perhaps cannot be proved. The same may be said of the very antiquity of the ponds. The archaeologist would be pleased were the feat possible, but it is entertainment enough to give reasons showing that the ancient and modern methods of the husbandman and the shepherd probably approximate.

CHAPTER XV

THE INCISED FIGURES OF OUR CHALK DOWNS

Our Chalk Downs, so dear to the antiquarian rambler, have yet another puzzling problem in store. No one can claim close acquaintance with the Chalk area of England without having seen one or more of those curious figures formed by the removal of the compact turfy covering. These figures, usually representing horses or men, or both, stand out, white and distinct, on many a steep hill slope. Once they were more numerous, for the invading plough, which levels earthworks, barrows, and linchets, has also scored and defaced many of these quaint pictures.

The question to be answered is easily stated. Some of these turf intaglios are known to be modern. Of others there is little or no written history—date and maker are unknown. When, and by whom, were these last-named examples constructed ?

Any folk-memory which may survive must be scrupulously tested, otherwise much perplexity will be wrought. Now and again, a magazine discussion is started concerning ' White Horses ', and thereupon some correspondent hurries forward, hot-foot, to say that he knows an old man who remembers the cutting of a particular ' Horse '. That this may be true in some instances is undeniable, but in others it is impossible. Usually, what the aged peasant remembers is most likely the renovation of a figure which existed long previous to his generation.

We have seen this freak of memory illustrated in earlier chapters. The human mind is miserable when no justification can be offered for the retention of a meaningless habit or the survival of ancient handiwork. Rarely is a tradition invented outright, much less is it the entire work of an individual person. But folk-memory, poor in direct initiative, is quick to pervert and garble a tradition which is really dying.

An example may be pardoned.   On ' St. Paul's Pitcher Day ' (St. Paul's Day, January 24) the Cornish tin-miners used to hold grotesque revelries, believed to be remnants of festive ceremonies connected with the early smelting of tin.   Some of the inhabitants allege that the mummeries were only a protest against the enforced water-drinking of the men employed in certain works.   The former explanation seems more probably correct, but as the custom was discontinued in 1859, there is now a difficulty in discovering which is the reason and which the afterthought.[1]

With one or two exceptions, the literature of 'White Horses' is both scanty and scrappy.   Conjecture has been heaped upon surmise, and confusion has become worse confounded.

One fact needs only to be stated in order to gain credence. The men who constructed later figures used the earlier ones as exemplars, though they did not necessarily make precise copies.   A bit of folk-lore, or a newly-created fashion, was the imitator's incentive in the first place, but always the modern artist had the antiques before him.   Yet he could not enter into the original spirit, for there had been a great break in the tradition.

An examination of the dated designs will help us to eliminate those which have only a pictorial or personal interest.

On the hill above the village of Preston, near Weymouth, there is a huge figure representing George III on horseback. It exhibits no little skill, since the constructor, said to have been a private soldier, had to accommodate the drawing to the curvature of the hill, at the same time preserving the true perspective effect.[2]   Another story gives the date about the year 1815, and ascribes the work, not to one man, but to a body of engineers.

The White Horse of Cherhill (Wilts.) was cut by Dr. Christopher Allsop, a physician of Calne, who intended it to serve as a landmark.[3]   We must observe, however, that close by there is an earthwork, of reputed Danish origin, and also, that from alternative interpretations of an old document, there is just a possibility that an earlier Horse existed on the spot.[4]

The White Horse of Marlborough is reported to be the work of schoolboys. They were pupils in a private school in the town (1804), and were familiar with the White Horses of Cherhill and Bratton.[5] Similar tales are attached to real antiques, but this particular account appears to be well authenticated.

An epidemic of imitation seems to have set in about this time. In 1812, a tenant farmer of Alton Barnes carved the White Horse of Pewsey (Wilts.). Another Pewsey animal, formerly seen on ' The Slopes ', has left no discernible traces.[6] The parish clerk and the publican of Broad Hinton (Wilts.) tried their skill at this kind of work in 1835. The Horse of Roundway Hill, near Devizes, cut in 1845 or 1848, is now no more.[7] Obliterated, too, is the White Horse of Hambleton (or Hambledon) Hills, East of Ripon (Yorkshire), although rumour says that it was of no great age.[8] This Horse, by the way, was cut in the Corallian rocks of the Middle Oolites. The Wootton Bassett (Wilts.) carving dates only from 1864, and about the same period was executed the White Horse design of Roulston Hill (Yorkshire), the work, it is said, of a journeyman mason.[9]

Away from the Chalk, there are figures of a horse and a stag at Mormond Hill, near Aberdeen. The first-named representation was made by a laird in memory of his favourite riding-horse, and goes back to the year 1700 ; the stag is as recent as 1870.[10]

With this example our cavalcade of modern horses may fitly end, though on the higher part of Dartmoor there is a bare patch on the granitic plateau, in form resembling a horse—whether the clearing is artificial is uncertain. The place is, however, known as White Horse Hill.[11]

We turn now to turf pictures of uncertain but ancient date and of obscure origin. The most famous White Horse—in fact the only one known to many people—is that which forms the centrepiece of the story told by the writer of ' Tom Brown's Schooldays '. This Horse was noted in the seventeenth century by Camden, Aubrey, and Baskerville. The figure is to be seen on the hill above ' Tom ' Hughes's native Uffington (Berks.), and covers an area of about an acre (Fig. 29). It has been periodically 'scoured', that is, cleared of all intruding vegetable growth, for generations, the records dating from 1738.[12] The Rev. Francis Wise, who in that year wrote a wordy treatise on the figure, says that the custom in his day was very old, and was observed once every seven years.[13] After the removal of the weeds from the 'Horse', Hughes says that there was general merry-making, accompanied by races, sword-play, and bouts with cudgels.

Traditionally, the Uffington 'Horse' is said to occupy the site, or to be in the neighbourhood of Alfred's victory over the Danes at Ashdown (A.D. 871). Wise argued for this theory in his two books (1738, 1741), and it was at first accepted by Hughes (1858). In a letter written in 1871, however, that perspicacious Berkshireman announced a change of view. 'I incline to believe that it was there long before,' he wrote, adding that the idea would be foreign to the Saxon period, nor would there be leisure in those days of strife to spend much time in ornamental work.[14] The true site of Ashdown forms a subject for dispute; to simplify matters, we may assume that the battle was fought in this district, since the casting vote is on that side of the controversy.

It would be singular, though not incredible, had a Christian monarch employed a pagan emblem to celebrate his victory. All circumstances considered, we may discount the old Berkshire ballad :—

> 'A was made a lang, lang time ago,
>   Wi' a good dale of labour and pains,
> By Alfred the Great, when he spoiled their consate,
>   And scaddled they warshirds [=rascals] the Danes.

The 'labour and pains' are undoubted.[15] The figure is 355 feet long from nose to tail, and is cut on a slope of 39°, while the declivity below is even greater.

The first authentic historical notice of the Uffington Horse occurs in the Cartulary of the Abbey of Abingdon, which may be seen in the British Museum. The exact date of the document is supposed to be A.D. 1171. The reference is to the 'Hwitceorce super flumen Tamisie'. Another cartulary of the same abbey, dating from the reign of Richard I,

Fig. 29. The White Horse of Uffington (Berks.). From a careful survey made in 1885 by the late Rev. W. C. Plenderleath. Length, from nose to tail, 355 feet; from ear to hoof, 120 feet. [By the courtesy of Commander C. W. M. Plenderleath, R.N., and Mr. R. S. Heath.]

contains the words, ' Prope montem ubi ad Album Equum scanditur . . . ' ; and the Close Rolls (1368–9) allude to ' la Vale de White Horse '.[16]

We have then, as a starting-point backwards, the year A.D. 1171, or thereabout, but no allusion to the Danes. Indeed, a conflicting tradition has to be examined. A manuscript of Bishop Pocock (1757), preserved in the British Museum, tells how that dignitary inspected the Uffington figure, and the hill below, where there was a mound called Dragon Hill. This mound was formerly deemed a barrow, but the idea is now disputed. The bishop found a story current that St. George slew the dragon on this spot, and that the chalk picture commemorated the deed.[17] Other writers have given the reading, Pendragon Hill, which may represent the British title Pendragon, of which the Dragon legend preserves a late version. The camp called ' Uffington Castle ', on the hill above the Horse, is supposed to be of pre-Roman date. The noteworthy point is that the dragon story may be older than the Ashdown tradition. And, indeed, the creature itself is almost as much dragon-like as equine.

Hard by the White Horse runs the ancient Icknield Way, and close to this old track is Wayland Smith's Forge, a ruined dolmen, representing the now uncovered framework of a long-barrow burial. Wise attempted to prove that the dolmen was Danish. Perhaps the White Horse is as much Danish as the dolmen, and not more so. In Uffington village is the Blowing Stone, with its legends and reputation in auguries. The presence of these antiquities may be of importance. Very noticeable, too, is the fact that other townships besides Uffington shared the duty of scouring the Horse. Such community of interest betrays an early origin.

From a figure published in 1735, it appears that the present Horse has undergone little modification since that date. It is at once seen that the head is bird-like in form, and hence analogies have been drawn between this creature and the ' Hen-headed Steeds ' of the Celtic goddess Ceridwen, the source of fertility and reproduction, as described in the poems of Taliessin, or Taliesin. Mr. W. F. Skene, in his ' Four

Ancient Books of Wales ', goes fully into the question of the age of these poems ; he believes that the groundwork is venerable, and that Taliessin was an actual personage of the sixth century of our era.

Certain British coins, debased copies, it may be, of the stater struck by Philip II of Macedon, also display a curious animal much resembling the Uffington Horse or ' Dragon '. The earliest of these pieces doubtless originally reached

FIG. 30. Ancient British coins, showing crescents and degraded representations of horses. a, b. ' Boduo ' coins, popularly associated with Boadicea. Notice the crescents, and the bird-like heads. c. Coin, with bird features more pronounced. d, e. Gold coins, displaying debased representations of the horse (Kent).

Britain from Gaul, but they tell us what were the prevailing artistic notions respecting horses.[18] Especially is the likeness observable in coins inscribed ' BODUO ' or ' BODUOC ', and popularly assigned to the time of Boadicea, though perhaps mistakenly (Fig. 30, a, b). The name has, however, been found on a Christian tombstone in Glamorganshire, and a probable variation, Boduogenus, on the handle of a Roman skillet. One of these Boduo pieces, it is interesting to note, has been discovered at Wallingford, barely twenty miles to

Fig. 31.   Late-Celtic bucket (Marlborough) showing how the figure of the
horse was depicted in ornamentation of the Early Iron Age.   [Reproduced
by the kind permission of Dr. C. H. Read, from the 'Guide to the Early Iron
Age'.]

the east of the White Horse Hill. In most of these coins, the horse, like the Uffington animal, faces sinister.

On the woodwork of a Late-Celtic bucket (Fig. 31) taken from a barrow near Marlborough, and supposed to belong to the first century B.C., there are curious ornamentations representing horses, comparable to those which are conspicuous features on coins of certain Gaulish tribes. Other finds, at Taplow and elsewhere, yield additional testimony to the prevalence of the horse cult.

Second in fame to the Uffington beast is the White Horse of Bratton Hill, near Westbury, in Wiltshire. This Horse was scoured so recently as 1903, but unlike its Berkshire neighbour, no story-teller has thrown around it a pleasing romance. Strictly speaking, the present figure dates only from 1778, in which year the old Horse was ' new-modelled ' by some unimaginative busybody of the district. No one would recognize in the altered Horse the quaint creature figured by Gough in 1772, which was most likely of a hoary antiquity. Truth to tell, Francis Wise, full of local pride in the Uffington animal, and weighed down by the burden of proving its great age, jauntily puts aside the Bratton Horse as modern, but the history of one creature seems to be practically that of the other.

The existing Bratton Horse measures 175 feet by 107 feet ; the eye alone is 25 feet in circumference.[19] Again oral tradition calls in Alfred, and declares that the figure perpetuates the victory over Guthrum the Dane at Ethandune (A.D. 878). Again, there is a clash of argument about the site, and the Wiltshire Edinton is but one of several claimants. Again, as at Uffington, there is a camp in the vicinity, ' Bratton Castle,' which has yielded evidence of Roman as well as Saxon occupation. Written history tells us nothing of the Bratton Horse, but a little help comes from a study of Gough's drawing. The original Horse had a crescent-shaped tip to its tail, and long ago Mr. J. Y. Akerman remarked that on British coins of the time of Cunobeline, crescents were associated with a horse (Fig. 30, a, e). Indeed, crescents are common on such coins. This coincidence led Mr. W. J. Thoms to assign a British origin to the Horse,[20] and recent writers are disposed to accept this hypothesis, especially as Taliessin sings of the 'strong horse of the crescent'.

Warwickshire possesses a Red Horse cut in the Marlstone Rock of the Lower Lias of the Edge Hills, near the village of Tysoe. The soil is there of a brown hue. The present figure is about a century old, but there existed a predecessor which was destroyed when the fields were enclosed in 1798. The former Horse was of ancient descent, and has been attributed to Guy of Warwick, who is alleged to have cut out the design in memory of his faithful steed, which he slew at Towton, preparatory to fighting on foot. This is doubtful, as any property which the Earl possessed hereabout passed to the Compton family before the Wars of the Roses. The Horse, which was noticed by Camden and Dugdale,[21] was formerly scoured each year on Palm Sunday, the expense being borne by the holder of 'Red Horse Farm'. The Rev. G. Miller has called attention to the possibility of communication by beacon-fires between the Vale of the Red Horse in Warwickshire and the Vale of the White Horse in Berkshire. Before the enclosures of fields were made, when there existed little hedgerow timber, the camp on Faringdon Clump would be visible from the Edge Hills, and the old fort on Sarsdon Hill would be an intermediate station.[22]

A White Horse, which was subjected to the usual periodical scourings, is said to have existed, generations ago, on the steep downs near the Cuckmere Valley, below Hinover (Sussex).[23] All traces have now perished.

Besides horses, the human figure has been engraved on our hill-sides. There is the huge Giant of Cerne Abbas (Fig. 32, B), in Dorset, which covers an acre of ground, is 180 feet high, and bears a club 121 feet in length.[24] Hutchins (1772) thought that the Giant represented the Saxon god Heil or Hayle, who, according to tradition, was worshipped in that part of the country. St. Augustine built Cerne Abbey to commemorate the downfall of this idol, Heil. Stukeley (1764) surmised that a Phoenician god was intended, and backed up the guess by a reference to supposed visits of tin merchants.[25] Dr. T. W. W. Smart, in his essay on

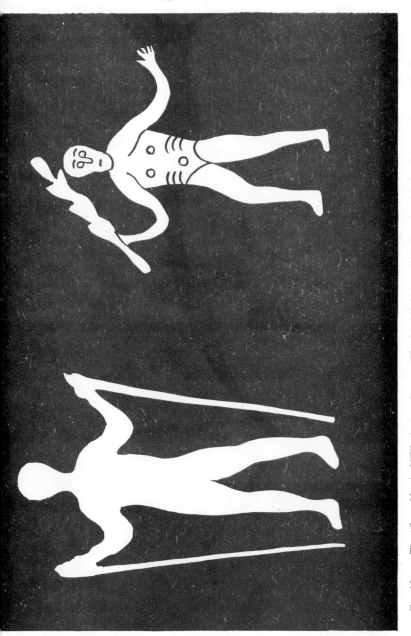

B

A

Fig. 32. A. The 'Long Man' of Wilmington, Sussex. Height, 240 feet; width, from hand to hand, 140 feet. B. The Cerne Abbas Giant, Dorset. Height, 180 feet; length of club, 121 feet. [By the courtesy of Commander C. W. M. Plenderleath, R.N., and Mr. R. S. Heath.] Cf. Drawing and detailed measurements of Cerne Abbas figure in C. Warne's 'Ancient Dorset' (1872), p. 319.

the Giant in Warne's ' Ancient Dorset ', supports the Heil theory, but otherwise does not further our quest. Finally, Dr. Sydenham considered the Giant to have a phallic signification,[26] and though we know little of possible phallic worship in Britain, the hypothesis may perhaps take its stand with others till better are put forward.

Another Giant, the Long, or Lanky Man, of Wilmington, Sussex, is 240 feet high, and holds in either hand an object, 230 feet in length, variously judged to be a staff, a club, a bow, or the old bundle of sticks of the widespread legend (Fig. 32, A). Who carved the Wilmington Giant ? The work was not done, urges Dr. J. S. Phené, by listless people in hours of idleness, for the device shows considerable care and arrangement. Neither would it be cut by monks or pilgrims, who deemed representations of the nude figure indecent. So far from the Church having carved the design, it is more probable, he argues, that the Church attempted to erase it. For here it must be explained that down to the year 1874 the Giant was covered with turf, and was only visible in a strong side light or after a thaw.[27] When the grass was removed, there were signs that the incised figure had been filled in.[28] The Giant is now clearly defined in white brick.

The two staves—if they be staves—borne by the Giant are taken to denote that he was a traveller. From incidental classical allusions, in the writings of Caesar, for example, it is conjectured that the Giant represented Mercury, the god of journeys. The figure is not at a great distance from Caesar's landing-place, and therefore, one would suppose, could scarcely be missed. Whether these surmises be correct or not, the trend of expert opinion is that the Giant is a Celtic legacy.[29]

There existed formerly a third gigantic figure on Shotover Hill, Oxfordshire ; Warne gives authorities in proof, but little else is known about it.

Dr. Phené is of opinion that figures of this kind are referred to by Caesar, in the passage wherein he describes the awful sacrifices offered by the Druids as propitiations to the gods in times of general distress.[30] The passage runs,

' *Simulacra habent, quorum contexta viminibus membra vivis hominibus complent*'; that is, the Druids had images of vast size, the limbs of which, when enclosed with wattles (osiers), they filled with living men. Then the willow fence was fired, and the victims perished amidst the hedge of flame (*circumventi flamma exanimantur homines*).[31]

From general considerations, Dr. Phené argues that the enclosure refers to an arena and not a basketwork idol.[32] The Rev. E. Conybeare contends for an interpretation of the word *simulacrum* agreeable with this hypothesis. A hollow idol of a size sufficient for the sacrifice would, however, have to be formed on an incredibly large scale. Spaces like that of the Cerne Abbas Giant, it is supposed, were probably marked out on the ground, and then shut in by palings.[33] Obviously, the two ideas of a human figure and of wattle-work may be combined. But a difficulty has to be faced. Strabo, the Greek geographer (*c.* B.C. 20), in a similar passage, says that the image (κολοσσός) was of hay, straw, or wood,[34] (χόρτος = enclosed strawyard, or feeding-place).

Is Dr. Phené's interpretation, then, admissible ? Plender-leath pertinently remarks that both modes of making enclosures are still in use. There is the fence of woven twigs, and the sheepfold, usually built of straw-covered hurdles, is a common sight in the wintry field.[35]

The older commentators of Strabo, at any rate, give no hint that the ' colossus ' means an area enclosed by hurdles. Rather do they spend their energies in discussing how the victims were burnt. The general conclusion is that a piece of lighted wood was thrown inside the basket-work. One old editor, however, A. J. Penzel (A.D. 1775), considered that the framework was made of hay covered over with wood, and that the structure was ignited as a whole: '*Häufen sie Ko-lossen Heu auf, die sie mit Holz umgeben* ' (They heap up hay on the colossus, which they surround with wood). The argument turns on a grammatical question, or more strictly on a doubt as to punctuation, and need not be further pursued.

We next note that whatever Strabo may affirm is discounted at the outset by the fact that he had no personal knowledge of Britain, little at all, says Sir E. H. Bunbury, beyond what he derived from Caesar, and this little was obtained from one or two unimportant authors. In fact, Strabo was only about ten years old when Caesar died. Hence Strabo's κολοσσός may be but a private gloss, standing for Caesar's *simulacrum*.

When, however, we have reconciled the passages in Caesar and Strabo, candour compels the admission that portable structures of wicker-work are prominent in certain Continental celebrations which Dr. Frazer considers counterparts of the old Druidical festivals.[36] There are a few classical references which also tell the same way; moreover, κολοσσός, according to the best dictionaries, always implies a gigantic statue. Town-dwellers will remember, too, another relic, the wicker cage of the Jack-in-the-green of May Day. Provisionally, one may suppose that if the incised ' Giants ' were not the actual *simulacra*, the two series of objects embodied similar root ideas, whether tribal, phallic, or totemistic.

What may be called the Hengist and Horsa theory respecting White Horses demands a word or two. John Aubrey seems to have been the first to suggest that the White Horse of Berkshire was made by Hengist, whose standard is reputed to have borne a representation of that animal.[37] Once accept Hengist as an historical personage, there is nothing inherently improbable in the theory. Both supposition and conclusion must then depend on deductive evidence. One group of disputants looks upon Hengist and Horsa as no more real men than were Cadmus and Remus.[38] The names, it is argued, symbolize the Teutonic race. ' Hengist ' means simply a horse or stallion, and ' Horsa ', a mare. Hengist and Horsa, consequently, were sometimes represented as two horses' heads, carried in front of the army as tutelary deities. Houses existed in Jutland in 1865, and probably exist to-day, which have gable rafters projecting in the form of a V, each limb of which is surmounted by a horse's head. Asked for an explanation, the natives exclaimed, ' Oh ! they are Hengist and Horsa; they are put up for good luck.'[39]

An analogy may be cited. There are sixth-century

records which tell how a Saxon chief, fighting against the Celts of the Scotch Lowlands, carried, as his standard, the fore-quarter of a headless wolf.[40] Horse-lore forms a wide subject, which I hope to examine in a future work. It will make a long story short, however, if we notice that the horse cult existed in England long before the Teutonic invasion.

To support the historicity of Hengist and Horsa, the White Horse on the banner and arms of Kent is invoked, but that creature is said to be due to a fiction evolved at a comparatively late period. From the banner to the inn sign, and thence to sacks and hop-pockets, imitation led the way.

The other parties to the dispute urge that, however true all this may be, there is no reason why actual persons bearing the names Hengist and Horsa should not have existed,[41] especially when we recall the principles on which early names were often given. Bede's statement, made while the folk-memory of the Jutish invasion of Kent was still presumably a little to be trusted, is also quoted on the positive side. That old chronicler says that Horsa was slain in battle by the Britons and buried in East Kent, where a monument bearing the warrior's name existed at the time of writing.[42] Mr. F. J. Bennett, too, has recently announced that the White Horse Stone, a huge sarsen on the chalk escarpment near Blue Bell Hill, Kent, has a rude resemblance to a human face, and that the stone has been roughly worked.

John Timbs asserts that the Saxons had adopted the White Horse on their standard before coming to England. It is found later in the arms of Savoy and the House of Brunswick. It is the proper emblem, if we may believe Ovid and other classical writers, of victory and triumph.[43] A reference to the Book of the Revelation will help to confirm this statement.[44] In Ireland there is often a prejudice against the white horse, probably because of its connexion with the Hanoverian dynasty, but also because the fanciful Celt sees therein the ' pale horse of death '.

As already indicated, a settlement of the Hengist and Horsa controversy will not decide the origin of the White Horse of Uffington, as Aubrey believed. That figure may

possibly have been executed by the Saxons, but the evidence
is altogether precarious. Let it be clearly grasped that the
Celtic races had their horse cult, that the Neolithic or
Magdalenian men who first domesticated the animal not only
used it for food but probably treated it with superstitious
veneration, that later religious customs were permeated by
horse traditions, then we shall find that a wider view must
be taken. The frequent geographical association of the
chalk intaglios with ancient remains can scarcely be for-
tuitous, and fuller knowledge may help to show connexion
between them.

It is strange that no replicas of our White Horses are
recorded from Ireland or the Continent. The absence may
not be real, the specimens may be grass-grown and indeci-
pherable. On the other hand, they may never have existed.
Our English Chalk Downs offered good scope to the artist,
yet the later Horses are not confined to that formation.
The Chalk formation is found on the Continent, though not,
perhaps, with its distinctive downland character.   There is
indeed a huge hammer roughly sculptured on a high hill
near Tours, dating beyond recorded memory. The inhabitants, who carefully keep the figure fresh and clear, associate
the hammer with Charles Martel's victory over the Saracens,
A.D. 732. (Note that Old French *martel* = hammer.) On
a hill in Hungary, too, there is cut an eagle, which is popularly connected with Eugene and the storming of Belgrade
(A.D. 1716).

From America, besides the famous raised cameo figures
of the mound-builders, there have also been reported
intaglios which seem to indicate the same purpose as those
of Britain.[45]   Among the designs in relief is one of a human
figure, carrying an implement in each hand. On the Western
shores of Lake Michigan there is actually a counterpart of
the Cerne Abbas Giant. There are, however, no records
of scouring. The mounds may shed some light on our own
figures, for some authorities believe the mound-builders to
have been the ancestors of the essentially totemistic Red
Indians. The ' animal-mounds ' are usually supposed to
be connected with totemism, and I see no great boldness

in the hypothesis that the shape of the British animal figures was partly determined by totemistic ideas. The evidence for the British case is inferential, and depends on many scattered facts, which may elsewhere repay collecting.

A recent discovery in the Raw Hide Mountains, on the Eastern spur of the Rockies, in the State of Wyoming, is worthy of a note. There, according to Mr. Robert F. Gilder, at a place popularly called ' The Spanish Diggings ', one may see prehistoric mines at which quartzite implements were once fabricated. On the almost insurmountable slope is a rude representation of the human figure, with arms upraised, the whole outlined with waste ' spalls ' of quartzite, carefully selected as regards conformity and size. The figure, known as ' the Man of the Mountains ', is covered with the lichens of ages. Twenty miles to the East is the figure of a serpent, formed in the same manner, and equally ancient.

Some authorities make much of the fact that Saxon and Roman writers do not mention the figures. The blank counts for little. The same writers tell us virtually nothing of Stonehenge, and are silent about other megaliths. They are also dumb respecting Silbury, that truncated cone of which the mass and outline are so striking, and which lies close to the old highway to the West.

Besides turf-monuments exhibiting animal figures, we possess several incised crosses. The White Cross of Whiteleaf, near Monks Risborough (Bucks.) is of the plain Greek pattern, and stands on a triangular base. The total height is 230 feet, of which the cross proper occupies 55 feet. The base is 340 feet wide.[46] Like the other colossal figures, it is visible over a large area. Like them, too, it faces West or North-West. Below are the Icknield Way and the remains of an earthwork, once known as the Black Prince's Palace.[47] This example is commonly assigned to the Saxon period, but several authorities believe that it is an earlier phallic emblem modified under Christian influences.[48] The local tale is that the cross commemorates a Christian victory over the Danes. To give all sides a hearing, it must be noted that the cross has been claimed as the armorial bearing of the Church and Priory of the monks of Christ Church, Canterbury, who held lands in the neighbourhood.[49]

The Risborough cross was formerly scrupulously scoured at intervals. At Bledlow, on a spur of the Chilterns, only a few miles distant, there is another cross, traditionally commemorating the usual 'victory over the Danes'. The name Bledlow, 'Bloody Field' or ' Hill,' is cited in corroboration, but one notices that the old Roman—and probably Celtic—road, the Icknield Way, runs near the spot.[50] As with the Risborough cross, scourings were formerly performed.[51]

Still another cross, by some deemed prehistoric, is cut in the chalk above Plumpton Place, Sussex. The arms, now turfed over, and visible only in certain lights, were originally 50 feet long. In the clear air of a summer evening, the cross could be occasionally seen a few years back. Some writers assert that the design celebrates the Battle of Lewes. Others contend that the monks of Southover cut the cross so that travellers in the distance, espying the figure, might offer a prayer for the slain.[52]

The reader will not fail to remember the crosses sunk into the barrows of the Yorkshire Wolds, nor the crosses in relief raised on old settlements (*vide* Chapter VIII). The North American figures, already alluded to, also supply instances of crosses and crescents in relief.[53]

Before dismissing hill-figures, we may profitably touch upon another class of carvings, namely, mazes and labyrinths. The Rev. G. S. Tyack, who has written an instructive paper on this subject, states that some twenty of these rustic labyrinths still exist, or are recorded by sound tradition to have existed in this country.[54]

Like the White Horses, the mazes appear to be of various ages. One at Hilton, in Huntingdonshire, has a stone pillar in the centre, giving the date of its construction as 1660. Comberton, in Cambridgeshire, has a maze 50 feet in diameter; the pathways are small trenches, 2 feet wide, the whole surface being gradually hollowed towards the centre. Mazes are also reported from Rutland, Northants, Essex, Hampshire, Nottingham, and other counties. The shapes and designs are very varied.[55]

On the Continent, mazes still exist in considerable numbers within churches and cathedrals. Generally they are found on the pavement of the building, but sometimes, when the scale is a small one, on walls and pillars. The larger ecclesiastical mazes, of which several were destroyed in France at the Revolution, are believed to have been used for 'devotional pilgrimages'. The worshipper, being unable to visit the Holy Places, could, by means of the labyrinth, follow in imagination the sufferings of the Cross. Again, the maze was probably an instrument of penance, the penitent laboriously tracing the pathways on his knees. Finally, the labyrinth had an intricate symbolism, and reminded the Christian of the difficulty of reaching heaven, that is *ciel* (the centre of the maze).[56]

Mr. Tyack says that there is but one known example of an English labyrinth within a church, and that is quite modern, being a reproduction of a local earth-maze. This is to be seen at Alkborough, or Aukborough, Lincolnshire (Fig. 33), overlooking the junction of the Ouse and the Trent, where the Humber begins. This maze, locally called 'Gilling Bore', which was noticed at length by Stukeley, continued to be frequently re-trenched during the first half of the nineteenth century.[57] Mr. J. Goulton Constable, through whose courtesy I am enabled to give a drawing of this maze, is confident that the work is to be ascribed to Benedictine monks, who had a cell or grange here from A.D. 1080 to 1220. The middle of the maze is always called Jerusalem. In Abraham de la Pryme's day (1671–1704) there was another maze at Appleby, eight miles distant. De la Pryme states that games were played in the maze, the spectators being seated on the slopes of the hill around.

Though not actually inside churches, our mazes are almost invariably adjacent to, or upon an ancient ecclesiastical site. Wing labyrinth, in Rutland, is hard by the parish church ; Sneinton (Notts.) and Boughton Green (Northants) are on spots once consecrated by chapels. Many of our turf-cut labyrinths were destroyed during the Commonwealth.[58] Not a trace remains of the celebrated Troy Town, which once existed near Guildford.

May we conclude that the turf-mazes are of ecclesiastical origin ? This is doubtful. Frequently they are called by such names as 'Troy Town' and 'Julian's Bower'; (OE.

Fɪɢ. 33.   The Aukborough Maze, Lincolnshire, believed to have been constructed by Benedictine monks in the twelfth century. The middle of the maze is called 'Jerusalem.' Total diameter, 42 feet. [From a drawing kindly made by Mr. J. Goulton Constable.]

búr=dwelling); Julian being variously understood as Julius Caesar, Julius Agricola (Vespasian's great general), or Julus, the son of Aeneas.   Some have argued that these are Mediaeval nicknames for a sport known as 'Troy Game', which arose in classic times. Doubtless many people, like the writer, can remember playing such a game as schoolboys. The idea is found in Virgil's 'Aeneid'. Strange to say, no maze seems to be connected with the name of Julian the Apostate, who was Emperor from A.D. 361–3.[59] Julian's Bower, on the Lincolnshire Wolds, overlooking the town of Louth, was formerly planted with trees, and served as a landmark to ships on the North Sea.[60] We may here compare the custom of planting trees on barrows. Moreover, we read that in 1540 the sum of three shillings was paid for the erection of a cross at the Louth ' Gelyan Bower '. The famous ' Blue Stone ', a boulder of dolerite, which stood for three or four centuries in Mercer Row, Louth, and which gave its name to an old hostelry, was brought thither from Julian's Bower.

Mazes have been recorded in proximity to holy wells, as in the Sneinton example—' Robin Hood's Race '—which was ploughed up in 1797.[61] By the way, one geometrical terrace-maze near Stirling Castle is connected with Arthur, for it has been known since the time of Barbour (c. 1375) as the ' Round Tabill '. A later name is the ' King's Knot '.

The Mediaeval mazes may possibly be developments of older ones. At any rate, the theory that dismisses the labyrinths as the result of shepherds' pastimes may itself be dismissed. Neither can we believe that the maze on St. Catherine's Hill, near Winchester, was cut by a boy who was debarred from going home for his holidays.[62]

On St. Martha's Hill, near Guildford, are some curious earth-rings, which may represent the remains of a maze. In olden times, the youths and maidens of the district met there on Good Friday, and indulged in music and boisterous dancing. Such observances could have no connexion with the solemnities of the Christian anniversary. History tells not of the origin of such celebrations. What people carved out the rings is likewise a mystery. Yet a comparison of general customs points to ceremonial dances of painted heathen around some early camp-fire.[63]

CHAPTER XVI

OLD ROADS AND TRACKWAYS

EVERY rambler is familiar with the Pilgrims' Roads, the Ridgeways, the Devil's Highways and Causeways, with which rural England abounds. It may repay us to stop and inquire how far these terms are chance nicknames and how far they may carry on ancient traditions.

Etymology, that fickle handmaid of science, gives here some little assistance. With field-names it is different. The origin of field-names is indeed surrounded with pitfalls. Decay of words, the jumble of personal names and descriptive terms, the expressions of measurements and areas, the recent date of particular boundaries, have produced fantastic designations, to which each succeeding generation of farmers seems to have contributed in turn.

Road-names are not so misleading. The very orthography often shows the real interpretation. Even where the names are so ancient that the archaeologist has to be consulted, the terms often sturdily retain their pristine force.

The Saltways tell of Mediaeval salt-works and of tributes paid to manorial lords. Old burial customs are permanently recorded in the Lyke Way (A.S. $l\bar{\imath}c$ = body) of the West Country and the Corpse Way of the Lake District. The Drove Way of Northumberland fills the imagination with pictures of Scotch shepherds bringing huge flocks and herds to English markets ; the Drove Road of Surrey speaks of the Mediaeval sheep-fairs of Wessex. The Pilgrims' Roads recall Chaucer's descriptions of gay companies, telling tales as they rode along. Of worse omen is the Tub Way of South-East Kent, dark, steep, and narrow ; it conjures up a weird vision of smugglers plying their craft. Lastly, there are roads which were repaired by the tolls collected by licensed hermits, or by individual churchmen, to whom were granted indulgences for this display of public spirit.

Some of these Middle-Age roads may be earlier pathways renamed. With the Pilgrims' Ways of South-Eastern England this is almost certainly the case. The Ridgeways, again, are, in some instances, known to be Roman.

It will be well to glance first at the Roman roads, and then to ask if they had predecessors. Frequently these roads, so marvellous in design and construction, are in regular use to-day, and are not surpassed in serviceableness by modern examples. Until the thirteenth century the Roman roads were used with little or no repair. Here and there we find lengths of a Roman ' strata ' (=*via strata*, the spread-out or levelled way), grass-grown and forgotten. Only by digging a section and noticing the careful disposition of the materials is the true nature of the foundation revealed.

Looking at the map, we find that some modification of our first axiom must be made. Watling Streets and Ermine Streets are liberally distributed over the country. The roads are generally ancient, but the folk of one region have obviously copied the names from a neighbouring district. The position appears to be as follows. Most of the names are really old. Three of them, Ermine Street, Icknield Street, and the Fosse Way, figure in the Inquisition of A.D. 1070. Together with Watling Street, about whose main course there is no dispute, these routes formed the ' Quatuor Chimini', the Four Royal Roads of England.[1] Very shortly after the date mentioned, all highways became Royal Roads, and the true course of the original four became a matter of antiquarian interest only.

Most of our information relating to these and other Roman roads comes from the ' Itinerary ' of Antonine, a work of the second or third century, but not printed till A.D. 1512.

Taking the ancient names, Geoffrey of Monmouth (d. A.D. 1154) assigned the chief of these to particular roads and localities, perhaps erroneously, and thus started a long-abiding controversy. Eighteenth-century antiquaries, especially Gale, Horsley, and Reynolds, took active part in the dispute, and conjecturally labelled other roads, whose hypothetical identification dates therefore only from this period.[2] These old writers often made free with the distances when harmonizing the 'Itinerary' with their own conclusions.

Dealing with general nomenclature, Mr. T. Codrington, in his admirable treatise, shows that certain recurring place-names point, though not unerringly, yet with tolerable certainty, to the presence of ancient Roman roads. Names like Old Street, High Street, and Green Street are self-explanatory, but sometimes, of course, they are modern. *Strata* is a better guide; it appears in Stretton, Stratton, Stretford, Stratford, and Streatham. Names referring to the paving or solid construction of the highways occur in Hardway, Stone and Stane Street, Staney Street, Stangate, Stanford, and Stony Stratford, the last being doubly significant. In Wales we get Sarn (Welsh, 'pavement'), but also the names *Heol* and *ffordd*, both of which mean 'street' or 'road' (*Hênffordd*=Old Road; *Heol lâs*=Green Road). Besides these, there are terms which tell of elevation, such as Ridge, Roman Ridge, Roman Ridgeway, Long Causeway, Devil's Causeway, High Dyke, and Atchling Dyke.[3]

Names like the foregoing show vividly how the engineering ability of the Romans impressed the imagination of the Britons. The elaborate construction, as taught in detail by classical writers like Vitruvius, may be frequently detected in the different layers of hard material, carefully graduated and rammed home. The poor islanders could only marvel; long after the withdrawal of the Romans, folk-memory retained traces of respect for the mysteries of the road-makers.

There is current a general supposition, seemingly well based, that some of the Roman roads represent older trackways straightened and adapted for rougher usage. Take the Icknield Way, which, though perhaps never made into a regular 'street', was the great war-path by which the British tribe, the Iceni, reached their East Anglian retreat. Indeed it was their only possible inlet and outlet. Marked by such place-names as Ickborough (Norfolk), Icklingham (Suffolk), Ickleton (Cambs.), and Ickleford (Herts.), all of which Dr. Guest connects with the A.S. *hild* (=war); and studded throughout its length with all kinds of British antiquities—barrows, forts, and megaliths—the pre-Roman origin is fairly manifest.[4]

Consider, again, the Kentish track known in Saxon times as Watling Street. The Rev. E. Conybeare, after describing the break-up of the British patriot confederacy under Caswallon or Cassivellaunus (B.C. 54), discusses the manner of the British retreat from Kent. Caswallon had actually fixed ' stations ' along the line of escape. The fleeing hosts kept to this route because they had an obvious objective, and this, Mr. Conybeare believes, was London, at which place there was a noted passage across the Thames. The stronghold, too, of Caswallon was in the forests near St. Albans. What, therefore, more reasonable than to suppose that the later Roman road through Kent—one of several converging ways to London—occupied the site of one of those earlier ' broad green ribands of turf ' representing olden trackways ? [5]

The old Roman road of Surrey, called on the Ordnance map Stane Street and Ermine Street, forming part of the thoroughfare from the Sussex coast to London, is believed to coincide with an earlier pathway, which the conquerors alined and metalled. Barrows and camps lie near its course, and it was probably a British track.[6] A part of the famous Pilgrims' Way, hereafter to be discussed, seems to have been converted in places into a Roman vicinal way, or by-road. No fewer than three paved portions have been discovered, and Roman villas dot its course.[7]

A broad, grassy road, marked off from the adjacent fields by low banks, passes above the Vale of the White Horse (Berks.), skirting Ashdown and Wayland Smith's Forge. This ' Green Road ', as the country-folk call it, became one of the ' Quatuor Chimini ' above-mentioned, and though probably used by the Romans, is believed to have been remade by them.[8]

Now what was the nature of the prehistoric trackways which the later roads sometimes superseded ? Hints have already been given, and these may be extended, for, happily, we have data which aid us in forming a reply.

First there are the ' hollow ways ', at one time merely

tortuous tracks, running up hill and down dale, after the unpremeditated manner of most primitive paths. Worn down ' by the traffic and the fretting of water ', as the great Selbornian puts it when describing such a road, now sixteen or eighteen feet beneath the level of the fields,[9] their appearance to-day is far different from what it was twenty centuries ago. The claim to prehistoric origin lies partly in the nature of such a path, and partly in the camps and ' locations ' which it connects. In some instances, as in the Selborne road just cited, the tracks were in use as cart-ways until within the last two hundred years.

Where carts have never been used, as in parts of the steep, bare, Chalk Downs, a little experience is needed to recognize these old by-ways. Oftentimes the primeval path is turfed over. Anon, what appears to be a long, narrow plantation, or wide, straggling hedgerow where clematis and hawthorn and honeysuckle run riot, and where a few old yews stand out as pickets, a close inspection shows that the prickly growth hides a deep, dusky track. This portion of the way never became re-turfed. Here and there is a scarred hedgerow, possibly the remnant of an ancient coppice. Other hedgerows there are, geometrically neat, except where hard times have caused neglect ; these hedges are no older, it may be, than the earlier Enclosure Acts. Follow the route patiently, and you may find it heading direct for some old earthwork. The path is again grassed over, or it becomes a streak of naked chalk rubble, or it widens into a trivial lane, along which the horse-bells of Mediaeval packmen and higglers once jingled, and the flocks of the wool-masters were driven by the shepherds.

What is needed for our enlightenment is the cutting of numerous sections through these old tracks, and the keeping of careful records of all objects of antiquity discovered along the route. Such work has been done incidentally on the Yorkshire Wolds by Mr. Mortimer. On the steep, uncultivated hill-sides, Mr. Mortimer has found hollow ways of pre-Roman age, and he believes that many others have been recently obliterated by the ploughshare.[10]

A slightly different class of prehistoric tracks comprises

those strips of turf, now broad, now narrow, which wind
around the shoulders of our hills and downlands, with little
regard to modern settlements, but with a clear relation to
those of primitive times. The wider, lower ways perhaps
were accommodated to the painted wooden chariots,[11]
whose ' crews ', armed with missiles, proved such formidable
opponents to the troops of Caesar.[12]   The straiter paths
are well described in Professor F. T. Palgrave's lines on a
Dorset trackway.   No Roman ' cemented mile-path ' was
this ; but a track which was trodden ' ere Roman and Saxon
were known '.   The poet thus sings :—

> It winds like a grassy streamlet
>   'Twixt hollies and hazels old,
> And the palms of silvery velvet,
>   Where the willow-wren twinkles in gold ;
>
> Where the wayside slopes are embosom'd
>   In gorse and feathery brake ;
> Where the round root-stems of the beeches
>   Coil like a gray old snake.' [13]

Even the narrower ways avoid the hill-tops, for there
a tribesman on the trail would be outlined against the sky,
so as to form a good target for his foe.   Midway up the
Southern slope, not only would he be better screened from
the enemy, but he would receive partial shelter from wind
and storm.   Occasionally, later users of the road made
a deviation to avoid a barrow or other sacred spot, and,
more recently, the system of enclosures produced further
diversions of the route.   Windings were also caused by the
abandonment of a soft track for a firmer one.   One remnant
of old use and wont stands out : the trackways often form
the boundaries of parishes and districts.   This is a clear
presumption of the antiquity of both boundary and pathway.   Mr. Codrington believes that a boundary running
along a lane, or hedgerow, or even across the country,
frequently indicates an ancient road when no other traces
can be discerned.[14]

As the primitive wayfarer kept away from the bleak hill-
crest, so likewise did he shun the marshy, clay bottoms.
Nor did he descend needlessly to the dry, chalk coombes—

another testimony to the former presence of a water-supply on the downs. Not for its own sake would even a savage, let alone a semi-civilized man, pursue an up-and-down route. Twice only does the course of the Pilgrims' Way in Surrey, the portion with which I am most familiar, drop down to the outcrops of the Upper Greensand and the Gault Clay, and then only for a very short space. In the one instance the Chalk escarpment has an extremely steep face,[15] in the other it has a Northerly trend, away from the direct route. The old path-finders knew that a track which would serve well in summer might in winter become a muddy rivulet or icy runnel.

Primarily, the general contours of the country, together with its geological features, would determine, not only the habitable sites, but also the trackways. Mr. R. A. C. Godwin-Austen once pointed out that the ' Stane Street ' of Sussex and Surrey strikes Northward across the Wealden area by the only practicable route, the line of the watersheds.[16] The Pilgrims' Way, too, leading from West to East, might conceivably have crossed Surrey on the Lower Greensand, had not that formation been seamed and furrowed by transverse valleys, which would cause unnecessary toil.

The avoidance of woodland ways seemed to be an instinct with the primitive Briton. Stone and bronze axes were not effective in woodcraft. To what period we ought to assign the first forest paths and rides I am at a loss to say. Scarcely to the Neolithic Age, for the needs of the Neolithic method of settlement did not correspond. Certainly not to the Palæolithic period, though that was pre-eminently the hunting stage. Yet hunters were probably the earliest agents in clearing the woods for the purpose of making roads. The chase, it must be remembered, was ever a popular occupation, even in the days of Aryan husbandry. Hence I look to the later Bronze Age and the early Iron Age for the commencement of forest roads. Even then much would depend on soil, fauna, and water-supply, and these all varied locally.

The fact remains that the dislike of woodland tracks lasted in many districts till the Middle Ages. It was found that

malefactors crouched among the brushwood as well as in
the ditches, so that in the Statute of Winchester (Edw. I,
1285) the king ordered the edges of highways to be cleared
of coppice for a distance of 200 feet on each side. A proprietor who neglected to do this was held responsible for
murders and robberies, and had to pay a fine to the king.
One exception was made, and the student should take
especial note of it. Large trees, such as oaks, might be left
standing.[17] We thus see a probable explanation of the
veteran oaks and sentinel yews which line old trackways.
We also infer that the tangled brushwood which often fills
hollow ways must frequently be of later origin.

Since we are touching upon forest roads, we may pause to
notice a mode of development suggested by Professor Patrick
Geddes. He supposes that the first clearings of the hunters
would be made in straight lines. During a great hunt, the
mounted men would ride down an avenue, while the followers
on foot, to avoid being ridden down, would run along behind
the first rows of standing trees on either side. Hence, in
the modern boulevard, the footpath is still behind the first
row of trees. Again, the Grande Étoile (= ' Star ') of Paris,
like other radiating avenues, brings back the forest to the
city. The *étoile*, so common in French forests, was the
hunters' trysting-place. Our London streets, on the other
hand, are often indirect, narrow and meandering ; they may
be derived from the primitive tracks of men and animals over
common land. With these thoroughfares we may contrast
the streets of an American city, planned in rectangles like
a ploughed field, essentially the arrangement of tillers of the
soil.[18] All these analogies are helpful, but one feels that
they must not be pressed too generally. Where there has
been direct continuity of site occupancy, these principles
may, indeed, explain the underlying folk-memory.

The detection of prehistoric tracks requires a little experience, especially where the modern agriculturist has been
at work, yet by patience one may piece out a long-lost route.
The so-called Ryknield Street, which ran from the very
heart of England and joined the Watling Street to the North
of the primeval Forest of Arden, still keeps, in places, its

Fig. 34.   The Pilgrims' Way, looking East, near Merstham, Surrey. Several 'guide' yews, with two beeches, are seen in the middle of a hollow way which has been worn in the chalk and is now overgrown with scrub and thorn.   Height, about 500 feet above the sea-level.   On the right, towards the South, the distant ridge of the Lower Greensand is faintly shown.

Fig. 35.   The Pilgrims' Way, near Little Willey Farm, Surrey.   The track. which here runs at a height of 650 feet, is represented by a rough cart-road, known as Pilgrims' Lane.   [Both photographs by Mrs. W. Johnson.]

ancient character.   Again, a narrow track near the top of
the Cotswolds, hard by the village of Broadway, and another
which crosses the fields between Alcester and Wixford, must
closely resemble in condition the road which was once
actually in use.[19]

The Portway, which passes along the top of the Longmynd,
near Church Stretton (Salop), and the Ridgeway, which
traverses the heights from Weymouth to Dorchester, are
other examples.[20]   There is another Ridgeway in Pembroke,
now metalled, and indeed many other tracks bear this name.
But of all the primitive roadways which have been discussed
of late years, none is so well known as the Pilgrims' Way of
the South of England.

The Pilgrims' Way, wherever it retains its priscan simplicity, is now all but deserted.   The poacher, the gamekeeper,
the gipsy, and the herbalist know it, and occasionally, note-
book in hand, comes the antiquary.   An old thatched cottage,
a red-tiled barn, a ruined ale-house, seemingly dropped
from the skies, are eloquent of the time when the road was
alive with traffic (Fig. 34).   Ask the peasant about the
path, and from the hidden corners of memory you may
drag some old road-name, or perhaps some fleeting tradition
of sheep-droves and pack-horses.   The track is obviously
ancient, it is of that period when, as ' in the days of Shamgar
the son of Anath, in the days of Jael, the highways were
unoccupied, and the travellers walked through the byways '.[21]
Aye, and the road is older still.

In brief, the Pilgrims' Way, as commonly understood,
leads from Winchester to Canterbury.   By general consent,
it is the road along which pilgrims travelled to the shrine of
Thomas à Becket at the great Kentish cathedral.   A stream
of visitors, from Normandy and Maine on the one hand, and
from the West Country on the other, converged by various
roads to the old city of Winchester, the erstwhile capital of
England.   Thence they proceeded along the Pilgrims' Way
to Alresford, Ropley, and Alton, entering Surrey at the
town of Farnham.   From this place they traversed the slope
of the Hog's Back almost to Guildford, thence by St. Martha's
Hill, and over Merrow Downs to Dorking, near which they

crossed the ' sullen Mole ' by a ford at Burford Bridge. The road then ascended Box Hill, passed by the afterwards notorious pocket-borough of Gatton (Gate-town), then touched the foot of Merstham Churchyard, where, hard by, was a bourne, or intermittent spring. Next it went across the shoulder of the Downs, flanked White Hill, and passing Titsey and Tatsfield, left the county of Surrey at Cold Harbour Green.[22] The last name is redolent of unending controversy, but, as the most widely accepted theory bears somewhat on our subject, I give it here. A Cold Harbour, then, was probably some kind of rough shelter, a poor tenement which provided sleeping accommodation only. In the North, its name and place are represented by ' Windy Arbour '.[23] From the Surrey border the road headed for Wrotham, Kits Coty House, and Hollingbourne, whence it passed through Charing to Canterbury.

Mr. Hilaire Belloc, after close personal investigation, asserts that, of the 120 miles covered by the old road, 60 per cent. of that distance is known. There is no gap greater than 7 miles, while stretches are continuous up to 15 miles.[24]

As soon as one attempts to prove that the Pilgrims' Way is a prehistoric road, the critic who is conversant with the facts may justly inquire, ' Which Pilgrims' Way ? ' Without doubt, in some portions of the area traversed, there are numerous intersecting tracks, and it would be rash to affirm which individual path is there the strict thoroughfare. West of Gatton, so complex are the crossways that it is difficult to favour one more than another. The reason is simple. Assuming that a previous road existed, Mediaeval pilgrims would naturally pursue its course where convenient, but they would constantly be branching off towards churches which lay at the foot of the hills, to visit a shrine, to worship, to procure water at a holy well. Unlike sheep, pilgrims would prefer spring water to that of dew-ponds, even if the latter kind were deemed potable by the easy-going Mediaevalists.

Lest the fact that the Way was used by pilgrims should itself be questioned, it may be said that folk-memory is still fairly sound on the matter. Peasants and townspeople, as the writer can avouch, still talk of the old track. Elderly

shepherds and quarrymen will tell one, as they told Sir Gilbert
Scott when he lived at the foot of White Hill, near Godstone,
the course taken by the ancient Way, though it is now obliterated by the plough.[25]   The pilgrim tradition, though the
older, is more vigorous than that of sheep-road.   Moreover,
the folk-names applied to particular stretches of the Way are
very significant.   We find Beggars' Lane, Beggars' Wood, and
Beggars' Corner, which tell of mendicants and almsgiving ;
Farthing Copse and Halfpenny Copse, reminiscent of tolls
and pilgrims' pence ;   Paternoster Row and Pray Meadows,
which   mark   devotional   spots.   Such   names   need   no
etymological comment.   Pilgrims' Lane, Pilgrims' Lodge,
and Palmers' Wood, are local variants of the usual title,
and could scarcely have arisen in different parts independently.[26]   Let us recall our previous experiences : economic
details, once obsolete, are soon forgotten ; but objects to
which mystery is attached live long in folk-memory.

Then there is the ecclesiastical evidence.   Dealing only
with Surrey, since one knows it best, we find that the
churches of Seale and Wanborough owed their existence to
pilgrims.   Other churches the travellers restored, such as
St. Catherine's and St. Martha's, near Guildford.   To the
twelfth-century church of Reigate the pilgrims added a
chapel, which they dedicated to Thomas à Becket.   The
former church at Gatton was of pilgrim origin ; the old
chapel at West Humble Lane was a shrine.   At Merstham
there are relics of mural paintings representing St. Thomas.
The Merstham spring may have been a ' Holy Well ', or
at least may have had sacred associations.   Near the Way,
in the parish of Oxted, is a spring known as St. Thomas's
Well.   At Puttenham and Wanborough the pilgrims made
offerings to the abbot in the churchyard.[27]

The dates of some of the local fairs are found to coincide either with the period of going to Canterbury or that
of the return journey.   Shalford Fair, and that held on
St. Catherine's Hill, caught the returning party.   Guildford
Fair was altered (A.D. 1312) from Christmas to September,
apparently for the same purpose.[28]   Testimony of this
nature is valid and far-reaching, for fairs, like corn-mills, are

among the oldest links between town and country, and are slow to accommodate themselves to change.

Little by little, the old thoroughfare was abandoned. First came the cessation of pilgrimages. Then, while the pilgrimages were but barely remembered, came the advent of paved roads. Soon followed turnpikes, with tolls and officialism. The first Toll-bar or Turnpike Act was passed in 1663, though tolls had been levied in London so early as A.D. 1267 and 1346.[29] The turnpike laws brought a slight reaction; drovers and carriers fell back on the old road as an alternative route. There are still living aged people whose parents could remember the use of the Pilgrims' Way as a pack-horse track and as a highway for flocks of sheep.[30] With the break-up of the great provincial sheep-fairs, and the construction of railways, the Way became finally deserted.

A generation hence, every genuinely traditional recollection of its industrial use will have disappeared. Even books cannot save such lore, so far as the rural mind is concerned. Says Cherry Grepe, the rascally old witch in Eden Phillpotts's novel, ' The things we'm taught was never in no books, so they'm living still. Print a thing and it dies.' [31] But the things remembered by the witch had a malign connotation and a present value. The Druids, as we have seen, knew the value of oral tradition, and were thus able to hand down their teachings with masoretic accuracy.

The reader waits impatiently to hear the case for the prehistoric road. The Pilgrims' Way, then, fulfils the elementary conditions demanded for such a track. It lies on the hill-side, not on the bleak crest. It lacks directness; never does it attempt to surmount obstacles openly. There is no relation between the Way and villages of the Teutonic settlement ; its one object is to connect East and West.

Mr. Hilaire Belloc admirably epitomizes other arguments for antiquity. First, there is the inherent suitability of geological and geographical conditions. Comparison with other known prehistoric tracks in Britain lends its help, and place-names supplement the evidence. Confirmation comes from the analogy of savage trails.[32] Among these analogies, Mr. Belloc notes these ' habits ' : The road never turns a sharp curve, except to avoid a precipitous rock or a sudden bend in the river. It does not climb higher than there is need. It keeps to the dry Southern slope, and to the Southern bank of streams. Where a river valley is crossed, the road makes for a spur of high ground. Wherever a hill must be taken, the shortest road to the summit is selected. Lastly, in passing from one valley to another, the track crosses the saddle of the watershed.[33]

To my thinking, the strongest argument for the prehistoric way lies in the plea expressed by the grim old earthworks and silent barrows which stud its course, and by the numerous relics dug up here and there, relics of which we may rest assured not one half has been put on record.

We will glance at some of the permanent remains, remembering that many others have doubtless been levelled. Beginning at the Western end, we notice that the Winchester district abounds in prehistoric handiwork. There are fine camps, probably Neolithic, at Anstiebury and Holmbury (Surrey). St. Martha's Hill, Guildford, has the earth-circles already spoken of. A Romano-British camp has been explored at Farley Heath (Surrey), and one of the Bronze Age at Oldbury (Kent). Another, dating from the early Iron Age, was explored by Boyd Dawkins at Bilberry Wood, Canterbury. Slight traces remain of the hill-fort at Bletchingley (Surrey). There is a large round barrow in Deerleap Wood, Wotton, near Dorking. 'Julaber's Grave', near Chilham Castle (Kent), has the reputation of having been the first barrow examined in England, the excavator having been William Camden.[34]

A Roman villa existed on Walton Heath (Surrey), not far from the Way. Although the villa was ruthlessly excavated in 1772, I have within recent years found red tesserae there. On the same heath, traces of three or four rectangular camps may be made out. Remains of a Roman dwelling, together with urns and pottery, turned up at Reigate. A similar building was discovered at Abinger. The Roman villa in Titsey Park is still in good preservation. Roman pottery has been dug up at Thurnham (Kent).

Kits Coty House, near Aylesford (Kent), is the only existing perfect dolmen in the South-Eastern part of England. Other rude megaliths are to be found in the Kentish districts of Trottescliffe, Coldrum, and Addington.

At Crooksbury a hoard of bronze celts was dug up. Puttenham Heath has furnished antiquities of the Neolithic and Bronze Ages. Worked flints have been found in the Rectory garden of Merstham, close by the Way, and in the Church Meadow below iron swords were unearthed. Flint implements have been turned up at Reigate, Gatton, Coulsdon, and at Titsey, not far from the Roman villa. From divers other spots come records of flint celts, arrow-heads, and pottery.[35] To extend the catalogue is but to bind clue to clue. Enough has been said to show that the Pilgrims' Way must correspond to a prototype which was known and used from Neolithic to Romano-British times at least. Where authentic history stops, proofs like those just tendered are the only ones possible ; taken as a whole, they indicate a probability not far short of certainty.

I have considered only the classic portion of the route. Mr. Belloc believes that old Western tracks converged toward Salisbury Plain, perhaps near Avebury or Stonehenge, but, for reasons which he fully discusses, Winchester afterwards absorbed the Western traffic, and the other termination was fixed at Canterbury.[36]

The last piece of testimony is supplied by the venerable yews which dot the Pilgrims' Way, and which, even in the bare stretches, occur somewhat freely. As the evidential value of these yews has been questioned, it is necessary that the objections should be considered. At once be it said that there is no written evidence of Mediaeval, much less of pre-Roman design, in the arrangement of these yews, or even of their existence as guides. Yet, reasoning from first principles, one can understand how valuable as guides these trees would be at dusk and dawn, and during foggy weather. The white chalk itself, where worn a little, would help travellers to keep the track, in the same manner as do the white stones set up by coastguards.[37] The yews, almost black, would accentuate this distinction. Dark on white,

or dark on the grey-green turf—either trail would be easily
picked out.

We turn to the facts which, being verifiable to-day, cannot
possibly be in dispute.   In Surrey, the yews occur at intervals
from St. Martha's Hill to the back of Albury Park.   At
Newlands Corner they are found but a few steps from the
path.   Then they occur intermittently from Wotton Church,
by way of Ranmore Common, to Dorking.   Just under
Box Hill, four ancient yews stand in a field by themselves.
The ridge East of Reigate is marked by another line, and
numerous fine specimens are met with from Merstham to
White Hill (Fig. 35).   In Titsey Park, which stands off
the Chalk, no yews present themselves, but a double line of
gnarled hawthorns and aged ash-trees borders the path.
Kent supplies a similar record of yews, occurring sporadically
or in rows, those about the village of Charing being specially
fine.[38]

Mrs. Ady thus explains the existence of the yews.   On
a chalk soil yew-trees spring up in every old hedgerow, being
for the most part sown by birds.   Concerning the lines of
yew-trees which are found apart from hedges, we are told
that, ' where the ploughshare has upturned the soil, and
the hedgerows have disappeared, three or four of these grand
old trees may still be seen standing by themselves in the
midst of a ploughed field, the last relics of a bygone age.' [39]

There is so much reason in this view that it may serve as
an antidote to some of the sentimental explanations which
are commonly accepted.   But there is another face to the
question.   Besides the straight, tolerably even hedges of
our rectangular fields—' hedges even pleached '—the products of quick-set planting, there is the other kind already
noticed.   A hedge which is high, rough, and straggling,
which dips into coombes and rain-channels and encircles the
chalk bluffs with bush and thicket, generally belongs to the
pre-enclosure period.   Such an unpruned, intractable hedgerow may by occasion be the vestige of a spinney or belt of
woodland, but that there should be a screen of this nature
for such considerable lengths as one finds on the Pilgrims'
Way must be more than coincidence.

Now it is demonstrably true that both sorts of hedgerow are added to by birds. When various kinds of fruit—hips and haws, the berries of privet, dog-wood, and spindle-tree— have passed through the digestive canals of birds, the seeds or kernels are without doubt encouraged to germinate. I have frequently observed that the missel-thrush, after having eaten greedily the red, glutinous, fleshy cups of the yew, or the scarlet berries of the rowan (*Pyrus aucuparia*), or the greenish-brown fruit of the wild-service tree (*Pyrus torminalis*), will repair to a neighbouring hedge to disgorge part of its meal. Fresh saplings consequently appear. But accretions of this nature cannot alone explain the sportive wild hedge, with its isolated yews, any more than they can altogether account for the ordinary farm hedgerow with its outstanding oaks, elms, and maples.

It has been submitted by Dr. J. Lowe that yews are found ' in rugged scars and clefts on the sides of hills ', because these positions are more inaccessible to browsing animals, or because in these spots there are peculiarities of soil and drainage. Very ingeniously, the writer argues that birds, after eating yew-berries, often go to their nests on these higher spots, and there eject the hard seeds.[40]

Two very different sites are here given as the nesting-places of seed-eating birds—that is, if ' scar ' is taken to mean a naked, precipitous rock. As a matter of plain observation, seed-carrying birds nest in various trees and at different levels. I have found the missel-thrush's nest in a yew—and actually in a yew on the Way near Merstham— but more commonly one meets with it in an oak, or elm, or tall hawthorn. The nest is seen alike in the valley and on the top of the escarpment. But whence came the first nucleus of scrub and bush, and was it destitute of yews at the start ? Whence came also the solitary yews, far apart from hedge-rows, yet roughly alined ? Why is not the spectacle of yew-studded hedges more frequently met with ?

Dr. Lowe proceeds, in some measure, to destroy the force of his own contention. He suggests that this Downland area was once covered with yews, and that those on the Pilgrims' Way have been left as guides.[41] There seem good grounds for accepting the second part of the suggestion, without entirely endorsing the first clause. Indeed, if the downland was once yew-clad, and if the present rows are mere remnants, the action of birds is reduced within narrower limits. But were the Downs ever clothed with yews ?

In preceding chapters, reasons have been adduced to show that the downtops have probably been bare and open country for ages. At various levels one indeed finds the yew growing in luxuriant abundance. Cherkley Court, near Leatherhead, is one locality; Norbury Park and Newlands Corner, also both in Surrey, are famous. Some of these yews are many centuries old, but the majority, as I have found by measurement, do not exceed 200 years, allowing the fairly liberal estimate of 75 years for each foot of diameter. The girth was, in each case, taken at a height of three feet from the ground. It may be that some of these patches represent primitive yew groves, but on the whole, one suspects artificial plantation. We are told that in the days of the long-bow, ending roughly with the early Stuart Period, yew groves and avenues were planted rather extensively. A general plantation was specifically commanded in 1483.[42] Strutt cites the remarkable yew wood on the island of Inchconakhead (L. Lomond) as a probable example.[43] And we know for certain that the planting of yew hedges for shelter also became fashionable.[44] Into this subject we must not now enter, but I hope to deal with it elsewhere.

Old inhabitants assure me that the mixed woodland around Horsley and Effingham (Surrey) was open downland —common fields—only seventy or eighty years ago. Time after time we are told that the yews in Norbury Park, at Newlands Corner, and Buckland, near Dover, are mentioned in Domesday Book, but it is now authoritatively asserted that no yews are referred to therein. Dr. J. Horace Round, in a letter to the writer (November 9, 1906), says, ' Individual trees are not mentioned in Domesday Book . . . least of all would yews be mentioned '—I suppose because yews are not serviceable for pannage. That there are a few yews older than Domesday is quite probable. That there are still primeval yew groves is also possible ; the examples at

Arely Hill (Staffs.) and Cranborne Chase may be representatives,[45] but the age of the latter group is seriously questioned. The argument is now being pressed merely against the assumed great extension of yew woods in Mediaeval and early historic times.

Beyond doubt the yew is indigenous. It is found in prehistoric peat bogs in Cambridge and Cumberland, in Scotland and Ireland. So well preserved are the specimens, that under the microscope the rich, brown-tinted timber shows distinctly its bordered pits and spiral vessels.[46] But the yew is older than these peat deposits. With oak and fir, it was found to accompany Palæolithic remains at Hoxne, in Suffolk.[47] At the seashore near Cromer, it has even been discovered in beds of glacial age.[48]

Being indigenous, then, at what period was the yew most flourishing ? It is admitted that the tree was once more common.[49] I think that this prevalence was in pre-Neolithic days. Professor James Geikie has pointed out that there was a decay of the ancient forests and an increase of peat mosses on the higher grounds after the final isolation of Britain on the Continent.[50]

If yew woods flourished largely in the Neolithic, Bronze, and Early Iron Ages, what existing deposits contain the relics ? Up to the present, so far as the Chalk Downs are involved, such deposits are looked for in vain. The New Forest proverb is almost literally true, ' A post of yew will outlast a post of iron.' Tough and durable, the living tree fears neither the storms above nor the damp below.[51] Therefore, if the yew ever clothed the Downs within the last 3,000 years, one ought occasionally to find either its stumps in the clayey pipes and pockets of the Chalk, or its trunks in the water-logged layers representing the ' run-of-the-hill ' or denudation-wash below—where this accumulation occurs.[52] Few such recumbent trunks or upright stools are yet recorded, and these are doubtless the ruins of trees felled or devastated by storm during our era.

If the Downs were among the sites mainly selected for plantations in the days of archery, again we should expect to find widespread remains, and these do not appear to be

forthcoming. Only a very small part, apparently, of the
plantations was laid out on the Downs. On the whole, the
yews of the Downs seem to have gained rather than lost in
numbers, but the gain probably belongs to modern times.
Mrs. Ady conjectures that some at least of the yews are
from 700 to 800 years old, and therefore anterior to, or at
least co-eval with, the visits to Becket's shrine (Becket died
A.D. 1170). Did bowyers cut down the yew woods, of which
these were the selvage ? If so, why were the odd ones left ?
From a perusal of a vast number of papers on the yew, it
seems well proved that the tree is poisonous.[53] Did herdsmen, then, hew down the groves to prevent injury to their
cattle ? Such an explanation is inadequate and far-fetched,
nor does it account for the sparing of isolated trees in prominent and easily accessible situations.

Only the novice needs to be warned against the bias of
the place-name or descriptive term, 'forest,' which formerly
often indicated waste land, having sometimes a certain proportion of woodland and pasture (French, _forêt_, from Latin,
foris = out of doors).[54] The evidence based on this word
is valueless in proving the existence of yew groves.

If it be asked why, on the same geological formation, and
on soils with practically the same physical texture, the yew
should be fairly common in some districts and rare in others,
one may reply—setting aside human agency—' The yews
are not there because they never got there.' This was the
answer given by Kingsley to the question why plants like
thrift and scurvy-grass are abundant on the seashore and
on certain mountains, but are not met with anywhere between these spots.[55] One might as well ask, Why is _Helix
pisana_ so restricted in its range and so loath to extend it ;
why are the natterjack toad and the nightingale not found
in counties which are equally as suitable as their actual
habitats ? And the list might go on.

A yew of 600 years is exceptional. A very small proportion of our North Down yews belong to the time of Becket.
Few yews anywhere antedate the Norman Conquest, and it
is virtually certain that none, unless it be the shell of the
Fortingal tree, goes back to the Roman period. Yet the

yew, as already shown, is native. We do not suppose that
there has been a vast extermination, followed by a reintro-
duction. The truth seems to be this : yews have been there
all the time ; here, a few ancient patches covering no great
area; there, stragglers, never really continuous, but still
numerous in favoured spots.

There is thus neither incentive nor justification for claiming
a great antiquity for any of the existing yews on the Pilgrims'
Way. They are merely the successors of others. Now,
how came these yews to be in lines ? Not by accident. Else
might also the fine row of large Scotch pines (*Pinus sylvestris*)
which are to be seen in a hedgerow near Sisters' Pond,
Coulsdon Common (Surrey), and which are not native in
Southern Britain, have come into their present situation by
natural agencies. No bird planted a chain of Scotch pines
in a hedge by chance—there are no other specimens in the
fields around. Plainly, the yews, like the pines, indicate
human purpose.

The Mediaeval churchman who could plant yews in his
churchyards, could plant them, or at least, retain them on
a Pilgrims' Way. The men who designed our Gothic
cathedrals could set out trees as guide-posts. One might
go further. The Christian syncretists who could see so much
derivative symbolism in the yew, probably got some tradition respecting its planting, in churchyards and elsewhere,
from their parents. So much for possible plantation in
historic times. But still further, the Britons who could
select the best route across a diversified country, who could
build forts in the most strategic positions, who could plant
trees on a barrow,[56] could, at discretion, preserve sentinel
yews along a trackway.

It is not, in fact, necessary to postulate so much the direct
planting as the preservation of yews which sprang up in the
hedgerow. Some proportion of bird-sown seedlings there
must be. On a well-worn hill-side path there would be
sufficient loose, ' pellety ' soil to allow young trees to get
root-hold. The wayfarers had only to take care that a
sufficient number of these were protected. A succession of
young trees would never be lacking.

Advocates of the theory that yews once largely covered the Downs are apt to overlook the possibility, even on that hypothesis, that the outpost yews are survivors, purposely preserved.   Indeed, were this theory more cogent, one would hasten to accept it, because the retention of the picket yews would be thereby more readily explicable.   So far as preservation is concerned the two hypotheses touch common ground.   And, of course, after the desertion of the Way, the rubbly hollows and steep screes would encourage the growth of seeds brought by birds.

On any view, the opponents of the ' guide-theory ' cannot, in Horatian phrase, ' quash the indictment with a laugh.' It may, indeed, be truly pointed out that there are other rows of yews.   If some alinements lie ' dead on ' a barrow or earthwork, other alinements lead nowhere in particular. Yew-trees line the Pilgrims' Way, therefore all such lines ought to mark old paths.   So runs the contention.   It is not incumbent on the upholders of the guide-theory to find an explanation of these exceptions.   In reality, however, the yew lines do frequently mark parish boundaries, and even old pathways, whose true nature is hidden from the unobservant by vegetation.   In other instances, the farmer has let the yews grow to maturity for the same reason that he allows oaks and elms their lease of power.

The yews have been considered at this length because they are always involved in a discussion on the Pilgrims' Way. The Way itself has occupied a large part of the chapter because it is so well known.

Mr. Grant Allen believed strongly in the prehistoricity of the Pilgrims' Way, and in his charming article on ' The Bronze Axe ' he argues that this was the route along which the ancients transported the tin from Cornwall to Mictis or Ictis, whence the metal was exported.   He therefore re-christened the track the ' Tin Way '.   The hoards of bronze unearthed here and there were considered confirmatory, and a parallel was drawn from the caches or hiding-places of treasure popular among Indian tribes.[57]   Other authorities have shared these views.   But it must be noted that much turns upon the hypothesis that Mictis (Ictis) was Sandwich, or some other Kentish port. This assumption has, until lately, had a somewhat general acceptance, but the tide of evidence has now turned in favour of the Isle of Wight, the Roman Vectis. The distance of the Isle of Wight from the source of the tin supply seems more in accordance with the accounts given by ancient writers, as elucidated by Mr. Elton, Professor Ridgeway, and others. In addition, the recent geological researches of Mr. Clement Reid have proved the former existence of a natural causeway between that island and the mainland, formed by a reef of limestone extending between Yarmouth and the Hampshire coast. It must be remembered, too, that in the Bronze Age the Solent would be much narrower and shallower than at present.[58]

Mr. Rudyard Kipling has thus sung of the Pilgrims' Way :

> There runs a road by Merrow Down—
> A grassy track to-day it is—
> An hour out of Guildford town,
> Above the river Wey it is.
>
> Here, as they heard the horse-bells ring,
> The ancient Britons dressed, and rode
> To watch the dark Phoenicians bring
> Their goods along the Western Road.
>
> And here, or hereabouts, they met
> To hold their racial talks and such—
> To barter beads for Whitby jet,
> And tin for gay shell-torques and such.[59]

The late Dr. J. J. Raven supposed that, at a later date, ' tinklers,' or *tintinnabula*, bronze bells of foreign manufacture, were carted along Roman roads and stored near crossways.[60] In fact, early land-routes were more important than is generally thought.

If Mr. Clement Reid be right, then the argument for the Tin Way is weakened, unless, indeed, there were more outlets than one. But the old road will not lose its attraction in any contingency. Clambering its seamed and worn hollows, or pacing with greater ease the elastic turf near its borders, ever there is in the mind of the rambler a feeling of remoteness, as of the presence of something primal, and he feels that he is nearer to the origin of things human. And as

poor Richard Jefferies said of these very Downs—though
the words had but half their force in his own sad case—
'Lands of gold have been found, and lands of spices and
precious merchandise, but this is the land of health.'

FIG. 36.   'Time, which antiquates antiquities, and hath an art to make
dust of all things, hath yet spared these minor monuments.'   (Sir Thomas
Browne, 'Urn Burial,' ch. v.)

CHAPTER XVII

REFERENCES AND BIBLIOGRAPHY

[The references marked by an asterisk roughly indicate the bibliographies of each respective subject.]

CHAPTER I

*1. E. B. Tylor, ' Researches into the Early History of Mankind,' 3rd edition, 1878, p. 218.

2. *Daily Chronicle*, Dec. 27, 1905.

3. *Notes and Queries*, 7th Ser., vi, p. 324. (See also p. 433.)

4. F. Lamennais, ' Esquisse d'une Philosophie,' 1840, t. iii, p. 42.

5. P. Stapfer, ' Shakespeare et L'Antiquité ' (1899), p. 99.

6. *Globe*, May 31, 1905.

*7. Grant Allen, ' Evolution of the Idea of God,' 1903 edition, p. 103.

8. Ecclesiasticus xxxviii. 25-6.

9. Ibid., xxxviii. 24.

10. *Naturalist*, 1895, p. 324.

*11. *Notes and Queries*, 10th Ser., iv, 1905, p. 247. See also 9th Ser., xii, 25, 134, &c.

12. R. Hudson, ' Memorials of a Warwickshire Parish,' 1904, pp. 287-306. Illustrative tables given. For hereditary parish clerks see P. H. Ditchfield, ' The Parish Clerk' (1907), pp. 90-104, 318-33.

*13. W. Marshall, ' Rural Economy of the Southern Counties,' 1798, ii, 180. R. Heath, in ' The English Peasant,' 1893, pp. 122, 167, deals with hereditary yeomen and shepherds.

*14. F. Seebohm, ' English Village Community,' 4th edition, 1896, p. 41.

*15. W. E. Roth, *N. Queensland Ethnography*, Bulletin No. 7, August, 1904, p. 8.

*16. G. L. Gomme, ' The Village Community,' 1890, p. 17.

17. Sir A. Geikie, ' Landscape in History,' 1905, pp. 13-15.

18. *Daily Chronicle*, Dec. 12, 1904.

19. Mrs. E. Burton-Brown, ' Recent Excavations in the Roman Forum,' 1905, pp. 93 et seqq.

*20. Rev. E. Conybeare, ' Roman Britain,' 1903, p. 180.

21. ' Roman Britain,' pp. 79-80. Also J. Haydn, ' Dictionary of Dates,' 1898, under ' Cables '.

*22. T. G. Bonney, ' The Volcanic Region of Auvergne,' 1901, p. 18. Also *Proc. Geologists' Association*, xvii, 1902, p. 276.

23. T. G. Bonney, op. cit., p. 16. *Geological Magazine*, Decade I, ii, 240. *Proc. Geol. Assoc.*, xvii, 1902, p. 289. Sir A. Geikie, ' Founders of Geology,' 1897, pp. 41-2.

*24. G. L. Gomme, ' Ethnology in Folklore,' 1892, p. 65.

*25. Sir J. Rhŷs, ' The Arthurian Legend,' 1891, p. 369. Cites *Hibbert Lectures*, pp. 195–9.

*26. See a remarkable article by Prof. C. Lombroso, *Daily Chronicle*, July 20, 1905.

27. ' Authority and Archaeology,' ed. D. G. Hogarth, 1899, p. viii.

28. ' Landscape in History,' p. 13.

29. See F. B. Gummere, ' The Popular Ballad,' 1907, pp. 31, 64–71 ; and C. J. Sharp, ' English Folk-Songs ; some Conclusions,' *passim*.

CHAPTER II

*1. M. Boule, *Comptes Rendus*, Paris Acad. of Sciences, June 26, 1905, translated in *Nature*, vol. 72, 1905, pp. 438–9.

2. See a good description in the *South-Eastern Naturalist*, 1902, p. 19.

3. B. C. A. Windle, ' Remains of the Prehistoric Age in England,' 1904, p. 7.

4. *Geological Magazine*, viii, 1901, p. 113.

*5. F. J. Bennett, in *Geol. Mag.*, 1906, Decade V, iii, 69–72, 143–4.

*6. S. H. Warren, *Jour. Anthrop. Inst.*, 1905, pp. 337–64.

*7. J. Russell Larkby, in *Antiquary*, N.S. i, pp. 130–1.

*8. *Proc. Geol. Assoc.*, xix, 1905, p. 92.

9. Ibid., p. 91 ; cf. *Q. J. G. S.*, lxxiv, 1908, No. 253, pp. 1–7.

10. A. Rutot, *Mém. Soc. d'Anthrop. de Bruxelles*, t. xxiii (quoted in *Proc. Geol. Assoc.*, xix, p. 76).

*11. W. Boyd Dawkins, ' Cave-Hunting,' 1874, pp. 353–9 ; see ch. iii. generally (cf. J. Logan Lobley, paper read at Vict. Instit., London, Feb. 18, 1907 ; *Naturalist*, 1907, pp. 137–43).

12. J. Deniker, ' Races of Man,' 1900, p. 308 n.

*13. ' Cave-Hunting,' pp. 136–8, 265–7.

14. *Naturalist*, 1904, pp. 102–4 ; 1906, pp. 420–4.

*15. A. Maskell, ' Ivories,' 1905, pp. 9–20. Tables of dated specimens, pp. 417 et seqq.

*16. A. Doigneau, ' Nos Ancêtres Primitifs,' 1905, p. 183.

17. M. Hoernes, ' Primitive Man,' trans. J. H. Loewe, 1900, pp. 31–2.

18. ' Cave-Hunting,' pp. 264–5.

*19. E. Piette, *Bull. de la Société d'Anthropologie*, 1895, pp. 235–67.

*20. ' Nos Ancêtres Primitifs,' p. 138.

21. Ibid., pp. 137–8.

22. Ibid., p. 136.

23. G. Hervé, *Revue de l'École d'Anthropologie*, 1894, p. 105. Quoted by Doigneau, pp. 124, 175–7.

*24. G. de Mortillet, ' Matériaux,' vii, p. 327 ; viii, p. 358, &c. ; also ' Le Préhistorique.'

*25. *Man*, 1903, p. 59.

*26. *Jour. Anthrop. Inst.*, xxiii, p. 142.

27. ' Cave-Hunting,' p. 351.

*28. C. H. Read, ' Guide to the Stone Age,' 1902, p. 9.

29. Ibid.

30. Ibid.

*31. W. Gowland, *Archaeologia*, lviii, 1902, pp. 37–118.

32. ' Remains Prehist. Age,' p. 39.

*33. ' Guide to Stone Age,' p. 65.

34. Ibid., p. 13.

*35. W. G. Smith, ' Man, the Primeval Savage,' 1894, p. 207.

36. Ibid., p. 220.

37. Sir A. Geikie, ' Geol. Sketches at Home and Abroad,' 1882, p. 357.

*38. *Proc. Geol. Assoc.*, xix, p. 94.

39. Ibid., p. 81.

40. W. J. L. Abbott, in *Proc. Geol. Assoc.*, xii, 1892, p. 349.

41. W. Johnson and W. Wright, ' Neolithic Man in N.-E. Surrey,' 1903, p. 146.

42. J. W. Brooke, ' Early Man in Marlborough ' (reprint, *Wilts. Archaeol. Soc.*), 1894, p. 2.

43. *Jour. Anthrop. Inst.*, xxii, p. 66.

*44. Cited by Windle, ' Remains Prehist. Age,' p. 15, from *Proc. Roy. Soc. Antiq. Ireland*. See also A. McHenry, ' Geol. of County Antrim,' p. 146 (reprint, *Proc. Geol. Assoc.*, July, 1895).

45. ' Guide to Stone Age,' pp. 56–7.

*46. ' Remains Prehist. Age,' p. 15. See also ' Guide to Stone Age,' p. 57.

*47. C. H. Read, ' Guide to the Bronze Age,' Brit. Mus., 1904, pp. 35–6 (illustrations given).

*48. A. C. Haddon, *Nat. Home-Reading Union Mag.* (Gen. Course), xv, p. 114.

49. *S.-E. Naturalist*, 1902, pp. 19–20.

50. A. C. Haddon, loc. cit., p. 91.

51. J. Fraipont, ' Les Cavernes et leurs Habitants,' 1895, p. 145. Quoted by Doigneau.

*52. Sir A. Geikie, ' Geological Sketches at Home and Abroad,' 1882, p. 359.

53. A. J. Jukes-Browne, ' Building of the British Isles,' 2nd edition, 1892, p. 404.

54. Ibid., p. 404 ; ' Cave-Hunting,' p. 272.

*55. Sir A. C. Ramsay, ' Geol. and Geography of Gt. Britain ' (5th edition, 1878), pp. 482, 586–7.

56. J. S. Flett, in Swiney Lectures, Nov. 10, 1905. For an able summary of the case of survival of pre-glacial fauna, see R. F. Scharff, ' Hist. of the European Fauna,' 1899, pp. 64–86, 104–14, 125–31, and ' European Animals,' 1907, pp. 18–19, 84 ; see also *Proc. Geol. Assoc.*, xx, 1907, pp. 53–7.

*57. R. Munro, ' Prehistoric Scotland,' 1899, pp. 62–5.

58. Ibid., pp. 57–9 ; ' Building of the British Isles,' p. 406.

*59. Gen. A. L. Pitt-Rivers, 'Excavations in Cranborne Chase,' 1887, *passim*.

*60. 'Remains Prehist. Age,' pp. 89–90; 'Guide to Bronze Age,' p. 27.

61. 'Remains Prehist. Age,' p. 86; 'Guide to Bronze Age,' p. 27.

*62. 'Guide to Bronze Age,' pp. 39–41; Gen. A. L. Pitt-Rivers, 'Evolution of Culture,' 1906, pp. 181–5.

63. 'Remains Prehist. Age,' pp. 70–1.

*64. A. C. Haddon, 'Evolution in Art,' 1895, p. 86 (illustrations given).

*65. Sir John Evans, 'Ancient Bronze Implements of Great Britain,' 1881, p. 22.

66. Ibid., p. 134.

67. Ibid., p. 312.

68. Ibid., p. 271.

*69. Reginald A. Smith, 'Guide to the Early Iron Age' (Brit. Mus.), 1905, pp. 82–3.

70. 'Guide to Bronze Age,' pp. 23, 87, &c.

71. 'Remains Prehist. Age,' pp. 284–5; 'Guide to the Early Iron Age,' *passim*.

72. Liddell and Scott, Greek Dict. (8th edition, 1901).

[Eolithic question also discussed in: *Knowledge*, N.S., iii, 1906, pp. 399–401; *American Anthropologist*, vol. vii, 1905; *Nature*, lxxiv, 1906, pp. 211–12 (Report of Internat. Congress on Anthropol. and Prehist. Archaeology, held at Monaco, April, 1906); Sir E. Ray Lankester, 'The Kingdom of Man,' 1907, pp. 15–22, 113; *B. Harrison, 'Eolithic Flint Implements,' 1904, pp. 1–24; *Knowledge*, N.S., iv, 1907, pp. 75–8; J. P. Johnson, 'The Stone Implements of South Africa,' 1907, pp. 1–9 (implements of aphanite, quartz, and jasper); *F. J. Bennett, 'Ightham: the Story of a Kentish Village,' 1907, pp. 12–14, 26–33.]

CHAPTER III

*1. J. Beddoe, 'The Races of Britain,' 1885, p. 9.

*2. Sir J. Rhŷs, 'Celtic Britain,' 3rd edition, 1904, p. 277; Sir J. Rhŷs and D. Brynmor Jones, 'The Welsh People,' 1902, pp. 617 et seqq.

3. J. Munro, 'Story of the British Race,' new edition, N.D., p. 38.

4. 'Celtic Britain,' p. 4.

*5. J. Deniker, 'Races of Man,' 1900, p. 348 *et passim*. [It is interesting to notice that Prof. G. Sergi, in 'The Mediterranean Race,' 1901, pp. v, vi, 2, &c., argues that the Neolithic folk came from Africa, and that the Aryans, after all, originated in Asia.]

6. 'Story of the British Race,' pp. 18, 338, &c.

7. 'Guide to Bronze Age,' p. 18, &c.

*8. E. T. Stevens, 'Stonehenge Excursion,' 1882, p. 142; J. B. Davis and J. Thurnam, 'Crania Britannica,' 1865, i, pp. 240–5.

*9. W. Z. Ripley, 'The Races of Europe,' 1900, pp. 307–8.

*10. 'Cave-Hunting,' p. 225.

11. B. C. A. Windle, 'Life in Early Britain,' 1897, pp. 210–11.

12. Beddoe, Huxley, and Thurnam, quoted in 'Cave-Hunting', p. 225.

13. 'Story of the British Race,' p. 109.

14. 'The Races of Europe,' p. 125 (references to Sir J. Rhŷs, 1892; Fita, 1893; Beddoe, 1893; *Academy*, Sept. 26, 1891); Sir J. Rhŷs, *Science*, xii, pp. 507–8, 516.

*15. Sir J. Rhŷs, 'Celtic Folklore,' ii. p. 681.

16. Ibid., ii, 665.

17. 'Life in Early Britain,' p. 64.

*18. *Science*, xii, p. 507.

19. 'Races of Europe,' p. 309.

20. Karl Pearson, Lecture at Birmingham, *Echo*, Nov. 23, 1903.

21. 'As You Like It,' Act iv, Sc. 4.

22. *Notes and Queries*, 1st Ser., vii, p. 86.

23. H. J. Moule, 'Old Dorset,' 1893, pp. 59, 139.

24. 'Life in Early Britain,' p. 117.

*25. Cf. Sven Nilsson, 'Primitive Inhabitants of Scandinavia' (3rd edition, trans. Lubbock, 1868), pp. 196, 203, &c.

*26. A. C. Haddon, *N. H. R. U. Mag.* (Gen. Course), xv, p. 178.

*27. *Science*, xii. p. 507.

*28. 'Celtic Folklore,' ii, pp. 664–5.

*29. Ibid., ii, pp. 663–4.

*30. L'Abbé Inchauspe, 'Le Peuple Basque,' 1894, pp. 10, 29, 30; *Archaeol. Jour.*, lii (2nd Ser.), p. 342.

31. *Notes and Queries*, 7th Ser., v, pp. 346, 412.

*32. 'Life in Early Britain,' p. 209; Eng. Dialect Dictionary, 'Keffel'; New Oxford Dict., 'Keffel,' also under 'Caple.'

*33. 'Celtic Folk-lore,' ii. p. 666.

*34. E. B. Tylor, 'Anthropology,' 2nd edition, 1889, p. 246.

*35. Sir J. Evans, 'Ancient Stone Implements of Great Britain,' 2nd edition, 1897, pp. 263–4.

*36. Sir C. Lyell, 'Antiquity of Man,' 4th edition, 1873, pp. 130–1.

*37. 'Nos Ancêtres Primitifs,' p. 178.

38. Mary H. Kingsley, 'West African Studies,' 1901, p. 218.

39. 'Anthropology,' p. 237.

*40. Pliny, 'Nat. Hist.,' l. viii, c. 48.

*41. E. Conybeare, 'Roman Britain,' p. 48; N. Annandale, 'The Faroes and Iceland,' 1905, p. 43.

*42. Owen M. Edwards, in 'Social England' (ed. H. D. Traill, 1898), i, p. 88.

43. 'Anthropology,' p. 241. References to the artificial shaping of heads in England may be found in a quaint booklet by Walter Vaughan (1793): 'Essay, Philosophical and Medical, concerning Modern Clothing'; pp. 46–53.

*44. 'Races of Man,' p. 306.

*45. Good description in J. G. Wood, ' Natural History of Man,' 1880, pp. 686-7 ; J. G. Frazer, ' Early History of the Kingship,' 1905, pp. 259-60.

*46. F. J. Bennett, ' The Antiquity of Man ' (reprint from *Rochester Naturalist*, 1901), p. 6 ; cf. Ex. xxiii. 16, Lev. xxiii. 34-36, &c. ; also Smith's Bible Dict., Art. ' Feast of Tabernacles.'

47. F. J. Bennett, op. cit., p. 6.

48. M. D. Conway, ' Autobiography,' 1904, ii, p. 77.

CHAPTER IV

1. Z. de Rouzic, ' Les Monuments Mégalithiques de Carnac et de Locmariaquer,' N.D., pp. 33-6.

2. See lists in ' Remains Prehist. Age '.

*3. New Oxford Dict., ' Cromlech,' ' Dolmen.'

*4. *Archaeologia*, lviii, 1902, pp. 37-118. (For stone bridges of Devon see *Notes and Queries*, 10th Ser., vii, 1907, p. 112.)

5. E. Clodd, quoted in ' Celtic Folklore,' ii, p. 607.

6. Rev. H. M. Scarth, ' Roman Britain,' N.D., p. 166. *Subject well dealt with in W. Howship Dickinson's ' King Arthur in Cornwall ', 1900, pp. 4-9.

7. ' Kenilworth,' c. xiii. Scott's authority seems to be Francis Wise, ' Letter to Dr. Mead, &c.,' 1738, p. 37.

*8. ' Remains Prehist. Age,' *passim*. Also *Notes and Queries*, 10th Ser., vi, p. 397.

9. *Reliquary*, xi, 1905, pp. 145-51.

10. T. Eley, ' Manual of Archaeology,' 1890, p. 40. Prof. Flinders Petrie, at Univ. Coll., London, June 29, 1907.

11. Grant Allen, ' Falling in Love : Essays ' (new edition, 1891), p. 301.

*12. H. D. M. Spence, ' Early Christianity and Paganism,' 1902, pp. 264 et seqq.

13. *Archaeologia*, xxxvii, 1857, pp. 456-7.

14. Ibid.

15. T. Wright, ' The Celt, the Roman, and the Saxon,' 2nd edition, 1861, p. 329.

*16. J. R. Green, ' The Conquest of England,' 2nd edition, 1884, p. 9.

*17. C. H. Read, in *Proc. Soc. Antiq.*, 2nd Ser., xv, p. 245. For accounts of moated mounds, and other pseudo-tumuli, see ' Victoria ' Histories : Warwick, 1904, i, pp. 351-3, &c. ; Nottingham, 1906, i, pp. 305-8. Also *Notes and Queries*, 9th Ser., 1900, v, pp. 309, 399 ; vi, pp. 11, 76, 134, &c.

*18. J. Grimm, ' Teutonic Mythology ' (trans. from 4th edition by J. G. Stallybrass, 1882), i. p. 85.

19. E. Conybeare, ' Roman Britain,' p. 144-5.

20. *Proc. Soc. Antiq.*, 2nd Ser., xv, p. 241.

21. E. Jesse, ' Gleanings,' 3rd Ser., 1835, pp. 244-5.

*22. ' Cave-Hunting,' p. 125.

23. ' Cave-Hunting,' p. 127.

24. Bede, ' Eccles. Hist.,' l. i, c. xiv ; ' Cave-Hunting,' p. 106.

25. ' Cave-Hunting,' p. 106.

26. *Reliquary*, xii, 1906, pp. 37–47.

*27. *Reliquary*, xi, 1905, pp. 25–35 ; *Proc. Soc. Antiq.*, 2nd Ser., xviii, pp. 259–60 ; ' Remains Prehist. Age,' p. 258.

*28. R. Munro, ' Lake-Dwellings of Europe,' 1890, *passim* ; F. Keller, ' Lake-Dwellings of Switzerland,' 2nd edition, 1878, 2 vols., *passim*.

29. ' Guide to Bronze Age,' p. 143 ; *Antiquary*, N.S., vii, 1906, pp. 267–8.

*30. F. W. Reader, in *Archaeol. Jour.*, lx, pp. 137–204.

*31. ' Lake-Dwellings of Europe,' pp. 460–4.

32. ' Anthropology,' p. 233.

33. ' Life in Early Britain,' pp. 72–3.

34. Ibid. ; ' Guide to Bronze Age,' p. 143.

*35. R. Munro, ' Archaeology and False Antiquities,' 1904, pp. 149–80, 221–65 ; *Antiquary*, Sept., 1905.

36. John Earle, ' Microcosmographie,' 1633, § 9.

*37. D. Wilson, ' Prehistoric Scotland,' 1899, pp. 343 et seqq.

*38. Lord Avebury, ' Prehistoric Times,' 5th edition, 1890, p. 57.

*39. E. Anwyl, in *Antiquary*, N.S., iv (1908), p. 7 ; Rev. R. Ashington Bullen, ' Harlyn Bay,' 1902, pp. 50 et seqq.

*40. R. Damon, ' Geology of Weymouth,' 2nd edition, 1884, pp. 164–6.

*41. M. Creighton, ' Carlisle,' 1889, p. 84.

42. Ibid., p. 187.

43. *Jour. Anthrop. Inst.*, 1890, xx, p. 4.

*44. S. O. Addy, 'Evolution of the English House,' 1898, pp. 11, 17, 199, 200 ; *Jour. Anthrop. Inst.*, xxix, 1899, p. 126 ; cf. A. Bulleid, ' Brit. Lake-Village near Glastonbury,' 1904, p. 21.

45. *Daily Chronicle*, Nov. 14, 1905 ; cf. Addy, pp. xix, xx.

*46. A. C. Haddon, ' Evolution in Art,' 1895, p. 115 ; also Addy, p. 10. See also Munro, ' Prehist. Scotland,' pp. 343 et seqq., and M. Haberlandt, ' Ethnology ' (trans. by J. H. Loewe, N.D.), pp. 26–33, for ancient types of dwellings.

47. 'Anthropology,' p. 231.

*48. Rev. J. C. Atkinson, 'Forty Years in a Moorland Parish,' 2nd edition, 1891, p. 174.

*49. Rev. T. Longley, *Louth Antiq. and Naturalists' Soc.*, March 19, 1900 ; cf. A. Ballard, ' The Domesday Inquest,' 1906, p. 182.

50. *Naturalist*, Sept., 1905, p. 266.

51. ' The Antiquary,' Black's edition, 1886, ch. iv, p. 40.

52. J. R. Green, quoted by Windle, ' Life in Early Britain,' p. 125.

53. G. T. Clark, ' Mediaeval Military Architecture,' ii. 406 (quoted by Gomme).

54. T. W. Shore, *Jour. Anthrop. Inst.*, xvii, 1889, p. 338.

*55. R. A. Smith, ' Guide to Early Iron Age,' 1905, pp. 122–3.

*56. ' Remains Prehist. Age,' p. 210.

57. C. F. Dowsett, ' Winklebury Camp,' 1904, p. 14.

58. *Notes and Queries*, 10th Ser., iv, pp. 394–5.

59. ' Remains Prehist. Age,' p. 210.

60. Vine, ' Caesar in Kent,' 1899, p. 171 (quoted by Conybeare, ' Roman Britain,' p. 111).

*61. Sir J. Rhŷs, ' The Arthurian Legend,' 1891, pp. 6, 8, 9, 23–4 ; S. Baring-Gould, ' A Book of the West,' 1899, ii, pp. 119–22.

62. *Notes and Queries*, 1st Ser., v, p. 231 (details and name given).

63. Isaac Taylor, ' Words and Places,' 3rd edition, 1873, p. 172.

*64. E. Guest, ' Origines Celticae,' 1883, ii, p. 150.

*65. Sven Nilsson, 'Prim. Inhabitants of Scandinavia,' 3rd edition, trans. Lubbock, 1868, p. 213 ; J. Grimm, 'Teut. Myth.,' 1882, *passim*. Rev. G. S. Streatfeild, ' Lincolnshire and the Danes,' 1884, p. 63.

66. *Notes and Queries*, 1st Ser., iv, p. 330.

67. Ibid., 1st Ser., iv, p. 372.

68. Ibid., 1st Ser., v. p. 43.

69. ' Remains Prehist. Age,' p. 209.

*70. J. R. Green, ' The Making of England,' 1885, p. 3, n.

71. Ibid., pp. 131–47. See splendid digest of the Teutonic theory in Prof. P. Vinogradoff's ' Villainage in England,' 1892, pp. 1–42.

*72. Grant Allen, ' Anglo-Saxon England,' 1884, p. 200. The true form and meaning of the place-name ' Londinion ' were discussed in the *Athenaeum*, March 7 and 14, April 11, 1908.

73. ' Anglo-Saxon England,' p. 200.

74. Ibid., p. 201.

75. T. K. L. Oliphant, ' Sources of Standard English,' 1873, p. 19.

*76. W. W. Skeat, ' Etymol. Dict.,' 1882 (under the various words).

77. See Address by E. Renan at Sorbonne, 1893.

78. ' Story of Brit. Race,' p. 63.

79. Ibid., pp. 71–2. On the question of the Norman tongue, see Prof. Kirchoff, *Geog. Jour.*, xxvii, 1906, pp. 510–11.

*80. Sir J. Rhŷs, ' Celtic Britain,' p. 111. See good summing-up by H. C. Wyld, 'Historical Study of the Mother Tongue,' 1906, pp. 242 et seqq.

*81. H. C. Coote, 'The Romans of Britain,' 1878, pp. 176–80, 186 et seqq. ; Rev. H. M. Scarth, ' Roman Britain,' N.D., pp. 229–30.

*82. G. L. Gomme, ' The Village Community,' 1890, p. 276.

83. Scarth, ' Rom. Brit.,' pp. 192–3.

84. ' Story of Brit. Race,' p. 76.

*85. ' Anglo-Saxon Britain,' ch. vii.

86. Ibid., p. 66.

87. Ibid., p. 66.

*88. F. York Powell, in ' Social England,' ed. H. D. Traill, 1898, i, pp. 124–5 ; * H. J. Mackinder, ' Britain and the British Seas,' 2nd edition, 1907, ch. xii.

*89. H. C. Coote, ' Romans of Britain,' pp. 187 et seqq.

90. ' A.-S. Britain,' p. 59.

91. Ibid., pp. 60–4. See also purport of passages in P. Vinogradoff, ' The Growth of the Manor,' 1905, pp. 41–2.

92. ' A.-S. Brit.,' p. 59.

*93. ' Life in Early Britain,' p. 173 ; ' Making of England,' p. 220.

94. Scarth, ' Roman Britain,' pp. 80–1.

*95. F. Seebohm, ' The English Village Community,' 1896, *passim.*

*96. G. L. Gomme, ' The Village Community,' 1890, *passim.*

*97. P. Vinogradoff, 'The Growth of the Manor,' 1905, pp. 37–8, 47–8, 85–7.

*98. Seebohm, ' Eng. Vill. Comm.,' pp. 424–37 (freely drawn upon in this and the two next paragraphs).

*99. Ibid., p. 435.

100. Ibid., p. 429.

[For a recent review of the extirpation theory, see T. Hodgkin, ' Hist. of England,' Vol. I of Longmans, Green & Co.'s Series, pp. 94–111.]

CHAPTER V

1. E. B. Tylor, ' Researches into the Early History of Mankind,' 3rd edition, 1878, p. 208.

*2. W. Bagehot, ' Physics and Politics,' 1885, p. 16.

3. Lucretius, ' De Rerum Natura,' v, 1283–8 (trans. Munro).

4. Bartholomew Anglicus, ' Mediaeval Lore,' trans. R. Steele, 1905, p. 38.

*5. R. Plot, ' Nat. Hist. of Staffordshire,' 1686, pp. 396–7, 403–4. Consult also Evans, ' Anc. Stone Impts.,' pp. 63, &c.

*6. Tylor, ' Researches . . . Mankind,' p. 190.

*7. ' Anc. Stone Impts.,' p. 145.

8. O. Schrader, ' Prehist. Antiquities,' trans. F. B. Jevons, 1890, p. 237.

*9. ' Anc. Stone Impts.,' pp. 146–7 ; G. L. Gomme, ' Ethnology in Folk-Lore,' 1892, p. 189 ; Wright, 'The Celt, the Roman, and the Saxon,' p. 72 ; *Archaeologia*, xli, p. 405. See also Dr. W. Smith's Latin Dict., under ' Jacto '.

*10. ' Anc. Stone Impts.,' p. 256.

11. R. Jefferies, ' Wild Life in a Southern County,' 1889, p. 59.

12. ' Anc. Stone Impts.,' pp. 233–4.

*13. Tylor, ' Researches . . .', p. 190.

*14. ' Anc. Stone Impts.,' p. 11.

15. J. G. Wood, ' Natural History of Man,' 1880, i, p. 97.

*16. New Oxford Dict., under ' Hammer '.

17. Fynes Moryson, ' Itinerary,' 1617, Part III, p. 161. Cited by Evans.

*18. ' Anc. Stone Impts.,' p. 258 ; * G. L. Gomme, ' Folk-Lore Relics of Early Village Life,' 1883, pp. 163–5.

*19. Sir A. Mitchell, ' The Past in the Present,' 1880, pp. 128-9.

20. ' Anc. Stone Impts.,' p. 440 (authorities given).

*21. ' Past in the Present,' p. 219.

22. ' Anc. Stone Impts.,' p. 140.

23. *Academy*, July 2, 1904.

*24. ' Anc. Stone Impts.,' p. 441.

25. Ibid., p. 440.

*26. E. T. Stevens, ' Flint Chips,' 1870, p. 101.

*27. ' Past in the Present,' pp. 122, 128-32.

28. ' Anc. Stone Impts.,' p. 442.

29. J. Lyly, ' Euphues and his England,' ed. Edw. Arber, 1868, p. 220.

30. Sir T. Browne, ' Vulgar Errors,' ed. S. Wilkins, 1884, i, p. 158.
' Anc. Stone Impts.,' p. 441.

*31. ' Century Dict.,' under ' Slick '.

*32. ' Anc. Stone Impts.,' p. 441.

33. Ibid., p. 442.

34. ' Flint Chips,' p. 74.

35. *Notes and Queries*, 1st Ser., x, p. 235.

*36. Question fully discussed in *Notes and Queries*, 1st Ser., x, p. 223 ;
2nd Ser., iii, p. 519, and iv, pp. 37, 95, 480.

37. B. von Cotta, ' Geology and History ' (trans. R. R. Noel, 1865),
p. 40.

38. ' Anc. Stone Impts.,' p. 439.

39. *Proc. Soc. Antiq. Scot.*, xv, pp. 149, 156 ; v, p. 313.

*40. ' Past in the Present,' pp. 126-7.

41. ' Anc. Stone Impts.,' p. 399.

*42. ' Flint Chips,' p. 112.   * For the decline of archery in England see
G. A. Hansard, ' Book of Archery,' 1840, *passim*.

43. J. T. Wheeler, ' Short History of India,' 1880, quoted in *Notes and
Queries*, 10th Ser., i, p. 225.

*44. E. B.Tylor, ' Anthropology,' 1889, p. 195. Chambers's Cyclopaedia,
1888, under ' Archery '.

45. ' Anthropology,' p. 197.

46. R. Heath, ' The English Peasant,' 1893, p. 141 ; R. Jefferies, ' The
Amateur Poacher,' 1879, ch. iii.   See also Eng. Dialect Dict.

47. ' Anthropology,' pp. 196-7.

48. ' Anc. Stone Impts.,' p. 348.

49. ' Memoirs of Leonora Christina,' p. 191 (quoted in *Notes and Queries*,
4th Ser., xi, p. 302).

*50. ' Past in the Present,' pp. 119-20.

*51. Ibid., pp. 128-9.

52. ' Anthropology,' p. 275.

*53. New Oxford Dict., under ' Bottle '.

*54. ' Anthropology,' p. 275.

55. Ibid., p. 273.

56. Ibid., p. 266.

*57. ' A Book of the West,' i, p. 165 ; Gomme, ' Folk-Lore Relics . . .,'
pp. 166–8.

58. Lucan, ' Pharsalia,' lib. iv, l. 136.

*59. C. I. Elton, 'Origins of Eng. History,' 2nd edition, 1890, pp. 13–75;
Conybeare, ' Rom. Brit.,' p. 37.

*60. Conybeare, ' Rom. Brit.,' p. 245, n.

*61. ' Anthropology,' p. 253 ; J. R. Larkby in ' Ightham, the Story of
a Kentish Village,' by F. J. Bennett, 1907, p. 27.   * Pitt-Rivers, 'Evolution
of Culture,' pp. 186 et seqq.

62. Virgil, ' Georgics,' i, l. 136 (Dryden's translation).

*63. W. W. Skeat, Etymol. Dict., 1888, under ' Punt ' (quotes Caesar,
' Bell. Civ.,' iii. 29).

*64. Sir C. Lyell, ' Antiquity of Man,' 4th edition, 1873, pp. 51–3.

*65. F. W. Reader, ' Handbook to Prehist. Objects, Essex Field Club
Museum,' 1901, pp. 19–21.   For facts as to the present use of thorn fish-
hooks or ' gorges' on the estuaries of the Thames and Towy see *Notes and
Queries*, 10th Ser., ix, 1908, pp. 385–95.

CHAPTER VI

*1. Quoted by E. Crawley, ' The Tree of Life,' 1905, p. 5.

*2. W. Ridgeway, ' The Origin of Metallic Currency and Weight
Standards,' 1892 (quoted by Haddon).

*3. A. C. Haddon, ' Evolution in Art,' 1895, p. 225.

4. Ibid., p. 226.

5. ' De Bello Gall.,' l. vi, c. 14–20.

6. Herodotus, l. ii, c. 86.

7. Livy, l. i, c. 24.

8. Diodorus, l. i, c. 9 (quoted in ' Anc. Stone Impts.,' p. 9).

*9. ' Guide to Stone Age,' p. 71.

10. ' Anc. Stone Impts.,' p. 8.

*11. Clodd, ' Story Prim. Man,' pp. 35–6.

12. Ibid., pp. 35–6.

13. S. Laing, ' Human Origins,' 1892, p. 181.   * W. M. Flinders Petrie,
' Illahun, Kahun, and Gurob,' ch. xi (by F. C. J. Spurrell), pp. 51–6.

14. Exod. iv. 25 ; Joshua v. 2.

*15. ' Researches E. H. M.,' p. 216 (name of informant given).

*16. ' Guide Bronze Age,' p. 7 ; ' Antiq. of Man,' p. 11.

17. ' Guide Bronze Age,' p. 8.

18. Exod. xx. 25 ; Deut. xxvii. 5.

19. Joshua viii. 31.

20. 1 Kings vi. 7.

21. Grant Allen, ' Evolution of the Idea of God,' ch. v.   J. J. Raven,
' The Bells of England,' 1906, discusses the Septuagint word translated
' brass,' pp. 3 et seqq.

*22. F. T. Elworthy, 'The Evil Eye,' 1895, p. 220.

23. Ibid., p. 220.

24. Ibid. Also, F. Bond, 'English Cathedrals,' 1899, p. 86.

25. 'Researches E. H. M.,' p. 190.

26. É. Souvestre, 'Le Chevrier de Lorraine,' ch. iii.

*27. 'Flint Chips,' p. 88.

28. Ibid., p. 87.

29. 'Anc. Stone Impts.,' p. 56.

*30. 'Nos Ancêtres Primitifs,' p. 16.

31. 'Past in the Present,' pp. 156 et seqq.

*32. J. G. Campbell, 'Superstitions of the Highlands and Islands of Scotland,' 1900, p. 27.

33. 'Story of Primitive Man,' p. 98.

34. 'Flint Chips,' p. 87.

*35. 'Anc. Stone Impts.,' p. 60.

36. Ibid.

*37. 'Flint Chips,' p. 88.   'Life in Early Brit.,' p. 44.

38. 'Flint Chips,' p. 89.

39. 'Nos Ancêtres Primitifs,' p. 16.

40. 'Story of Prim. Man,' p. 99.

*41. 'Life in Early Brit.,' pp. 44–5.

42. 'Flint Chips,' p. 88.

43. 'Life in Early Brit.,' p. 45.

44. 'Cymbeline,' Act iv, Sc. 2.

45. 'Julius Caesar,' Act iv, Sc. 3.

*46. 'Anglo-Saxon Britain,' p. 77.

*47. Cited in 'Researches E. H. M.,' p. 224.

*48. F. Kauffmann, 'Northern Mythology,' trans. M. Steele Smith, 1903, p. 57.

49. For example, see the discussion in *Nature Notes*, xiv, 1903, pp. 17, 36, 56.

*50. 'Celtic Folklore,' i, pp. 224–5.

51. 'Story of Prim. Man,' p. 122.

*52. 'Evol. of Idea of God,' ch. vi.

53. 'Story of Prim. Man,' p. 134.

*54. T. Hughes, 'The Scouring of the White Horse,' 1889, pp. 115, 118.

55. R. White, 'Popular Romances of the West of England,' 1881, p. 176.

*56. A. C. Haddon, *N. H. R. U. Mag.*, xv, pp. 28, &c.

*57. W. G. Wood-Martin, 'Traces of the Elder Faiths of Ireland,' 1902, ii, pp. 226, 237, 242, &c.

*58. G. White, 'Nat. Hist. Selborne' (Harting's edition, 1880), pp. 222–3; see also Harting's references.

59. *Notes and Queries*, 8th Ser., vii, p. 413. J. Brand, 'Popular Antiquities,' ed. Sir Henry Ellis, 1841, vol. iii, 'Physical Charms.' * W. Henderson, 'Folk-Lore of the Northern Counties,' 1879, pp. 156, 164–5, 166, 194. J. J. Hissey, 'Over Fen and Wold,' 1898, p. 397.

*60. A. C. Haddon, *N. H. R. U. Mag.*, xi, pp. 28 et seqq.

61. *Notes and Queries*, 8th Ser., viii, 1895, p. 52.

62. ' Researches E. H. M.,' p. 193.

*63. ' Past in the Present,' pp. 124–5.

64. *Notes and Queries*, 8th Ser., viii, p. 52.

65. ' Hudibras,' pt. ii, canto iii, ll. 291–2.

66. J. Aubrey, ' Miscellanies,' 1784, p. 197.

*67. Pliny, ' Nat. Hist.,' l. i, c. 66.

68. *Notes and Queries*, 8th Ser., ii, p. 243.

*69. Pliny, ' Nat. Hist.,' l. xxvi, c. 29 ; l. xxix, c. 13.

*70. Ibid., l. xxxvi, c. 38.

71. *Notes and Queries*, 8th Ser., vii, p. 485 ; viii, p. 431.

72. *Notes and Queries*, 8th Ser., viii, p. 482.

CHAPTER VII

1. J. Earle, ' Microcosmographie,' 1633, § 9.

*2. S. Baring-Gould, ' A Book of Dartmoor,' 1900, pp. 64–6.

3. Ibid., pp. 56–7, 66.

*4. A. Rimmer, ' Ancient Stone Crosses of England,' 1875, p. 15.

*5. See, for example, Z. le Rouzic, ' Les Monuments Mégalithiques,' *passim.*

6. ' Evolution of the Idea of God,' p. 147.

7. *Notes and Queries*, 4th Ser., ii, pp. 292, 451.

*8. S. Baring-Gould, ' A Book of Brittany,' 1901, p. 27.   * Excellent works for study are A. G. Langdon's ' Old Cornish Crosses,' 1896 ; W. Crossing's ' Ancient Stone Crosses of Dartmoor.'

*9. ' Evol. of Idea of God,' p. 147.

*10. J. Romilly Allen, ' Celtic Art in Pagan and Christian Times,' 1905, p. 186.   * Cf. A. G. Langdon, ' Old Cornish Crosses,' 1896, pp. 4–7. Cornish inscribed stones shown to date from seventh century.

*11. ' Story Prim. Man,' p. 136.

*12. ' Evol. of Idea of God,' pp. 50–1.

*13. ' Story Prim. Man,' p. 136 ; ' Evol. of Idea of God,' p. 41.

14. ' Story Prim. Man,' p. 136.

*15. J. Anderson, ' Scotland in Pagan Times,' 1886, pp. 135–6.

*16. Rev. G. S. Tyack, ' Lore and Legend of the Eng. Church,' 1899, pp. 11–12.

*17. Lord Avebury, ' Origin of Civilization,' 4th edition, 1882, p. 307.

*18. ' Story Prim. Man,' pp. 129–30.

*19. ' A Book of Brittany,' p. 16.

*20. F. G. Jackson, ' The Great Frozen Land,' 1895, pp. 84, 88, 89.

21. Ibid., pp. 88–9.

22. ' Life in Early Britain,' p. 56.

23. J. Borwick, 'Irish Druids, and Old Irish Religions,' 1894, pp. 211–24.

24. Tyack, ' Lore and Legend,' p. 36.

25. W. Borlase, ' Antiquities of Cornwall,' iii, p. 162.

26. *Notes and Queries*, 1st Ser., viii, p. 413.

27. Ibid.

*28. A. C. Haddon, *N. H. R. U. Mag.*, xv, p. 28.

29. Ibid.

30. Earl of Roden, ' Progress of the Reformation in Ireland,' cited in *Notes and Queries*, 1st Ser., v, 1852, p. 121.

31. M. Martin, ' Western Isles of Scotland,' 1703, p. 88.

*32. Gomme, ' Ethnology in Folklore,' pp. 165–72.

33. Gomme, ' Vill. Comm.,' p. 113.

34. Gen. xxviii. 18, 22.

35. 1 Sam. vii. 16.

36. Gen. xxxi. 45–6.

37. Gen. xix. 26.

38. Josh. iv. 5.

39. 1 Sam. xi. 14.

40. 1 Sam. vii. 12.

*41. See Smith's ' Bible Dict.,' Art. ' Stones.' Also Grant Allen, ' Evol. of Idea of God,' pp. 48, 49, &c.

42. Deut. vii. 5, xii. 3, &c.

43. 1 Sam. x. 3, 4.

44. Cited by Grant Allen, ' Evol. of Idea of God,' p. 48.

45. Isa. lvii. 6.

*46. Rev. H. N. Hutchinson, ' Prehist. Man and Beast,' 1896, p. 258.

47. G. L. Gomme, ' Prim. Folk-Moots,' 1880, pp. 33–4.

48. Michelet, ' Origines du Droit Français,' liv. iv, c. 11 ; cited by Gomme, op. cit., p. 43.

*49. Gomme, ' Vill. Comm.,' pp. 218–20 (authorities given).

*50. ' Prim. Folk-Moots,' pp. 192, 227–33.

51. Ibid., p. 192.

52. Ibid., pp. 108–9.

*53. Mr. G. L. Gomme in *Notes and Queries*, 2nd Ser., ii, p. 33.

54. Ibid. Concerning ' blue stones,' see also 10th Ser., 1907, vii, p. 94.

55. Ibid.

56. Ibid.

57. *London and Middlesex Arch. Soc.*, iv, p. 62 (quoted by Gomme).

58. '2 Henry VI,' Act iv, Sc. 6.

59. ' Vill. Comm.,' pp. 218–20.

60. See *Notes and Queries*, 3rd Ser., i, 1862, p. 13.

*61. *Arch. Jour.*, liv, pp. 201–25 ; *Blackwood's Mag.*, March, 1902, pp. 50–1 ; ' Neolithic Man in N.-E. Surrey,' pp. 116–17.

62. ' Neol. Man in N.-E. Surrey,' p. 116.

63. *Notes and Queries*, 1st Ser., v, p. 122.

*64. ' Past in the Present,' p. 265.

65. Ibid., pp. 263–5.

66. Ibid., p. 120.

*67. Brand, ' Pop. Antiq.,' ii, p. 302.

*68. *Folk-Lore,* 1893, pp. 13–14.

*69. ' Celtic Folklore,' i, pp. 344–5 (authority given).

70. Ibid.

*71. Rev. R. Ashington Bullen, ' Harlyn Bay ' (2nd edition, 1902), p. 36.

*72. ' Celtic Folklore,' i, pp. 344–5.

73. Rev. ii. 17.

*74. Pliny, ' Nat. Hist.,' l. xxix, c. 12.

75. Ibid. (trans. Bostock and Riley), n.

76. Conybeare, ' Roman Brit.,' pp. 70–1.

*77. Gen. A. L. Pitt-Rivers, ' Excavations in Cranborne Chase,' 1887, &c., ii, pp. 68, 78, 79–86, &c.

*78. Pitt-Rivers, op. cit., ii, pp. 93, 94, 98, 102, 103, 106, &c.

*79. J. G. Frazer, ' Early Hist. of the Kingship,' 1905, pp. 157–8.

CHAPTER VIII

1. Quoted by Sir J. Rhŷs, ' Celtic Folklore,' ii, 683–4, n.

2. ' Guide to Bronze Age,' p. 16.

*3. Canon W. Greenwell, ' British Barrows,' 1877, pp. 122, 127–9, 482, 543, 549.

*4. Dr. W. Wright, in *Jour. of Anatomy,* N.S., xix, 1905, esp. pp. 441–2. Cf. G. Sergi, ' The Mediterranean Race,' 1901, pp. 240, 277.

*5. J. R. Mortimer, ' Forty Years' Researches,' 1905, pp. xix, xx, lxxviii, &c. * Report of Brit. Assoc., 1906 (*Nature,* lxxiv, pp. 457–8).

*6. Sir J. Rhŷs, ' Celtic Folklore,' ii, p. 683 ; Sir J. Rhŷs, *Science,* pp. 508 et seqq. For an account of the Neolithic dwarfs of the Continent, Sir John Rhŷs recommends an article in the *Zeitschrift für Ethnologie,* xxvi, 1904, pp. 189–254.

*7. ' Celtic Britain,' pp. 240–2 ; cf. S. Baring-Gould, ' Deserts of Southern France,' 1894, i, pp. 174–9.

8. ' Celtic Folklore,' ii, p. 685.

*9. W. F. Skene, ' Celtic Scotland,' i, pp. 194–227. * H. Zimmer, ' Das Mutterrecht der Pikten,' pp. 209 et seqq. (quoted by Frazer, ' Early Hist. of the Kingship,' pp. 246–7, n.)

*10. *Antiquary,* N.S., ii, 1906, pp. 172–5.

*11. ' Celtic Folklore,' ii, p. 685.

12. Ibid., ii, p. 679.

13. Ibid., ii, pp. 663–4, 669. Campbell, ' Superstit. of the Highlands,' pp. 35–6, &c.

14. ' Merry Wives of Windsor,' Act v, Sc. 5.

15. ' Celtic Folklore,' ii, p. 667. * See E. S. Hartland, ' Science of Fairy Tales,' 1891, ch. v.

*16. ' Superst. of the Highlands,' pp. 90–2, 38–9.

17. Ibid., pp. 15–16, 35–6.

18. Ibid., pp. 27–8.

*19. *Antiquary*, N. S., ii, 1906, p. 174; 'Science of Fairy Tales,' ch. iii—Fairy births and human midwives.

*20. Rev. J. C. Atkinson, 'Forty Years in a Moorland Parish,' 2nd edition, 1891, pp. 52–3.

*21. 'Superst. of the Highlands,' pp. 9–11.

22. Ibid.

*23. D. F. Kauffmann, 'Northern Mythology' (trans. M. S. Smith, 1903), p. 17.

*24. B. Thorpe, 'Northern Mythology,' ii, p. 115. * W. A. Craigie, 'Scandinavian Folklore,' 1896, p. 93.

25. 'Tempest,' Act v, Sc. 1.

26. 'L'Allegro,' ll. 102, 105–9.

27. P. H. Ditchfield, 'Memorials of Old Oxfordshire,' 1903, pp. 34–5.

*28. Craigie, 'Scand. Folklore,' pp. 91–2.

29. Ibid., p. 97.

*30. J. O. Halliwell, 'Rambles in Western Cornwall,' 1861, pp. 227–32.

*31. 'Celtic Folklore,' i, pp. 342–3.

32. 'Superst. of the Highlands,' p. 13.

33. 'Celtic Folklore,' i. 683.

*34. W. Henderson, 'Folklore of the Northern Counties,' 1879, p. 2.

*35. W. Boyd Dawkins, 'Early Man in Britain,' 1880, p. 388. Cf. similar account from Devon, Baring-Gould, 'A Book of the West,' 1899, i, p. 193.

36. *Daily Chronicle*, Aug. 18, 1905.

*37. Canon A. Jessopp, in *Nineteenth Century*, Jan., 1887, pp. 40–59.

*38. 'Early Man in Britain,' p. 433.

39. R. Chambers, 'Popular Rhymes in Scotland,' 1826 (quoted fully in *Notes and Queries*, 9th Ser., viii, p. 151). *Reliquary*, xi (1905), pp. 258–62.

*40. 'Celtic Folklore,' ii, pp. 457–8, 467–8. Authorities given. (Chapter viii is full of cave legends.)

41. 'Celtic Folklore,' ii, p. 494.

42. Craigie, 'Scand. Folklore,' p. 265.

*43. B. Thorpe, 'Northern Mythology,' 1851, ii, pp. 50–1.

*44. G. L. Gomme, 'Prim. Folk-Moots,' 1880, pp. 62, 105, 112, &c. *J. R. Mortimer, 'Forty Years' Researches,' pp. lxxxv, lxxxvi.

*45. Rev. R. W. Eyton, 'A Key to Domesday,' 1878, p. 143.

*46. S. O. Addy, 'Evolution of the English House,' 1898, pp. 177–9, &c.

*47. 'Forty Years' Researches,' pp. 388–94.

*48. 'Superst. of the Highlands,' p. 83. References to the deiseal are very numerous: see, for example, C. F. Gordon-Cumming, 'In the Hebrides,' 1883, pp. 241–5.

CHAPTER IX

*1. e.g., St. J. V. Day, 'Prehist. Use of Iron and Steel,' 1877, pp. 225– *et passim*.

*2. 'Guide to Iron Age,' p. 3.

3. ' De Bell. Gall.,' l. v, c. 12.

*4. G. Clinch, ' Early Surrey Industries ' (? 1895), p. 3.

*5. Canon J. C. Atkinson, ' Forty Years in a Moorland Parish ' (2nd edition, 1891), p. 174.

6. Ibid., p. 166.

*7. Murray, ' Handbook to Cornwall ' (11th edition, 1893), p. 138. * J. O. Halliwell, ' Rambles in Western Cornwall,' 1861, pp. 51–2. See also Eng. Dial. Dict. under ' Jew '—an excellent series of quotations given.

*8. ' Victoria History of Surrey,' 1905, ii, pp. 268–9. * Surrey Archaeol. Coll., xxiii, pp. 11–61. * H. E. Malden, ' Hist. of Surrey,' 1900, ch. xx.

9. ' Vict. Hist. Surrey,' ii. p. 278. The Essex ' Red Hills ' are discussed by I. Chalkley Gould in ' Vict. Hist. Essex,' 1903, i, pp. 307–9; and Home Counties Mag. ix (1907), pp. 75–6.

*10. Conybeare, ' Roman Britain,' p. 177, n. (Quotes Gesner, Catullus, Beckmann's ' History of Inventions', &c.)

*11. L. Jewitt, ' Grave-Mounds and their Contents,' 1870, p. 264.

*12. W. de Gray Birch, ' Domesday Book,' 1877, p. 274. *A. Ballard, ' The Domesday Inquest,' 1906, p. 156.

*13. J. E. Thorold Rogers, ' Six Centuries of Work and Wages,' 1899, pp. 87–8.

*14. Reliquary, xi, 1905, p. 223. Cattle were also shod when taken long distances to fairs. See J. J. Hissey, ' Over Fen and Wold,' 1898, p. 127. Instructions for shoeing cattle are given in W. Youatt's ' Cattle ', new edition (1876), pp. 569–70.

*15. ' Excavations in Cranborne Chase,' i. p. 84.

*16. ' Superst. of the Highlands,' pp. 46–7.

17. Ibid., p. 246.

18. Ibid., p. 152.

*19. ' Celtic Folklore,' i. pp. 35, 40, 46, 70, &c. ; ii, p. 583. Also Hartland, ' Science of Fairy Tales,' pp. 305–9.

*20. Craigie, ' Scand. Folklore,' pp. 166–7.

21. Ibid., pp. 168–9.

*22. F. T. Elworthy, ' The Evil Eye,' 1895, p. 22.

23. Ibid., p. 22.

*24. ' Scand. Folklore,' p. 388.

*25. ' Superst. of the Highlands,' p. 235.

26. Notes and Queries, 8th Ser., xi, 1897, p. 138.

27. ' Evil Eye,' p. 22. Discussion in Notes and Queries, 10th Ser., 1906, vii, pp. 230–1.

28. J. Aubrey, ' Miscellanies ' (4th edition, 1857), p. 142.

29. ' Evil Eye,' p. 220.

*30. Mary H. Kingsley, ' West African Studies,' 1901, pp. 459–78.

31. ' Evil Eye,' pp. 216–25.

*32. See, for example, Notes and Queries, 10th Ser., iii, pp. 9, 90, 214–16, &c.

33. J. Aubrey, 'Miscellanies,' quoted by J. Timbs, 'Things not Generally Known' (new edition, N. D.), p. 144. [I cannot trace the passage in any available edition of Aubrey.—W. J.]

34. R. Herrick, ' Hesperides ' (ed. Hazlitt, 1869), p. 305.

*35. ' Evil Eye,' pp. 216–25. A well illustrated paper on ' Horse Brasses,' in the *Reliquary*, xii, 1906, pp. 108–13 and 247–262, deals with the crescent ornament.

*36. ' Folk-Lore of the Northern Counties,' pp. 117–19; ' Folk-Lore Relics of Early Vill. Life,' p. 163.

37. ' Evil Eye,' p. 22.

38. Ibid., p. 220.

39. Bacon, ' Essays'—' True Greatness ' (ed. H. Lewis, N. D.), p. 168.

*40. O. Schrader, ' Prehist. Antiquities,' pp. 158–61.

CHAPTER X

*1. H. B. Woodward, ' Geol. of Eng. and Wales ' (2nd edition, 1887), p. 420. ' Vict. Hist. of Essex,' ii, 1907, p. 413. * S. B. J. Skertchly, ' Manufacture of Gun Flints ' (Mem. Geol. Survey), 1879, *passim.*

*2. J. Wyatt, in ' Flint Chips ', by E. T. Stevens, 1870, pp. 578 et seqq.

3. A. J. Jukes-Browne, ' Cretaceous Rocks of Britain' (Mem. Geol. Survey, 1904), iii, pp. 241–2.

*4. *Notes and Queries*, 4th Ser., v, p. 446 ; *Knowledge*, N.S., v, (1908), pp. 4–6. * ' Cret. Rocks of Britain,' iii, p. 385.

5. C. Roach Smith, ' Collectanea Antiqua,' 1861, v, p. 200.

*6. ' Manuf. of Gun Flints,' *passim.*

7. Ibid., pp. 36–7.

*8. ' Anc. Stone Impts.,' p. 315.

9. Ibid., p. 16.

10. Ibid., p. 314.

11. Ibid., p. 314.

12. Ibid., pp. 313–14.

*13. ' Neol. Man in N.-E. Surrey,' pp. 181–4. For flints found on Roman sites, see ' Anc. Stone Impts.,' p. 283; *Knowledge*, N. S., v, (1908), pp. 4–6.

*14. Conybeare, ' Roman Britain,' p. 37.

15. Ibid., p. 37, n.

*16. ' Prim. Culture,' i, p. 82.

17. F. J. Bennett, in *Rochester Naturalist*, iii, 1906, p. 362.

*18. See description and plan in ' Vict. Hist. Sussex,' 1905, i, pp. 314–16.

*19. J. J. A. Worsaae, ' Industrial Arts of Old Denmark,' 1882, p. 17.

*20. Windle, ' Life in Early Brit.,' pp. 46–8. *Antiq.*, N.S., iv, 1908, pp. 137–9. The writer of the article contends that the Grimes Graves pits belong to different periods of the Neolithic stage.

*21. ' British Barrows,' p. 231 ; ' Guide Bronze Age,' p. 93.

*22. *Essex Naturalist*, xi, 1899, p. 111. (Illustrations given.)

23. *Rept. of Roy. Inst. of Cornwall*, 1871, p. xxii, quoted in Avebury, 'Prehist. Times,' p. 87.

*24. 'Anc. Stone Impts.,' pp. 233–4.

*25. 'Manuf. of Gun Flints,' pp. 41, 72.

*26. Ibid., p. 72.

*27. 'Guide Stone Age,' pp. 80–1.

28. R. F. Scarff, in *Nature*, lxxiv, 1906, p. 138.

*29. 'Manuf. of Gun Flints,' pp. 39, 71.

30. Ibid., pp. 39, 72.

31. Ibid., pp. 70–72.

32. Ibid., p. 39.

33. J. Beddoe, 'Races of Britain,' 1885, p. 254.

34. J. Beddoe, op. cit., pp. 255–6. Windle, 'Life in Early Brit.,' p. 214.

*35. 'Manuf. of Gun Flints,' p. 43.

*36. For this section, see New Oxford Dictionary, Skeat's Etymol. Dict., Century Dict., Eng. Dialect Dict., under the respective words.

37. H. G. Archer, in *Wide World Magazine*, xvi, 1906, p. 533.

38. *Notes and Queries*, 7th Ser., v, p. 85. (Authority given.)

39. 'Manuf. of Gun Flints,' p. 39.

[These authorities will also be found helpful : — Canon W. Greenwell, *Trans. Ethnol. Soc.*, 1870, p. 429. A. Rees, 'Cyclopaedia,' 1819, Art. 'Gun-flints, economical and industrial.' A. C. Haddon, Paper prepared as guide for Brit. Assoc. at Cambridge, 1904. Sir J. Evans, 'Anc. Stone Impts.' (2nd edition, 1897), ch. ii. Also works of Windle, Avebury, &c. Good popular accounts in *Wide World Magazine*, xvi, 1906, pp. 527–33. *Penny Magazine*, xviii, 1903, pp. 349–53.]

CHAPTER XI

1. M. Tusser, 'Five Hundred Points of Good Husbandry,' 1562.

*2. W. Fream, 'Text-Book of Agriculture,' 1892, pp. 15, 19, 36.

*3. H. G. Seeley, 'Handbook of the London Geol. Field Class,' 1892, pp. 120–1, 155.

*4. A. J. Jukes-Browne, in *Q. J. G. S.*, lxii, 1906, pp. 132–65.

*5. H. G. Seeley, loc. cit. *A. J. Jukes-Browne, *Proc. Yorks. Geol. and Polytechnic Soc.*, N. S., xii, 1895, pp. 385–95. Also 'Vict. Hist. Yorks.,' i, 1907, pp. 63–4.

6. W. Fream, op. cit., p. 36.

*7. A. J. Jukes-Browne, 'Handbook Physical Geology' (2nd edition, 1892), pp. 361, 364.

*8. Ibid.

*9. Century Dict., under 'Marl'.

10. O. Pughe, Welsh Dict., 1832, under 'Marl'.

*11. J. C. Morton, 'Cyclopedia of Agriculture,' 1865, ii, p. 371 et seqq. * R. Holland, in *Nature Notes*, iii, 1892, p. 149.

12. Morton, loc. cit. ; Holland, loc. cit.

*13. G. W. Young, *Proc. Geol. Assoc.*, xxix, 1905, pp. 189, 193; xx, 1908, pt. 7. Clement Reid, ' Geol. of Holderness ' (Mem. Geol. Survey), 1885, p. 120, distinguishes between marling and chalking. For the Lincolnshire discovery, see *Naturalist*, 1906, pp. 207–12. For marling in Lincs. and the I. of Wight, see A. W. Rowe, *Proc. Geol. Assoc.*, xx, 1908, pp. 249-51.

14. Conybeare, ' Rom. Brit.,' p. 40.

*15. Tacitus, ' De Moribus Germaniae,' c. 26.

*16. Pliny, ' Nat. Hist.,' l. xvii, cc. 3–4 (trans. Bostock and Riley, 1865, iii, pp. 452 et seqq.).

*17. ' Nat. Hist.,' l. xvii, c. 4.

*18. Pliny, ' Monument. Hist. Brit.,' l. viii, c. 9. * Seebohm, ' Eng. Vill. Com.,' pp. 247–8.

*19. ' Nat. Hist.,' l. xvii, c. 4 (Bostock and Riley, iii, pp. 451, 453).

*20. J. G. Keysler, ' Antiquitates selectae septentrionales et Celticae . . .,' 1720, pp. 246, 284 (' Germania,' § xviii). Also Keysler, ' Exercitatio de dea Nehallenia,' 1717, pp. 15–16; 56–7. * Father B. de Montfaucon, ' Antiquity explained ' (tr. D. Humphreys, 1721), vol. ii, pt. 2, pp. 283-4.

*21. Kauffmann, ' Northern Mythology,' p. 91.

*22. J. R. Green, ' The Making of England,' 1885, p. 150.

*23. T. Pennant, ' Journey from London to I. of Wight,' 1801, i, p. 53.

*24. Ibid., i, pp. 55–7.

*25. Keysler, ' Antiq. select.,' p. 285 [cf. W. Camden, ' Britannia,' (ed. R. Gough, 1789), iii, p. 7].

*26. T. Reinesius, ' Epistolae ad Rupertum,' 1660, pp. 300–1 ; ' Epistolae ad Daumium,' 1660, lxiii, p. 161.

*27. Camden, ' Britannia ' (Gough's edition, 1789), i, p. 90.

*28. Pennant, op. cit., i, pp. 55–7.

*29. New Oxford Dict., under ' Chalk '.

*30. H. B. Woodward, ' Geol. of Eng. and Wales,' p. 419.

*31. *Archaeol. Cantiana*, i, 1858, pp. 141–2. W. de Gray Birch, ' Cartularium Saxonicum,' 1893, ii, p. 114. J. M. Kemble, ' Codex Diplomaticus aevi Saxonici,' 1845, iii, p. 227.

*32. R. E. Prothero, ' Pioneers and Progress of English Farming,' 1888, p. 45.

33. *Notes and Queries*, 2nd Ser., 1856, ii, p. 195.

*34. Seebohm, ' Eng. Vill. Comm.,' p. 88.

*35. J. C. Morton, ' Cyclopedia of Agriculture,' 1865, ii, pp. 371 et seqq.

36. *Archaeol. Cant.*, i, p. 142. J. Thorpe, ' Registrum Roffense,' 1769, p. 227.

37. Morton, loc. cit.

38. Morton, loc. cit.

39. Prothero, op. cit., p. 45.

*40. G. Markham, ' Inrichment of the Weald of Kent,' 1625, p. 4.

*41. Sir Anthony (=Maister) Fitzherbert, ' Book of Husbandry, ' 1523, ed. Skeat, 1882, p. 132. * Rogers, 'Six Centuries of Work and Wages,' pp. 92–3, 476.

*42. F. J. Bennett, 'History of Eng. Farming,' 1889, p. 14.

*43. W. Lambarde, 'Perambulation of Kent' (publ. 1520), edition 1826, pp. 401–2.

*44. G. Markham, 'Inrichment,' p. 4.

*45. W. Blith, 'Survey of Husbandry,' 1649, p. 58.

46. Ibid., p. 60.

*47. S. Hartlib, 'Legacie . . . Discourse of Husbandry,' 1651, p. 43.

48. Ibid., p. 44.

49. J. Aubrey, 'Nat. Hist. and Antiquities of Surrey,' quoted in 'Vict. Hist. Surrey,' ii. p. 277.

50. Morton, 'Cyclop. of Agric.,' p. 371.

*51. C. W. Hoskyns, 'Talpa, or the Chronicles of a Clay Farm' (4th edition, 1857), p. 52 (1st edition, 1835).

52. R. P. Cruden, 'Hist. of Gravesend,' 1843, p. 442.

53. *Essex Naturalist*, xii, p. 250, n.

54. Prothero, 'Pioneers . . .,' p. 45. Cf. A. M. W. Stirling, 'Coke of Norfolk and his friends,' 1908, i, p. 253.

*55. W. Cobbett, 'Rural Rides' (ed. Pitt Cobbett, 1886), 'i, pp. 165, 177, 200, &c. (Cobbett refers to 'chalk-wells'.)

*56. C. Vancouver, 'Agric. Survey of Hampshire,' 1813, i, p. 342.

57. Vancouver, op. cit., i, p. 341. * Cf. W. Cobbett, 'Rural Rides,' i, p. 165.

58. Vancouver, op. cit., i, p. 336. (See also *Hampshire Antiquary and Naturalist*, i, 1891, p. 8.)

*59. Gomme, 'The Vill. Comm.,' ch. iv. * W. Topley, in *Jour. Anthrop. Inst.*, iii, 'Parish Boundaries in the S.E. of England.' * F. J. Bennett, *Proc. Geol. Assoc.*, x, No. 7.

*60. Rogers, 'Six Centuries of Work and Wages,' pp. 14–16, 92–3.

*61. F. T. Richards in Traill's 'Social England', 1898, i, p. 92.

*62. R. L. Galloway, 'Annals of Coal Mining,' 1898, pp. 5–20; also 'Earliest Records connected with the Working of Coal,' 1879, pp. 1–6. (Authorities cited.) *Naturalist* (1905), p. 313.

*63. Sir H. Jekyll, evidence before Royal Commission on Canals, March 21, 1906. See also Art. 'Canals,' 'Encyc. Brit.,' 10th edition.

64. *Home Counties Mag.*, ii, 1900, pp. 43–4.

65. *Notes and Queries*, 2nd Ser., 1861, xi, p. 167; *South-Eastern Naturalist*, 1907, p. lxiv.

*66. F. J. Bennett, in *Essex Naturalist*, i, 1887, pp. 261–5.

*67. T. Pennant, 'Journey from Chester to London,' 1811, pp. 302–3, (1st edition in 1782).

*68. *Essex Nat.*, xi, p. 261. * A. J. Jukes-Browne, 'Cret. Rocks of Britain' (Mem. Geol. Surv.), 1904, iii, pp. 391–2. Daines Barrington, in *Archaeologia*, vii, 1785, pp. 236–43, describes pits at Little Coxwell (Berks.) which were apparently chalk-wells.

69. *Essex Nat.*, i, p. 261.

*70. 'Geol. of Eng. and Wales,' p. 419.

*71. '*Gentleman's Magazine*,' 1822, pt. ii, p. 416.   * F. J. Bennett, ' Guide to Newbury,' 1890, p. 85.

*72. W. Whitaker, ' Geol. of London ' (Mem. Geol. Surv.), 1889, i, p. 115.

*73. *Jour. Brit. Arch. Assoc.*, N.S., x, 1904, pp. 64–74, 87–102.   Cf. previous account, N.S., ix, 1903, pp. 147–60.   Summary in *Academy*, Feb. 27, 1904 ; see also an authoritative description in *Standard*, Jan. 14, 1908, followed by correspondence, Jan. 16, 18, 22, 24, Feb. 7 ; and W. T. Vincent, in *South-Eastern Naturalist*, 1907, pp. lxiii–lxiv, and 50–1.

74. Caesar, ' De Bell. Gall.,' l. v, c. 42.   For a good account of the rock-shelters of France see S. Baring-Gould's ' Deserts of Southern France,' 1894, i, pp. 231–65.

CHAPTER XII

*1. F. C. J. Spurrell, in *Arch. Jour.*, xxxviii, pp. 391–409 ; xxxix, pp. 1–22, &c., as hereafter quoted.

*2. T. V. Holmes and W. Cole in *Essex Naturalist*, i, 1887, pp. 225–76.

*3. *Surrey Arch. Coll.*, xvii, pp. 181–3.   * *Reliquary*, xi, 1905, p. 33. ' Neolithic Man in N.-E. Surrey,' pp. 37–8.

*4. New Oxford Dict., ' Dene-hole.'

*5. Skeat, Etymol. Dict., ' Dene-hole.'

*6. F. C. J. Spurrell, *Arch. Jour.*, xxxvii, p. 333.

*7. Ibid., xxxvii, p. 334.

*8. Ibid., xxxviii, p. 401.

*9. Ibid., xxxviii, pp. 397–8.

*10. *Essex Naturalist*, i, 1887, p. 235.

*11. Ibid., i, pp. 240, 247, 259–60.

12. Ibid., i, p. 246.

13. ' Victoria Hist. of Essex,' i, p. 320.

*14. W. Camden, ' Britannia ' (ed. Philemon Holland, 1610), p. 440. J. Childrey, ' Britannia Baconica,' 1660, pp. 69, 99.

15. *Essex Nat.*, i, pp. 246–7.

16. ' Vict. Hist. Berkshire,' 1906, i, p. 283.

*17. ' Vict. Hist. Essex,' i, p. 310.

*18. T. Wright, ' The Celt, the Roman, and the Saxon,' 2nd edition, 1861, p. 63.

*19. E. King, ' Munimenta Antiqua,' 1799, i, pp. 44–60.   W. Stukeley, ' Palaeographia Britannia,' 1795 (devoted to the Royston caves).

20. *Essex Naturalist*, i, p. 248.

21. Ibid., i, pp. 248–9.

*22. *Jour. Anthrop. Inst.*, 1876, v, p. 361.

*23. ' Victoria Hist. Sussex,' 1905, i, pp. 326–7.

24. *Arch. Jour.*, xxxvii, p. 194.

*25. See Rev. G. S. Streatfeild, ' Lincolnshire and the Danes,' 1884, *passim*.

*26. *Arch. Jour.*, xxxviii, p. 399.

*27. Ibid. (cf. New Oxford Dict., under 'Clapper' and 'Kidnapper ').

28. Chaucer, ' Romaunt of the Rose,' ed. Bell, 1855, vii, p. 60.

*29. W. Lambarde, ' Perambulation of Kent,' ed. 1826, pp. 401-2.

*30. *Archaeologia Cantiana,* xviii, pp. 317-18.

*31. Mr. Spurrell's excellent papers have been largely used here : he gives his authorities. See also C. Dawson, in *Geol. Mag.*, 1898.

*32. Victor Hugo, ' Quatre-vingt-treize,' pt. i, bk. 4, cc. 2, 3.

33. *Essex Nat.*, i, pp. 227-8.

34. Gen. A. L. Pitt-Rivers, in *Times*, Sept. 25, 1884 (quoted in *Essex Nat.*, i, p. 251, n.).

35. *Essex Nat.*, i, p. 245.

*36. Ibid., i, pp. 249-50.

*37. Roach Smith, ' Collectanea Antiqua,' vi, pp. 243-7.

38. Pliny, ' Nat. Hist.,' Bostock and Riley's edition, 1865, iii, p. 454.

39. Conybeare, ' Roman Brit.,' p. 41.

40. *Essex Nat.*, i, p. 250.

*41. Seebohm, ' Eng. Vill. Comm.,' p. 247. (References given.)

*42. Ibid., p. 248 (translation). Cf. A. J. Church, ' Early Britain,' 1889, p. 1, n. Sir E. H. Bunbury, ' Hist. Anc. Geography,' 1879, i, pp. 590-601, for favourable review of Pytheas. * C. I. Elton, ' Origins of Eng. Hist.' (2nd edition, 1890), p. 32. Conybeare, ' Roman Brit.,' p. 40. For a full discussion of the voyage of Pytheas, see T. Rice Holmes, ' Anc. Britain and the Invasions of Julius Caesar,' 1907, pp. 217-26.

*43. Diodorus Siculus, ' Geog.,' l. v, c. 21.

*44. ' Eng. Vill. Comm.,' p. 248.

*45. Martin Martin, ' Descrip. of the Western Isles of Scotland,' 1703, p. 204.

*46. *Arch. Jour.*, xxxix, p. 8.

*47. ' Collectanea Antiqua,' vi, p. 246.

*48. *Proc. Geol. Assoc.*, viii, p. 408.

*49. *Essex Nat.*, i, pp. 266 et seqq.

*50. Tacitus, ' De Moribus Germaniae,' c. 16.

*51. *Essex Nat.*, i, p. 273.

*52. Quoted by E. King, in ' Munimenta Antiqua,' 1799, i, pp. 44-60. Valuable details on elevated Scotch *daisses* are given by Robt. Chambers in *Proc. Soc. Antiq. Scotland*, i, 1855, pp. 127-33.

*53. Jer. xli. 8.

54. *Essex Nat.*, i, p. 273. For the passage in the 'Perceval', see *Antiquary*, N.S., iii, 1907, p. 407.

*55. ' Munimenta Antiqua,' i, pp. 40-61 (for store pits generally). For silos of Southern France, see Baring-Gould, ' Deserts of S. France,' i, pp. 255-6.

56. *Essex Nat.*, i, p. 273.

57. *Proc. Geol. Assoc.*, viii, pp. 404-10.

*58. ' Excav. in Cranborne Chase,' ii, p. 33.

59. 'Excav. in Cranborne Chase,' i, pp. 24–5.

60. Century Dict., under 'Saracen'.

61. Eng. Dial. Dict., under 'Saracen'.

*62. *Essex Nat.*, xiii, 1904, pp. 275–9.

63. Gentleman's Mag. Library, 'Archaeology,' ii, p. 93 ; also Sir R. C. Hoare, 'Anc. Wilts.' [Quoted by T. V. Holmes, loc. cit.]

64. *Notes and Queries*, 4th Ser., ix (1872), pp. 95–6.

65. *Essex Nat.*, xiii, pp. 275–9.

66. J. Gerard, 'Herball,' 1579, fol., p. 347. Cf. F. Wise, 'Further Observations upon the White Horse, &c.,' 1742, p. 53.

*67. J. Larwood and J. C. Hotten, 'Hist. of Sign-Boards,' 1867, pp. 100, 430–1.

68. J. Selden, 'Table Talk,' quoted in *Notes and Queries*, 3rd Ser., iv, p. 226.

*69. A. Evans in *Folk-Lore Jour.* (Folk-Lore Soc.), vi, 1895, pp. 6–51.

*70. E. A. Freeman, 'Hist. and Conquests of the Saracens,' 2nd edition, 1876, pp. 161–6.

[Additional references to Dene-holes :—*Arch. Cantiana*, i, pp. 137–43 ; xi, p. 126 ; xiii, pp. 11–12. *Home Counties Mag.*, ii, 1900, pp. 43–4, 167. *Trans. Essex Arch. Soc.*, iii, p. 49 ; iv, p. 87 ; vii, N. S., 1900, pp. 206, 252–5, 400. *Reliquary*, i, N. S. (1875), pp. 65–82 ; ii, N. S., p. 37. *Idler*, March, 1898. *Proc. Woolwich Dist. Antiq. Soc.*, iii, 1890, pp. 20, &c. E. Hasted, 'Hist. of Kent,' 1778, i, p. 211. Murray, 'Handbook to Kent,' 5th edition, 1892, pp. 6–7, 21–2, 228–9. Murray, 'Handbook to Essex, Suffolk, &c.,' 3rd edition, 1892, pp. 7–8. W. T. Vincent, 'Records of the Woolwich District,' ii, pp. 531–2, 615. C. Dawson, 'Ancient and Modern Dene-holes and their Makers' : in *South-Eastern Naturalist* (1898). Mr. Spurrell (p. 276, vol. i, *Essex Nat.*) gives references to several French sources *re* the storehouse theory. *T. V. Holmes, in 'Vict. Hist. of Kent,' 1908, i, pp. 446–55. **Athenaeum*, Mar. 7, April 18, May 30, 1908. In the issue of April 18 (p. 479), it is argued that the *puis* of Chrestien de Troyes may represent 'hills'. *The Stone Court dene-hole is fully discussed in *Proc. Geol. Assoc.*, xx, 1908, pt. 6.]

CHAPTER XIII

1. W. Cobbett, 'Rural Rides' (ed. Pitt Cobbett, 1886), ii, p. 114.

2. Cent. Dict., under 'Linch'. Cf. New Oxford Dict.

*3. Seebohm, 'Eng. Vill. Comm.,' p. 382.

*4. Eng. Dial. Dict., under the respective words.

5. 'Eng. Vill. Comm.,' p. 381.

6. Ibid.

7. D. Wilson, 'Prehist. Annals of Scotland,' 2nd edition, 1863, i, pp. 492–4.

8. H. Rider Haggard, 'Rural England,' 1902, i, pp. 107–10.

9. S. Baring-Gould, 'Book of Dartmoor,' pp. 56, 162, &c.

10. T. Hardy, ' Desperate Remedies,' ch. x, § 6.

*11. D. Mackintosh, ' Scenery of Eng. and Wales,' 1869, p. 89.

12. Mortimer, ' Forty Years' Researches,' 1905, p. 381.

*13. *Notes and Queries*, 3rd Ser., vii, 1865, pp. 241, 301, &c.

14. *Gent. Mag.*, 1796, p. 821.

15. H. B. Woodward, ' Jurassic Rocks of Britain' (Mem. Geol. Surv.), 1893, pp. 313-14.

*16. Mackintosh, ' Scen. Eng. and Wales,' pp. 85-6. Cf. W. G. Maton, ' Observations . . . Western Counties of England,' 1797, ii, pp. 186-7.

17. Mackintosh, pp. 85-6.

*18. ' Geol. of Eng. and Wales,' p. 609.

19. Quoted in *Notes and Queries*, loc. cit.

*20. Gomme, ' Vill. Com.' ch. iv.   * *Wilts. Archaeol. and Nat. Hist. Mag.*, xii, 1869, pp. 192-3.

21. F. J. Bennett, ' Marlborough in Neolithic Times,' 1892, p. 8.

22. T. Pennant, ' Tour in Scotland,' 1779, iii, p. 283.

*23. ' Vill. Com.,' ch. iv.

*24. H. Rider Haggard, ' Rural England,' 1902, ii, p. 98.

25. Haggard, ' A Farmer's Year,' 1899, p. 20 et seqq.

26. ' Rural Eng.,' ii, 158.

*27. W. de Gray Birch, ' Domesday Book,' 1887, p. 241.
* A. Ballard, ' The Domesday Inquest,' 1906, p. 183.

*28. F. W. Maitland, ' Domesday Book and beyond,' 1897, pp. 375-6.

29. William of Malmesbury, ' Gesta Pontif.,' pp. 292, 326.

*30. C. I. Elton, ' Origins,' p. 221, n.

31. Conybeare, ' Rom. Brit.,' p. 192 n.

*32. R. W. Eyton, ' Key to Domesday,' p. 39.

*33. Rogers, ' Six Centuries,' p. 101. M. Drayton, in ' Poly-olbion ' (1613), pp. 234-5, n., discusses why wine was not made in England in his day.

34. The question of British vineyards is further discussed in * *Wiltshire Archaeol. and Nat. Hist. Mag.*, xvii (1869), pp. 292 et seqq. * *Notes and Queries*, 5th Ser., xi, pp. 185, 256 ; xii, pp. 55, 172, 397. 6th Ser., i, p. 45 ; vi, p. 389 ; vii, p. 56.   7th Ser., vi, pp. 321, 476 ; xi, p. 409 ; xii, pp. 10, 91. * *Archaeologia*, iii (1775), pp. 53-95: Full statement. S. Pegge favours vineyards ; Daines Barrington argues against them.

*35. ' Eng. Vill. Com.,' pp. 1-5.

*36. Ibid., pp. 5-6.   Cf. Gomme, ' Vill. Com.,' p. 85, n.

37. H. J. Moule, ' Old Dorset,' 1893, p. 81.

38. T. Wright, ' Celt, Roman, Saxon,' p. 209.

*39. *Wilts. Archaeol. Soc. Trans.*, xii, pp. 186-7.

*40. ' Eng. Vill. Com.,' p. 113.

*41. P. Vinogradoff, ' Villainage in England,' 1892, pp. 235-7.

*42. ' Domesday Book and Beyond,' pp. 339, 346-7.

*43. ' Rural Rides,' i, pp. 14, 50, 105, 177, 310, 331 ; ii, p. 212, &c.

*44. *Quar. Jour. Geol. Soc.*, lxii, 1906, pp. 132–65. * *Proc. Geol. Assoc.*, xix (1905), pp. 191–2.

*45. A. J. Jukes-Browne, 'Cretaceous Rocks of Britain,' 1904, iii, pp. 423–4. * G. W. Young, *Proc. Geol. Assoc.*, xix, pp. 191–2.

*46. 'Anglo-Saxon Brit.,' p. 154. 'Vict. Hist. Sussex,' i, pp. 9, 24–5.

*47. Prothero, 'Pioneers and Prog. of Eng. Farming,' pp. 1–2.

*48. W. Topley, in *Jour. Anthrop. Inst.*, iii, pp. 34, 39, 43–5, 49. Cf. 'The Domesday Inquest,' pp. 169–70. * 'Geol. of the Weald' (Topley— Mem. Geol. Surv., 1875), pp. 396–8.

*49. 'Eng. Vill. Com.,' pp. 107–8 (charters quoted).

50. G. Boate, 'Ireland's Naturall History,' 1652, pp. 83, 87.

*51. 'Eng. Vill. Com.,' p. 20.

52. 'Vict. Hist. of Berkshire,' 1906, i, p. 284. The Argyle terraces are referred to in A. Campbell's poem, 'The Grampians Desolate' (1804), p. 8, and long note, p. 168.

*53. Gomme, 'Vill. Com.,' ch. iv.

*54. *Jour. Anthrop. Inst.*, xvi, 1887, pp. 72–3.

*55. Gomme, 'Vill. Com.,' p. 91.

56. H. Graves, 'Way about Berkshire,' N. D., p. 82.

*57. *Jour. Arch. Assoc.*, xiii, p. 109.

*58. W. Marshall, 'Rural Economy of the Southern Counties,' 1798, ii, p. 301.

59. W. Fream, 'Agriculture' (4th edition, 1892), p. 51. * W. L. Rham, 'Dict. of the Farm,' 1858, pp. 282, 433. * Chambers's Cyclopaedia (1904), art. 'Plough'.

*60. L. C. Miall, 'Round the Year,' 1896, pp. 103–4.

61. Prothero, 'Pioneers and Progress,' pp. 1–2.

62. Cited in 'Vill. Com.,' p. 94.

63. *Wilts. Arch. and Nat. Hist. Mag.*, xii, 1869, p. 191.

*64. 'Eng. Vill. Com.,' p. 6, n. Cf. 'Rural Rides', ii, p. 114.

*65. 'Past in the Present,' p. 95.

*66. 'Vill. Com.,' pp. 279–80.   67. Ibid., p. 279.

*68. Evans, 'Anc. Stone Impts.,' p. 71. * *Jour. Anthrop. Inst.*, xxix, 1899, p. 130.

*69. 'Eng. Vill. Com.,' pp. 303, 409, 411, &c.

*70. Ibid.,' p. 411.   *71. Ibid., pp. 180, 437–9.

*72. Gomme, 'Vill. Com.,' pp. 132–47.

*73. 'Eng. Vill. Com.,' pp. 180, 437–9.

*74. F. W. Maitland, 'Domesday Book and Beyond,' pp. 337–8.

*75. P. Vinogradoff, 'The Growth of the Manor,' p. 175.

76. 'Domesday Book and Beyond,' pp. 339, 346–7.

77. 'Vill. Com.,' p. 287.

*78. Ibid., pp. 137, 293.   79. Ibid., p. 133.

*80. For drawings and descriptions of early ploughs, see *Reliquary*, xi, 1905, pp. 218–19.

*81. Grant Allen, 'Falling in Love : Essays ' (new edition, 1891), p. 291.

*82. ' Forty Years' Researches,' p. 388.

*83. Ibid., pp. 385–7.

*84. A. J. and G. Hubbard, in *Cornhill Mag.*, No. 119, N. S., 1906, pp. 608–22.

CHAPTER XIV

*1. For old theory, see W. C. Wells, ' Essay on Dew,' 1818 (preface dated 1814). Also good summary, T. H. Huxley, 'Physiography,' 1885, p. 54.

*2. *Trans. Roy. Soc. Edinburgh*, xxxiii (1886), pp. 9–64. * Summary in Chambers's Cyclopaedia, 1904, iii, p. 782.

3. Eng. Dial. Dict., under ' Mist-pond'.

*4. *Rept. Brit. Assoc.*, 1900, pp. 585 et seqq.; *Nature*, lxiii (1900), pp. 20–1.

*5. W. Marshall, ' Rural Econ. of the Southern Counties,' 1798, ii, p. 398. Wiltshire dew-ponds are noticed in *Wilts. Archaeol. and Nat. Hist. Mag.*, xvii, 1878, pp. 299–300.

*6. *Spectator*, Nov. 16, 1901 (lxxxvii, pp. 755–6).

7. *Nature*, lxii, 1900, p. 495.

*8. G. White, 'Selborne' (Harting's edition, 1880), pp. 225–6. Gideon Mantell, in 'Geol. of S.E. of England,' 1833, p. 9, n., quotes White, and mentions the natural stocking of ponds with animal and vegetable life.

9. *Spectator*, lxxxvii, p. 990.

10. E. A. Martin, in *Knowledge*, N. S., iii, 1906, p. 481.

*11. A. J. and G. Hubbard, ' Neolithic Dew-Ponds and Cattle-Ways,' 1905, pp. 2–4 (speak of wandering band). Stationary workers referred to in *S.E. Naturalist* (1906), pp. xxxix, xl, 20.

12. ' Neolithic Dew-Ponds,' p. 3. *13. *Nature*, lxiii, 1900, pp. 20–1.

14. *Knowledge*, N. S., iii, 1906, p. 481.

*15. H. P. Slade, ' A Short Practical Treatise on Dew-Ponds,' 1877, p. 30.

16. Ibid., p. 12. 17. Ibid., p. 6.

*18. R. Jefferies, ' Wild Life in a Southern County ' (new edition, 1889), pp. 25–8.

*19. ' Rural Econ. of S. Counties,' ii, p. 398. Cf. E. Lisle, ' Observations in Husbandry ' (ed. by T. Lisle, 1757), ii, p. 406.

*20. C. Reid, in Miall and Fowler's edition of White's ' Selborne,' 1901, p. 166, n.

21. *Proc. Geol. Assoc.*, x, p. 377. Cf. Cobbett, ' Rural Rides,' i. p. 20.

*22. J. Clutterbuck, in *Jour. Roy. Agric. Soc.*, i (2nd Ser., 1865), p. 273. Cf. T. Davis, ' Wiltshire Agric.,' 1811, p. 13.

*23. A. Collett, in *Macmillan's Mag.*, N.S., i, 1906, p. 217.

24. Slade, ' Treatise on Dew-Ponds,' p. 20. 25. Ibid., p. 31.

*26. C. J. Cornish, ' The Naturalist on the Thames,' 1902, pp. 129–30. A capital summary given in the *Spectator*, lxxxvii, 1901, pp. 775–6.

27. ' In Memoriam,' c. xi, v. 2.

*28. White's ' Selborne ', Harting's edition, 1880, p. 226. The damp, foggy atmosphere of the Downs is well described in J. H. Shorthouse's ' John Inglesant ', 1887, p. 20.

29. 'Selborne,' p. 226.

*30. White's 'Selborne', annotated by Miall and Fowler, 1901, p. 164. *Rept. Brit. Assoc.* (1900), pp. 585 et seqq.

*31. 'Neolithic Dew-Ponds,' pp. 2, 3. 32. Ibid., pp. 3–4.

33. *Macmillan's Mag.*, N. S., i, 1906, p. 216.

*34. *Jour. Roy. Agric. Soc.*, 2nd Ser., i (1865), pp. 281–7.

35. Ibid. Cf. Davis, 'Wiltshire Agric.,' p. 13, and account in Woodward's 'Geol. of Eng. and Wales,' p. 421. (The Calcutta custom is recorded in *Nature*, v, p. 189.)

*36. *Spectator*, lxxxvii, 1901, p. 798.

*37. *Nature*, lxii, 1900, p. 495.

*38. White's 'Selborne' (Miall and Fowler), pp. 165–6.

*39. Ibid., p. 166.

40. 'The Naturalist on the Thames,' pp. 130–1.

*41. W. C. Wells, 'Essay on Dew,' p. 225.

*42. Ganot, 'Physics' (12th edition, Atkinson, 1886), p. 961.

43. Ibid., p. 316; White's 'Selborne' (Miall and Fowler), p. 165.

*44. *Proc. Geol. Assoc.*, x, p. 377. 45. Slade, 'Treatise,' p. 6.

46. *Jour. Roy. Agric. Soc.*, 2nd Ser., i, pp. 281–7.

*47. *Macmillan's Mag.*, 1906, pp. 216–17.

*48. C. Vancouver, 'Agric. Survey of Hampshire,' 1813, i, pp. 47–8.
* Cf. W. Cobbett, 'Rural Rides' (1886), i, p. 20.

*49. C. Packe, 'Philosophico-Chorographical Chart of East Kent,' 1743, pp. 87–8.

50. Murray, 'Handbook to Kent,' 5th edition, 1892, p. 37.

*51. C. F. Dowsett, 'Winklebury Camp,' 1904, pp. 4, 7; also *Times*, Nov. 26, 1900.

*52. 'Excavations in Cranborne Chase,' ii, p. 237.

*53. Ibid., i, pp. 10, 27–8. 54. Ibid., ii, p. 237. 55. Ibid., i, p. 28.

*56. 'Neolithic Man in N.-E. Surrey,' pp. 25–6.

*57. *Jour. Roy. Agric. Soc.*, i, N. S., p. 273.

*58. *Trans. Newbury Field Club*, iii, pp. 257–8.

*59. R. Jefferies, 'Wild Life in a Southern County,' 1889, pp. 25–8.

*60. 'Neolithic Man in N.-E. Surrey,' pp. 83–4.

61. *Trans. Newbury Field Club*, iii, pp. 257–8.

*62. 'Vict. Hist. Sussex,' 1905, i, pp. 460–1. The Sussex ponds are dealt with in the abstract of a paper by A. H. Allcroft, *Morley College Magazine* (London), xvi, 1906, pp. 40–3.

*63. *Jour. Anthrop. Inst.*, 1889, xviii, pp. 336, 338, &c.

64. *Cornhill Mag.*, No. 119, N. S., 1906, p. 617.

*65. 'Neolithic Dew-Ponds,' p. 17.

66. Ibid., pp. 60–1. 67. Ibid., p. 59.

68. King, 'Munimenta Antiqua,' i, pp. 150–1.

NOTE.—Since this chapter was written, I have seen Mr. E. A. Martin's excellent articles in *Knowledge*, iv, N.S., 1907, pp. 108–9, 126–8, 197. Some slight additions have been in consequence incorporated, but in the main

Mr. Martin's authorities are the same as those here quoted. The reader may, however, do well to compare Mr. Martin's summary with that of the text.

CHAPTER XV

1. *Daily Chronicle*, Jan. 24, 1906.

2. Murray, 'Handbook to Wilts. and Dorset' (5th edition, 1899), p. 85.

3. Ibid., p. 50.   H. B. Woodward, 'Geol. of Eng. and Wales,' p. 421.
* W. C. Plenderleath, 'The White Horses of the West of England' (2nd edition, 1892), p. 28.

4. But see Plenderleath, 'White Horses,' pp. 14, 28.

5. Murray, 'Handbook to Wilts. and Dorset,' p. 85.

*6. 'White Horses,' pp. 32–4.   7. Ibid.

8. *Notes and Queries*, 2nd Ser., vi, p. 49.

9. 'White Horses,' p. 35.

10. Murray, 'Handbook to Scotland' (7th edition, 1898), p. 292.

*11. 'White Horses,' p. 36.

*12. T. Hughes, 'The Scouring of the White Horse' (new edition, 1889), p. 97.   (1st edition, 1858.)   * 'White Horses,' pp. 17–18.

*13. F. Wise, 'A Letter to Dr. Mead . . . White Horse,' 1738, *passim.*
* F. Wise, 'Further Observations upon the White Horse, &c.,' 1742.

14. *Times*, June 10, 1871.

15. Quoted by H. Graves, 'Way about Berkshire,' N.D., p. 123.

*16. Hughes, 'Scouring,' p. 255.

*17. *Notes and Queries*, 6th Ser., x, p. 325 ; Wise, 'Letter to Dr. Mead,' pp. 45–6.

*18. 'White Horses,' p. 15.   Consult also W. F. Skene, 'The Four Ancient Books of Wales,' 1868, for discussion on Taliessin and Ceridwen, i, pp. 184, 498 ; ii, p. 324, &c.   * 'Vict. Hist. Berks.,' 1906, pp. 188–92.
* Sir J. Rhŷs, 'Celtic Britain,' p. 19 and plate.   * 'Guide to Early Iron Age,' pp. 28–9.   * *Jour. Brit. Arch. Assoc.*, l (1884), pp. 64–6.

19. Murray, 'Wilts. and Dorset,' p. 151.

*20. *Archaeologia*, xxi, pp. 289–98.

*21. W. Camden, 'Britannia' (Gough's edition, 1789), ii, p. 333.   Wise, 'Further Observations,' pp. 48–9.

22. G. Miller, 'Rambles around the Edge Hills' (2nd edition, 1900), pp. 4–5, 8–10.

23. 'Vict. Hist. Sussex,' 1905, i, p. 323.

24. *Notes and Queries*, 8th Ser., ix, p. 30.

*25. 'White Horses,' p. 40.   * C. Warne, 'Anc. Dorset' (ed. T. W. W. Smart, 1872), pp. 319–25.

26. *Notes and Queries*, 8th Ser., ix, p. 30.   * J. Sydenham, 'Dissertation on the Antient Colossal Figure at Cerne,' 1842.   * J. Hutchins, 'Hist. and Antiquities of Dorset,' 1774, ii, pp. 293–4.

*27. J. S. Phené, in *Sussex Arch. Coll.*, xxvi, 1885, pp. 63–4.

28. Ibid., pp. 97–111.

*29. Phené, *Trans. Roy. Inst. Brit. Architects*, 1872, p. 381, &c.

30. Ibid. Also, ' Vict. Hist. Sussex,' 1905, i, pp. 323-4.

*31. Caesar, ' De Bello Gall.,' l. vi, c. 15 (cf. Bohn and M'Devitte's translation).

32. *Sussex Arch. Coll.*, loc. cit.

33. Conybeare, ' Rom. Brit.,' p. 65.

*34. Strabo, ' Geog.,' l. iv, c. 4, § 5.   Also trans. by Hamilton and Falconer, 1887, i, p. 295, and see Liddell and Scott, ' Greek Dict.,' 8th edition, under the words cited. Concerning Strabo's information, see Sir E. H. Bunbury, ' Hist. Anc. Geog.,' 2nd edition (1883), p. 249.   See also a general discussion in the ' Géographie de Strabon ' (Paris, 1809), t. ii, pp. 71-2 ; cf. Greek and Latin versions, ed. by C. Müller and F. Dübner (Paris, 1853).

35. ' White Horses,' p. 41.

*36. ' Golden Bough,' ii, pp. 280-1.

37. ' Scouring of the White Horse,' p. 256.

38. *Notes and Queries*, 2nd Ser., i, p. 475.

39. *Notes and Queries*, 3rd Ser., vii, p. 10.   * J. Grimm, ' Teut. Myth.' (tr. Stallybrass, 1883), iv, p. 1482.

40. *Notes and Queries*, 3rd Ser., vii, p. 64.

*41. S. J. Low and F. S. Pulling, ' Dict. Eng. Hist.,' 1889, p. 576.

*42. Bede, ' Eccles. Hist.' (ed. J. A. Giles, 1887), p. 24.

43. J. Timbs, ' Curiosities of Science ' (6th edition, 1862), p. 191.

*44. Rev. vi. 2 and xix. 11.

*45. *Sussex Arch. Coll.*, xxvi, p. 110.   * Sir D. Wilson, ' Prehistoric Man ' (1876), i, pp. 307, 318-19.   For the Wyoming figure, see *Putnam's Monthly* (1907), pp. 277-84.

*46. ' Vict. Hist. Bucks.,' 1905, pp. 189-90.   ' White Horses,' pp. 43-4. *Proc. Geol. Assoc.*, x, p. 373.

*47. ' Vict. Hist. Bucks.,' pp. 189-90 ; Wise, ' Further Observations,' pp. 34, 35, 39, &c.

48. ' Vict. Hist. Bucks.,' p. 189.

49. ' White Horses,' p. 44.

50. H. Graves, ' Way about Buckinghamshire,' N.D., p. 65.

51. ' Vict. Hist. Bucks.,' pp. 189-90.

52. H. Cheal, ' Parish of Ditchling (Sussex),' 1901, pp. 135-6.

53. Sir D. Wilson, loc. cit.

*54. G. S. Tyack, in ' Eccles. Curiosities ' (ed. by W. Andrews, 1899), pp. 186-205.

55. Ibid., pp. 195-6.   Cf. *Notes and Queries*, 10th Ser., ix, 1908, p. 475.

*56. Tyack, op. cit., pp. 190-1.

*57. *Notes and Queries*, 3rd Ser., x, p. 398 (good description).   See also * *Rep. Associated Archit. Socs.*, iv, p. 258 ; * *Gent. Mag.*, 1786, part I, pp. 474-5 ; ' Hist. and Descrip. Acct. of Lincolnshire,' 1834, p. 238 ; ' Diary of Abraham de la Pryme ' (Surtees Soc.), 1870, p. 164.

58. Tyack, op. cit., pp. 199-200.

*59. Tyack, op. cit., p. 201 (cites ' Aeneid,' l. v, v. 583 et seqq.). Cf. *Nature Notes*, xviii (1907), p. 33.

*60. *Notes and Queries*, 1st Ser., xi, pp. 132, 193 ; J. Britton, ' Magna Britannia ' (1720–31), vii, pp. 677–8 ; * W. Stukeley, ' Itinerarium Curiosum,' 1724, p. 91. There is a good account of the Louth ' Julian's Bower ' in ' Notitiae Ludae ', R. S. Bailey, 1834, pp. 238–42.

61. Tyack, pp. 198–9.

62. G. P. Bevan, ' Tourist's Guide to Hampshire,' 1881, p. 27.

63. ' Neol. Man in N.-E. Surrey,' p. 113. T. F. Thiselton Dyer, ' British Popular Customs,' 1876, pp. 156–7.

CHAPTER XVI

*1. T. Codrington, ' Roman Roads in Britain,' 1903, p. 27. * Conybeare, ' Rom. Brit.,' p. 167.

*2. Conybeare, op. cit., p. 167 ; Codrington, op. cit., p. 16.

3. Codrington, p. 35.

*4. Conybeare, pp. 140, 170 ; ' Vict. Hist. Berks.,' 1906, i, pp. 192–3.

5. Conybeare, pp. 117–18.

*6. ' Neolithic Man in N.-E. Surrey,' p. 88.

*7. *Notes and Queries*, 2nd Ser., xii, p. 109. E. R. James, ' Notes on the Pilgrims' Way,' 1871, *passim*. * H. E. Malden, ' A History of Surrey,' 1900, p. 29, &c. G. Thompson, ' Wolfe-Land,' N.D., pp. 144–5.

8. Windle, ' Life in Early Britain,' p. 122.

*9. White, ' Selborne ' (Harting's), pp. 12–13 (cf. *Notes and Queries*, 10th Ser., vii, 1907, pp. 111–13).

*10. ' Forty Years' Researches,' pp. 117–18.

11. Propertius, l. iv, cc. 3, 7.   *12. Conybeare, pp. 50, 92, 99, &c.

13. F. T. Palgrave, ' A Dorset Valley.'   *14. Codrington, p. 38.

15. *Surrey Arch. Coll.*, vi (1874), pp. 301 et seqq.

*16. R. A. C. Godwin-Austen, in *Surrey Arch. Coll.*, v, p. 21.

*17. J. J. Jusserand, ' English Wayfaring Life in the Middle Ages ' (tr. Toulmin Smith, 4th edition, 1892), p. 151.

18. P. Geddes, Lecture at Horniman's College, Forest Hill, Jan. 1, 1905.

*19. Windle, ' Early Brit.,' p. 121.   20. Ibid., p. 121.

21. Judges v. 6.

*22. H. Belloc, ' The Old Road,' 1904, *passim*. * J. Cartwright (Mrs. H. Ady), ' The Pilgrims' Way ' (new edition, 1901), *passim*. ' Neolithic Man in N.-E. Surrey,' pp. 89–91.

23. Codrington, p. 35.   *24. ' The Old Road,' p. 59.

25. *Surrey Arch. Coll.*, vi (1874), pp. 301–4.

*26. Cartwright, ' The Pilgrims' Way,' pp. 34–5, 41, 43, &c.

*27. Ibid., pp. 26, 27, 113, &c. On this section see E. R. James, in ' Three Surrey Churches,' N.D., pp. 169–210.

28. Cartwright, p. 26.

29. J. Haydn, Dict. of Dates (22nd edition, 1898), under ' Tolls '. A useful work to consult for roads generally is ' Bibliography of Road-Making and Maintenance,' by S. and B. Webb, 1906.

*30. ' The Old Road,' pp. 46, 56.

31. E. Phillpotts, ' Sons of the Morning,' 1900, p. 207.

*32. ' The Old Road,' pp. 60 et seqq.

33. Ibid., pp. 61 et seqq.   34. Ibid., p. 155.

35. References to these discoveries are very scattered : e.g. ' The Old Road,' pp. 94, 155, &c. ; Cartwright, p. 43, &c. ; ' Neol. Man in N.-E. Surrey,' pp. 71, 72-82, 91, &c. ; ' Three Surrey Churches,' pp. 167 et seqq. ; *Surrey Arch. Coll.*, *passim*.

*36. ' The Old Road,' pp. 18, 28, &c.

37. F. J. Bennett, in *Rochester Naturalist*, iii (1905), p. 348.

*38. Cartwright, pp. 36, 42-3, 49 ; Belloc, *passim*.

39. Cartwright, p. 4.

*40. J. Lowe, ' Yew-Trees of Great Britain and Ireland,' 1897, pp. 131-2.

41. Ibid., p. 28.

*42. Ibid., p. 103 ; * cf. G. A. Hansard, ' Book of Archery ' (1840), pp. 330, *et passim*.

*43. J. G. Strutt, ' Sylva Britannica,' 1822, p. 1.

*44. J. Evelyn, ' Sylva,' 1664, p. 65, and ' Diary ', 1684, iii, p. 274.

*45. G. S. Boulger, ' Familiar Trees,' N.D., 2nd Ser., pp. 57-8 ; Murray, ' Handbook to Hants,' 1898, p. 57 ; ' Handbook to Surrey' (1898), p. 185 ; *Notes and Queries*, 1st Ser., xi, p. 166.

*46. ' Familiar Trees,' 2nd Ser., p. 58.

47. Evans, ' Anc. Stone Impts.,' p. 575.

*48. Sir A. C. Ramsay, ' Geology and Geography of Great Britain ' (3rd edition, 1878), p. 358.

*49. G. Rolleston, ' Scientific Papers and Addresses,' 1884, ii, pp. 785-6.

*50. Woodward, ' Geol. Eng. and Wales,' p. 523.

51. A. J. Harrison, in *Naturalists' Jour.* (1895), p. 99.

*52. See Jukes-Browne, ' Handbook of Physical Geology,' 1892, pp. 190-1.

*53. See, for example, *Jour. Board Agric.*, x (1903), pp. 235-6 ; *Trans. Chem. Soc.*, lxxxi (1902), p. 874 ; *Science Gossip*, vols. xxii, xxiii, xxiv ; &c., &c.

54. New Oxford Dict., under ' Forest '.

55. C. Kingsley, ' Scientific Lectures and Essays,' 1890, p. 158.

*56. Concerning trees on barrows, see Grant Allen, ' Evolution of the Idea of God,' ch. vii.

*57. Grant Allen, ' The Bronze Axe,' in *Cornhill Mag.* (1889), pp. 526-7.

*58. ' Guide to Early Iron Age,' pp. 84-5. * Clement Reid in *Archaeologia*, lix (1904), pp. 281-8. * W. Ridgeway, in *Folk-Lore*, vol. i (March, 1890), pp. 82-107, ' Greek Trade-Routes to Britain ' ; see especially p. 97.

59. R. Kipling, ' " Just So " Stories.'

60. J. J. Raven, ' The Bells of England,' 1906, pp. 14-15.

ADDENDA

PAGE 28. *Eoliths.* The improbability of our reaching a complete settlement is admirably expressed by Mr. F. J. Bennett, in the *Geol. Mag.*, iii, 1906, p. 72 : ' The difficulty of the whole question consists in this, that we are trying to decide where no final decision seems possible. For those who hold that certain flints are due to natural causes have never seen, or can see, Nature doing what they would refer to Nature, and those who uphold the human origin of the flints can never, of course, have seen them actually made by man.' But we have actual knowledge, urges Mr. Bennett, that man does fashion certain stone tools : ' The difficulty will lie in fixing the starting-point of his 'prentice hand.'

Among the types of Eoliths worthy of attention is that which Sir E. Ray Lankester has called the 'trinacrial', from its resemblance in form to the island of Sicily (Trinacria).

PAGE 30. *Æneolithic.* This mode of spelling has been adopted by the sponsors of the term. The word ' Neolithic ' does not enter into the compound. Dr. William Wright informs me that the etymology is Latin *aēnĕus,* adj., made of bronze or copper, and Greek λίθος = stone. The term is applied to the period when copper and bronze were equally in use with stone.

PAGE 37. *Continuity of implements.* Dr. Holmes, ' Anc. Brit. and the Invas. of Jul. Caes.,' 1907, pp. 38 et seqq., discusses the French types of implements and compares them with the drift and cave implements of England. He concludes (p. 41) thus : ' On a general review it should seem that the French chronological classification of palæolithic implements, even applied to England, contains a measure of truth. The implements which are commonly found in the river drift and other deposits in the open field undoubtedly began to be manufactured before those which are characteristic of the caves ; and those of the Mousterian type were first made, both in England and in France, long before the development of the elegant Solutrean forms and the period in which flourished the artists of South-Western France. But both in France and in England Mousterian implements were still used during the latter period ; and even drift implements of the latest kind continued to be used by palæolithic hunters of the latest generation.' (Authorities cited.)

PAGE 42. *Overlap of Palæolithic and Neolithic implements.* Messrs. Baldwin Spencer and F. J. Gillen, in ' The Northern Tribes of Central Australia,' 1904, p. 635, show that the Central Australian natives use implements which are typical of both the Palæolithic and the Neolithic periods. Some of the tools are as crude as those of the extinct Tasmanians, while others are as well chipped as those found in European barrows. It is largely a question of material : where quartzite alone is available, the implements are merely chipped ; if diorite can be obtained, the worker makes a ' Neolithic ' ground axe.

PAGE 43. *Mesolithic Period.* Dr. T. Rice Holmes (op. cit.) makes some pertinent remarks concerning the supposed total disappearance of Palæolithic man :—

1. pp. 59–60. Out of the 48 mammalian species belonging to the Palæolithic Age, 31 are admitted by Professor Boyd Dawkins to have survived into Neolithic times.

2. Some strange difficulties arise, if we accept the popular theory. What a remarkable cataclysm, which drove away, or exterminated man, and yet allowed the 31 other mammals to thrive ! Was it a pestilence that spared

none ? Did the race die out, though no civilized people entered the country to expedite its fate ? Or did the inhabitants, for some unexplained cause, decide to emigrate ? If Palæolithic man was driven away by Neolithic invaders, there was no hiatus (p. 60).

3. p. 387. To Professor Boyd Dawkins's insistence on the gulf between the rude hunting stage and the pastoral and agricultural civilization of Neolithic man, Dr. Holmes replies with a parallel. The gap is no greater than that between the Red Indian civilization and that which the Pilgrim Fathers introduced ; ' yet the Red Indian lived on.'

4. In reply to the objection that domesticated animals alone appear in the uppermost (Neolithic) strata, Dr. Holmes urges that the fact proves merely that Neolithic man domesticated beasts while Palæolithic did not do this (p. 386).

PAGE 44. Dr. T. Rice Holmes, ' Anc. Brit. and the Invas. of Jul. Caes.,' pp. 19 et seqq., argues that Britain was connected by a land bridge with the Continent during some part only of the Palæolithic Age. That Britain was continental throughout that Age is, Dr. Holmes contends, a ' dogma '. He cites Mr. Clement Reid (p. 59) to the effect that at the time when the Hoxne (Suffolk) implements were lost [by their owners] the land stood at only a few feet above the present level ; and (p. 19) that, during the Palæolithic Age, England never rose more than seventy feet above this datum line. He concludes that man entered Britain across a narrow strait during the earlier period of glaciation.

PAGE 71. *Barrow-digging in Roman times.* During the year 1907, Mr. H. St. George Gray examined the Wick Barrow at Stogursey, Somerset. The relics, among which were a flint dagger and a ' beaker ', indicated an early Bronze interment. The skeletons were of the Transitional type, exhibiting both Neolithic and Bronze Age features. But most important was the discovery of Roman remains, arranged in such a position as to afford—so the explorer considers—' definite evidence that the chief interment had been excavated for, and found by the Romans.' (*Antiquary*, N. S., iv, 1908, p. 161.)

PAGE 81. *Evolution of the rectangular house.* Dr. Xanthoudides has recently discovered a farmstead at Sitia, in Eastern Crete, dating from the ' Middle Minoan I ' period. An elliptical boundary-wall about 85 feet by 49 was divided into several rooms by means of party walls of small stones and clay. The discoverer suggests that here we have a survival of the old round hut divided into apartments by walls of wood and wickerwork. Both round and square houses occur very early in Crete. Whether the different types imply different races is a debated point. (R. M. Burrows, ' The Discoveries in Crete,' 1907, pp. 169, 181.)

PAGE 189. *Early use of flint as a strike-a-light.* The New Oxford Dictionary, under ' Flint ', gives references to early glossaries : A.D. c. 700, *Petrafocaria*, flint ; A.D. c. 1050, *Petra focaria*, fyrstan, flint. In A.D. 1330 we get an allusion to ' fer of flint '.

PAGE 192. *Use of iron pyrites as a strike-a-light.* That nodules of iron pyrites were also used for ignition purposes in early times is very probable. Mr. F. W. Rudler (*Essex Naturalist*, xiii, pp. 309–10) notes that *Kies* is still the German word for this mineral ; and he cites Henckel, who suggests that this word may be connected with *Kiesel* (flint), because both minerals were employed for striking fire. It appears also that the Greek πυρίτης has also been used in connexion with both flint and pyrites.

PAGE 206. *Liming and chalking.* The value of chalk as a dressing is assessed very highly by the writer of Leaflet No. 170 (revised edition) issued by the Board of Agriculture and Fisheries. P. 3: ' The fertility of many farms to-day is undoubtedly due to the liming and chalking that

was done by the farmers of the eighteenth and earlier centuries ; they,
indeed, made the soil, for it is through their labours that it remains in
profitable cultivation at the present time.' A warning is issued that we
are at present living on capital thus accumulated, and that the supply
of lime in many soils is running ' dangerously short '.

PAGE 208. John Houghton, in his ' Collection of Letters for the Improvement of Husbandry and Trade,' No. 11, 1682, p. 120, publishes a long
account of the Cheshire marls and their mode of extraction. Preparing
a roadway to give descent to the pit was called ' shooting the pace ',
removing the material was known as ' feying the Marle '.

PAGE 231. *Chislehurst chalk-mines.* A writer in the *Standard*, Feb. 11,
1908, contends, erroneously, as I believe, that the inner circle of galleries
exhibits tool-marks of two kinds : (*a*) those showing traces of iron oxide—
made by iron picks ; (*b*) those which are ' clear and white '—made by
bronze picks. He further asserts that the entrance to the outer series
of passages has been enlarged in comparatively recent times, and that the
inner series was formerly only accessible by a low opening through which
the visitor had to crawl on hands and knees. If these current assertions
about the outer galleries be well founded, we must conclude that the
original workings were the inner ones, and that they were reached by
a dene-hole shaft or a draw-pit. With this conclusion we may compare
Messrs. Forster's belief that the dene-holes of star-fish ground-plan are
missing links between the primitive bell-pit and the pillared and galleried
mine seen at Chislehurst. But, as Dr. Holmes relevantly asks (' Anc.
Brit. and the Invas. of Jul. Caes.,' p. 516), Is the bell-pit primitive ?

The visit to the Chislehurst galleries paid by the Essex Field Club on
Feb. 15, 1908, gave rise to a discussion which should greatly assist in
dispelling the romantic legends which have grown up around these curious
old mines.

PAGE 237. *Dene-holes.* There is an expression used in a charter dated
A.D. 958 which may refer to dene-holes. The actual words are ' dene
pitte ', and they occur in the description of a grant of land by King Edred
at Boxora, or Boxford, near Newbury. (W. de Gray Birch, ' Cartularium
Saxonicum,' 1893, iii, p. 222.)

PAGE 265. *Lynches.* Near Ilfracombe, the untilled portions of the field
are called *launchers* (=land shares). In Dorset the ploughed strips are
termed *lawns* ; in Cheshire and North Wales, *loons, lawnds,* or *lownts* (G.
Slater, ' The English Peasantry and the Enclosure of the Common Fields,'
1907, pp. 20, 250). These terms evidently refer to lowland cultivation.

PAGE 271. Was the original purpose of linchets generally understood
in the early eighteenth century ? This seems unlikely, for, so far as I can
discover, Jethro Tull (1674–1741), who was born at Basildon, Berks.,
makes no allusion to linchets in any edition of his works. The omission
is the more noteworthy because he gives elaborate rules for cultivating
hill-slopes. In ' The New Horse-Houghing [*sic* ; a later edition has
' hoing '] Industry', 1731, pp. 86 et seqq., he advocates the ploughing
of a hill ' across its descent ', that is, not up and down hill, but along its
contours. The ridges (=furrow slices) are to be raised in pairs, so that
the water will drain into the trenches. At the next ploughing the double
ridge and the trench are to change places. On p. 88, n., he admits that
even this plan is not quite practicable on a hill of great declivity, in which
case ' it may be sufficient to plough the ridges obliquely'. Surely, if Tull
had understood terrace cultivation he would have mentioned it, especially
since he imbibed his ideas of thorough tillage when studying foreign
vineyards, where he observed that intensive ploughing and hoeing took
the place of manure. One is bound to conclude that though Tull and

his contemporaries must have noticed linchets, they knew no current tradition, and deemed the shelves natural features.

PAGE 277. *Loss of soil on downs.* Downland pastures near Mickleham, Surrey, were treated in the way described in the early spring of 1908. Soil from the vale was carted uphill to replace that which had been washed away.

PAGES 278, 282. *Linchet.* The name 'linchet' may be much more recent than the object denoted, having superseded an earlier British term. (Cf. Teutonic words, *barrow, house, hut*; *chalk-pit, plough*; *knife, arrow*, &c.) Again, is Professor Seebohm's etymology of 'linch' (p. 264) tenable? The New Oxford Dictionary, indeed, says that *link*—a variant of *linch* (A.S. *hlinc*)—may 'possibly' be a derivative from the root *hlin* (= to lean); but Professor Skeat, after noticing that the A.S. *hlinc* means a hill, and especially a balk or boundary, connects this word with A.S. *hring* (=a ring) and O. Latin *clingere* (=to surround). [See N. O. D. and Skeat's Etymol. Dict., 3rd ed. (1898), s.v. 'Link.'] Either origin would harmonize with the description of terraces, but it is not plain whether hill-foot shelves or elevated linchets are denoted—setting aside the alternative meaning of an unploughed, grassy strip as the level.

PAGE 287. *Turnwrest plough.* A scrap of evidence has just come to light showing that the turnwrest plough is nearly four centuries old, at least. Maister Fitzherbert, 'Book of Husbandry,' 1534 (ed. by W. W. Skeat, 1882), p. 9, says: 'In Kente they haue other maner of plowes, somme goo with wheles, as they doo in many other places, and some wyll tourne the sheldbredth [=shield-board; the termination *th* is corrupt] at euery landes ende, and plowe all one waye.'

See also 'Vict. Hist. of Kent,' 1908, i, pp. 457–8.

PAGE 299. *Puddling ponds.* I have found an early reference to this practice in J. Houghton's 'Collection for the Improvement of Industry and Trade', 1693, iii (No. 68), where he shows how to make ponds hold water. 'If Clay be well ram'd [he is speaking of light soils] and upon that a good pitching of Stones be laid, Water may be preserv'd to great purpose.'

PAGES 344, 356. *Preservation of trees.* The student may compare the scrupulous preservation of 'Gospel Oaks', which stood on the boundaries of parishes, and which were formerly prominent in the ceremonies connected with annual perambulation of the bounds on Ascension Day. Cf. also the Statute of Edward I (1307), '*Ne rector prosternat arbores in coemiterio,*' forbidding the rector to cut down churchyard trees except for the purpose of repairing the chancel.

PAGE 357. *Early trade in tin.* Dr. T. R. Holmes, 'Anc. Brit. and the Invas. of Jul. Caes.,' pp. 483–96, discusses thoroughly 'The Cassiterides, Ictis, and the British Trade in Tin.' On p. 497 he says, 'The real Cassiterides—the "tin islands" which were known to the mariners from whom the ancient writers ultimately derived their notions—were, speaking generally, the British Isles, and particularly the tin-producing districts of Cornwall and perhaps also the Scilly Islands.' The Scilly Isles have, however, yielded tin to a very limited extent only. See G. Barrow, 'Geol. of Isles of Scilly' (Mem. Geol. Survey), 1906, pp. 10–11. William Borlase's 'row of shallow Tin-pits' (1754) seem to have been very insignificant.

Dr. Holmes (op. cit., pp. 499–514) fully reviews the vexed question of Ictis or Mictis. He claims that this spot was different from Vectis, and that the tin was not shipped from the Isle of Wight but from St. Michael's Mount. With some force he combats Mr. Clement Reid's proposition that St. Michael's Mount was, in pre-Roman times, an isolated rock with no real harbour, and contends that it fulfils all the conditions named by Pytheas and his successors.

INDEX

A.

Abbotsbury (Dorset), 276.

Abbott, Mr. W. J., terrace implements, 39.

Abingdon, Abbey of, 322.

Abinger (Surrey), Roman villa, 349.

Abinger Hammer (Surrey), 171.

Achilles, tradition, 120.

Adam's Grave, barrow, 74.

Adder-stones, 107, 158.

Adder's glass, 148.

Addington (Kent), 350.

Addy, Mr. S. O., early huts, 81; open-air courts, 166.

Ady, Mrs. H., yews of Pilgrims' Way, 351, 355.

Ælfric, Saxon glossary, 102.

'Aeneid', reference to the, 336.

Æneolithic period, 30, 45, 68, 153, 155, 156.

Æschylus, use of iron, 120.

Africa, West, Miss M. H. Kingsley on, 62.

Agricola, 335.

Agriculture, ancient, 184, 258, 275. (See also under Marling, Linchets, &c.)

Aitken, Dr. J., theory of dew, 295.

Akerman, Mr. J. Y., on British coins, 325.

Alcester (Oxon.), 105, 170, 345.

Aldershot, 87.

Alfred, translation of Boethius, 70; victories over the Danes, 322, 325.

Alfred's Castle, earthwork, 87.

Alfriston (Sussex), 298.

Alinements, 66.

Alkborough maze, 334.

Allcroft, Mr. A. H., on South Down earthworks, 308-9.

Allen, Mr. Grant, on the peasant, 15; Roman place-names, 89; Thor and Thunor, 125; stake monuments, 136; Saxon agriculture, 280; linchets, 292; the Tin Way, 357.

Allen, Mr. J. R., evolution of the cross, 135.

Allison, Dr. J. M., on flails, 19.

Allsop, Dr. C., Cherhill White Horse, 320.

Altagore (co. Antrim), 140.

Alton Barnes (Wilts.), 321.

Ambidexterity of Neolithic man, 167.

Ambresbury Banks, 87.

Amesbury, 260.

Amiens, 248.

Amulets, 124.

Anchors, 21, 114.

Anderida, forest, 89, 94, 170.

Andreas of Chislehurst, 215.

Anemone pulsatilla, 261.

Anglesey, huts, 80; dolmen superstition, 164.

Anglo-Saxon Chronicle, on Anderida, 89; on coal, 222; on Saracens, 261.

Animal mounds, 331.

Anstiebury camp (Surrey), 349.

'Antiquary' (Scott's) quoted, 83.

Antiquities, false, 79.

Antonine's Itinerary, 338.

Antrim, 129.

Anwyl, Prof. E., on huts of Anglesey, 80.

Appleby (Lincs.), 334.

Arabs, amulets of, 124; and iron, 177.

Arden, Forest of, 280, 344.

Areley Hill, 354.

Argyle, 274, 284.

Aristotle, on red hair, 57.

Arran Island, use of coracles, 113; holed stone, 128.

Arrow-heads, in Ireland, 107; 'wingers', 108; in medicine, 122; as elf-shot, 122-3, 158; as amulets, 124; at Brandon, 200.

Art, of cave-man, 33, 35, 43; of Neolithic man, 33, 35; shown on bronze celts, 48; of pottery, 49.

Arthur, King, in folk-lore, 69-70, 73; legend, 85, 164-5.

Arthur's Stone, 69; Hall, 69; Round Table, 73, 85; Seat, 286.

Arts, lost, 17, 18.

Aryan, use of term, 54; settlement, 280-1.

Ashantee, 177, 179.

Ashbourne (Derbyshire), 75.

Ashburnham (Sussex), 170.

Ashdown (Berks.), 87, 322, 340.

Ashley, Mr. W., 200.